{ THE BEST SCHOOL
IN JERUSALEM }

HBI SERIES ON JEWISH WOMEN

Shulamit Reinharz, General Editor | *Sylvia Barack Fishman, Associate Editor*

The HBI Series on Jewish Women, created by the Hadassah-Brandeis Institute, publishes a wide range of books by and about Jewish women in diverse contexts and time periods. Of interest to scholars and the educated public, the HBI Series on Jewish Women fills major gaps in Jewish Studies and in Women and Gender Studies as well as their intersection.

For the complete list of books that are available in this series, please see www.upne.com.

PUBLICATION OF THIS BOOK

IS SUPPORTED BY A GRANT FROM

Jewish Federation of Greater Hartford

LAURA S. SCHOR

The Best School in Jerusalem

{ ANNIE LANDAU'S SCHOOL
FOR GIRLS · 1900–1960 }

Brandeis University Press · Waltham, Massachusetts

Brandeis University Press
An imprint of University Press of New England
www.upne.com
© 2013 Brandeis University
All rights reserved
Manufactured in the United States of America
Designed by Mindy Basinger Hill
Typeset in Adobe Jenson Pro

University Press of New England is a member of the Green Press
Initiative. The paper used in this book meets their minimum
requirement for recycled paper.

For permission to reproduce any of the material in this book,
contact Permissions, University Press of New England, One Court
Street, Suite 250, Lebanon NH 03766; or visit www.upne.com

Library of Congress Cataloging-in-Publication
data available upon request.

5   4   3   2   1

IN LOVING MEMORY OF

Joseph Martin Schor

CONTENTS

ILLUSTRATIONS

FOREWORD

Given the sophistication of contemporary Jerusalem, the capital of the State of Israel, it is difficult to imagine that a little more than a century ago, the holy city to which Jews face three times a day in their prayers was in truth a city of squalor. Beggars and disease were rampant. Food was unhygienic and in short supply. As historian Laura Schor explains, the city suffered from social problems as much as from physical ones. Jerusalemites were divided sharply between Sephardi and Ashkenazi communities; girls in both ethnicities married at twelve or thirteen with almost none of them having received any education at the time of their weddings; and 50,000 of the 60,000 Jews who lived in Jerusalem were supported by welfare. Into this maelstrom of misery stepped Annie Landau (1873–1945), an Orthodox Jewish British optimist who believed in "the critical role to be played by women in the development of the Jewish people" (8). Guiding the activity of the rest of her life was the belief that the only way to harness the untapped potential of women was to educate the girls!

Current attitudes toward education in the twenty-first century are generally so positive that, again, it challenges the imagination to think that the people of Jerusalem did not welcome Landau's commitment to build a school that truly educated girls. And yet she succeeded. Her ability to implement her mission-driven work rests on her intelligence, extraordinary energy, single-mindedness, and perhaps also the fact that she remained unfettered by a family of her own. Like the American Zionist Henrietta Szold, Annie Landau never lived to see the State of Israel declared. Nevertheless, the State of Israel is deeply indebted to both of them.

Annie was one of eighteen children born to her father whose first wife bore him the first five. Annie was the oldest of the children to whom the second wife,

Chaya, gave birth. Again, stretching the bounds of the plausible, the Landau family was committed to educating every single one of those children in secular subjects while simultaneously imbuing them with Jewish knowledge at home. Neither of her parents—Chaya and Marcus—saw any contradiction between high-quality secular and Jewish education. Annie adopted this approach in all of her subsequent educational enterprises. It is notable that Marcus and his friends were highly critical of the standard of Jewish education in London and developed a plan for a strong alternative. Annie's views as an adult mirrored those of her father. As he wrote in an editorial in the *Jewish Standard*, a newspaper he founded, "There is no reason to assign to woman an inferior position either in religious or intellectual matters" (20). Not surprisingly, the nine daughters of the Landau family achieved as much as did the nine sons.

Both in Great Britain and the United States, the end of the nineteenth and the start of the twentieth century were preoccupied by discussions of girls' education. This is no surprise since it was also the period when people were wrestling with competing concepts of women's roles in society, specifically their right to vote. Prominent physicians argued that educating young [white] women represented race suicide, as educated women would not marry or have children. Others argued that exposing women to liberal ideas would make them irreligious and promiscuous. Added to this was the general confusion among Jews concerning the appropriate response to modernity. Should they embrace or shun new opportunities? The Hirsch School that Annie attended as a teenager came down clearly on the side of integration, an approach she would later advocate in Jerusalem. Her subsequent training to become a teacher underscored this approach and also taught her the essential and complex skills of school administration.

Supported by funds from the Ladies' Committee of the Anglo-Jewish Association and regularly evaluated by prominent figures of the London Jewish community, the Evelina de Rothschild School existed long before Anne Landau arrived in Palestine. The school, like many institutions in the early twentieth-century *yishuv*, reflected effective partnerships between the Jews in the diaspora and those in the holy land. These outside influences compelled earlier administrators in the school to decrease crowding, enhance healthy behaviors, and upgrade instruction. The growing excellence of the school, it was also hoped, would protect Jewish students from the missionary institutions always eager to baptize Jewish girls.

As the nineteenth century came to a close, Annie was offered a teaching position in the Evelina School in Jerusalem. Soon after she took her place among the teaching staff, however, the headmistress left and Annie was put in charge. The conditions she inherited, as described colorfully by historian Laura Schor, were abominable. One can see easily that the school Landau was beginning to lead had many—possibly competing—objectives: to be an antidote to early marriage, to ward off missionaries, to teach girls to live healthy lives, to provide a bilingual education, to train the students in marketable skills, and to imbue them with a love of Orthodox Judaism, among others. Given this great array of purposes, it is not surprising that the demand for admissions rose precipitously. In the spring of her first year as headmistress, "300 children applied for 200 places" (46). To its credit, the new graduates were getting jobs rather than living off welfare. Nevertheless, opposition to the school also grew, sometimes for ludicrous reasons. To her Ashkenazi rabbinical critics, for example, "Arithmetic was deemed an inappropriate subject because the plus sign looked like a cross, while geography was forbidden since pupils would have to learn about cities with names like St. Augustine or San Francisco" (47). Landau had a unique view of education—not only did she intend to develop the minds of the students, she also strove to minister to their physical, spiritual, and communal needs. She took particular satisfaction in the girls' learning by example to help each other.

And there was one more administrative role she immediately adopted—director of fundraising. Landau used her frequent trips "home" to London to address individuals and groups about the needs of the school. Laura Schor makes good use of the transcripts of these speeches to trace the record of the school's setbacks and victories. Landau's 1902 report, for example, ended with a plea to expand the physical plant of the school to accommodate the four hundred girls who were denied admission. The following year's evaluation described the physical features of the school in very harsh terms, including a comment about the shocking ratio of six latrines for nearly six hundred students. Landau used this information in her persuasive fund-raising.

Grounded in meticulous archival research and interview data from her discussions with Rothschild School graduates, Dr. Schor's vivid description of the school and its children transported me mentally to those trying days in Jerusalem, two decades before the ground was broken for the Hebrew University and Hadassah Hospital and nearly five decades before the creation of the State of Israel. Landau stressed repeatedly and doggedly that the greatest need of Jerusalem was the education of women (66). Likewise her enthusiasm for and definition of her work can serve as a model for current school principals. Landau cared not only for the children themselves but also for their parents, whose homes she visited. And beyond that, she cared for the graduates, especially for their continued commitment to religious Judaism and to gainful employment. Moreover, "when the girls who finished the program were hired abroad, they became her ambassadors to the homes of potential donors to the school" (65).

Laura Schor rounds out her portrayal of Landau with vignettes about many other aspects of her life. She explains, for instance, why Landau did not identify as a Zionist—it stood in the way of her religious identity and of her commitment to teaching the girls English. Schor describes the communal living arrangement for single women teachers with no family in Jerusalem. In doing so, Annie Landau reminds me of Jane Addams and her creation of settlement houses in the United States. Schor sketches the monthly salons attended by Jewish, Christian, and Muslim residents of Jerusalem, along with professionals and artists, established in Miss Landau's shared home. Throughout her life, Annie loved to dress for parties and to open her home for social events.

Nevertheless, violence was never far away. The chaotic, debilitating conditions of World War I, in which the Ottomans sided with the Germans, led to the closing of the school and Miss Landau's relocation to Egypt. The war years saw the population of Jerusalem cut in half on account of starvation, disease epidemics, emigration and deportation, reducing the population to 26,000 Jews of whom 3,000 were orphans. Half of these young people—the girls—had become prostitutes. The new occupiers, the British, saw this as a *necessity* for the 26,000 British soldiers stationed in Palestine (86). Annie engaged the debate about the legalization of prostitution, thereby preventing the Orthodox leadership of Jerusalem from denying the very existence of prostitution and drunkenness in holy Jerusalem. She also turned to women as strong as she was to form organizations that would address the ills of the city.

The ills of World War I were revisited on Jerusalem a little more than a decade later during the Arab Riots of 1929—disease, murder, lack of food, lack of housing, and as Landau saw it, "periodic Zionist agitation" (123). People fled *to* Jerusalem, even though Jerusalem had a hard time taking care of its own citizens. Schor characterizes the 1930s as a time of rapid growth and modernization of the city, alongside Arab violence against Jews. And shortly after the decade of the 1920s ended, and World War II erupted, Landau faced the new challenge of integrating refugee girls into the school. So successful was she that her successor, Ethel Levy, gushed: "Nobody was more helpful in bringing Jews out of Hitler's hell after 1933 than Miss Landau" (152).

But the story was not so simple. Annie was torn as to where the future of world Jewry lay. Was it in Europe, particularly her beloved England, which ironically was engaged in bitter conflict with the Jews of Palestine? Or was it in Palestine, the homeland of the Jewish people? Or was it—God forbid—neither? And what should her attitudes be to the Arab population of Jerusalem? Was there an opportunity for "inter-communal cooperation" (161) and social service? Or were the various sides stuck in mortal combat with each other? And could she, as a "proper British and Orthodox" Jew continue to lead "her girls" who increasingly hoped for the creation of a Jewish state in Palestine?

Annie Landau was one of the few fortunate people who live to see their dream realized. By actually tackling the true challenges of the children while teaching them to believe in themselves, the Evelina de Rothschild School under Landau's leadership created several generations of talented women who contributed enormously to the welfare of the Jewish people and the development of Jerusalem. We, as readers, are fortunate to have Laura Schor embrace the project of describing the school in a way that makes its leader come alive and that allows the history of the school to illuminate the changing nature of the city.

Founded in 1997, the Hadassah-Brandeis Institute is devoted to telling the stories of countless chapters in Jewish and women's history so that we may learn from our past. Laura Schor has gifted us with the story of one such chapter, and we can all benefit from studying it.

Shulamit Reinharz

ACKNOWLEDGMENTS

It would have been impossible to write this book without the help of several individuals who agreed to be interviewed and in some cases provided substantial sources from their personal collections. I am deeply indebted to each of them.

Ruth Sless, the daughter of Ethel Levy, graciously allowed me to read papers that were saved by her mother. These papers, referred to in the book as the Ethel Levy Collection, were an invaluable source. In addition, Sless gave generously of her time during several interviews over a period of three years. Her sparkling recollections of Jerusalem, the Evelina de Rothschild School, and Annie Landau are central to my narrative.

I also interviewed twenty graduates of the Evelina de Rothschild School and spoke more casually with several others. The twenty are named in the list of sources. In particular, I must single out Rachel Harris Babad Pirani, who during the course of several interviews patiently recounted her experiences and ultimately gave me a copy of her diary to use in my research. Adaya Hochberg Barkay gave me copies of her poetry and also agreed to comment on the manuscript at an early stage. Her support for the project has been unflagging. Elisheva Shifman Baram spoke with me at length and sent follow-up materials about herself and her classmates that were very useful. Shulamit Kishik-Cohen spoke with me twice and gave me a copy of the book about her life. Marta Zayonce Shamir was generous with her time and also gave me a copy of her memoirs as well as photos, copies of report cards, and other school memorabilia.

Two distant members of the Landau family—Chaim Ashkenazi, the widower of Helen Landau, Annie's niece; and noted neurologist, Oliver Sacks,

Annie's nephew—shared family records and photos that helped me to understand Annie Landau's family life.

Shalva Weil, a colleague and a friend, interviewed her father, David Dimson, about the 1930s, when he attended Landau's parties in Jerusalem. She also shared family letters from the Mandate period. Shira Leibowitz Schmidt, another colleague and friend, interviewed Miriam Bujowsky in Bnei Brak about her years at the Evelina School.

Hannah Newman, who taught for many years at the Evelina School and is now retired, shared memories of her mother, Esme Aaronson, a teacher of the 1930s. Liza Slutsky, who taught for several years at the Evelina School and wrote a thesis about its early years, invited me to burrow through an old closet in the school library, where we found old reports, prayer books, and report cards.

In addition, I was helped by the professional and courteous support of archivists and librarians in London and Southampton, in Jerusalem and Tel Aviv, and in New York City.

Ela Greenberg and Michal Ben Yakov, both historians who have worked on the educational history of Jerusalem, were careful readers of early drafts of the manuscript. Shula Reinharz, a colleague and a friend, read a later draft and provided useful suggestions. Jessica DeCoux assisted in bringing the manuscript to a final draft through careful editing, thoughtful questions, and attention to detail.

INTRODUCTION

Annie Landau, the headmistress of the Evelina de Rothschild School from 1900 until her death in 1945, aspired for her school to become the best girls' school in Jerusalem. Landau, educated in London and Frankfurt, arrived in Jerusalem in the last decades of Ottoman rule. The city she found was impoverished, and the education of girls was of little importance to its residents. Most girls were illiterate; they learned to cook and to care for children by assisting their mothers. The fortunate ones learned to read and write in small, short-lived schools created by European Jewish philanthropists and missionaries.

The Evelina de Rothschild School, opened in 1854, was unique among this group of schools, both in its inclusive outreach to the typically divided Sephardi and Ashkenazi communities and in its longevity. Despite the elevated status of the school, when Landau arrived, she found squalor and a lack of discipline. She soon set about creating standards for pupils and for teachers.

Landau's plans did not find favor with the Orthodox Jewish community, which rejected her modern curriculum. Nor did her plans find favor with Zionists, who approved of her modern approach but firmly rejected her bilingual program of study. Nevertheless, Landau persevered. Her vision for the school was fully realized during the years of British rule (December 1917–May 1948), when many considered her school the best school in Jerusalem. Beginning in the 1920s, Landau was assisted in her work by the highly competent Ethel Levy, who continued to implement her predecessor's vision when she assumed the leadership of the school in 1945.

The Evelina de Rothschild School taught the daughters of old Jerusalem families alongside the daughters of new immigrants; religious and secular girls learned Jewish and modern texts together; those from poor families dependent on charity and those from affluent families shared double desks. Girls who were educated at the Evelina de Rothschild School in the 1930s and 1940s made significant contributions to the early history of Israel. The achievements of Landau make it clear that she was dedicated to bringing a new spirit to Jerusalem, specifically to the girls of the city.

Landau was not a great national leader; she steered clear of political parties, but she was an innovator in the realm of girls' education and in understanding its significance in creating a new civic model in Jerusalem. During her years at the helm of the school, she demonstrated extraordinary talent and developed a variety of strategies to overcome enormous difficulties: financial shortfalls, persistent malnutrition, public health crises, periodic violence, and two world wars. Through it all, she persevered steadfastly. In doing so, she acted as a new role model for the Jewish girls of Jerusalem, teaching them self-reliance, self-esteem, accomplishment, and a vision of a better future.

In July 1911, Annie Landau set sail from Jaffa for London. She had lived in Jerusalem since 1899, where she had already won a reputation as an educational leader and a charming hostess. In London, her childhood home, she gathered her friends and supporters to tell them stories about her school and her pupils in Jerusalem. The tales she shared were designed to convince those who had little knowledge about her school of its importance to the future of the Jewish people. She wanted their support for her plans to further develop the girls' school that had become her life's work.

Landau's stories were collected and published as a booklet titled *An Appeal to Jewish Women on Behalf of the Anglo-Jewish Association*. Writing with a dramatic flair, she ushered her readers into the fetid dwellings of her malnourished pupils:

> Shall I take you with me into these homes of our children, into narrow and steep courts where the children herd in holes, without light, without air, without covering, old and sick and young crouching together upon the dank and reeking earth? Everyone in Europe has a dim idea that the economic condition of Jerusalem is a sad one. Sixty years ago there were but a few thousand Jews in Jerusalem. But since then the influx of our brethren from those countries where Jews were persecuted has been very great. The Jewish population of Jerusalem has risen to 60,000, of whom at least 50,000 are supported by charity, of that kind of which a French writer said, "Charity creates the misery it tries to relieve and can never relieve half the misery it creates."[1]

With this evocative description, Landau sought to engage British Jewish women in her project not only to educate but also to modernize the Jewish girls of Jerusalem. She was determined to refashion them in her own image, creating religiously observant women who would be self-supporting and who would contribute to their families and their people. Landau knew that she had set a difficult task for herself. She explained that for centuries, Ashkenazi Jews had lived in the holy cities of Jerusalem, Hebron, Safed, and Tiberias, surviving on *chaluka*, charity sent by those who remained in Europe. Immersed in Jewish learning and prayer, the small numbers of Jews in the Holy Land continued to believe that they should be supported by those who lived in the Diaspora. The Sephardi communities, living apart from their Ashkenazi coreligionists, were equally poor and devoted to study and prayer, with the exception of a few families who engaged in commerce and local businesses and supported the poor of their community.[2]

In Jerusalem both of these communities educated their sons in schools that were very similar to those in their countries of origin, where learning was limited to the study of religious texts. The schools for Ashkenazi boys were called *cheder* or *Talmud Torah*, and the language of instruction was Yiddish. The schools for Sephardi boys were called *kuttab*, and the languages of instruction were Ladino and Arabic. Hebrew was not spoken in either of these schools but was taught as a sacred language. Girls of both communities were typically married at age twelve or thirteen, had many pregnancies, lost many babies, and remained dependent on their husbands and their families of origin. They were given no formal education, although some Sephardi girls were sent to the home of a *maestra*, a woman who took care of little girls and taught sewing to older ones.[3]

Seventy-two years before Annie Landau arrived in Jerusalem, Sir Moses and Lady Judith Montefiore had first traveled to the city seeking ways to address the poverty, disease, and ignorance that appeared to be endemic in the city. The Montefiores, and the Rothschilds who followed in their footsteps, responded to the needs of the Jews of the Holy Land as part of their growing concern for the Jews of North Africa, the Levant, and eastern Europe.

They were joined by other modern Jews who were moving into positions of greater influence in London, Paris, Vienna, Frankfurt, and Amsterdam. These leaders, new members of the middle class, felt a responsibility toward their impoverished kin. Still struggling to determine their own identities as Jews living and working in Europe's most advanced societies, these well-educated men and women wanted to help, but they rejected the system of *chaluka*. They hoped to change the traditional relationship between the Jews of Jerusalem and the Jews in Europe.[4]

The catalyst for the reexamination of this relationship was an incident that came to be known as the Damascus Affair. In 1840, dozens of Syrian Jews were imprisoned and tortured, charged with murdering a priest and his servant in order to harvest Christian blood to bake matzo for Passover. The specious allegation that Jews required Christian blood to make matzo had been the cause of much violence in earlier centuries, but this blood libel, as it was called, had been dormant in Europe for hundreds of years. When it emerged in Damascus, it was taken up by French officials who were protectors of the Catholic Church in Syria. Antisemitic Catholic newspapers in Europe began to circulate the unsubstantiated story of Jewish perfidy, spreading fear among the newly emancipated Jews of western Europe.[5]

In the early decades of the nineteenth century, Jews had become citizens and participants in the economic and cultural life of the great European capitals. Sensitive to the charge of dual loyalties, emancipated Jews proclaimed that they had only one nationality: French, English, or German. Judaism, they affirmed, was a religious practice, not a national identity. The Damascus Affair challenged this paradigm. Using the vehicle of the newly founded Jewish newspapers, they lifted their voices to protect their far-flung brethren living in squalid conditions who endured periodic outbursts of violence. By 1860, Western Jews had grown into a group of well-educated and concerned men and women committed to ameliorating the conditions of impoverished Eastern Jews. The first organization they formed was the Alliance Israélite Universelle in Paris.[6]

Though eschewing the term *nationality*, these Jewish leaders expressed solidarity with their people and were determined to spread the benefits of modern education to them. Through education, Western Jews hoped to raise the status of Eastern Jews in their local communities. The Alliance quickly started building French Jewish schools in North Africa and in the Levant in the areas where France had influence. A decade later, the Anglo-Jewish Association replicated the endeavors of French Jews, building schools in areas of British influence. Several decades later, German Jews launched the Hilfsverein der Deutschen Judens with similar objectives. Beginning in 1848, there was a sharp growth in missionary activity in Jerusalem, drawing the attention of European Jews to the needs of that city. All three philanthropic groups turned their focus to Jerusalem, where legal restrictions were imposed on all non-Muslims and where disease was endemic.[7]

Building on the work of the Montefiores and the Rothschilds, the new European Jewish organizations continued the effort to replace reliance on foreign charity with investment in education for self-sufficiency. They established schools that taught vocational skills and modern Western languages as well as Hebrew and some Arabic. The goal was to provide youngsters with technical expertise in order to promote a culture of participation in the local economy.

However, Sephardi and Ashkenazi community leaders, fearful that the recommended changes would lead their children away from strict religious practices, rejected these new ideas. Ottoman authorities, wary of increased Western influence, also viewed these new schools with suspicion. Hence, Jewish teachers and other emissaries from the English, French, and German Jewish organizations were viewed with hostility by local authorities.

Annie Landau was among those recieved little welcome upon their arrival in Jerusalem, and like many leaders, she created a foundation myth to justify the bold actions she took in her first years as headmistress. She continued the story of her project with a description of the establishment of the Evelina de Rothschild School:

> More than half a century ago, . . . Albert Cohn, visiting the city with Sir Moses Montefiore, and noting the utterly uncared for condition of the girl-children of the Holy City, provided the means with which a room was hired, and a Spanish Jewess—quite without education herself (it would have been hard to find an educated woman in Jerusalem at that time)—was engaged to look after the five little girls whose mothers were courageous enough to let them form the "School." . . . On the death of Baroness Evelina, the young daughter of Baron Lionel and the wife of Baron Ferdinand de Rothschild, the institution took her name and received . . . a large annual donation, sufficient then to cover its upkeep. Gradually, the school widened its scope, and a regular curriculum was introduced.[8]

Landau's account was a mixture of truth and legend. Her picturesque description of the Spanish Jewess and the five little girls was repeated in many articles and stories about the school, although the actual history is somewhat more prosaic. Albert Cohn, the philanthropic consultant to the French Rothschild family, arrived in Jerusalem in 1854 with fifty thousand francs and plans to establish a hospital, schools, a maternity clinic, and a loan fund. He rapidly achieved each of these goals, adding a soup kitchen to care for the hungry.

The combined social assistance—medical care, schooling, and assistance for women in childbirth—had a great effect on the impoverished Jerusalem-ites. Even parents who resisted the idea of educating their daughters were not indifferent to the benefits of free food, clothing, and boots. Those who were suspicious of doctors and medicine were reassured by the presence of a synagogue established in the hospital. The maternity program also provided a layette for new babies, which was a great benefit for poor families. Since all these programs were viewed as related, good experiences with one had an influence on attitudes toward the others.[9]

It is not surprising that most of the schools supported by European Jew-ish organizations that opened in Jerusalem in the decades before World War I were short-lived. Foreign-born teachers who faced difficulties from the authorities, from community leaders who didn't share their values, and from illness caused by unhygienic conditions and poor-quality food arrived in the city full of hope but then left when their health deteriorated or their spirits flagged. Even the Evelina de Rothschild School, by far the most stable of the schools, knew decades of uncertainty caused by short-term teachers, irregular attendance by the pupils, and the lack of a proper school building.[10]

The school founded by Albert Cohn was quite different from previous efforts to provide a bit of education for the girls of Jerusalem. The earlier attempts frequently involved a woman with no educational qualifications opening a room in her home to a small number of pupils of mixed ages. At-tendance was restricted to either Sephardi or Ashkenazi girls. Learning was limited to recitation of prayers and some reading, writing, and basic arithmetic. Most of the time was spent sitting on the floor sewing or embroidering. In contrast, the Evelina de Rothschild School featured vocational training and secular education as well as prayers and Hebrew. Ashkenazi and Sephardi pupils were taught together, a new practice that would continue to be unique among Jerusalem schools for many years. Finally, the rooms in which this education took place were called a school, not a *cheder*, the room where tra-ditional learning took place.

The original Evelina de Rothschild School in the Old City had five rooms in which five women taught about fifty girls. It was located adjacent to the new Rothschild Hospital and was supervised by the hospital director. The pupils received free supplies for their academic subjects and materials for vocational education. They also received clothing and shoes, often for holidays. When new secular subjects—history and nature studies—were introduced in the 1870s, several Ashkenazi families removed their daughters. French was added to the curriculum in 1872.[11]

Unlike most of the girls' schools, which remained small and were short-lived, the Evelina de Rothschild School, funded at first by the French Rothschild family and later by their British relations, endured. The school, which started with fifty pupils, grew to serve more than triple that number by the end of the nineteenth century. In 1889 Fortunée Behar, formerly a teacher for the Alliance in Constantinople, was hired as the first professionally trained headmistress of the Evelina de Rothschild School. Under her leadership, the school moved out of the Old City to temporary headquarters on the Street of the Prophets.

A few years later, the administrative supervision of the school was passed to the Anglo-Jewish Association. With its approval, in 1896, Behar arranged for the purchase of Frutiger House, located nearby, about equidistant from the Damascus Gate and the growing community of Meah Shearim. This forty-room building housed the Evelina de Rothschild School for many years. As soon as the new building opened, a kindergarten for girls and boys was added to the program; it was the first modern Jewish kindergarten in Jerusalem.[12]

Landau continued the history, explaining her effect on the mission of the school:

> I was sent to Jerusalem by the Anglo-Jewish Association at the beginning of 1899 with orders to reorganize the school on English lines . . . the task at first seemed almost an impossibility, so great were the practical difficulties on every side. How great the task, how heavy the responsibility, is apparent from the fact that it was then (and remained till a few years ago) the one and only institution in Jerusalem which had for its aim the upbringing of a generation of women firm in their faith, modern in education, and sound in their knowledge of those life principles so essential to the motherhood of a strong and independent people. [Because I was] Entrusted with the inner organization of the school and the creation of a new curriculum, it soon became clear to me that the education of the Jewish girls of Jerusalem must be animated by a deep and ardent religious spirit in order to produce strong Jewish personalities. Through the stress we lay upon religion and religious tradition, the moral standard and tone of the

school are heightened and strengthened, while the secular education not only does not suffer, but is, on the contrary, all the more conscientiously carried out.[13]

Once again, Landau's story was a bit of a gloss on the actual record. She was, in fact, hired to teach English at a pivotal moment in the school's history, when efforts at modernization were beginning to influence cities under Ottoman control. In the early years of the school, when it was located in the Old City and supervised by the head of the Rothschild Hospital, pupil attendance was erratic and the curriculum was constantly revised to reflect the availability of teachers. In the last years of the nineteenth century, under the supervision of Fortunée Behar, the school moved into the more hygienic new city, and school attendance, though still erratic, improved. Landau's arrival in Jerusalem marked the beginning of a new period in the school's history.

Within a few months, Landau was appointed to take over for Behar. She quickly reorganized the administration and the curriculum in keeping with recommendations from the Anglo-Jewish Association.[14] These measures satisfied the Anglo-Jewish leadership, but Landau saw the need for even more: a complete overhaul of the program, beginning with a clear statement of purpose. She did not want to be the headmistress of a school that taught only those skills that would help girls to earn a bit of money to help their families. Although the need for additional income was real, Landau had a larger objective.

In her view, the girls of Jerusalem were an untapped resource that had to be developed if the goal of Jewish regeneration in the Jewish homeland was to succeed. She envisaged her program as a merger of faith and modern education. This dual education created women who provided leadership of all sorts: in educating the young, improving social conditions, and fostering cultural development. These leaders were young women and old, married and single, mothers and those without children. In the early decades, Landau included boys in her kindergarten classes—she wanted them to be well educated, too—but her special interest was girls' education. Once other opportunities for boys existed in Jerusalem, she removed them from the school.

Landau was unusually perceptive in recognizing the critical role to be played by women in the development of the Jewish people. She was at odds with traditional Jewish communities in Jerusalem that adhered to strict limitations on women's dress and movements so as not to "lead men astray." She questioned Zionist leaders who spoke of equality for women but failed to provide opportunities for them to develop beyond traditional roles. Landau never wavered from her belief in women's abilities and in the necessity of harnessing their talents. She began her life's work of creating and constantly modifying curricular and extracurricular programs to prepare her pupils for the roles she imagined for them. In the process, she met with stiff opposition. She was able to continue in the face of adversity because of the loyal support of Claude Montefiore, the great nephew of Sir Moses and Lady Judith, and the Ladies' Committee of the Anglo-Jewish Association.

Although Landau's program was buttressed by the financial and moral support she received from London, in Jerusalem she was on her own to solve problems for which she had no previous experience. Not long after she became headmistress, a camel found its final resting place at the entrance to her school. Landau sent a request to the Ottoman governor of Jerusalem asking him to arrange for the removal of the decaying carcass. After a few days, having received no reply, she sent a second letter that revealed her growing confidence:

> Your Excellency, as the presence of a dead camel outside my School is a grave danger to the health of our several hundred children, I must beg to inform Your Excellency that if the carcass is not removed before 5 o'clock this evening, I shall be compelled to have it removed at my own expense and placed outside Your Excellency's door, as I do not know how to dispose of dead animals.[15]

This letter resulted in the quick removal of the carcass. Landau paid no bribes, nor did she turn to a male teacher to intercede with the authorities. She addressed the issue firmly and clearly. As a result of this and many similar actions, Landau became a force to be reckoned with in Jerusalem. She reported her successes to her benefactors in England to demonstrate her capability in dealing with local matters.

Landau found allies for her work in an unanticipated quarter: the mothers of Jerusalem. These deeply religious, overworked women, many suffering from malnutrition and illness, were minimally educated and often superstitious. Landau, who met socially with European community leaders—doctors, professors, and bankers—also made time to call on her pupils at home, engaging their mothers and trying to educate them in basic hygiene, nutrition, and preventative medicine. She understood the important role that mothers played in the traditional family, in which men supervised the education of the sons and women that of the daughters.[16]

Yet even while Landau understood the importance of the mothers' help, she was not afraid to confront them about beliefs and practices she considered antithetical to her mission. The mothers, survivors of early marriages, multiple pregnancies, and the loss of many babies, resorted to amulets and magic phrases to ward off the "evil eye." Landau recognized that she would have to convince them to work with her if she hoped to rid her pupils of such ideas and usher them into the modern world. She relied on her knowledge of Jewish practice to separate superstition from Jewish observance, and she had no hesitation about removing all amulets from her pupils as soon as they entered the school. Landau enforced standards of personal hygiene that were at first opposed by the parents. In cases of suspected malnutrition, she sent letters home, to be read aloud by the girls to their illiterate mothers.

She also negotiated with mothers about keeping their daughters in school past the age of twelve or thirteen, when many were betrothed. She urged her pupils to delay marriage for several years for health reasons (many infants and mothers died during early pregnancies) and so that they could complete their education. At first, the mothers remonstrated with Landau, fearing that if their daughters waited to marry until they were seventeen or eighteen, they would be considered too old. In time, recognizing the improved health of their "late-marrying" daughters, they became Landau's staunch supporters.

Landau's British friends did not understand her passion for her adopted city. They frequently asked why she remained in Jerusalem when she could have returned to a more comfortable life in London. Landau's attempts to explain focused on her sense of mission:

> We are very happy in Jerusalem, happy because of something attempted, something done. We see every day more and more, notwithstanding that many a disappointment is not spared us, how beautifully our girls' lives begin to unfold, how day by day some dormant sense of feeling and honor is quickened. Our pupils do not sever their connection with the school once they are out of its walls. In order to keep in touch with our girls after they have left, we instituted our "Old Girls' Club" which, meeting once a week, has always a crowded attendance. Good books in Hebrew and English are discussed, we sing and drill a little, and, above all, the girls are encouraged to speak freely to us about their

joys and their sorrows, thus enabling us to help them with advice they know to be well meant and sincere.[17]

She reminded them of the big picture, the underlying reason for her work:

By educating the girls of Jerusalem, however, we are slowly but surely improving conditions in the Holy Land. For when these girls are mothers they will teach their children a new creed of independence, of self-help, and these children will not wait for charity to help them. With the Almighty's help they will create industries for themselves—they will live, not merely exist. It is my firm conviction that the pitiful state of things in Jerusalem has come about because the education of women has been neglected.[18]

Annie Landau was a builder. She created a school that introduced a new, modern spirit to Jerusalem. Her pupils articulated the belief that they were part of a joint venture with their headmistress to improve conditions in the city. Using distinctly British terms of reference, one alumna said that she felt that she belonged to a "royal family." Another commented that Landau dubbed her and her sisters "treasures." A third used the term "angels," while a fourth said that she was encouraged to feel as though she wore a "halo."[19] By echoing her words, these pupils demonstrated their feeling of belonging to Landau and to her world of high-mindedness and purpose. Landau called on her girls to join her in building their homeland using their new skills.

The Evelina de Rothschild School, popularly known as "Miss Landau,"[20] was not the only school for Jewish girls in Jerusalem, but it educated the largest number of pupils and is the only one to survive to the present day. Several other schools were founded in Jerusalem by Jewish organizations from western Europe at the end of the nineteenth century. The Lamel School, funded originally by Elise von Herz-Lamel and later by the Hilfsverein, taught in German and later in Hebrew. For several years it responded to community pressure by teaching only traditional subjects, but ultimately it turned to a more modern curriculum. The Alliance Israélite Universelle, which established a large network of schools throughout Palestine, taught in French, with Hebrew reserved for sacred studies.[21]

Although each of these schools and the missionary schools enrolled numbers of Jewish girls in Jerusalem, none of them influenced the history of the city and of the country as much as the Evelina de Rothschild School. Part of the effect of the Evelina School derived from the values and leadership of Annie Landau. Her unique vision and her persistence in the face of adversity became legendary. The good fortune of the pupils to become fluent in English without compromising their abilities in Hebrew at a time when English language skills were demanded by the Mandatory government was another reason that they became influential women in Palestine and later Israel.

"Miss Landau's girls," as they were called, modeled themselves after their headmistress and their teachers. Like these adults, the girls expected to work hard to help in the development of their country. They understood that they were growing up at a special moment in the history of their people, and they were encouraged to contribute their skills and talents, nurtured during their school years, to build a bright future.

The story of the graduates is a little-told narrative of young girls who grew to womanhood in Jerusalem during years of struggle, strikes, riots, and war. Within this environment of severe hardship, these girls found a garden oasis in the Evelina de Rothschild School. Here they learned about a world beyond sandbags and barbed wire, beyond poverty and disease, and beyond religious hatred. They learned poetry and chemistry; they studied Bible and horticulture; they practiced sports and recited daily prayers. They viewed slides of Baroque and Renaissance masterpieces and learned to sing classical music in a choir. They learned popular English girls' songs and games as well as Hebrew songs and games. They were encouraged to write in English and Hebrew in the *School* magazine. The Evelina School afforded them time and space to develop mature adult identities and roles appropriate for building families, communities, and a nation.

The girls entered the school from vastly different backgrounds. In the 1930s and 1940s, refugees from Hitler's Europe joined the already eclectic group of girls. They spoke different languages at home; their parents were of different socioeconomic and educational levels; some families were religiously observant and others were not; and, like all children, they had a variety of skills, talents, and ambitions. Their stories reflected the complicated times in which they grew.

In their later lives, most Evelina graduates were remarkably aware of the effect that their school, teachers, and classmates had on their development. Former classmates kept in touch with one another and frequently compared notes on the influence of the school on their lives. Class photos adorned their family albums. Leather-bound volumes of the Bible, of English poetry, and of stories and novels in English and Hebrew were inscribed by the teachers and Landau and kept as treasures on their bookshelves. All the women who were approached to share their memories and reflect on their school experiences for this book were eager to do so.

Annie Landau died in 1945, but her legacy lived on at the school under the guiding hand of her associate, Ethel Levy, and in the lives of her thousands of graduates who worked for the welfare of Jerusalem and the nation of Israel. Many continued their education, practiced nursing and other aspects of medicine, taught at all levels, and achieved important positions in government and business. Most served in the Haganah, the clandestine Jewish defense movement, and later in the Israel Defense Forces. A small group joined kibbutzim.

Some abandoned Landau's principles of firm in faith and modern in education. Finding the two principles incompatible, they adhered to the second principle while abandoning the strict religious practices of their youth. Nevertheless, these graduates report being happy to have learned the weekly Torah reading and remember with fondness special holiday and Sabbath programs. All continue to feel privileged to have lived a purposeful life with goals that were larger than individual fulfillment.

Nearly seven decades have passed since Annie Landau was buried on the Mount of Olives. The Jerusalem in which many of the Evelina graduates now live is very different from the city in which they attended school. Frutiger House, which housed the Evelina School, is still a beautiful building surrounded by gardens. It has merited a place on the historic register and today serves as offices for the Ministry of Education.

Sitting in Landau's former office, the education minister looks out over the same purple-hued hilltops, now dotted by many more buildings. His problems include ongoing conflict between religious and secular Jews who want to control the national education agenda as well as the dilemma of an inadequate education budget. Both of these problems have deep roots in the period of the Mandate. Landau believed in her ability to solve problems. The problems of today's leaders are of a different order, and in a postmodern world, the belief in solutions has been shaken. Nevertheless, I believe that her story and that of her pupils provide important historical lessons, both cautionary and inspirational, for those committed to building the future of the Middle East.

[1]

ANNIE LANDAU'S ROAD
TO JERUSALEM

Hannah Edith Landau, called Annie, was born in 1873 on Leman Street in the rapidly expanding, vibrant eastern European Jewish community in the East End of London. She was the eldest daughter of Marcus Israel Landau and Chaya Kohn, both immigrants to London who were raised in Orthodox families that scrupulously observed Jewish law, traditions, and customs. In London, Marcus and Chaya encountered established Jews who were less observant and who were invested in a particularly British model of self-reliance and hard work.

Annie imbibed both traditions and became a true Englishwoman as well as an Orthodox Jewess. This dual identity served her well in her extraordinary career as an educational leader in Jerusalem during the late Ottoman Empire and through the years of the British Mandate in Palestine. The beginning of Annie's life is somewhat obscured by the passage of time, yet the limited information about her childhood and her schooling provide significant clues to her future life and work in Jerusalem.

Annie's father, born Mordecai Fredkin in 1837 in Gomel, Mogilev, Russia, was exceptionally bright and energetic. Faced with conscription into the czarist army, which entailed lengthy service as well as pressure to convert, Mordecai fled his home and country, seeking a place to live where he could practice his religion freely. He acquired a forged passport that had been issued to a man named Marcus Landau. Upon Landau's death shortly thereafter, Mordecai assumed his identity.

Mordecai/Marcus lived for a short while in Paris, moving later to Frankfurt, where in 1853 he married a woman named Hannah, who was also from Mogilev. Both bride and groom were only sixteen. Shortly after their marriage, Hannah and Marcus moved to the East End of London, where Marcus started his first career as a shoemaker. The young couple had five children: John, Rose, Charlie, Henry, and Esther. Hannah died in 1871 at the age of thirty-five, leaving her husband with two teenage children and three younger ones.[1]

After the mourning period, Marcus returned to Frankfurt, then a vibrant center of Orthodox Judaism, to seek a new bride. There he met and married Chaya Kohn, originally from Kleine Erdlingen, Bavaria. Chaya was nineteen when she married the widower Marcus, now in his midthirties. She came from a highly educated family and had received an unusual education. Chaya's family eschewed the secular and vocational focus of the Philanthropin, a school that opened for the Jewish children of Frankfurt in the early nineteenth century. Instead, Chaya studied in a Catholic girls' school in Frankfurt and later was sent to Paris, where she attended a convent school under the supervision of her uncle, Rabbi Moses Weiskopf. She was tutored in Jewish subjects at home.

The strong family commitment to education continued in the next generation as Marcus and Chaya raised their children in London. Marcus soon changed his occupation to grocery shop owner, a step up from the smelly work of tanning hides, which was repugnant to his new wife. The family lived above the shop, which was located at 96 Leman Street, next to Wechsler's well-known wine store, in the heart of London's Jewish East End. Chaya gave birth to eleven children in that house. Two more children were born after the family had moved to the more fashionable Highbury Park.[2]

Like most immigrants, Marcus and Chaya Landau aspired to join the middle class. They worked hard in the grocery shop, especially before Passover, when the picture of Marcus on packaged food was accepted as a guarantee that it was kosher for Passover. Over time, Marcus expanded his business, soon adding kosher meat to his inventory in order to provide the increased income he needed for his growing family.[3]

With the older Landau siblings, there were eighteen children, nine boys and nine girls, to be fed, clothed, sheltered, and educated. All the children, girls as well as boys, were encouraged to excel in both secular and Jewish studies. Already imagining themselves in the middle class, Marcus and Chaya did not join the thousands of poor immigrants who sent their children to the Jews'

Free School. They selected schools that offered a middle-class curriculum in secular studies, while the family provided Jewish education at home.

Marcus and Chaya also taught their children by example. Marcus was an autodidact who continued to study all his life. Unlike most Jews in London, he understood Hebrew and amassed a large Hebrew library of Jewish law and tradition as well as Hebrew books on mathematics. He was fascinated by arithmetic calculations and became interested in the young science of aeronautics and in the invention of lamps. During the 1870s he invented safety lamps for mines, carriage lamps, and street lamps, and he patented some of these inventions. It is not surprising that several of the Landau children studied science and that others went into medicine.[4]

Less is known about Chaya Landau's continuing education. Unlike her husband, Chaya had many years of formal schooling and was undoubtedly influential in deciding where her children would study. She was deeply involved in charitable work. Her husband was one of the founders of the Society for Providing Sabbath Meals and also of the Poor Jews' Temporary Shelter. Both of these activities required extensive support from Chaya. Decades later, in a memorable lesson to her pupils, Annie Landau reflected on her mother's concept of charity:

> When I was a young girl people came to our house to collect toys for poor orphans. I offered to give an old doll that I didn't like. My mother asked me, "Do you want to make the poor orphan girl happy?" I answered, "Yes, of course." She asked, "If someone brought you this doll, would you be happy?" I said, "No! I don't like it." "If so," my mother said, "give a doll that you would be happy to receive."[5]

Chaya practiced philanthropy as an ethical obligation to treat others, especially the poor, with respect and compassion. When Annie Landau told this story to her pupils, she demonstrated that she not only had learned the lesson, she also honored her mother for teaching her this ethical approach to giving. Landau's lifelong dedication to the girls of Jerusalem was further proof that she was guided by the values taught by her mother.

Chaya's teachings influenced her eldest daughter in other ways, too. Long after Annie left home, she maintained the Landau family tradition of celebrating the Sabbath and Jewish holidays with special rituals, songs, and foods, and she shared them with the friends she invited into her circle. One of these friends later observed the following:

Seder, Succoth, Purim, the High Holydays found her salon or dining room buzzing with guests of all origins, British, locals, Arabs and Jews, Army, the Jewish Agency, the Synagogue, and the Church . . . traditional dishes on every commemoration; golden Sabbath Eves in the finest Frankfurt fashion, with unabridged choral introduction and envoi. We learnt the zemiroth which still trip easily from our tongues today. We learnt the essential loveliness and melody of Psalms and piyyutim, the beguiling charm of candlelight and snowy Jewish linen, delicate china, burnished brass and glittering silver.[6]

It is not clear what conversations took place around the Landau family dinner table. There must have been some discussion of the inventions that occupied Marcus and of the charitable work done by Chaya, and there was certainly concern about the welfare of family members and of the Jewish communities of France, Germany, and Russia. It is likely that there was some discussion about the conditions of Jews in the Holy Land, since reports about the poverty and disease of Jews living in Jerusalem, Safed, Hebron, and Tiberias were found in the established German, French, and English Jewish newspapers.

By the time Annie reached her teen years, Marcus's strong interest in community affairs was documented in the editorials of the *Jewish Standard*, a newspaper that he began with a few friends in 1888 and printed in the basement of the Landau home for three years. Marcus Landau and his fellow editors took exception to the basic approach of the *Jewish Chronicle*, founded nearly half a century earlier. They advocated a periodical that would express a different point of view:

> Many of us have felt the need of an English journal which should represent our feelings and aspirations as earnest Jews. While recognizing the ability with which the existing Jewish newspapers published in this country are conducted, we are compelled to feel that their views are entirely opposed to those which we hold. . . . Our contemporaries contend that Judaism has been formed in a plastic mould, and requires to be re-modelled according to the shifting needs of every age. We believe, on the other hand, that the written and oral law, as revealed on Sinai, is fixed and unchangeable, and was vouchsafed not for one age, but for all time. We cannot, therefore, allow any considerations of expediency or interest to make us acquiesce in changes which are based on the negation of principle, which is the foundation of our faith.[7]

Marcus Landau's interest in mathematics and his dedication to inventing did not lead him to question Orthodox beliefs. His commitment to Orthodox Judaism was expressed in the way he led his life and in the newspaper he launched. Intrigued by many aspects of secular studies, Marcus saw no conflict between excelling in those fields and practicing his religion. Annie followed his example, integrating modern ideas and religious observance throughout her life. Like her father, she was determined to teach her ideals. He worked through the editorials of the *Standard*, whereas she developed a school for girls in Jerusalem.

The first editorial of the *Standard* addressed education. Marcus and his colleagues advocated a new type of comprehensive education that challenged the basic objective of the Jews' Free School, which provided elementary school education for poor Jewish youth so that they could find employment after graduation. The school also sought to change the stereotypical image of immigrants as dirty, ill-mannered, and imbued with questionable ethics by introducing the children to English manners and elements of secular culture. In recognition of the Orthodox practices of many of its pupils, the school was closed on all Jewish holidays and provided strictly kosher lunches. The *Jewish Chronicle* regularly documented the successes of the graduates of the Jews' Free School in finding employment or continuing education.

Marcus and the editors of the *Standard* perceived a different and more pressing challenge to the Jewish community in the area of education—specifically, a profound deficiency in Jewish learning. Unwilling to pose a direct challenge to the Jewish leadership of the city, which supported the Jews' Free School, the *Standard* presented a plan that was designed for middle-class Jewish children. The editors pointed out that previous generations of Jews were much more knowledgeable about the history and culture of their people; they lamented that "modern English Judaism bears so faint a resemblance to the sturdy faith, which once flourished notwithstanding the fiercest onslaughts of its foes from without."[8]

The solution promulgated by Marcus and his friends was the establishment of a new type of Jewish school designed for the growing middle class in every district in London in which there was a large Jewish population. They asserted that the object of education was not only to supply skills for practical use but also to give mental and moral training to make "our children better men." In these new schools, Hebrew and religion would be fundamental subjects in the curriculum, replacing Latin and Greek. The editors asserted, "The Torah is surely at least as efficient an instrument as the Latin and Greek Classics, which absorb so much time in an ordinary school."[9] In addition, all the subjects usually included in a commercial education would be taught in the same manner that they were taught at non-Jewish middle-class schools. The editors, aware that they were newcomers to England, also advocated deep study of the history and literature of the English people.

As headmistress of the Evelina de Rothschild School in Jerusalem, Annie Landau struggled to create a curriculum that included religious values and modern ideas. She adopted educational reforms from England and Germany, introducing music and sports to the course of study, which also included a course in Jewish history taught in Hebrew. Landau's curriculum reflected her father's values, but it went beyond the ideas of the *Jewish Standard*, introducing the importance of developing self-sufficient Jewish girls who would contribute to their families and their people.

The editors considered several other topics in the weeks that followed: Judaism and art, Jews and politics, and the observance of the Sabbath.[10] Each of these topics played a role in the Landau family worldview that shaped young Annie's education. Unlike many Orthodox Jews who banned the study of the visual arts, Marcus believed that all true art is the result of religious sentiment and proceeds from joy in the beauty of God's works. Years later, Annie developed an innovative art history curriculum for her school. Like her father, she saw no contradiction between Orthodox Judaism and appreciation for the arts.

In the public arena, Marcus criticized the view of some religious Jews who believed that the Jewish community should keep apart from non-Jews. He thought that Judaism should not only benefit Jews but inform the whole world as well. Annie shared her father's idea that Jews were not living up to their obligations if they did not work for general social improvement. Her school pioneered and promulgated civic engagement in Jerusalem. Not long after the founding of the Jerusalem Society for the Prevention of Cruelty to Animals, Landau boasted that her pupils were the first to establish a student group associated with the society.

Sabbath observance was a problematic issue for English Jews, since work on Saturday was then the norm. Some Jews gave up regular Sabbath observance and limited their religious practice to major Jewish holidays. Nevertheless,

Marcus and his colleagues advocated regular Sabbath observance as a requirement of Jewish life. Annie was similarly committed to teaching the values of Sabbath observance to all her pupils in Jerusalem; she developed a weekly program that taught generations of the city's young women how to welcome the Sabbath, and this service became a hallmark of the Evelina School.

Another controversial issue that was addressed in the *Jewish Standard* was the role of women in synagogue rituals. An editorial that appeared on April 27, 1888, responded to a number of issues then under debate: Should women be counted in the minyan, the quorum for communal prayer that traditionally consists of ten men? Should female choirs be established in synagogues? These issues were certainly of concern to Chaya as well as to Marcus. With their eldest daughter, Annie, attending the Hirsch School in Frankfurt and about to begin a career as a teacher in Jewish schools, the Landaus thought about the role of women in all aspects of Jewish life. The editorial read as follows:

> There is no reason to assign to woman an inferior position either in religious or intellectual matters. Her spiritual insight is indeed at least as keen as that of man, and the quality of her mind has often a power of intuitive judgment not found so often in man. . . . She should therefore study nearly the same subjects as man, but in a somewhat different manner, so as to call into play the particular qualities of heart and head which she possesses.[11]

To further elucidate their views, the editors added, "We fully approve of the proposed confirmation of girls, provided it be preceded by real and substantial instruction, and not be a mere occasion for display." Annie Landau was inspired by these discussions to create a daily program of communal prayer in the Evelina de Rothschild School. In a break with tradition, prayers were led by one of the girls; similarly, the weekly program to welcome the Sabbath featured a girl reciting from the Torah reading, with a commentary offered by Landau. These practices reflected Landau's belief that girls should be required to learn and be given opportunities to lead in all areas of life.

Annie grew up in a home where girls were encouraged to pursue their dreams. She was educated with the goal of serving her people and humanity. She saw no conflict between religious Orthodoxy and public roles for women. Annie treasured her English upbringing along with the traditions and teachings of her strictly Orthodox home. She chose to be called "Annie," a proper English girl's name, even after she moved to Palestine, where many immigrants adopted Hebrew names.

Landau was not an intellectual. In the face of adversity, she did not examine the values she had learned in childhood; she held them close as she approached the many challenges of life in Jerusalem. Throughout her years as the headmistress of the Evelina de Rothschild School, she returned home regularly to renew ties with her family and friends. Until 1923, when her mother died, Landau stayed at 20 Highbury Park, the large house purchased by her father in 1895. In later years, during her visits to London she stayed with her sister Elsie.

The special character of the Landaus' culture and their clear dual identity as English and Jewish are visible in a program printed for the celebration of Marcus's seventieth birthday in 1907. The musical evening, which took place at home, included presentations by the choir of the Dalton Synagogue as well as piano performances, songs, tableaux, comedies, and dances by many family members. Annie participated in several sets in Hebrew, English, and German with her sisters and other family members. Some of the pieces were biblical in origin; others were influenced by Gilbert and Sullivan. One piece, which had an Ottoman motif, was certainly written by Annie; titled "Turkee Turks," it included Syrian dancers.[12]

Annie's full sisters—Dora, Helena, Birdie, Ruth, Elsie, and Violet—and two of her brothers, David and Joe, participated in this event. The family remained remarkably close despite the fact that several of them lived abroad for many years. David lived in South Africa, and Joe practiced medicine in Singapore. Abraham and Michael worked together during World War I to invent luminous gunsights and plates for taking deep X-rays. Isaac remained in London where he served as president of the London shechita (ritual slaughter) board; there is no information about Sydney.

Elsie, who married, obtained an MD and became the head of the Elizabeth Garrett Anderson Hospital in Bloomsbury. Dora became an actress, although she restricted her performances to the Jewish Drama League and the Delphic Dramatic Society out of respect for her parents' Orthodoxy. Helena became the principal of the Jewish Fresh Air Home and School at Delamere, Cheshire. Birdie and Violet were both teachers. Ruth, the youngest, was a warden with the Air Raid Precautions in north London during World War II.[13]

As the eldest of Chaya and Marcus's children, Annie played an important role in the family. She set an example for her younger siblings, three of whom also entered the field of education. As a sister and an aunt, her visits from Jerusalem were important occasions. In the 1930s she stayed in Mapesbury, where her sister Elsie kept a large room for her visits. Elsie's son, Oliver Sacks, recalled, "She would arrive periodically in England with steamer trunks so enormous they needed six porters to lift them." Thirty years after her death, the room was still called "Annie's room."[14]

The close ties between Annie and her sisters continued throughout Annie's years in Palestine. In the early 1930s, Annie sent fruit from Jerusalem to her sister Helena's school in Delamere. The familiar style of the letter written by Annie to Helena in November 1942 is another illustration of the strong family connections:

Dear Len,

So delighted to get your airgraph of Oct. 19. Got here very quickly. I'm glad you've heard from Marjorie [Annie's and Helena's niece from Australia]. Strange that none of us get any news of Joe. . . . I've turned our garden into vegetables and we are having summer weather again after a brief spell of what was looking like mid-winter. Aubrey Eban [Annie and Helena's nephew, later Abba Eban] is lecturing for the British Council to packed audiences in addition to his Army work. He is with us most Friday nights. He overworks too tremendously. As my heart is behaving itself badly and I am doing without my two nurses now, I have a thoroughly good medical masseuse twice a week or so to pep up my muscles. I've done no walking for practically two years now. I hardly ever leave the house and then only by car. We listened yesterday to the bells pealing all over England, Scotland, N. Ireland, and Wales. It made me cry. How I wish the end of this conflict was in sight. I'd so love to be with you all once again. Miss Raphael, the old headmistress of the Manchester Jewish School, has just been here talking to me of the old time. I know so many of her old pupils.
All my love, Len dear, keep well. Don't overwork.

Affectionately,
Annie[15]

Annie's Education

Annie remained close to her parents and siblings but was also influenced by her teachers. As a young girl, she attended an elementary school for middle-class girls, the Bishopsgate Ward School, which was quite close to the family home in the East End. Little is known about this school, formerly St. Ethelburga's Society School, which enrolled 280 girls in 1887.[16] The school was formed as the result of the passage of the Endowed Schools Act of 1869, which responded to reports on the inadequacy of girls' education by permitting endowments to be set up for girls' schools similar to those previously established for boys' schools.

One of those who invested in this new school was the Baroness Mayer de Rothschild.* Like many women of the Rothschild family, she shared the emerging belief that women had a special role to play in the world, whether at home or in the community. This idea was espoused by educational reformers like Frances Buss and Dorothea Beale, who demonstrated that middle-class girls could be given a liberal education, similar to that of boys, that would prepare them to be better mothers as well as for greater involvement in the community. The skills they learned would also prepare those who needed to work for jobs. These ideas, developed first in secondary education, soon influenced elementary schools as well.

Buss founded the North London Collegiate School for Girls at Camden in 1850. Her school became the inspiration for girls' schools all over the English-speaking world. She created a model curriculum for girls' high schools that closely followed the curriculum of boys' high schools: English subjects (scripture, history, literature, and geography), languages (French, German, and Latin), sciences (mathematics and natural science), and aesthetic subjects (music, singing, and drawing).[17] The new curriculum replaced the practice of teaching refinements like sewing, embroidery, and singing. New teaching methods replaced rote memorization with classroom engagement and the use of new classroom materials, including visual aids.[18] Several of the teachers hired at the Evelina de Rothschild School in later years were graduates of this school.

---

* Baroness Mayer de Rothschild, née Juliana Cohen, used her husband's name in public. As historians regularly refer to her as Baroness Mayer, I have continued to use this appellation to avoid confusion.

Another woman who contributed to the discussion of girls' education in this period was Caroline Franklin, a member of a leading Jewish family, whose work with the Ladies' Committee of the Anglo-Jewish Association would bring her into close contact with Annie Landau. Landau frequently spent weeks of rest in Franklin's guesthouse in Aylesbury. Franklin noted that girls' education had been neglected for the greater part of the nineteenth century, but this state of affairs had changed at the end of the century. The education of girls became recognized as very important since women's role in the state and the household had become more highly esteemed.

Previously, only girls of affluent families received excellent educations, but as it became obvious that poor women bore responsibility for the early mental, moral, and physical training of the nation, it became equally clear that it was important to prepare women for this important task. Franklin assumed that girls possessed intellectual abilities. In her discussion of girls' education, she emphasized the importance of educating girls to help those in need beyond their families, observing, "There is so much to be done in the world that I don't see how it can be done unless each one is prepared to help a little."[19]

Annie came of age at a time when educational opportunities for girls of all classes were expanding. She was held to a high standard of performance by her family and by her schools—first by Bishopsgate Ward and later by the Jewish High School for Girls, established by Rabbi Samson Raphael Hirsch in Frankfurt. Annie was sent to Frankfurt to pursue the type of education advocated in the editorials of the *Jewish Standard*. Hirsch's views about Orthodoxy and modern life were remarkably similar to those held by Marcus Landau. Chaya's natal family, which had remained in Frankfurt, supervised Annie.[20] Chaya had set an example for Annie by going to Paris for continuing study in her youth.

The Jewish High School for Girls, also known as the Hirsch School, proved an ideal place for Annie to spend her formative years. Here she continued to develop a modern Jewish identity that prepared her for the challenges she would face as headmistress of a Jewish girls' school in Palestine. Hirsch established his school as a modern Orthodox response to the challenges of Jewish emancipation. For more than half a century, Jewish schools in western European cities were funded to teach immigrant communities to integrate into the economic lives of their new cities.

One of the earliest examples of these schools was Philanthropin, founded in

1804 by Mayer Amschel Rothschild. By midcentury, this school had educated thousands of children, preparing them for jobs and ultimately for citizenship. Despite the clear success of these schools in achieving their objectives, many Orthodox Jews were concerned about the eclipse of Jewish education. By the 1870s there was a strong feeling in Frankfurt that another kind of education for Jewish youth, a combination of religious education and secular studies, was needed.

Strictly Orthodox Jews in Frankfurt continued to maintain traditional Jewish schools that included little secular learning. They were unwilling to support Rabbi Hirsch's approach, fearing that it was not sufficiently traditional. Their threats and demands did not deter Hirsch from his conviction that it was possible to teach Jewish children to engage with the world while remaining loyal to Jewish traditions.

Hirsch's school was designed to educate "a new generation of knowledgeable and loyal Jews for whom Judaism is their life's purpose."[21] This was a very different objective from most Jewish communal efforts, which remained committed to "regenerating" poor Jewish children by teaching them skills to enable them to participate in the changing economic conditions brought about by industrialization. Thus, schools for poor Jewish children, primarily immigrants, continued to teach speaking, reading, and writing in the language of their new country; these children also learned arithmetic and geography. They studied some religious subjects, but their education was decidedly secular, with a supplementary course on Judaism aimed at eliminating superstition and practices deemed to be at variance with modern life.

As a devout Jew, Hirsch was enthusiastic about secular studies—not because they might lead to jobs and further integration of Jews in the gentile communities of Europe but rather because he believed that the combination of secular and traditional subjects was more intellectually powerful than either one alone. Before emancipation, Jews had lived a traditional, segregated life and were disengaged from any knowledge of natural and historical processes. Hirsch anticipated that in the new era, Europe's understanding of and relationship to natural and historical processes were changing, and he reasoned that to survive this epic change, the Jewish people would have to develop interest in the study of both the traditional and the worldly.

Hirsch called on Jewish educators and parents to try a different approach— not one that perpetuated the dualism of religion and secularism but one that united within a weltanschauung the qualities and duties applicable to both domains.[22] Hirsch was not surprised when the school he started in Frankfurt to implement his approach was attacked by both traditionalists and progressives. Undaunted, he replied to his critics, "Our institute devotes the same care and attention to general educational subjects as to the specifically Jewish and, in fact, it is one of the declared principles that both should be put on the same footing."[23]

Hirsch believed that his school would educate Jewish youth to be better citizens by introducing them to Jewish culture and to be better Jews by introducing them to general culture. For Hirsch, the fundamental aim of the Torah, and thus of Judaism, was to promote knowledge and to improve the moral and intellectual standards of humanity. Thus, in the modern age there should be no estrangement between general culture and Jewish culture. Judaism should welcome every advance in thinking while also infusing an ethical-religious spirit into all aspects of the curriculum.

Annie Landau thrived in a school created on these principles, which closely mirrored the ideas she heard at home. Years later, she would apply Hirsch's ideas to the Evelina de Rothschild School in Jerusalem. One of her early colleagues at the Evelina School would be a friend from Frankfurt, Ella Schwartzstein.

When Annie returned home to London in 1892, she registered at the Graystoke Teachers' Training College to complete her education. In this training program, she was brought up-to-date on the new teaching methods that permeated the curriculum of the college. The endeavor to reform girls' education included lessons in hygiene, home economics, sports, and the importance of volunteer work for girls. Later, she would adopt all of them at her school in Jerusalem.

First she had to take the exams that would give her a teacher's certificate. Landau did not shrink from expressing her concerns about the exam schedule in a strongly worded letter to the editor of the *Jewish Chronicle* on December 7, 1894. She pointed out that some of the exams were scheduled for late Friday afternoon, which made it impossible for an observant Jew to take them:

I am sitting for the Certificate on December 10th and on receiving my time-table from the Department on November 27th I found that one of the languages I intend to take was timed Friday, 4 to 6. I immediately wrote to the correspondent of the school at which I am an assistant, requesting him to communicate with the Department on the difficulty. Hearing rumours that it was too late to make any alteration this year, I determined to use every means in my power to secure justice, for it would certainly be an injustice if a candidate had to forego marks on account of religious views. I wrote to the Chief Rabbi and to Mr. Acland, Vice-President of the Educational Council, stating the facts, and asking them to bring their influence to bear upon the matter.[24]

Four months later, the *Jewish Chronicle* reported the following about the Westminster Jews' Free School, where Landau had gotten her first teaching job:

Miss Annie Landau of this school has been placed in the first class (first year papers) at the Government Certificate Examination held last December. Miss Landau took Hebrew and German as optional subjects; a special examination in the latter language having been permitted by the Education Department on January 15th instead of the original date which was timed for Friday afternoon, after Sabbath had commenced.[25]

Annie's protest was characteristic of her lifelong behavior. She did not take shortcuts when it came to religious observance, nor did she apologize for her right to the accommodation of her needs. Moreover, she made her concerns a public matter, using the exam schedule as an opportunity to demonstrate the possibility of living according to Orthodox practice while entering the modern world of exams and licenses. She was now a credentialed teacher working at the Westminster Jews' Free School on Hanway Place, a beautiful building that housed separate boys' and girls' schools. The headmistress of the girls' school was Hannah Herzon, who had been taught by Moses Angel, the legendary leader of the Jews' Free School in the East End and the trainer of scores of teachers for Jewish schools and London School Board schools located in Jewish communities.

By the time Landau began teaching in Westminster, the school enrolled three hundred girls and received annual government grants. Government inspectors measured student success regularly.[26] The Westminster school had an excellent library and the funds to provide children with dinner in winter months as well as clothing and boots. Annie's experience at Westminster enabled her to put into practice some of the theoretical principles she had learned at Graystoke.

Westminster had ample playground space, which was fitted with gymnasium equipment. In accord with modern practices, the physical comfort of the pupils was considered in deciding to provide adequate heating and ventilation for the classrooms. The safety of the pupils was a priority in planning corridors and staircases that were fireproof. Great care was taken with plumbing and drainage; drinking water was filtered.

Landau observed all the details of school administration, including enrollment management, curriculum planning, student assessment, student support services, and the planning and management of the buildings and grounds. Years later, when she was confronted by the chaos of the Evelina de Rothschild School, Landau remembered the organization and planning that had led to success at the Westminster school.

The Evelina de Rothschild School, Jerusalem, 1854–1899

While Annie Landau was still learning her craft in London, Dr. Yitzchak Schwartz, head of the Rothschild Hospital in the Old City of Jerusalem, continued to supervise the adjacent Evelina de Rothschild School. In 1886, he submitted a report to Leopold Rothschild explaining the use of school funds during the previous six months:

> 150 girls—6 to 14 years of age—attended the school. 100 of them received a daily meal of soup, vegetables, and bread, and twice weekly of meat. One teacher gave lessons in Hebrew reading and writing, likewise two mistresses gave lessons in French reading and writing as well as math, also during the summer term there were some lessons in geography and natural history and three mistresses taught needlework, including dressmaking and sewing . . . the most industrious girls, 30 altogether, got a prize, one dress for each.[27]

Schwartz noted that the pupils came from both Ashkenazi and Sephardi backgrounds; there were also some Moroccan and Karaite pupils and one Armenian Christian. He expressed satisfaction that the girls' needlework surpassed expectation and reported that the *hakham-bashi*, the chief rabbi appointed by the Ottoman government, expressed deep gratitude to the founders of the school.

In 1888, the Rothschild Hospital, which suffered from overcrowding, moved out of the Old City to a larger, new building on the Street of the Prophets.

The next year, the Rothschilds decided to appoint a headmistress for the school, since the hospital administration was no longer in close proximity. They selected Fortunée Behar, an experienced teacher at the Alliance school in Constantinople and a member of a leading Sephardi family in Jerusalem, to administer the school. Fortunée's brother Nissim was the head of the Lionel de Rothschild Technical School in Jerusalem, and he most likely brought her skills to the attention of the Rothschild family. Simultaneously, the Anglo-Jewish Association, an organization devoted to helping poor Jews who lived outside England, began to devote increased attention to the need for girls' education in the East.

The association had first discussed the topic of establishing a Jewish girls' school in its meetings of 1886. Alarmed by the backwardness of the Jewish community of Baghdad, the board members concluded that Jews in the city would not be able to raise their status or make any substantial progress unless girls received an appropriate education. They reasoned that educating boys for modern life while neglecting girls would be ineffective because the useful work done in the boys' schools would be overturned at home, and they were convinced that educating the Jewish girls of Baghdad to become modern would yield results for their families and for the Jewish community of Baghdad as well as for the image of Jews in London.[28]

The Anglo-Jewish Association opened its first girls' school in Baghdad, followed by a second in Mogador, Morocco. Eager to evaluate the school, the association asked Charles Payton, the British consul in Mogador, to inspect the pupils. In 1891, he reported as follows:

> The general proficiency and progress shown in the English language (including grammar, writing and translation, dictation, analysis, etc), and also in geography, history and arithmetic, were all very pleasing; and I was glad to notice among new subjects in your curriculum drawing and music, though doubtful as to the desirability of these more elegant subjects for all classes of your scholars. Some excellent specimens of needlework were submitted for Mrs. Payton's inspection.[29]

Nevertheless, the magnitude of the task was daunting. In addition to relying on reports by British consuls, the association sent one of its leaders, Alfred Cohen, to review opportunities to establish new schools. Cohen went first to Damascus, where he reported the prevalent view among Muslims and

Christians that the Jewish population of the city had low moral standards. He was surprised to discover that Jewish women in the Levant, unlike their Western sisters, were assumed by the non-Jews around them to be of low moral character:

> It is curious that while in Western countries the purity of the Jewish woman has been so marked and honourable a characteristic, that while in epochs of persecution foul and unfounded charges have often been made against Jewish men, no aspersions have ever been cast on the general honour of Jewish European women, nevertheless in cities like Damascus, and perhaps other Mussulman cities, the Jewish woman, as far as I can gather, is not on a level with her Muslim or Christian sister.[30]

Cohen continued his journey to Jerusalem. The concern of the Anglo-Jewish Association with the deficiency in Jewish girls' education in the East was particularly acute in their review of the situation in the Holy City. In addition to describing the dirt, disease, and ignorance in Jerusalem, Cohen reported on the activity of Christian missionaries. He described two of the missionary schools for girls: the London Jews' Society School for Girls and the Soeurs de Sion School. The London Jews' Society School enrolled only Jewish pupils. The superintendent, Elizabeth Fitzjohn, asserted that no attempt was made to baptize the girls against their parents' will. Nevertheless, the pupils learned Christian dogma, sang Christian hymns, and were expected to join in Christian worship; they received free room and board, clothing and food, and tuition and were taught to be neat and clean. Cohen found the level of instruction to be poor. There were about forty girls in the school, and Fitzjohn reported that about 10 percent of the pupils asked to be baptized.[31]

Cohen was convinced that the children attending this school experienced a life of constant hypocrisy; he assumed that those who agreed to be baptized believed that they owed this to the institution that fed, clothed, and educated them. He contrasted the emphasis on conversion in missionary schools with the mutual respect he believed existed in European schools, where Jewish and Christian children might join in ecumenical prayer. He cited this verse as an example:

> He prayeth best who loveth best,
> All things both great and small.

This brief prayer, something that Annie Landau might have recited at Bishopsgate Ward, was in Cohen's view the outcome of tolerance and breadth of mind, virtues he found to be in short supply in Jerusalem.

Cohen continued his school report with observations about the French convent of the Soeurs de Sion, which accommodated one hundred pupils, about thirty of whom were Jewish. These pupils also received room and board, clothing, and an education. Here the expectation of baptism was more definite.[32] In Cohen's view, the education received at the French school was superior to that of the English school; he assumed that the conversion of these girls was based on faith.

Cohen reserved most of his time for a visit to the Evelina de Rothschild School, the largest school for Jewish girls in Jerusalem. His assessment of the school was of great importance, as the Anglo-Jewish Association was in the process of taking over its management from the Rothschild family. Recognizing the growing expertise of the association in school management, the Rothschild family had entered an agreement in 1894 with the association whereby the family would continue to fund the school at the level of eight hundred pounds per year, while the supervision of the school would pass to the association. The agreement included a provision that additional funds would be provided for the purchase of a building for the school. The association promptly created its Ladies' Committee to supervise the Evelina de Rothschild School. The committee enthusiastically took up the challenge, declaring, "There is room for women from the West to help their sisters in the East."[33]

Under the management of Fortunée Behar, the Evelina School had made some important strides. Nevertheless, Cohen believed that it was not as strong as the other schools supported by the association. While in Jerusalem, he ranked the Evelina School behind the Soeurs de Sion and ahead of the London Jews' Society School. Needlework was well taught at the Evelina School, and French instruction was fair, but English instruction was poor. He explained that it was difficult to find competent teachers in Jerusalem. One of the best teachers at the Evelina School had been educated at the English mission and was leaving to get married.

Cohen noted that the pupils were of various nationalities—Russian, Persian, and Palestinian—and that Behar had adopted French as the common language. A rabbi taught Hebrew, but there was no attention given to religious values or ethics. Cohen's review of the Evelina School may have reflected his lack of comfort with Behar, whose Sephardi background and French culture were foreign to him.

Before Cohen's arrival, Behar had been successful in moving the school to temporary quarters outside the walls of the Old City on Street of the Prophets near the new quarters of the Rothschild Hospital. Cohen found the area much healthier than the Jewish areas within the walls. Nevertheless, crowding and hygiene remained a problem. Behar explained that she often had to send pupils home on account of their dirty condition. Unpaved streets remained a problem until the mid-1930s; girls who walked long distances to school arrived dusty or muddy, depending on the season. Cohen recommended hiring a woman to wash the girls, but Behar refused.

Cohen also recommended that girls who could afford tuition should pay. Behar agreed that some of the families could afford tuition, but she opposed charging tuition since she feared that it would create a distinction between paying and nonpaying pupils. Cohen noted a different concern: he feared that the attendance of too many girls from affluent families would prevent the enrollment of poor girls, who would be ashamed to appear in their ragged garments next to the well-garbed girls.

Finally, Cohen suggested that Behar work with a local committee to create school policy and that she hire an accountant to keep an organized record of the expenditures of the school. Behar was reluctant to work with an accountant. Cohen also pointed out that the school kept no attendance records or any records of student progress.

After discussing Cohen's report, the Ladies' Committee was convinced of the need for reform, so it invited Behar to London to visit English schools and to learn English school management practices. By the time of her visit, the Anglo-Jewish Association had substantial experience administering schools in the East. Since its establishment in 1870, it had provided schooling for forty thousand children.[34] The Ladies' Committee discussed Cohen's report with Behar and instructed her to purchase a suitable school building, increase the hours of English language instruction, and start collecting tuition from pupils whose families could afford to pay. Behar reluctantly agreed.

Despite Behar's reluctance to accept these changes, a few months later she reported progress in several areas and noted that the demand for admission remained high. She pointed out that fifty fee-paying pupils were enrolled;

most were the daughters of the old Sephardi Jerusalem aristocracy, whereas others were daughters of the new intelligentsia. There were also several non-Jewish girls. The women on the committee were delighted that the school year ended with a credit balance and that a portion of the surplus would be devoted to support a senior student who would be trained as a teacher in London and then return to teach at the Evelina School.[35]

Behar was especially proud of the growing reputation of the Evelina School. She informed the Ladies' Committee of the following:

> On several occasions I have had the honour to report on the esteem in which the School is held by high Mohammedan functionaries, as we have among our pupils nieces and nephews of the President of the Municipality. A month ago, Mousbah Effendi, President of the Criminal Tribunal, placed his three daughters with us. He had withdrawn them from a Christian school in order to place them among us, for among Jews, he said, there is no proselytism, but a wide spirit of tolerance. He personally came to express his goodwill towards the School, and begged me to communicate his sentiments to you.[36]

A few months after her visit to London, Behar learned that a splendid property, Frutiger House, had become available for purchase. Built by a Protestant Swiss banker named Frutiger as a private mansion in 1885, the house, valued at 4,960 pounds, was put up for sale by the Latin Patriarch of Jerusalem after Frutiger went bankrupt. Behar applied to Salim al-Husseini, the mayor of Jerusalem, for authorization to use the building for a school; his approval made the Evelina de Rothschild School one of the first schools to have a permanent building in Jerusalem. Husseini explained that he wished his action to be regarded as recognition of the good work done by the school and of the kindness shown to his nieces, who were pupils there.[37]

The purchase was quickly approved by the Anglo-Jewish Association; the Rothschild family donated twenty-five hundred pounds toward the purchase price, and the balance was provided by the association. Leopold de Rothschild and Ellis Franklin were designated trustees of the property; power of attorney was given to Constantine Tadros, an interpreter from the British Consulate. It took several years for the deed to finally be registered to the Anglo-Jewish Association.[38]

The mansion was one of the most beautiful buildings in the city, with more than forty rooms, a walled garden, two wells, a gatekeeper's house, and a gazebo. There was a spectacular view of the Old City from a widow's walk around the roof. The house, designed by prominent architects Conrad Schick and Theodore Sandler, was on St. Paul Street (now Shivtei Yisrael), a mixed neighborhood near several hospitals, monasteries, churches, and consulates that became, after the turn of the twentieth century, the neighborhood of intellectuals and artists, including many German and Russian Jews.

Dr. Albert Ticho, a noted ophthalmologist who treated Turkish and Arab leaders, and his wife, Anna, an artist who painted Jerusalem landscapes, were both from Vienna. They lived near the school in a house previously owned by the Nashashibis, a prominent Arab family. Dr. Moshe Wallach, the head of Shaare Tzedek Hospital, who arrived from Frankfurt, lived nearby. Dr. Helena Kagan, originally from Tashkent, studied medicine in Switzerland and was the first pediatrician in Jerusalem; she joined the neighborhood before World War I.[39]

Enrollment climbed after the move to the new Evelina School building in 1895, reaching 280 pupils. Although Frutiger House could accommodate 400 children and the demand remained very high, it was impossible to increase the number of pupils further, since there were insufficient seats and desks for them. The Ladies' Committee reported that there was great improvement in the school since the move to the new building.

As a result of the larger number of separate rooms, work was more varied and the pupils were not kept at one subject as long as they used to be. Cooking, gardening, and gymnastics, subjects that encouraged active learning, were added to the curriculum. The building was large enough to accommodate workrooms where the older girls learned to make dresses and underclothes; to wash, iron, and mend; and to make fancy articles and lace. Some of the fancy articles and lace were sold to a shop in Paris, but most were sold in Jerusalem, primarily to foreign women.[40]

In addition to the new subjects and to the workrooms for older girls, there was now a separate kindergarten, taught by Emma Jungnickel, a Christian pilgrim who had arrived in Jerusalem a few years earlier after studying the Froebel method of teaching in Dresden.[41] Previous programs for young children in the city were separated by community and did not encourage a child's development. Sephardi toddlers were taken to a *maestra*, where children were crowded together on mats in enforced idleness, whereas Ashkenazi toddlers were brought to a *cheder*, where children were expected to behave like adults.

The prevailing belief in both communities was that little children should remain quiet and do nothing.[42]

The Evelina kindergarten was based on new methods that emphasized the importance of encouraging children to learn through play. Mothers were told to promote children's play at home as well. As a result of Jungnickel's efforts and the possibilities provided by the garden and outdoor equipment left by the Frutiger family, the first modern kindergarten in Jerusalem began to grow, and it remained an important part of the school for decades. The following year, Mlle Sitton,* a local Sephardi woman, was hired to assist in the kindergarten. Classes were taught at first in English, but from 1900 on, the kindergarten was taught mostly in Hebrew.[43]

Within a short time, Behar reported remarkable moral improvement in the girls now installed in their new school building. They were much more amenable to the rules of cleanliness and order than they had been previously, and they showed camaraderie and expressed a desire to help those less fortunate than themselves. Some children asked permission to give clothing to fellow pupils whose clothes were in rags. The Ladies' Committee was clearly pleased by these changes and, in addition to the regular subsidy, sent gifts of English books and magazines to the school. Mrs. Leopold Rothschild† and Lucy Cohen sent funds to purchase additional desks and seats, and the Rothschild family sent maps and pictures for the new building.[44]

In 1896, the purchase of more classroom furniture made in Jerusalem by students in the Lionel de Rothschild Technical School permitted the enrollment of 350 students. Finding appropriate teachers for all the subjects remained difficult. At first, the American colony provided part-time teachers for English, drawing, and music,[45] while Fortunée Behar, Emma Jungnickel, and Yosef Meyuhas, a leading member of the Sephardi community, taught the balance of the program. The Evelina School continued to provide opportunities for older girls to study dressmaking and embroidery. These girls worked under the supervision of additional part-time teachers, and the school established a savings bank for these girls so that they took a modest sum with

---

* In the period under discussion, teachers and most notables were known by their titles and last names; married women were frequently addressed using *Mrs.* and their husband's first names; thus written records frequently do not include women's first names.

† Née Maria Perugia.

them when they left. Poorer girls were given presents when they left school. About a hundred girls were given free lunches, and some also received shoes and clothing at Passover.[46]

In 1898, Behar reported that the number of girls enrolled continued to grow. Israel Abrahams, noted Jewish scholar and member of the London Committee for Training Jewish Teachers who was travelling to Palestine for historical research, was asked by the Anglo-Jewish Association to inspect the school. His report confirmed that of the headmistress. Since moving to Frutiger House, there had been improvements in cleanliness and general decorum, but Abrahams saw the need for better-trained teachers as well as for a local inspector. The Ladies' Committee and the association, recognizing the importance of the school to Jerusalem, were ready to take this advice. Claude Montefiore, the leader of the association who had hired Annie Landau at the Westminster Jews' Free School, offered her the opportunity to join the teachers at the Evelina School.

Landau's Arrival in Jerusalem

Annie Landau did not hesitate to accept the job. She was twenty-five years old when she agreed to leave her family and friends to build a life in Palestine. Perhaps she chafed at the limited vision of the Westminster education, which had favored secular studies and job skills and had kept religious education to a minimum. She may have recognized that there were few opportunities for her in London; she was ambitious and, like several of her siblings, looked overseas for challenges and opportunities to advance.[47]

Whatever the reason, she left her comfortable existence in Highbury Park for Jerusalem, a city about which she had no practical knowledge aside from what could be gleaned from a study of the Bible and Jewish prayers. Nonetheless, Claude Montefiore saw in Annie Landau a determined young woman who was a strictly observant Jew as well as a modern educator. He thought she was exactly the right person for the job. The Rothschild family agreed, increasing its annual subsidy to the school to nine hundred pounds to defray the cost of the additional teacher.[48]

Landau left for Jerusalem in the middle of the academic year, eager to take up her new job. She was unaware that a few months earlier the Ottoman administration had issued strict orders to prohibit entry to Palestine to all foreign Jews unless they gave assurances that they would leave within thirty days. Theodor Herzl, who arrived in late October 1898, had jumped ashore and managed to evade the Turkish police. Landau recounted her harrowing experience in an article that appeared a few years later in the *Jewish Chronicle*:

> I arrived at Jaffa, then the chief port in Palestine in February 1899. . . . My troubles began when some young men from Mikveh Israel, the Jewish Agricultural School near Jaffa, came on board to meet me. The agent who had taken my landing ticket realized only then that I was a Jewess. My Salisbury passport, of which I was inordinately proud, being the first I ever held, of course said nothing of religion. The agent evidently saw his opportunity for baksheesh and informed me that although there was an *irade* [official edict by Muslim ruler] in force forbidding the entrance of Jews, he had recently arranged for several to be admitted for a consideration.[49]

Annie told how she had refused to pay the customary *baksheesh*, or bribe, and commented on her immediate desire to rid the East of this ancient custom. When the agent replied that she would have to remain on board and return to Marseilles, she replied, "I paid 12 [shillings] / 6 [pence] in London for my landing ticket; I insist on being landed." The agent sent her on shore, warning, "At your own risk!" She recounted that she was ferried to shore in a *felucca*, a small boat—a most unpleasant journey.

Once on shore, she entered the custom house, where everyone spoke Arabic; she understood not a word. Finally, an official asked her, *"Etes-vous Chrétienne, Mademoiselle?"* Annie replied obliquely, *"Je suis Anglaise."* He then asked pointedly if she was a Jewess. She replied in the affirmative and stated that she was proud to be one. He told her that she would have to deposit her passport and half a pound as guarantees that she would leave within the month. Landau refused to do either. Since she was not in compliance with the law, she demanded her consul and was marched off to a hut on the quay that was used as a smugglers' prison.

Five hours later, the British consul, John Dickson, arrived from Jerusalem and found her locked up, surrounded by a group of curious children who were amused to see an Englishwoman in prison protected by an armed sentry. Dickson arranged for her release. In reply to Landau's account of her travail, Dickson explained that he had been in communication with the authorities regarding her arrival but that the official Ottoman edict, or *firman*, entitling her to live in Palestine had not yet arrived. He added that the Anglo-Jewish Association should have waited to send her until the *firman* had been received.

Landau's entry to Jaffa was difficult. She had expected to be treated in Palestine as she had been in England, where she was recognized as English in public while her Jewish identity was considered a private matter. In Jaffa, she was agitated at first by the prevalence of bribery and later by being forced to reveal her religion to a state official and singled out as a Jew to guarantee that she would leave the country within thirty days.

Once she had been rescued by Dickson, Landau was reassured that the civility she had come to expect could be achieved in Palestine. As with many Western visitors who arrived in the Holy Land, her frustration was tempered by the novel beauty of the people and the places. In recollecting her arrival, she noted that Dickson had been accompanied to Jaffa by his *kawass*, a grandly uniformed soldier-servant. At first glance Annie thought that the *kawass*, "resplendent in blue and plenty of gold," was the consul in diplomatic uniform. When she went forward to shake his hand, the *kawass* smiled and pointed to Dickson, making her aware of her error.

Landau moved into the modest home across from Frutiger House that was the residence of the foreign teachers at the Evelina School, and she got to work. As a single woman with no relations in the city, she created a new life for herself that was built around her duties at the school but that soon encompassed a broad range of social activities as well. Coming from a traditional Jewish family, Landau was accustomed to celebrating the Sabbath and holidays at home with special food and traditional songs. Her new surroundings were bleak by comparison.

A few weeks after her arrival, she was visited by a Turkish official who brought the *firman* that had been lacking at the port. He asked her pardon for the events in Jaffa and, as a gesture of friendship, invited her to visit his harem. Landau later described the women with their painted faces, their henna-colored hair and nails, and their languishing poses. One of them passed her a narghile, but Annie politely refused, explaining that English women didn't smoke.

In these early weeks in Jerusalem Annie learned a lot about the Evelina de Rothschild School. She noted that she was obliged to use the green painted walls as blackboards. Even more troubling to her than the lack of teaching tools was the lack of general decorum and sense of purpose. She wrote the following:

> There were 250 pupils in the school. The main activities centered around the workroom where beautiful embroidery was done. I would meet girls walking down the corridor from classrooms to the workroom and in answer to my query as to where they were going they would say, "J'ai récitée," meaning that they had picked a number out of their master's tarbush which enabled them to say their piece, after which, their scholastic requirements for the day being ended, they were free to go to the workroom.[50]

This general lack of order was pervasive in all aspects of the school. Although Behar reported that there were 350 pupils enrolled, Landau commented that the attendance rates were so poor that 250 was a more accurate number. In the admission of new students, Landau learned, birth certificates were almost unknown. When she asked a child's age, she was told, "She was born in the year it snowed soon after the Feast of Lights." Landau remembered that she began to remove the amulets worn by her students on her first day:

> I remorselessly cut blue beads, silver tokens, camphor bags, and pieces of dried garlic from the hair of wide-eyed little girls with which the mothers had sedulously endeavored to keep off the evil eye from their offspring. It was hard work trying to convince parents that our medical inspection, newly arrived nurse, our eye treatment and dental clinic were more efficacious than their amulets.[51]

While Landau was still adjusting to her new surroundings, Behar, who had directed the school for a decade, was called away to care for her ailing mother, leaving Landau temporarily in charge. The months that followed were a challenge to the young teacher. Few of the basic practices with which she was familiar from her years at the Westminster Jews' Free School were employed at the Evelina School.

There were virtually no systems. Admission to the school took place several times a year. Attendance was not compulsory. Pupils were not advanced to higher classes based on completion of a body of work; rather, they were grouped by available space. Many teachers were part-time and showed marginal interest in the pupils. The poverty of Jerusalem was worse than anything she had witnessed in London. Perhaps the biggest surprise to the energetic and determined Landau was the complacency of the population and the general lack of resolve for self-improvement.

Having taught at Westminster, where the immigrant dedication to self-improvement was a major reason for the pupils' success, Landau was determined from the beginning not only to teach but also to change the culture of the Evelina School and of her new city.

〖 2 〗

AN ENGLISH GIRLS' SCHOOL
IN OTTOMAN JERUSALEM

Annie Landau initiated several changes during the months she spent at the helm of the Evelina de Rothschild School while Fortunée Behar was away. Shortly after Behar's return, Olga d'Avigdor, the honorary secretary of the Ladies' Committee of the Anglo-Jewish Association, arrived in Jerusalem to review the conditions of the school. She was accompanied by Lucy Haynes, an expert in school administration, whose presence was an indication of the increasing professionalism with which the association approached its management responsibilities. D'Avigdor was empowered to make some changes on the spot and to recommend others to the association. It is possible that Landau had communicated some of the shortcomings of the school to the association, precipitating this inspection. D'Avigdor spent nearly three weeks in the city, most of the time at the Evelina de Rothschild School. She was a keen observer, and in addition to collecting personal impressions, she interviewed many people connected with the school.

Her report, filed in February 1900, raised several concerns not addressed in previous reviews of the school, including its administration, finances, and accommodations for teachers.[1] It also noted several concerns that had been indicated previously, such as deficiencies in the curriculum and the incompetence of some members of the staff. D'Avigdor's comments were given serious attention by the Anglo-Jewish Association. Indeed, her visit established a pattern of close cooperation between the Ladies' Committee and the leadership of the school that facilitated support in the face of repeated challenges in the coming decades.

The first two items in d'Avigdor's report were the admissions and promotion procedures, both areas of concern noted by Landau. D'Avigdor pointed out that there was no regular procedure for admitting children, who were simply enrolled whenever they were presented by their parents for admission and placed in any classes that happened to have vacancies. Similarly, there was no procedure to promote pupils. As a result, some pupils stayed in the same class for two or more years, repeating the lessons learned during the previous year, while girls in the top class were allowed to repeat that class as many times as they liked, usually until they were betrothed.

D'Avigdor recommended substantial changes in the admissions and promotion policies: only young children were to be admitted and thereafter promoted regularly. Wary that this change in procedure was likely to lead to disappointment in influential quarters, d'Avigdor reviewed the recommendation with the British consul, who diplomatically suggested that exceptions be made for the daughters of Turkish officials. In recognition of the importance of continued cooperation from local officials, d'Avigdor agreed.[2]

The lack of any system in admissions and promotion was also discovered in the accounting department. D'Avigdor found the accountant's report to be useless because it failed to distinguish between credits and debits. She fired the accountant and arranged for Landau to take over the task of recording the school accounts in addition to her teaching duties, a move that was a clear vote of support for the young teacher. Behar's casual disregard for maintaining academic and financial records would not have been tolerated by the Alliance Israélite Universelle, where she had been trained. In view of her earlier accomplishments in moving the school out of the Old City and later into Frutiger House, her negligence in later years remains a mystery.

In addition to its administrative problems, the school had difficulty keeping experienced teachers. Foreign teachers who had no family in Jerusalem were hired with room and board, but the domestic arrangements for them were very poor. Since Behar lived with family members, she was unaware of the conditions in the teachers' home. D'Avigdor's investigation revealed that there was one servant to cook and clean, but the woman had little knowledge or skill in either area. Landau, who complained that the food was inedible, once became quite ill.

The kitchen in the teachers' lodging had none of the basics—no kitchen cloths, no plates, and only three teacups—and food was placed, Eastern style, on the floor, since there was no table. D'Avigdor fired the servant and hired Sophie Marx, an Orthodox German Jew, who took over the domestic arrangements and did some of the cooking. In addition, she soon became responsible for training pupils in cooking and housework.[3]

At the time of d'Avigdor's visit, there were eight full-time and three part-time teachers working at the Evelina School. Some were highly effective, whereas others were, she stated bluntly, useless. Her criticism began with Behar, who did very little administration and taught only one hour of French each day. Gavison, a Hebrew teacher who spoke no English was found to be weak in the classroom. Although he contributed to the school by making designs for the embroidery workshop, d'Avigdor thought he should find a new job.

Three American part-time teachers taught English; they were not regular in their attendance, nor were they trained teachers. D'Avigdor judged them to be without any merit and recommended replacing them with full-time teachers. Miss Goltmann, who had just arrived from England, knew very little Hebrew and was somewhat lacking in general information, although d'Avigdor thought that she would probably manage the older pupils well enough. Mlle Cohen, who taught dressmaking and needlework, was unable to control her class, whereas Behora Baruch, the pupil-teacher (an older pupil trained as a teacher), had little aptitude for teaching and knew very little English.[4]

In contrast, d'Avigdor had very good things to say about the remaining teachers, particularly Landau, who was singled out for praise. Considering the short time that had elapsed since Landau's arrival, it was clear that her pupils had already made great progress in English, singing, and drill. D'Avigdor noted with approval that the pupils' attendance and work were documented in class record books and progress reports.

D'Avigdor also noted that Yosef Meyuhas, a senior member of the staff who taught Hebrew, Arabic, and French in the upper classes, generally had good results, especially in Hebrew. In later years he became a national leader in Hebrew language instruction; he wrote Hebrew textbooks, including the first reader designed for girls, *Bat Hayil* [Daughter of Valor]. Mme Assoul, another capable teacher, taught the older girls embroidery and lacework. The other skilled teachers in the school were both in the kindergarten: Emma Jungnickel, a certified teacher, and Mlle Sitton. D'Avigdor reported that both did excellent work under very difficult circumstances.

D'Avigdor was receptive to the teachers' suggestions for the improvement of the school. She listed their ideas on the duration of lessons, the division of the school into seven classes, the alteration of several small classrooms to create larger ones, the continuation of workshops, the need for better facilities for the kindergarten, and the problem of early marriages among pupils. Her recommendation regarding class time was as follows:

> In agreement with Miss Landau, I have suggested that the experiment should be tried of 40- to 45-minute lessons, with an interval of sufficient duration to allow the children to go downstairs . . . to the garden which is large and very pretty to amuse themselves on some gymnastic apparatus, which was left by the late owner of the house.

No previous report by a school inspector had identified and supported staff suggestions. By giving credit to Landau and some of the other teachers, d'Avigdor signaled her intention that the Ladies' Committee and the teaching staff should work as partners in creating school policy.

Nevertheless, d'Avigdor did not support all the teachers' suggestions. While the teachers urged retaining French and Arabic classes in addition to English and Hebrew, d'Avigdor recommended dropping French, even though it was the language of commerce and culture in the Middle East. The Evelina School, which had been founded by the French Rothschilds and managed by Fortunée Behar, the product of an Alliance Israélite Universelle education, was now to become thoroughly British. D'Avigdor supported Hebrew instruction: "Hebrew must be thoroughly taught, for it is the only language the many varieties of Jews who meet at Jerusalem have in common."[5] Regarding Arabic, she recognized that the modest amount of literary Arabic that was taught to older students was ineffective and thought that the only reason to continue teaching it was to please the Turkish authorities.

D'Avigdor recommended gradual elimination of the school workshops, which provided fifteen- and sixteen-year-old girls with very limited general instruction while supervising them in embroidery and other needlework. About twenty girls worked in these shops, which were established partly to prevent early marriages.[6] Those who participated in the workshops also did housework in the school in return for modest wages. The benefits of these workshops were, according to d'Avigdor, not sufficient in view of the cost. The work failed to provide useful skills for the girls to earn an income in later life. D'Avigdor urged the Jewish Colonization Association—which was established in 1891 by Baron Maurice de Hirsch to facilitate the emigration of Jews from Russia (primarily to agricultural communities in South America) and also provided limited funding for projects in Palestine—to create workshops that would teach girls useful trades outside the framework of the Evelina School. She recommended that the school continue to teach basic cooking, housecleaning, and plain needlework, such as darning, patching, and cutting out simple garments.[7]

D'Avigdor also addressed the subject of free school lunches, an increasingly expensive item in the school budget. Although she was aware of the precarious condition of many of the pupils and knew that the missionary schools provided free lunches, she noted that the association was reluctant to fund free lunches to all pupils. At the time of her visit, 270 of the 400 pupils were provided a free lunch. In view of budgetary constraints, she told the school not to offer free lunch to new pupils until a new source of funding could be identified.[8]

These last two recommendations, closing the workshops and limiting free lunches, were in line with the practices of the Jews' Free School in London. D'Avigdor believed that the Evelina School should be modeled on that London school rather than on the Alliance and the missionary schools, which continued to offer workshops.

D'Avigdor's report concluded as follows:

> To sum up: I regret to state that in spite of the large sums annually spent on the School, in spite of the exertions of the Committee to regulate its affairs, in spite of the time and trouble spent on it, we appear at present to have no school, only bits of one. We have only a kindergarten and two upper standards—no classes in between. We have not sufficient desks nor school materials. We have very few teachers of any value, and too many, alas! of very little use. I cannot resist the conclusion that it would be more to the advantage of this very important School if a change were made in the Head-mistressship, and I have no hesitation in asking the Committee to consider this question besides that of a further increase of staff.[9]

A few months after this critical report was filed, Behar tendered her resignation. Her experience, garnered while teaching for the Alliance, and her connections to the Sephardi community had served the school well for several years. Enrollment had grown under her leadership, and girls from affluent

Sephardi families had begun to attend for the first time. Behar facilitated the move out of the Old City and negotiated the purchase of Frutiger House.

Nevertheless, she was not prepared to establish an efficient bilingual English-Hebrew school. Landau, who had arrived from London only fifteen months earlier, had both the vision and the personality to take on this challenge. The Anglo-Jewish Association named her headmistress in 1900. In time, she would turn the "bits" of a school described by Olga D'Avigdor into a model for bilingual instruction. Landau brought enormous energy as well as superior leadership skills to the task.

Annie Landau, Headmistress

During Landau's first year in office, the demand for Jewish girls' education continued to grow. At the time, 292 girls were enrolled in the school, and an additional 225 children were placed in the kindergarten classes. Despite the institution of a small application fee, applicants continued to exceed the space available. In the spring, more than three hundred children applied for two hundred places. Ashkenazi and Sephardi girls applied in equal number. Two English teachers, Cohen and Reinman, who had arrived from London, were added to the staff, and fifty dual desks were added to the classrooms. Classes in domestic science, cooking, and gardening were taught, and steps were taken to train some of the older girls as teachers.

Landau was pleased to report to the Ladies' Committee that the skills attained by the graduates in domestic science had an immediate effect on their usefulness in the city.[10] When Augusta Victoria, the grand new German hospital on Mount Scopus, opened, several older pupils recently trained in modern housekeeping methods were hired as practical nurses, an unanticipated source of employment and income that was appreciated by the girls' parents. Landau also reported progress in volunteer work. The girls used their new cooking skills to bake cookies for the annual bazaar, proudly selling all they made in support of the Evelina School. The Ladies' Committee was pleased with both of these developments, which exhibited a new spirit in the pupils.

Ashkenazi rabbis, however, continued to criticize Landau and kept the school under a perpetual *cherem*, or ban. They broadcast their opposition to the curriculum of the school in posters on the walls of Meah Shearim, a neighborhood with many girls who attended the school as well as others who

FIGURE 2.1 Cookery class, 1910 *Courtesy of the Jerusalem Municipal Archive*

were forbidden to attend. Arithmetic was deemed an inappropriate subject because the plus sign looked like a cross, and geography was forbidden because the pupils would have to learn about cities with names like St. Augustine and San Francisco.[11] In these rabbis' view, all secular knowledge was unnecessary and potentially dangerous. They remained a constant irritant to Landau, who considered her curriculum to be in keeping with strict adherence to an Orthodox way of life.

Landau also battled with parents who elected to send their daughters to the London Jews' Society School or the Soeurs de Sion, which provided their pupils with much-needed free food, clothing, and boots. These parents were certain that their daughters would not be affected by the missionary teachings. Landau did not agree and was opposed to this arrangement. She wanted the Jewish girls of Jerusalem to learn to be leaders of their people, and she knew that this would not happen if they attended missionary schools.

Landau therefore campaigned tirelessly to match the social benefits of the missions. Aware that the Anglo-Jewish Association had limited funds, she began to seek additional funds from individuals. Beginning in 1905, her reports often mention gifts like pairs of boots and special treats for Purim and Chanukah donated by visitors to the school. Fees continued to be collected from pupils whose families could afford to pay, and these assisted in defraying some school costs. Finally, the proceeds of an annual bazaar and contributions from friends and teachers were placed in the school fund. In general, Landau was able to provide food only for orphans and the children of deserted wives, but in times of crisis, she managed to stretch her budget to include all hungry children.

Landau was committed to addressing the physical needs of her pupils, but she was even more dedicated to their spiritual needs. Thus, while she was providing periodic food and clothing assistance, she was delighted to report that the pupils were beginning to look after one another. She worked to create an esprit de corps in her classrooms that cultivated mutual responsibility.

For example, she created an attendance banner that was awarded to the class with the fewest absences, which sparked keen competition among the older girls. When it appeared that a girl had to miss school because of a lack of boots, for example, her classmates scavenged among their possessions until they came up with a usable pair. The girls understood that they were being held to a new standard that encouraged school spirit and brought together classmates from different communities. Some saw this idea as British and wished to live up to the new standard. When one of the older girls did not bring her school fee, one of her classmates approached the headmistress and said the following:

> You think we are not like English girls—honourable; please let me pay for her. I have brought a franc to school today for a pencil-box; I can wait for another time for it. Melke will not be able to pay herself; she has a step-mother, and her father is nearly blind and cannot work.[12]

Indeed, Landau was eager to impart the values of initiative and mutual responsibility that she had learned in the Bishopsgate Ward School in London. She didn't share the common view that her pupils were inherently different from English girls. She believed that they were capable of learning new values, and she took great pride in their accomplishments. She expected the future mothers of Jerusalem to become caring, motivated, and actively involved in self-improvement.

In October 1901, Landau returned to London to continue the dialogue with the Ladies' Committee and with the council of the Anglo-Jewish Association about the needs of her school and the importance of educating Jewish girls in Jerusalem. In what would become a regular practice, her address to the association was printed in the *Jewish Chronicle*, increasing her visibility in the wider community and allowing her to comment not only about the school but also more broadly about life in Jerusalem.

Landau began by citing her pupils:

> The keynote of my words to you today must be the sentence which occurred in every letter, in every address, presented to me by my children when I left Jerusalem a few weeks back. "Dear Headmistress, Please thank the good ladies and gentlemen who so kindly help us to be taught." It was a sacred trust, this message; and it is with a feeling of intense responsibility, of a sincere and earnest desire to do my whole duty, that I rise to deliver it. For the very act of thanking you for the generosity, which enables a very real and tangible act of mercy to be carried out, entails pleading the cause of these 520 poor children, who cannot speak to you themselves and so have deputed me to speak for them ... you would understand could you see just once what I have before my eyes every day when I go into the schoolroom to bid the children, "Good morning." ... If you could but see the intense love and gratitude in the upturned faces, alive with emotion and intelligence, ... you would feel rewarded. Let me take you with me in imagination through the picture-hung classrooms. Listening to the fluent Hebrew ... let us observe the teaching in English of the pupils of Domestic Economy and Hygiene, hear the naively bright answers to the inductive questioning of the object lessons. Watch the graceful movements of these lithe Oriental children in this wonderful new thing for Jerusalem—the daily drill lesson.[13]

Landau continued her address with references to the lessons in cooking and baking; to the playing of the children in the kindergarten; to the work of the six pupil-teachers, the eldest of whom applied for a King's Scholarship; and to the efforts of the working girls, those who were fifteen years old and remained in the school to learn and practice domestic skills. Her address concluded as follows:

> When deciding to revisit my home this year, I had intended asking you a great many boons for our school. But I am abashed and shall go back with most of my petitions unvoiced. For I have repeatedly during my stay here listened sadly to the words, "The School is a great burden; the sum asked for its maintenance is such a great one." I own at first sight it does seem a great deal of money that we need for the proper maintenance of our School. For the current year, 1901, we need ... approximately 1,210 pounds. And yet let us for a moment consider

what is done with this 1,210 pounds. . . . It has provided for the education and instruction of 520 children, furnishing them with every school requisite, paying the salaries and wages of a staff of nine teachers, six pupil-teachers, a house-keeper, a porter and fellah [agricultural laborer], and sixteen working girls. It has provided for full board and residence, with attendant expenses of firing, lighting, etc., for six teachers, and a daily meal for 125 orphans and children of deserted wives. We paid 750 francs as taxes to the Turkish Government, and in this 1,210 pounds, 60 pounds was included as estimate for the repairing of all outer walls and re-painting of shutters, doors, etc., and it paid for the vaccination of our whole school and staff. . . . Although surrounded by sick parents and relatives, not one of our children was stricken with small-pox. . . . The School gave no dresses, no books this year even to the poorest, and the dinners are limited to the orphans and the children of deserted wives.[14]

Landau then pleaded for donations to reinstate achievement awards: "Our earnest little workers should be accorded some sign of our appreciation of their good will." She wanted money to provide every child with a prayer book and to be able to distribute toys at Chanukah. She noted, "Children in London Jewish schools are so well off in the manner of treats, and I should like our Jerusalem children to have one sometimes. Their lives are very sunless as it is."[15]

Landau understood the value of communicating regularly with the Ladies' Committee. She wasn't able to travel home every summer, but beginning in 1902, she submitted a formal, typed annual report to the Anglo-Jewish Association. Her reports included a financial section, typically referring to funds resulting from school fees and from local efforts such as the annual bazaar; some reports included photographs of the girls and some of the products of their workshops.

None of the other principals whose schools received support from the Anglo-Jewish Association submitted formal reports. The report was Landau's way of demonstrating the progress made on the goals she developed in discussion with the Ladies' Committee during her visits to London. Shortly after initiating these reports, Landau began to include general reflections on the situation for Jews in Jerusalem and to write of the role to be played by the Evelina School in the development of the city.

Landau's evocative descriptions of the girls and the school were influential in forging close ties between the headmistress and the members of the Ladies'

Committee, many of whom were involved with local education projects in England. For example, Landau wrote the following:

Keen delight has been manifested during the year by the children in the scheme of object- lessons in plant life connected with practical gardening, and the domestic economy connected with practical cookery. The well-cared-for plots of ground tended by the children won the commendation of Mr. A. Simon Ahlem, who visited the School during the Passover vacation. Object-lesson teaching in our School, made attractive by simplicity of treatment and variety of illustration, has been a decided success, and has certainly laid the foundation for the right direction of the activity and intelligence of these imitative and acutely imaginative Oriental children, as well as influencing for good their moral conduct.[16]

Landau explained that teachers tried to instill the values of obedience, love, honesty, and cleanliness in all their lessons. She reported with pride the "touching sign" of the growing love and good fellowship among the children that they had pooled their tiny resources to create a small Hebrew library in memory of three schoolmates who had died within the previous two years.[17] Despite Landau's efforts to provide medical care, the death of youngsters from disease and malnutrition was commonplace in Jerusalem, but the act of creating a Hebrew library to honor the memory of classmates was not. It was the result of the new spirit inculcated by Landau. She continued to nurture this new spirit and to nourish those who were in need, with acts as simple as providing each of her students with a cup of warm cocoa on cold winter afternoons.

Finally, Landau concluded her report of 1902 with a plea for funds to enlarge the school. She had been forced to deny admission to four hundred girls in April because of a lack of space. She vividly described her dilemma:

It taxed all the energy I could muster to cope with the supplicating crowd of mothers and fathers who assembled on the day advertised for admission of pupils and for the whole week following. The disappointed parents would not listen to reason and to my answer: "The School is full." It was even more painful to say nay to those who had patiently waited their turn in the burning sun for hours—only to be told the same thing. Many a mother said: "I learnt nothing—I cannot write my name—but I want my child to learn." From six o'clock in the morning until dusk the gates were besieged and notwithstanding the recent addition to the height of the walls and their iron palisadings, there were attempts to scale them by fathers and brothers holding sobbing children under their arms, each one eager to be first. Did space permit, we should have a thousand children. We have accommodation for 350 and we have 567 children on the books.[18]

Landau explained that in the summer she arranged many classes in the open air, but she hoped that in the near future a new wing would be built to provide a proper kindergarten, more classrooms, a drill hall, and a big water cistern to meet the needs of the growing student body.

In August 1902, the headmistress was able to reinstate the practice of public prize distribution that had been started decades earlier by her predecessor. Pupil-teachers as well as a group of monitors (girls who supervised the play area) received awards in 1902. The school also gave out prizes for those who excelled in housework and those with perfect attendance.

Punctuality, which was expected of all pupils in the school, was also expected of the parents and guests attending the ceremony, which started at precisely 2:30 p.m. It included Hebrew readings, a Japanese costume song, a scene from Shakespeare's *King John*, and a play entitled *The Little Cooks*. "God Save the King" was sung to the accompaniment of the pianoforte, played by two pupil-teachers. As in previous years, the awards were distributed by Edith Dickson, the wife of the British consul, and the event was presided over by the *hakham-bashi*, the chief rabbi.[19]

Disease, Poverty, and Crowding

A few months after the awards ceremony, a cholera epidemic raged in the villages surrounding Jerusalem. The authorities sprayed the streets of the city with a dilution of carbolic acid, required houses to be cleaned and whitewashed, and levied fines for accumulating rubbish. The government closed all its schools but allowed private schools to use their own discretion about whether to close. The Evelina de Rothschild School remained open.[20]

Landau seized the opportunity to share modern health instructions with the mothers of her pupils by distributing printed instructions in Hebrew and English: "Precautions against Cholera," compiled by Dr. R. J. Petri. Since not all the parents were literate, Landau encouraged advanced pupils to read the instructions to their families, and she held public lectures to review the information. Mothers were urged to be calm, to focus on personal cleanliness as well as the cleanliness of their surroundings, and to avoid feasting and large gatherings as well as contact with people coming from cholera-stricken places. The instructions warned, "Do not bring objects other than food or drink near or in the mouth."[21]

Children were reminded not to put their fingers in their mouths when turning the pages of a book; likewise, pens and pencils were never to be placed in the mouth. Instructions were given to boil water for several minutes before drinking it, using it to rinse the face or the mouth, or washing dishes in it. Cholera germs were found in butter and fresh cheese, which were to be avoided for the duration of the crisis; and milk, fruits, and vegetables were all to be boiled.

During the worst time of the panic, when food prices were exorbitantly high, all the children received their meals at school. This brought the number of free meals to a total of 36,860 for the year, but it provided much-needed relief for the pupils. Aware of the vulnerability of her children to disease, Landau was pleased that 256 children were vaccinated during the year at the school's expense.[22]

The next year, 1903, Landau reported that there were 606 pupils in the Evelina School: 333 in the elementary school and 273 in the kindergarten. A result of her success in developing a sequential curriculum and demanding regular attendance was the ability to train older pupils to become teachers. Landau reported with pride that the majority of female teachers in elementary schools in all the Jewish colonies of Palestine had been trained at the Evelina School. In 1903, there were eight girls in training as teachers, one of whom came from Bulgaria to study Hebrew with Yosef Meyuhas.[23]

The growing British character of the school can be seen in the announcement that prize distribution day would also celebrate the coronation of King Edward VII. The efforts of the children in a long and varied program were further proof of Landau's success in raising the level of instruction in the school. The pupils received warm words of commendation from more than four hundred guests, who assembled in a tent lent to the school by the British hotel and guide company Thomas Cook & Sons.[24]

Four-year-old Tova Rosenbaum was one of the pupils admitted that spring. Sixty years later, she continued to treasure an English-language Bible with gold lettering on its spine reading THE EVELINA DE ROTHSCHILD SCHOOL FOR GIRLS, JERUSALEM. Inside was a dedication from Landau: "A gift to Tova Rosenbaum for not being absent from school and not being late over the course of two years. Jerusalem 3 April 1913."

Tova recalled that there were three schools for Jewish girls in Jerusalem in 1903: one where the principal language was German, one where French was spoken, and Evelina, which taught English. Tova's parents were eager to see her enrolled at the Evelina School, since they agreed with Landau that it was the best school in Jerusalem. Tova lived too far away to walk to school and there was no public transportation, so she was carried "like a sack of flour" on the back of one of her older brothers to school each day. Classes started at 8 a.m. and concluded at 3 p.m. At the end of the day, she remembered lining up by neighborhood for the long walk back home.[25]

Tova remembered that discipline was unusually strict but that the girls accepted it as characteristic of their school. She also remembered with great fondness Yosef Meyuhas, who taught prayers and Bible in Hebrew. Each day started with communal prayer, but the highlight of the week took place on Thursday afternoon, when the whole school participated in a ceremony in honor of the Sabbath. One of the older girls recited part of the weekly Torah reading in Hebrew, then Landau commented on the reading in English. In 1964, Tova Rosenbaum, by then Tova Menirav, recalled, "Every word that came out of her mouth still rings in my ears."[26]

Tova particularly remembered the care that Landau exhibited toward her pupils. She wanted them to learn from the vast array of world knowledge, but she also wanted them to learn essential skills for household management, including cooking, baking, and child care. Tova remembered a nurse who was hired to teach first aid while another woman taught infant care to the older pupils; these subjects were added to the curriculum of history, geography, mathematics, and psychology. In addition, Tova recalled that the school enrolled girls of different ethnicities and taught them to forget their differences and to work and play together. In Tova's view, all these lessons were planned to develop strong Jewish women who would contribute to their families and to their communities.[27]

In the summer of 1903, Landau returned to London to recuperate from a bout of rheumatism. The *Jewish Chronicle* reported that she seemed as anxious to return to Jerusalem as her pupils were to have her back. Her English friends, in contrast, were rather surprised at Landau's protracted stay in a city that was indeed historic and holy but that was also a wilderness socially. Its climate was especially trying to those used to western Europe, and the danger of cholera would certainly try the courage of a comfortable Londoner or Parisian. Landau replied to their concerns this way: "But somehow Jerusalem has its own peculiar charm. Upon one who has worked there it seems to have a magnetic influence, and one yearns to go back."[28]

Landau provided a few details about the socioeconomic conditions of Jerusalem for readers of the *Jewish Chronicle*. Of the sixty thousand inhabitants of the city, there were forty thousand Jews, fourteen thousand Muslims, and six thousand Christians.[29] Three-quarters of the Jews lived on charity. She noted that "England, in the worst days of the old poor-law system, could never allow such an appalling situation" and added the following:

> The Moroccan Jews, especially, are in a state of shocking poverty. You can see them living in holes made in the wall—without light, air, or furniture, or covering. . . . I have come across Jewish families where the father has no work, the mother is blind, and there are eight or nine children to support. Perhaps all are herded in a single room; and diphtheria is raging among them. . . . In my school there are 190 children of deserted or widowed mothers who receive a free dinner every day. It is a touching sight to see these little girls save half the bread they get, in order to take it home to their people.[30]

And yet given a chance to learn, these girls did very well. Landau shared some of the letters she received from her pupils, written with passion and with poetry, urging her to return to Jerusalem. In describing her sadness after visiting the school bereft of its headmistress, one wrote: "My eyes were gloomed and my heart discouraged." The reporter for the *Chronicle* commented, "These girls are naturally born rhetoricians."[31]

Boyd Carpenter's Recommendations

A few weeks after Landau returned to her post, Boyd Carpenter, an experienced English school inspector working in Egypt, was asked by the Anglo-Jewish Association to visit the Evelina School. He was the first inspector to report on Landau's brief tenure as headmistress. In his report, filed in

March 1904, Carpenter began with a review of the premises and the school equipment:

> The site does not strike me as being a very good one. . . . The house itself was a good dwelling house, but not really suited for a school, and it would be difficult to really satisfactorily adapt it, and in any case, if successfully altered, would not be sufficient without considerable enlargement for the proper instruction of the present numbers.
>
> The kindergarten classes are taught on the ground floor, [the rooms of] which are best described as rather superior cellars, and the walls and divisions are of such a nature that one class can hardly work without disturbing, if not distracting, the attention of the neighbouring class. The rooms are small, not always well lit, and the children much crowded. I understand that a plan has been entertained of providing extra accommodation for the Kindergarten department, but even if this were done, the main school would remain without sufficient room space. The class-rooms are uncomfortably full, and the ventilation of the rooms is not of a character to really secure a proper supply of pure air.[32]

Carpenter concluded that there were about a hundred children in the elementary classes for whom space was not available. The feeling of crowdedness was intensified by the lack of a cloakroom or a lunchroom. The garden, he observed, was nice, but it lacked any shelter for very hot or wet days. He also noted the lack of sufficient latrines; there were only six for nearly six hundred pupils. The lack of a proper sewage system was a serious problem. He noted, "The present system would not be tolerated in an English community, nor under the present Egyptian Administration."[33] In addition, he judged the number of cisterns to be insufficient to provide adequate drinking water.

The present building did not have any place for the girls to assemble, so entry to the building and dismissal were problematic. Lack of space made physical exercise quite difficult. Nevertheless, Carpenter credited Landau with skill in arranging some space for exercise. He recommended that the Anglo-Jewish Association provide a musical instrument to accompany exercise and singing lessons.

The next section of the report focused on instruction. Carpenter reported that the level of speaking English was generally good:

Even in the lowest classes the actual speaking was exceedingly good, and in power of speech the girls undoubtedly are much superior to the girls in the Egyptian schools. Reading was, on the whole, very good, and the Recitation well and intelligently given. The English writing was of a good average, but not so markedly good as the Reading.

The grammar in English was not up to the same standard, but this is partly accounted for by the recent changes in the staff, and will no doubt improve as the new mistresses get more accustomed to the character of their work and surroundings.[34]

Carpenter observed that the level of arithmetic was not good and noted that Landau was aware of the need to improve this area of instruction. He found that object lessons, the use of visual aids to enhance story-telling, singing, and needlework were all well executed. The embroidery and fancy work done by some of the older girls was, according to Carpenter, undoubtedly above the level of work done by girls of similar age in England. He noted the lack of geography lessons and recommended that they be included, perhaps replacing some of the classes in domestic science.

Carpenter's comments about the weakness in arithmetic and the absence of geography lessons might reflect the Orthodox community's opposition to these subjects, noted earlier. His report also provides evidence of the continuing turnover of staff. There is no mention of the three teachers who had arrived from London within the previous two years: Goltman, Reinman, and Cohen. Sophie Bondi, a new arrival from Frankfurt, had taken over two classes from Landau. Carpenter was concerned that Bondi's mastery of English showed some gaps. Miss Faber, another newcomer, taught arithmetic adequately. Mme Assoul continued to perform an excellent job with needlework. Carpenter recommended that Rachel Adhan and Liza Tagger, both pupil-teachers, apply for scholarships to study in England. He noted that Ella Schwartzstein, also newly arrived from Frankfurt, had promise as a teacher, and he also wrote favorably of Emma Jungnickel's work.

In general, Carpenter thought that the teachers worked satisfactorily but that they were burdened with too many hours of teaching. Bondi and Faber were teaching thirty hours per week, with extra hours of supervision. The limit in Egypt was twenty-five hours per week, to give teachers time to prepare lessons. He advised the Anglo-Jewish Association to authorize Landau to hire additional teachers in order to lighten the burden on her existing staff.

Carpenter concluded his report with recommendations for the future. He noted that he was struck by the excellent work being done by the school as an agent for good in Jerusalem, a city afflicted by poverty, dirt, and disorder. In contrast, he observed the neat and tidy appearance of the Evelina pupils, many of whom came from very poor homes and did not receive sufficient food. Carpenter suggested two primary changes: first, to select a better site for the school and erect a building more suitable for educational purposes; and second, to develop the school into three departments—kindergarten, primary school, and secondary school or training college.[35]

Carpenter's recommendations touched on areas of great concern to Landau. As headmistress, however, she had an accurate understanding of the limited funding that would be provided by the Anglo-Jewish Association. Thus, she avoided asking for a new building and limited her request to extensions on the existing building. Similarly, she experimented with adding classes to meet the needs of older pupils for technical training, but she did not create a separate division for this purpose until after World War I.

Progress and Setbacks in the Continuing Struggle against Poverty and Disease

The lack of sufficient space remained a top concern for the next two decades. Despite the rabbis' *cherem*, Landau faced continuing demand from Ashkenazi and Sephardi families who wished to secure admission to the school. Her report of 1904 concluded with her observations from visits to her pupils' homes:

> Knowing well the sordidness of the home surroundings of the poor here, the absolute inability of the parents to train their children properly, and the real danger for a girl who spends most of her time in the streets, it is as painful for me to have to refuse admission as it is for the mothers to hear the continual: "We have no more room."[36]

Despite the frustrations of crowding, poverty, and periodic outbreaks of disease, Landau was keenly aware that the school was making significant strides in improving the lives and aspirations of the girls of Jerusalem. In her 1904 report she boasted that one of the girls trained at Evelina had been selected to be headmistress of the Infants' School in Jaffa, whereas several others who had been required to leave school at age fifteen because of a shortage of classroom space were employed as teachers in Jerusalem.

Furthermore, she reported, in order to provide an additional means of livelihood to those reaching the compulsory leaving age, a millinery class had recently been added after hours. The class had achieved great success at its first exhibition of work, selling more than four hundred francs' worth of hats, with more orders arriving for the future. In addition, the organizers of a Palestinian exhibition in Vienna had purchased all the embroidery and handmade lace on hand at the time of their visit, and a newspaper account of the event attested to the fact that it had all been immediately sold.[37]

Thus, Landau slowly won the confidence not only of the Anglo-Jewish Association but also of the mothers of Jerusalem. She felt their hesitation as they watched her—an outsider, a European—closely. She surprised them by not desecrating the Sabbath or trampling on the religious tenets that they and she held dear, and their confidence in her grew as they watched their daughters learning new ways but remaining faithful to their religious practices. Landau's value to their daughters was obvious in her ability to help them find jobs. In the area of health and hygiene, however, Landau still had a lot of convincing to do.

Beginning in the autumn of 1903, Dr. Michaelovitch of the Rothschild Hospital came regularly to the school, treating an average of eighty pupils per week, mostly for malaria and eye disease. The mothers wondered about the efficacy of medical treatment. Shortly after the doctor began to attend the Evelina School pupils, an epidemic of scarlet fever erupted in Jerusalem, lasting for nine months and reviving the mothers' beliefs in amulets and home remedies. Control, isolation, and exclusion from school attendance were impossible in the city, since there was no sanitary inspector and no medical officer to keep track of infectious cases.

Thus, following medical advice, the school closed for January 1904. Many of the students who contracted scarlet fever received treatment at Shaare Tzedek Hospital, the only hospital in Jerusalem that had facilities to treat infectious disease. The hospital was under the direction of Dr. Moshe Wallach, Landau's friend and neighbor. Ella Schwartzstein, one of the new teachers, volunteered to work as a nurse while the school was closed. The mothers and their daughters viewed the united front between doctors and teachers skeptically. Periodic outbreaks of diseases that resulted in the death of young children left the mothers uncertain about the efficacy of medical treatment. Four pupils died during this epidemic.[38]

Like her pupils, Landau suffered from ill health periodically during her years in Jerusalem. In the summer of 1904 she returned to London to recuperate after an extended stay at Shaare Tzedek Hospital, apparently for a respiratory ailment that became a chronic problem in later years. Despite her weakened state, she summoned the energy to address the annual meeting of the Anglo-Jewish Association. Landau explained that she had left Jerusalem with a heavy heart and regretted the time spent away from her girls. She knew that their holidays were often not pleasant because their home surroundings were difficult. She reported getting batches of mail from pupils who saw her not only as their teacher but also as their friend, to whom it was natural to come with their troubles, both little and big. Finally, she addressed a topic that continued to intrigue her family and old friends:

> People wonder what it is that keeps me in Jerusalem, in dreary, bleak Jerusalem, with its present-day scenes of the ruin of human life which so much overshadow its ruins of historic interest. And my answer to the wondering questions is always the same, the Jerusalem children keep me there despite troubles of all kinds, not the least of which are intrigue and overwork, and consequent ill-health. I cannot leave these children, because I know they need me, and they love me as I do them.[39]

Thus, Annie Landau's vision for the future of the city and the country emerged from her concern for the welfare of her pupils. Although she was certainly aware of the struggles within the Jewish community regarding the future of Palestine, she did not line up with any of the Zionist groups or with the anti-Zionist groups. She chose to live in Jerusalem out of the conviction that she could develop the best girls' school in the city, one that would improve the lives of Jewish girls and their families. She was motivated by religious convictions and by her belief in education, specifically the education of girls. Landau was simultaneously learning to manage her school and becoming a reporter on the conditions of Jerusalem for the Anglo-Jewish Association and the readers of the *Jewish Chronicle*. She expressed the wish that the Ladies' Committee could accompany her back to Jerusalem so that its members could see for themselves what she had been reluctant to communicate in her previous reports:

> We are diffident about touching upon the inner life of Jerusalem. We do not like to show the world how deep are our wounds, how awful the state of things. But I feel that I ought to be silent no longer, that the veil must be put aside a little, even at the risk that my work personally may become even more difficult than it is. Everybody has a dim idea that the economic condition of Jerusalem is a shocking one. Sixty years ago there were but a few thousand Jews in Jerusalem. But since then the influx of our brethren from those countries where the Jews are so shamefully treated—Russia and Romania—has been very great. The Jewish population of Jerusalem has risen to 40,000 souls, and the *chaluka*, once meant to support our students of Hebrew literature, and rightly so, has degenerated to a great extent into a degrading charity. We English cry out at the *chaluka* system as it stands at present—a cancer eating away at the vitals of Jerusalem—but we cannot alter it, we contribute little or nothing towards it. But we are doing something far greater and better than giving *chaluka*—we are educating the girls of Jerusalem, and in so doing we are slowly but surely solving the problem of the future of the Holy Land. For when these girls are mothers they will teach their children a new creed—unknown to present-day Jerusalem—the creed of independence, of self-help.[40]

Employment Opportunities

In her 1905 report, Landau described the continuing difficulties facing graduates of the Evelina School. The school tried hard to prepare the girls for useful and strong lives, but there were few jobs available for graduates in Jerusalem. Evelina girls were able to read, write, and speak in both Hebrew and English; they were able to cut out and make their own underclothing and simple blouses and skirts; they were proficient at mending and cooking; they understood gardening; and they had completed a course in first aid and hygiene. Some were skilled embroiderers, making the beautiful linens for which the school was known, but Jerusalem was a town of poor people, with few opportunities for such skilled workers.

There were a few jobs available for domestic servants and nurses, but these jobs were not favored by the girls' parents. Since there were few job opportunities in the city, Landau maintained a lace-making atelier that employed twelve to eighteen girls and served European customers. Despite Olga d'Avigdor's recommendation to discontinue this program, these girls, who were all orphans, continued to do the laundry and cooking in the school as well as produce lace and embroidery for many years. They were paid five to twenty francs per month and received one hot meal a day as well as additional lessons in various subjects.[41]

Later, Landau added millinery and dress workshops to the previously established lace and embroidery shops as a form of continuing education that also provided the girls with a small nest egg to help them establish families.[42] She was keen to have her graduates work so that they would become accustomed to being self-reliant. Providing jobs for her graduates for a few years was also a strategy she employed to convince parents to agree to postpone the marriages they had planned for their daughters. These arranged marriages, at age twelve or thirteen, were typical for Jewish, Muslim, and Christian girls in Jerusalem, although all the Western schools fought this tradition. Landau's efforts to address the immediate issue of early marriages were also part of a larger plan to shape the future fortunes of women in Jerusalem.[43]

Despite the ongoing health problems of the pupils, the crowded condition of the school building, and the lack of central heating during a very cold winter, six years after her arrival in Jerusalem, Landau recognized the enormous importance of the school to all the Jewish girls of the city. She was committed to bringing her girls into her world, the modern world. She saw them as "waifs and strays" and was determined to transform them into model pupils who would become builders of their people:

> The School, the only Jewish Girls' School in Jerusalem, with its cleanliness, its discipline and order and loving-kindness, its work and play, its upbuilding of Faith and Character, is, indeed, a haven of refuge, and, let us hope, a beginning of better things for the poor demoralized waifs and strays of humanity tossed hither from Russia, Romania, and Galicia. It is a veritable Garden of Eden to the native Jerusalem child, to the little Yemenites, Moroccans and Persians who fill our rooms, to the little Georgian "savage" from the Caucasus, who in common with her fellow pupil, our one little Jewish negress (an infant of five), does not see why she should sit at a desk, and is therefore giving us terrible trouble until she is transformed into an "Evelina School" girl.[44]

Unlike the missionary schools, whose curriculum was dictated by church authorities, the Evelina School was not provided with a model curriculum by the Anglo-Jewish Association. Landau's experience teaching at the Westminster school had introduced her to a curriculum for poor immigrants, but physical conditions in Jerusalem were far worse. The families of the pupils she taught in London were eager to see their children succeed economically in England. In Jerusalem, some of the families of pupils were recent immigrants to the city, and others had been there for generations, but none had any expectations of economic improvement. All the graduates were faced with meager opportunities for economic self-sufficiency.

Nevertheless, Landau created a school culture that encouraged self-reliance as well as cooperation and mutual aid. She reported with pride each year as her former pupils found work as teachers in Jewish colonies all over Palestine. Some of the colonies, impressed by the work of Evelina graduates, sent their girls to the Evelina School for teacher training, too. Other graduates of the school went to Europe and the United States to work as teachers, dressmakers, and bookkeepers. She encouraged all of them to help one another find employment. She started a club for former students, the Old Girls' Club, in 1905, which facilitated continuing education and job referrals.[45]

One pupil who went to Paris for additional teacher training wrote to Landau, demonstrating how well she had learned the headmistress's lessons of self-reliance and adherence to religious practice:

> You cannot imagine how proud I am, dear Headmistress, to write to you like a quite grown-up friend, because although I am in Paris, I am still your own pupil. I thank you very much for your advice; but I can assure you, dear Miss Landau, that I keep my religion just as I used to in Jerusalem. What you said to me before I went away came true; some girls did laugh at me, but it is not that which will prevent me to do what is right. I can also tell you that your kind words which you used to employ, when encouraging us to be good Jewesses, are too much engraved in my heart to be forgotten so quickly.[46]

In the first decade of the twentieth century, Landau continued to develop opportunities for employment for her graduates in Jerusalem, in the Jewish colonies, and abroad. In 1906, a Constantinople firm ordered a large quantity of lace. The order posed a challenge, because Landau realized that she did not have sufficient space to create all the lace requested. Nevertheless, she accepted the order and employed her former students, both single and married Old Girls, to work from their cramped homes. She organized pattern distribution at the school and regular inspection of the work as well.

Since the price paid was small, Landau gave all the proceeds to her former students. The teachers supported this endeavor, volunteering their time to assist in the inspection process. These extra efforts were reported to the Ladies' Committee, and photographs of the lace made were included in Landau's report. She was also pleased to report that the needlework, millinery, and embroidery workrooms in the school had become self-sufficient, though not yet producing a surplus for the school coffers.[47]

Although Landau was keenly aware of her pupils' need to develop skills that would provide employment, she was even more concerned with their moral transformation, believing that to be the most important aspect of their education. She reported proudly that the girls were becoming not only more self-reliant but also more cooperative. She noted that even the little ones in the kindergarten helped one another in play; the stronger girls helped the weaker ones to lift a watering can to tend to their garden plots.

While nurturing these developments, Landau constantly reminded the Ladies' Committee and a growing group of international friends that her pupils still needed boots for winter, hot meals, books, and warm clothing. Her reports listed special gifts made by a growing number of friends in London, Frankfurt, Hong Kong, Bournemouth (England), and Baltimore. She was grateful to the Rothschild Hospital, which continued to provide medical care, including smallpox vaccinations, without remuneration. Because of all her initiatives, Landau was always short of money and space. The persistent needs of her pupils periodically caused her to make unanticipated expenditures to meet emergency needs:

> The children enter their work with a zest which is little short of marvelous, considering the semi-starvation to which so many of them are subjected, added to the unhygienic conditions under which we work. During the summer I often have to interrupt the lessons in the overcrowded rooms on the east side of the house, on finding a large percentage of the children from them in our "sick room" down with fever, the remainder in the classrooms languid and

pale, and the teacher with a bad headache. In summer we turn as many classes as possible into the garden for lessons, but as we have very little shade in our big grounds it is not easy to arrange this. Last winter was a bitterly cold one in Jerusalem and I was forced to buy ten stoves and fix them up in the school rooms. It was a very expensive proceeding as the only fuel at our command is wood, charcoal fires in school-rooms being out of the question, and wood is exceedingly difficult to obtain now.[48]

The Anglo-Jewish Association continued to support Landau, adding small sums to her annual budget each year. The Rothschild subsidy of nine hundred pounds was more than matched by the association in 1906. The funds given to the Evelina School now equaled the amount given by the Anglo-Jewish Association to all the other schools combined. In addition, the Ladies' Committee provided special gifts, presenting the school with a piano and a typewriter. Landau continued to build bridges to affluent Jewish families, which provided support as well.

Landau was developing plans for the future of her school, but she also learned to respond quickly to unanticipated opportunities. Her ability to think about long-range plans while executing short-range projects served her well throughout her career. Learning of a demand for Jewish governesses in French- and German-speaking countries, for example, she created a new class for girls who had finished the regular program. This class, called the Selecta, offered lessons in Hebrew, English, German, French, history, geography, domestic science, typewriting, shorthand, and bookkeeping. Girls paid five francs per month to attend twenty hours of class per week; they often earned the fee money by working in the school workrooms during the day. When the girls who finished this program were hired abroad, they became Landau's ambassadors to the homes of potential donors to the school.

Although Landau was always working to increase the limited finances of the school, she was no less devoted to recruiting and keeping excellent teachers. In 1907 she was pleased to report that the Anglo-Jewish Association supported sending four European teachers—Ella Schwartzstein, Miss Faber, Sophie Bondi, and her sister—home for a summer holiday. Landau recognized the importance of rewarding foreign teachers with periodic visits home, because a frequent turnover of teachers was not conducive to developing a school rich with traditions and esprit de corps. By attending to her teachers' needs, she succeeded in keeping many of them in Jerusalem for years. Landau continued to build a dedicated and stable staff, both European and local.

In June 1907, Landau returned to London after a three-year absence. Her address to the Anglo-Jewish Association, reported in the *Jewish Chronicle*, revealed her growing self-confidence. She began by stating that the greatest need of Jerusalem, "the city which was, and which, please God, will once more be the centre of our Jewish life," is education, and specifically the education of women.[49]

She noted that since her last report, both German and French schools had been opened for Jewish girls in Jerusalem, adding, "I gladly accept the help they give me in taking some of the many hundreds to whom I have yearly to refuse admission." She continued dramatically, "But is our School—the doyen of all girls' schools in Palestine—to stand back, to retrogress while others go forward? No! emphatically no!" Landau explained that the French and German schools were high schools, whereas the Evelina School was the only Jewish girls' elementary school in Palestine. She concluded, "I have been accused of making our girls unfit for their surroundings. I admit the impeachment. I was sent to Jerusalem to do just that and I hope I may succeed."[50]

Despite Landau's commitment to change, she did not identify as a Zionist. Like most of the Anglo-Jewish leaders who supported her, she eschewed nationalist rhetoric, focusing instead on the daily needs of her pupils. She had lofty aspirations for them and for the future of Jerusalem, but she was wary of becoming involved in the struggle between the traditional leaders of the English Jewish community, who encouraged Jewish integration in England, and the Zionists, who rejected what they called assimilation and demanded that those leaders focus on the challenge of settling the Holy Land. Another important difference between Landau and the Zionists was that whereas most Zionists were secularists devoted to agricultural settlements, Landau remained religious and devoted to educating her girls to contribute to the transformation of the historic city of Jerusalem.[51]

She explained her point of view as follows:

I have lived too long in Jerusalem and among Jerusalemites to believe that the holy city is ready for its national destiny. I am only a Zionist in that I give my life's strength to my work in Zion, and I shall account that work a success if I can help my girls to better and purer lives; if I can make them true and steadfast daughters in Israel, in truth unfit for their surroundings, but with the conviction that they will make their surroundings better.[52]

Zionists who applauded her views about self-improvement denounced her for her commitment to continue teaching English. When challenged, Landau reminded her critics that Jews had no legal right to live in Palestine; they could be ordered to leave at any moment. English, therefore, was a practical language that must be taught in case Jews were obliged to evacuate the Holy Land (as was indeed her fate in 1915). In addition, she was aware that many men emigrated in search of work abroad, often leaving their wives and children behind to a fate of terrible poverty. She reasoned that if the wives knew English, they would be employable abroad, too, and all the family members might emigrate together.[53]

Landau's growing success in educating her pupils for employment in a variety of settings was a vindication of her philosophy both to the Anglo-Jewish Association and to the parents of the girls. In the last years of the Ottoman control of Jerusalem, graduates of her school found work in the United States—one as a clerk, another as a teacher, and two as nurses—and in Austria as a governess; several others continued their studies in Berlin, Frankfurt, and Paris. Several more remained in Jerusalem, engaged in weaving at the newly founded Bezalel Art School or employed as assistants in the kindergarten of the Hilfsverein.

Finally, one graduate had become the first female dentist in Jerusalem. Her list of donations included special gifts from the philanthropic Kadoories of Hong Kong and the Schiffs from New York. Smaller gifts arrived from Landau's sisters, indicating family support for her efforts, as well as from her neighbor and friend Dr. Wallach. Alumnae who lived in Jerusalem continued to meet weekly to read and discuss books; some attended dressmaking and cooking classes, and others used the school library.[54]

In 1908, Emma Jungnickel, the kindergarten mistress and one of the school's senior teachers, retired after twenty years of service to the children of Jerusalem. Landau had prepared for her departure by establishing connections with European schools that trained kindergarten teachers. Within a few months she found the ideal replacement: Rivka Mitshanik, born in Rehovot and educated in Berlin, where she had studied the Pestalozzi method of teaching and received a certificate as a kindergarten teacher.

Mitshanik was offered the job of kindergarten teacher and, as an additional inducement, was invited to live with Landau and the other foreign teachers in the building across the street from Frutiger House. This communal living arrangement for single women, the teachers with no family in Jerusalem, was a pragmatic solution to the shortage of adequate housing in the city and continued until Landau was awarded her own apartment at the top of the remodeled Frutiger House in 1931. From that time on, the communal living arrangement was modified. Two or three single teachers sometimes rented an apartment together, and a married teacher sometimes rented an extra room to a single teacher.

Mitshanik was both the youngest teacher in the teachers' house and its chronicler. She was appreciative of the helpful spirit of her fellow teachers and noted with gratitude the maternal concern that Landau showed for the young teachers. Fearing for their safety if they went out alone, Landau took the teachers on trips to the fashionable German Colony; they took sandwiches and drank coffee in the Hollander Café. Sometimes she hired a horse-drawn carriage and they ventured as far as Motza, a Jewish settlement outside Jerusalem. Mitshanik remembered these convivial occasions with pleasure.[55]

Mitshanik also commented on the monthly salon that Landau held in the house. On the first of every month, the residence was turned into a meeting place for the most cultured of the Jewish, Christian, and Muslim residents of Jerusalem. Landau was friendly with the doctors, professors, and artists of the city, and she included European visitors, whom she was eager to introduce to her teachers and her school.

These were propitious years for attempting to forge better intergroup relations in Jerusalem. A Jerusalem branch of the Young Turk Committee of Union and Progress was established in early 1909, and so was the Jerusalem Patriotic Society, a literary and political club. David Yellin, a teacher, wrote optimistically to a friend in Berlin that "we see for the first time in these societies Muslims associating with Christians and Jews."[56]

Landau shared Yellin's enthusiasm for bringing together the different communities of the city to improve living conditions. She encouraged her teachers to participate in the conversation, seeing them as partners in the endeavor to achieve the civic mission of the school. Inspired by her leadership, Mitshanik

and the others held fast in the face of epidemics, insufficient funds, and su-
perstitions. They continued to encourage their pupils to believe in themselves
and in their ability to improve their conditions and those of their city.

Nevertheless, there were those in Jerusalem who viewed Landau's gatherings with suspicion. She shared the criticism with her supporters in England:

> In an institution like ours, trying and delicate situations must of necessity arise,
> and I am glad and proud to say in my own name and that of my staff that never
> once have our President, Committee, and Council failed us. None but the well-
> nigh despairing worker in Jerusalem, fighting the hard fight against ignorance,
> prejudice, superstition, atheism, apathy and personal enmity, can fully appreciate
> what such help, advice and encouragement mean.[57]

Although Landau failed to elaborate on the "trying and delicate situations,"
it is clear that her goal of transforming lives and her methodology were not
viewed positively by all. On the eve of her tenth year in Jerusalem, she was
still opposed by Ashkenazi leaders who feared that her teaching would lead
their children astray. She was grateful for the continuing support of the Anglo-
Jewish Association, and she also appreciated the support of the chief rabbi
of the United Kingdom, Hermann Adler, who had earlier served for two
years as the head of the Jews' Free School in London. Rabbi Adler offered
to read and review all the books being considered as texts for the Evelina de
Rothschild School. When he celebrated his seventieth birthday, the Evelina
School presented him with a beautiful piece of lace created for the occasion.
Upon his death in 1910, Landau lost a trusted advisor.[58]

A few months later, Landau reported that the association had decided to
expand Frutiger House, a plan that she had advocated for several years. The
president of the association approved a budget of ten thousand pounds for
that purpose. The Rothschild family responded to the new challenge with a
donation of twenty-five hundred pounds, and additional smaller gifts were
collected as well. While planning for a brighter future, Landau was forced to
turn her attention to yet another health crisis that threatened Jerusalemites:
meningitis.

The Evelina School was singled out by medical authorities to stay open
during this crisis because its premises were judged to be cleaner than the
homes of the students. Shaare Tzedek Hospital lent the necessary apparatus
to disinfect the classrooms and the library, which were washed twice a day.

Each child was provided with an individual drinking glass and told not to share it with anyone, clean handkerchiefs were distributed daily, and extra meals were given to destitute and weak children. Despite all the precautions, five pupils died during this epidemic.[59]

While she was focused on these health precautions, Landau continued to support the millinery, lace, and embroidery workrooms, whose income now funded the needlework requisitions of the rest of the school and left a fair profit margin for the workers. Berlin department stores requested lace-trimmed handkerchiefs and dress trimmings; simple, modern dresses designed in Amsterdam to be comfortable, healthy, and beautiful were made in the dressmaking shop; and the embroidery workroom was commissioned to make epaulettes for the officers of the Turkish garrison in Jerusalem. The girls loved embroidering *Kuds-es-shaarif*, or "Jerusalem the Holy City," in Aleppo pure silver thread on red cloth. Landau was so proud of their work that she commissioned small silver wire brooches with the same words to be made as presents for the embroiderers.[60]

At the Abyssinian Palace

In January 1911, to meet the urgent need for more classrooms, the Evelina School temporarily moved desks and chairs, libraries, and science equipment across the street into rented quarters in the Abyssinian Palace. Built for the Abyssinian queen in 1902 but never used as her residence, this large house resembled the kind of magnificent villa typically seen on the Riviera. It was larger than Frutiger House, and some of the classrooms were large and airy, but others were quite small, creating crowded conditions.

However, the children had a playground on which they could assemble before moving into the classrooms in the morning. Landau and the teachers moved to an apartment at the top of the palace. In this magnificent setting, Landau continued to entertain, and her reputation as a hostess grew. At this time she began to be called the "Queen of Sheba" in the press.[61]

The building had bathing facilities, which Landau could use to address the problem of girls who arrived at school dirty. Many had to walk on unpaved roads that were dusty most of the year and muddy on rainy days. Landau found it hard to convince destitute mothers, themselves dressed in rags, to send their children to school clean and tidy. After a gift of clothing from

Landau Ladies' Committee member Nellie Nissim, Landau announced that girls who arrived with clean bodies and hair every day for three months would be given free clothing. This system worked very successfully.[62]

Although the Abyssinian Palace was intended as a temporary residence, the Evelina School remained there for two decades while Frutiger House was leased to tenants to generate income. The planned construction of additions to Frutiger House was delayed because of budget shortfalls in London and the failure to win permits from the disintegrating Ottoman Empire in Constantinople. While the Anglo-Jewish Association in London struggled with budget and permit issues, in Jerusalem Landau was faced with severe water shortages that were detrimental to her battle to improve basic hygiene among her pupils. Characteristically, Landau experienced each obstacle as a challenge that could be overcome, and she expected her students to do the same.[63] Treating the water shortage as a temporary setback, she redoubled her efforts to inspire her pupils to join her in the modernizing of Jerusalem.

Part of her vision included working with the various communities of Jerusalem for the common good. Hence, Evelina girls participated with several of the Jerusalem schools in a series of concerts and drill performances to raise funds for the Ottoman-sponsored Red Crescent League.[64] This medical relief organization, founded in 1868, opened a Jerusalem branch in the early years of the twentieth century. Landau and the Ladies' Committee of the Anglo-Jewish Association were supportive of the activities of the Red Cross in London and saw support of the Red Crescent as a worthy endeavor for the Evelina pupils.

Nevertheless, many traditional Jerusalemites were alarmed at the sight of their daughters performing drill exercises and raising funds for a Turkish cause. Similarly, the establishment of the Evelina de Rothschild School League for the Prevention of Cruelty to Animals was not understood by some parents. The league, which had its origin in England's Society for the Prevention of Cruelty to Animals (SPCA), soon had eighty student members, each of whom paid a half-penny per month and wore a badge. The members promised to be kind to every living thing; in a city where stray cats were ignored and camels were beaten, this was a decidedly new idea. The girls wrote essays on kindness to helpless creatures and read them at their monthly meetings.[65]

Landau believed that her pupils would learn about serving the common good through their work in organizations like the Red Crescent and the SPCA, but her primary objective was to uplift Jewish life in Palestine. She believed that the Evelina School was already a prime mover in this effort as a result of its record in serving as a training ground for other schools in Palestine. In 1912 Landau provided free training to a pupil of the Hilfsverein school in the embroidery workrooms so that the girl could return to her school and teach others what she had learned.

Likewise, Landau sent one of the teachers trained at the Evelina School to the village of Petah Tikvah at the request of the school authorities. Landau received grateful acknowledgment that the young teacher was doing excellent work in the new school. She explained, "It was a sacrifice to relinquish the services of a good teacher to another institution. . . . We felt, however, that as pioneers of women's education in Palestine, we should do all we could to help those following in our footsteps."[66]

In the spring of 1911, Landau returned to London to visit with her family and to meet with the Ladies' Committee and the leadership of the Anglo-Jewish Association. Once again, she was determined to demonstrate the merits of her project and the need for additional funds to establish the school in a proper school building. The Ladies' Committee, chaired by Mrs. Leopold de Rothschild, supported her efforts to raise additional funds with the publication of the booklet titled *An Appeal to Jewish Women on Behalf of the Anglo-Jewish Association*. The booklet was distributed in pamphlet format and was simultaneously printed in the *Jewish Chronicle*.[67]

Additional efforts at fundraising were launched in London the next year with the creation of the Palestine Exhibition and Bazaar. This event, announced on May 10, 1912, in the *Jewish Chronicle*, was a project supported by many of the leaders of the Anglo-Jewish Association and other Jewish leaders who wished to acquaint the public with the recent advances made in industry and the arts in Palestine.

The stalls at the exhibition primarily showed the work of the Evelina de Rothschild School and the Bezalel Academy for Art and Design, opened in Jerusalem in 1906 by Boris Schatz. The Evelina School exhibited lace, art needlework, gold and other embroideries, and various accessories for a woman's wardrobe. The Bezalel Academy showed art metalwork, wood carvings, carpets, rugs, cushions, filigree work, and jewelry. Most of the work was for sale. The *Jewish Chronicle* reported that the sales were a great success.[68]

The patrons for the event paid for the publication of a commemorative booklet, *Awakening Palestine*, which declared the following:

The progress of Jewish education in Palestine has not hitherto been followed very closely in England, yet the efforts of those who have engaged upon the task of transforming, often in the face of difficulties and disappointments, the whole character and spirit of the Jewish population, should appeal to every section of the Jewish people.[69]

The anonymous author expressed the optimistic assessment that in the previous decade, education in Jewish schools had changed to reflect changes in life in Palestine. The schools, originally intended to provide paupers with the skills that would make them into English, French, or German Jews, had changed as Palestine had developed industrially and agriculturally, providing opportunities for Jewish development. However, the conclusion glossed over the real difficulties identified by Landau. It read as follows:

> What is needed is an education that shall enable the boys and girls of today to develop into useful members of the Palestinian Jewish community. For this purpose they need on the one hand a knowledge of the Hebrew language, which is becoming more and more the speech of everyday life in Palestine; and on the other hand a practical training in manual work.[70]

Landau had discovered that it wasn't enough to teach Hebrew and practical skills in Jerusalem. She understood that it was even more important to change deeply held beliefs and that little would be gained without a basic change in values. Teaching the merits of self-reliance and the commitment to civic responsibility was the foundation of her educational approach.

While Landau focused on changing her pupils' lives, the world around them was becoming less stagnant. By 1913 there were 150,000 Jews in Palestine living in sixty colonies as well as in cities, the largest of which was Jerusalem, with 80,000 Jews. In the previous three decades, domestic industries had grown—among them, wine, silkworms, olive oil, and soap. Orange, almond, and apricot orchards spread across the landscape. Perfume plantations with roses, geraniums, and other flowers were in development. Machine shops and factories were producing construction tools, household utensils, and agricultural implements. Arts and crafts were developing as well: knitting, weaving, basketry, metalwork, pottery, lace, wood carving, and jewelry. The Hebrew language was becoming a unifying factor for the immigrants involved in these developments.[71]

Landau believed that teaching Hebrew to the diverse Jewish populations of Jerusalem was important to break down barriers among the communities. She realized that Hebrew would be the language of the Jews in Palestine. The school was fortunate to have Yosef Meyuhas as the senior Hebrew teacher. In the last years before World War I, Landau hired Hemda Ben-Yehuda—the wife of Eliezer Ben-Yehuda, the author of the first modern Hebrew dictionary—as the second Hebrew instructor in the Evelina School. Landau also emphasized the value of Hebrew in teaching Bible and religion. However, she remained convinced of the importance of simultaneously teaching English to provide her pupils with a broad education and to increase their ability to find jobs.

Thus, Annie Landau opposed the demands of a group of young Zionists who had successfully convinced the teachers of the Hilfsverein schools to teach only in Hebrew, temporarily putting an end to their bilingual program. Landau refused to follow their lead; although she staunchly supported excellence in Hebrew instruction, she refused to change the program of bilingual education that was the hallmark of the Evelina School. The debate became more energetic as the Hebrew advocates urged the closing of all Jewish schools to show support for their position. This action, known as the Palestinian Language Strike, resulted in negative publicity for the Evelina School in Zionist circles.[72]

Landau's teachers remained in class while most of the Jewish schools participated in the strike that year. The curriculum continued to be carried out in Hebrew and English in equal proportions in the girls' school and in three of the five kindergarten classes, while in the two lowest kindergarten classes the work was entirely in Hebrew.[73]

The next year, Landau reported the arrival of two excellent teachers from London: Rebecca Portnoi and Deborah Lazarus. Simultaneously, she reported that two former pupils had been hired to teach abroad, one in South Africa and the other in Switzerland. In addition, a former pupil, Batsheva Hirschensohn, who had spent three years as a governess teaching Hebrew in Hungary, returned to Jerusalem in response to a shortage of qualified teachers there. Hirschensohn possessed ideal qualities to teach at Landau's school, since she brought back to Jerusalem ideas and behaviors that could be modeled by her pupils. These additional teachers proved indispensable, for Landau was soon obliged to accommodate one hundred extra pupils who were "rescued" by young Zionists. Landau described the circumstances:

A group of enthusiastic young Zionists in Jerusalem determined to place in Jewish schools about 200 Jewish girls attending the Day School of the London Jews' Society (for promoting Christianity amongst the Jews). Forming a cordon around the school building, they took charge of the pupils as the latter left the school, accompanied them home, and obtained the consent of the parents to their being placed in Jewish schools on the understanding that they received the same benefits as at the mission school (free tuition, clothing, food). Each of the two other Jewish girls' schools in Jerusalem was asked to take 50 children, while to the Evelina School, which is regarded as *the* educational establishment for the poor, 100 children were sent, each with a written and signed request from the newly formed "War Committee against the Conversionists," to be admitted, clothed, and fed. As the cases were really genuine—the mothers in most cases being widows quite destitute, or washerwomen earning but a few piastres a day—we had no alternative but to accede to these requests, in spite of the additional financial burden.[74]

Despite the limitations of space and of budget, when faced with the demands of the War Committee, this time Landau did not refuse the Zionist activists. Although she did not approve of their methods, she was opposed to the enrollment of Jewish girls in missionary schools. She wanted to build strong mothers for the Jewish people and saw the mission schools as a serious obstacle to her plan.

Landau's report focused on the needs of the additional pupils, who were from the poorer segment of the population. In her 1914 report, she noted that 180 children received daily eye care in the school, courtesy of two nurses—supported by Hadassah, the American Zionist women's organization—under the supervision of Dr. Albert Ticho. Landau was delighted that three pupils now wanted to study nursing, and she gratefully accepted the assistance of Eva Leon of New York City, who volunteered to convince the parents of these girls that it was a respectable field. Dr. Braun provided dental treatment for hundreds of children that year, filling teeth, curing gum disease, removing tartar, and extracting rotten teeth. In addition, 57,693 free meals were served to three hundred needy children from May 4, 1913, to July 30, 1914. The average rate of attendance during the 1913–1914 school year was 86 percent.

This was a very impressive record, considering the generally primitive hygiene conditions and widespread disease described by Dr. Helena Kagan, a recent arrival in the city who soon became a good friend of Landau's. Kagan described the conditions in Jerusalem in April 1914:

> Boundless ignorance and superstition were added to extreme poverty. The sanitary situation was at its lowest ebb. . . . Rubbish was thrown into the streets and piled up in the corners, attracting rats and millions of flies and mosquitoes. Public lavatories did not exist and usually there was one neglected and filthy privy in the courtyard of a house inhabited by numerous teeming families.
>
> No central water supply existed and taps were a rare sight. Water was collected during the rainy season, running from the roofs into cisterns. . . . Sometimes these cisterns were so infested that the bad smell and taste of the water made it unsuitable for drinking. In such cases water had to be bought, from water vendors who carried water in sheep skins supposedly fresh from the spring at Silwan.
>
> Food hygiene was on a particularly low level: vegetables were irrigated with sewage and were the main cause of dysentery, typhoid fever, and enteric diseases of all kinds . . . meat often came from tubercular and sick animals, slaughtered in the final stages of disease. . . . Cows' milk was often dangerous, infested with bacteria.[75]

Dr. Kagan quickly got to work to improve the situation. She bought a cow and began to distribute fresh milk to mothers with young babies. Around her, Jerusalem experienced its last spurt of growth before the scourge of war took over. It was the biggest city in Palestine and the cultural center of the country. While Jaffa and Haifa were dominated by working-class and business concerns, Jerusalem was a junction for religious, social, cultural, economic, and government activities in which Jews, Muslims, and Christians took part.

In February 1914, the last Ottoman mayor, Hussein al-Husseini, announced a new contract between a French company and the city to build a tramway from Jerusalem to Bethlehem. The same company announced plans to illuminate the city with electric lights and to bring water from nearby fountains to the city. The editor of *Ha-Herut*, a Zionist newspaper, commented that "the mayor makes sure that the city of Jerusalem will become a nice, clean and organized European city."[76]

Landau's last report before the outbreak of war illustrated her continued efforts to provide her graduates with employment. The workshops of the Evelina School produced ornamental curtains for the ark of a synagogue in

Perth, Australia; embroidered Torah mantles for a community in Hungary; and sewed a banner for a school in Jerusalem. Individual orders arrived for lace from Baroness Edmond de Rothschild* in Paris, Caroline Franklin in London, Augusta Rosenwald in Chicago, and Josephine Morgenthau in Constantinople, while A. Kimchi in St. Gall, Switzerland, Eva Leon in New York, and Birdie Friedenwald in Baltimore all purchased embroidery.

Many of those who bought items from the workshops also visited the school and used the opportunity to make donations. Baroness Edmond de Rothschild provided funding for two hundred pairs of boots for needy children, Caroline and Arthur Franklin and their daughter Helen supplemented the meals for needy children with an egg for each girl three times a week for six months. The U.S. ambassador to Turkey, Henry Morgenthau Sr., and his wife, Josephine, paid two visits to the school and donated funds to clothe poor kindergarten children.[77]

The Disruption of War

The school and the city appeared poised for development, but as had so often happened in the past, hostilities from abroad were about to cause great damage to Jerusalem. With little warning, in August 1914 the Ottoman authorities announced that all British, French, and Russian nationals would have to leave Palestine immediately or be detained. Visitors ceased coming to Jerusalem, and Jews living in the city who hailed from enemy countries were given the option of applying for Ottoman nationality. Immediately, the price of food and fuel rose steeply as a result of hoarding, speculation, and panic.

Zaki Bey, the military commander of Jerusalem, called on all residents to unite, regardless of nationality or religious belief, to cope with the crisis.[78] Ottoman male subjects between the ages of seventeen and forty began to be drafted. Rose Kaplan and Ray Landy, the two American nurses supported by Hadassah who provided medical assistance at the school, left Jerusalem, one to work with Palestinian Jewish refugees in Alexandria and the other to join U.S. naval forces in the Pacific.[79]

On October 30, 1914, the Ottoman Empire joined the war on the side of Germany and Austria-Hungary, and a week later the Ottomans declared that

---

* Née Adelaide von Rothschild

the war was a jihad, a Muslim holy war. Forty Circassians brandishing scimitars rode through the streets of Jerusalem to impress the public with their fierce determination. Banks stopped providing credit and selling gold. All foreign post offices and banks closed, with the exception of the Anglo-Palestine Bank, which was permitted to open intermittently as a result of pressure from Ambassador Morgenthau. The foreign press ceased to arrive, schools and relief institutions closed, and food imports stopped. Jerusalem was cut off.[80]

In November, at a joint meeting of Jewish and Muslim residents of the city, Eliezer Ben-Yehuda and David Yellin appealed to foreign Jews to stay on and to accept Ottoman nationality. Both began to wear the red tarboosh as a sign of their loyalty to the Ottoman Empire. Dr. Kagan became an Ottoman subject as well.

With Britain and Turkey at war, Landau faced serious problems in keeping her school open. At first, the British government permitted the Anglo-Jewish Association to continue to send funds; the money was remitted through the American embassies in London and Constantinople. In recognition of the important work done by the Evelina School to combat the rampant cholera and persistent hunger faced by the city's children, Turkish authorities allowed it to remain open after all the other British schools were closed. Rivka Mitshanik remembered that the teachers took care of the pupils: telling them stories, washing them, and feeding them. Dr. Ticho and Dr. Kagan, who lived near the school, volunteered their help.[81]

In May 1915, after all other British nationals had been evacuated, the Turkish authorities informed Landau that she would either have to become an Ottoman subject or leave Palestine. Landau reluctantly left her school in the care of Ella Schwartzstein, whom she appointed acting headmistress. Officially, the Ottoman minister of education took over the administration of the Evelina School.

Albert Montefiore Hyamson, a Zionist who later played an important role in the Mandatory government and whose daughter attended the Evelina de Rothschild School in the 1940s, described the school Landau left in 1915 as follows:

It is the finest type of English girls' school, above the rank of elementary, but somewhat lower than secondary. At the same time it has managed to secure a thorough Jewish atmosphere. The position it has attained is shown by the support and approval given to it by the best Turkish families in Jerusalem, who send their daughters to be educated there. The school is attended by children of all classes, but only from the more prosperous are fees required. . . . The institution is, however, far more than a school. At times of epidemic it is partly a hospital, partly a place of refuge for the avoidance of contagion. It is always a centre for the distribution of relief, without discrimination. The position which the Evelina School has attained could never have been reached if it had not been for the personality of Miss Landau and the devotion of her staff. She has made for herself, and incidentally for the school, a position of great influence in Jerusalem.[82]

During the years leading up to World War I, the Anglo-Jewish Association had supported Landau as she struggled to create "the finest type of English girls' school" and give it a "thorough Jewish atmosphere." The Association had worked with Landau as she tried to place greater emphasis on education only to be repeatedly forced to spend funds and time on basic social services in the face of disease and poverty. She won the support of affluent Sephardi families, who sent their daughters to the school alongside girls from impoverished backgrounds. The presence of these new families allowed Landau to aspire to higher levels of education in her school; at the same time, she created a true oasis for those from poor families. After she left for Alexandria, her colleagues did their best to maintain the school.

For the next several months, despite the exile of the headmistress and about 100 children whose parents were enemy subjects of Turkey, the staff continued to teach and manage the school, providing much-needed food and education for the 650 or so remaining girls. Children who had been on waiting lists for admission replaced those who left.

In addition to suffering the deprivations caused by war, Palestine experienced an infestation of locusts in the summer of 1915. Turkish officials turned to Aaron Aaronson, a noted agronomist working near Zichron Ya'akov. Aaronson recommended using chemicals to combat the plague, but they were not available in wartime. He next requested eight thousand soldiers to work to eradicate the locust eggs, but his petition was denied on the grounds that a Jew could not be allowed to command Turkish soldiers. Aaronson therefore mobilized the entire population of Jerusalem, including children, some of whom were pupils at the Evelina School, to dig in the soil to find the locust eggs and burn them. Aaronson returned to the Galilee and was soon engaged as a spy for the British.[83]

Landau relocated to Alexandria, responding to a request from the Anglo-Egyptian authorities to organize a school for the hundreds of refugee children from Palestine and Syria. Rose Kaplan, the Hadassah nurse, ailing with cancer, had left Jerusalem earlier to seek treatment in the United States. Arriving in Alexandria, she learned that thousands of Jewish refugees were stranded there, and she stayed on to assist Landau in serving them. She remained head nurse for these refugees until her death in August 1917.[84]

Nellie Nissim, who had provided clothing for Evelina girls, now tried to secure funds and teachers to assist Landau in Alexandria.[85] Despite Nissim's aid and the fact that Landau was devoted to the children in Alexandria, Landau's heart remained with her pupils in Jerusalem. With help from the Anglo-Jewish Association, she obtained permission from the British Foreign Office to send funds she collected in both London and Alexandria to feed her girls in Jerusalem. When she ran out of money, the Foreign Office agreed to Landau's contracting a loan for the same purpose, and the Anglo-Jewish Association agreed to repay the debt at the conclusion of hostilities. Thus, the school stayed open and fed its destitute pupils for another year.[86]

In the face of growing difficulties, the German teachers, including Ella Schwartzstein, gradually returned home. The young kindergarten teacher, Rivka Mitshanik, and the Hebrew teacher, Yosef Meyuhas, both Ottoman subjects, were the last to remain at their posts. They were aided by Jonas Marx, the honorary director of Shaare Tzedek Hospital, who served as an unofficial accountant for the school in Landau's absence.

Finally, the Turkish authorities closed the school and confiscated both the Abyssinian Palace and Frutiger House. Mitshanik struggled to protect school furniture and supplies from destruction by Turkish soldiers. Marx was able to secure a shelter for 170 desks in the Monastery of St. Anne.[87] In the winter of 1916–1917, Landau's girls were left to wander the streets in the increasingly bleak Jerusalem. Bertha Spafford Vester of the American Colony, a religious community engaged in social welfare that was permitted to remain open during the war, reported on the harsh conditions, noting that many women offered to sell their babies for a pittance, just to be sure of a few more meals. One desperate mother left her skeletal twin babies at midnight hanging from the Colony's front gate. Equally alarming, many women and young girls sold themselves to Turkish and German soldiers.[88]

The Evelina School was closed through the early months of 1917, leaving destitute girls with paltry supervision. Some Evelina students had been able to find places in other schools, but many were left to wander around aimlessly, receiving no education and no food. On September 9, 1917, a group of seven teachers still living in the city wrote to the Jewish education authorities lamenting the condition of their pupils since the closing of the school, begging the authorities to find places for them and offering their services to teach the girls.

The teachers also spoke of the need for continued medical treatment for the girls and for the teachers and their families. The teachers themselves had fared no better than their pupils. Beginning in October 1915, the teachers received only two-thirds of their salaries, and that in worthless paper currency; in May 1917, their salaries ceased to be paid. Yet even as their incomes were being greatly reduced, there was a significant inflation in the prices of basic necessities.[89] Landau's teachers and her pupils suffered greatly; the oasis she had created had reverted to an arid lot.

In Jerusalem, the school that had begun to transform the lives of Jewish girls was closed, and its buildings were being used by wounded Ottoman soldiers. In Alexandria, Landau solicited financial aid from a network of English women who were her friends and supported her work. She followed the progress of the war with keen interest and planned her return to her school and her pupils.[90]

As soon as General Edmund Allenby marched into Jerusalem on December 9, 1917, Landau requested permission to go home to Jerusalem. Allenby, keen to restore order and to bring cleanliness to the destitute city, was happy to bring back the "Queen of Sheba" to aid in his project.

[3]

REBUILDING IN

BRITISH JERUSALEM

Jerusalem surrendered to General Edmund Allenby in early December 1917, one month after the Balfour Declaration, promising the Jews a homeland in Palestine, had been issued in London. Allenby's humble walk through the Jaffa Gate into the Old City marked the beginning of a new phase in the history of the Middle East.[1] Jerusalem, denuded by the retreating Turkish army of food, money, drugs, surgical instruments, furniture, records, and archives, became the responsibility of the British.

General Allenby, anxious to reassure the residents of the city of the benign intentions of his government, announced that the status quo would prevail regarding all holy places. He decreed that henceforth all official business would be conducted in three languages: English, Arabic, and Hebrew. This news immediately raised the ire of Arab leaders, who were happy to drop the use of Turkish but were alarmed by the inclusion of Hebrew, the language advocated by nationalist Jews. The general appointed Colonel Ronald Storrs as the first military governor of Jerusalem.

Storrs noted in his diary that the residents of the city were starving and suffering from cold and that there was not a single private car or private phone in the city when he arrived. Storrs's request for emergency food aid was met by General Allenby with alacrity: wheat and other essentials arrived daily by rail from Cairo for the next few months. Storrs established food control with rations for flour, sugar, and kerosene. Further help came from relief agencies that arrived in the first weeks of 1918. The Syrian Relief Fund, founded by Assistant Archbishop Rennie MacInnes in 1916 to provide relief in Syria and Palestine, donated food as well as wool to make blankets and warm clothing.

The American Zionist Organization and the American Red Cross contributed personnel, equipment, and funds.[2]

Although the war was not over, Annie Landau, exiled in Alexandria, was eager to return home. She appealed to General Allenby and became the first woman permitted to return to her beloved Jerusalem, arriving in February 1918. Knowing the desperate plight of the city, she arranged to bring with her four tons of food and clothing supplied by her supporters Jack Mosseri of Cairo and Sir Elly Kadoorie of Shanghai. British authorities acceded to Landau's request to ship the goods free of charge on the military train from Cairo.

Upon her arrival, she distributed food and clothing to the needy. She soon learned that there was an additional scourge in the city: starving young women were selling themselves as prostitutes to the thousands of soldiers stationed in Jerusalem. Landau, who had maintained good relations with the Turkish authorities, now began to develop ties to the British administration. She was determined to get as many girls and women off the streets as possible. One way she could help was to reopen her school quickly.

The obstacles to reopening the Evelina de Rothschild School were many. Frutiger House had been requisitioned as an annex for the British military hospital, which operated out of the Italian Hospital across the street.[3] The Abyssinian Palace, which had been used by the Turkish army, was now empty. The school furniture that had been salvaged by Jonas Marx remained in storage. None of the foreign teachers who had fled during the war had returned to Jerusalem. The coffers of the Anglo-Jewish Association were depleted as a result of the war. Nevertheless, Landau met with Governor Storrs and asked for the immediate return of Frutiger House. Storrs recorded his first impression of the headmistress:

> When, early in 1918, a lady, unlike the stage woman of Destiny in that she was neither tall, dark, nor thin, was ushered, with an expression of equal good humour and resolution, into my office, I immediately realized that a new planet had swum into my ken. Miss Annie Landau had been throughout the War exiled in Alexandria from her beloved Evelina de Rothschild Girls' School, and demanded to return to it immediately. To my miserable pleading that her school was in use as a Military Hospital, she opposed a steely insistence: and very few minutes had elapsed before I had leased her the vast empty building known as the Abyssinian Palace.[4]

Landau's unique combination of resolve and charm, tested earlier in her dealings with Ottoman representatives, worked well with British officials. Storrs offered the Abyssinian Palace for immediate occupancy, and he agreed to clean up Frutiger House and remove the remaining convalescent soldiers. Frutiger House was soon returned to the Anglo-Jewish Association for use as rental property. Landau searched for graduates who would be able to teach and arranged for desks to be brought to the Abyssinian Palace.

Three months after she had returned to the impoverished city, Landau greeted five hundred former pupils and many guests at a grand reopening ceremony, a tea hosted by the headmistress and presided over by Governor Storrs. In a city still struggling with famine and occupied by British soldiers, the reopening of the school was a major event and a sign of optimism.

To mark this occasion, Landau's pupils, who remembered their English lessons well, expressed their gratitude to Storrs in verse:

> We thank you all kind gentlemen,
> For coming here today
> And hope you'll not forget our School
> When you are far away.
> How can we prove our gratitude,
> A School of Jewish girls?
> How can we show we're happy
> As Britain's flag unfurls.
> We know that you have fought for us
> But brave lives it has cost
> And in some way we would repay
> A part of all that's lost.
> We love our land of Palestine,
> And England we love too,
> The land that's fighting hard to make
> A home for every Jew.
> We wish God's blessing on our King.
> We pray that peace is near,
> And that you'll soon be joining hands,
> With those who are so dear.[5]

Storrs was clearly moved by the girls' sentiments. The poem remained with his personal papers and was among those donated to Pembroke College after his death.

Following the tea, Landau escorted the governor to a class taught by Tova Rosenbaum, the girl whose older brother had carried her to school like a sack of flour in 1903; she was now one of the young women hired by Landau to replace the foreign staff members who had not returned. Storrs watched as Rosenbaum began her class for beginners in English with the poem "A Day in May." When the lesson was completed, Landau introduced Rosenbaum to the governor, who was quite surprised to learn that the young teacher was a native of Jerusalem and a former pupil of the Evelina School. He marveled at her command of English. This classroom visit was the catalyst for new employment opportunities for the graduates of Landau's school.

Storrs needed people proficient in English to staff the offices of the Occupied Enemy Territory Administration (OETA), as the military government was called. He turned to Landau to help him locate graduates like Rosenbaum whose command of English was exemplary.[6] Landau quickly understood that this was a splendid opportunity for her former students. OETA offices were located in Government House, formerly the German hospital Augusta Victoria, on Mount Scopus, where young graduates of the school trained as housekeepers had worked before the war. In response to the request of the governor, Landau quickly identified several graduates for positions as office assistants with the Mandatory government. To ensure the safety of the young women, the government hired a vehicle to drive them back and forth every day.[7]

Landau realized that the British needed clerks who not only were fluent in English but also knew shorthand. Encouraged by Storrs, she introduced a shorthand class for older girls at the Evelina School taught by an assistant to the governor, Warrant Officer John Owen. Within four months, the first fourteen girls who had finished the course took the Pitman Examination for Elementary Certificates and passed, some with distinction. Three weeks later, they passed the Theory Examination. Storrs, in presenting the certificates to the successful candidates, expressed his pleasure at presiding at this function at what he considered to be "the best school in Palestine."[8]

Landau established close ties with the British administration, partly as a result of the success of her graduates who worked for the government. The addition of shorthand marked the beginning of a new phase in the school's history. Girls who finished the Evelina course of study were soon offered an additional option, the commercial class. Here, fourteen- and fifteen-year-old pupils learned shorthand and other business-related skills, which kept them in school for an additional year and thereby delayed the early marriages that were still common in Jerusalem and opposed by Landau.

The Evelina de Rothschild School was unusual in its level of cooperation with British authorities. Rachel Elboim-Dror, who has studied the resistance to British influence on education in the Jewish community, found opposition to the British in Orthodox groups who continued to oppose modernization, labor groups who used schools for party indoctrination and recruitment, and the Teachers' Union, which advocated cultural autonomy and nationalism. Jews who supported British involvement were mainly western European immigrants and academics who advocated modern, secular, Western culture.[9]

The only other girls' school in the city that provided graduates to serve the British administration was the English High School for Girls, later known as the Jerusalem Girls' College, a Christian school opened in 1918 by Mabel Warburton to serve Christian, Muslim, and Jewish girls. This school produced graduates who worked for the British administration in Jerusalem as well as teachers who worked for government Arab schools.[10]

Postwar Challenges

During the summer months, the military government looked beyond education to solve serious problems created by the war. The Jewish community had lost approximately half its population, partly from starvation and epidemics and partly from emigration and Turkish deportations, leaving approximately twenty-six thousand Jews, including about three thousand orphans. Half the orphans were girls, many of whom in desperation had turned to prostitution. Major General Arthur Money, the chief administrator of OETA in Palestine, believed that prostitutes were a necessity for the twenty-six thousand British soldiers stationed in Palestine. In June 1918, he published regulations to limit brothels in Jerusalem to the neighborhoods of Nahalat Shiva and the Milner Houses; both of these were Jewish neighborhoods and were close to the Evelina School.

The leading women of Jerusalem disapproved of legalizing prostitution in their city and soon created the Social Service Association to address the problems of girls and women in the streets. Its founders were Salmah Salameh, a Greek Orthodox Arab and the wife of Demetri Salameh, the local manager of the travel agency Thomas Cook & Company; Marianne Hoofien, a Dutch Jew and the wife of the director of the Anglo-Palestine Bank; and Bertha Spafford Vester of the American Colony. These three women had worked together during the war and had experience assisting vulnerable women and children in the city.

Now they called on the Syria and Palestine Relief Fund, the American Red Cross, and the Hadassah Medical Units to join in an effort to rid the city of prostitution. Landau, whose commitment to social service was part of her educational vision, was one of the first members of the group; she remained active in its work for the rest of her life. Mary Anne MacInnes, wife of the Anglican bishop and one of Landau's friends, became the first president of the Social Service Association.

The existence of Jewish prostitutes was a topic for debate among ultra-Orthodox and Zionist leaders. The former fervently denied the presence of Jewish prostitutes, whereas the latter were outspoken critics of the policy of denial. Chaim Weizmann, the leader of the Zionist Commission, incurred the wrath of ultra-Orthodox leaders when he informed the European Jewish community that prostitution and drunkenness had become widespread in Jerusalem. He estimated that there were five hundred Jewish girls and women who refused to accept jobs in workshops, preferring to earn their living through prostitution. Ultra-Orthodox leaders in Meah Shearim protested his comments and criticized Weizmann, who "defame[d] the daughters of Jerusalem."[11]

Yosef Meyuhas, the senior Hebrew teacher at the Evelina School and the scion of a distinguished Sephardi family, joined the debate. As a concerned citizen and a member of the newly formed Jewish Municipal Committee, he reluctantly acknowledged the truth of Weizmann's comments. He urged action against pimps and prostitutes in the Holy City. A letter from members of the municipal committee to Governor Storrs depicted the blight of prostitution as both an economic loss to the householders who lived adjacent to the brothels and a moral injury to the city's children.[12] Storrs, who hired Landau's graduates, knew the poverty of Jerusalem's girls and their families and was sympathetic to the special nature of the city. He responded to the letter of the municipal committee by removing prostitutes who were not local residents; this act immediately cut their number in half.[13]

Amid the controversy surrounding the issue of prostitution in Jerusalem, the embers of hostility to learning English and wearing school uniforms were stoked. Landau's pupils became the target of special criticism because they knew "how to chat in English" and "went out all pinned up, wearing silk stockings up to their knees."[14] Orthodox leaders objected to Jewish girls working in a Christian professional environment, whereas Zionist leaders may have been jealous that these highly competent young women worked for the British administration rather than for them.

In sharp contrast to the image of loose morals ascribed to Evelina girls, perfect behavior was demanded by Landau from her pupils. She forbade them to have any contact with boys while they were in school, and she continued to admonish them about proper behavior after graduation. Malicious gossip about Landau's girls coexisted with the very high regard in which the school and its graduates were generally held. Despite the criticism, Landau remained steadfast in her commitment to bilingual education for her students and encouraged her graduates to work for the British government, presciently believing that these jobs were good training for future leaders of the Jewish people.

Landau was not flustered by the attacks. She and the members of the Social Service Association continued to focus on the real problems of poor girls and women in Jerusalem. They were pleased with the progress made in diminishing the presence of prostitutes in the city, but they recognized that some women would need more assistance to restart their lives. Helen Bentwich, who had arrived in Jerusalem a few weeks after Landau's return from exile in Egypt, offered to use her skills as a social worker to address these needs.[15]

Bentwich, the daughter of Caroline Franklin, a member of the Anglo-Jewish Association's Ladies' Committee, had visited Jerusalem as a young teenager traveling with her parents. When she returned in 1918, she joined her husband, Norman, a lawyer who worked for the OETA and later become attorney general under the British Mandate. Bentwich had volunteered during World War I with the land army and was eager to support the effort to improve conditions for women and children in Jerusalem. She met with Landau; with Alice Seligsberg, a Hadassah leader and social worker from New York; with the pediatrician Dr. Helena Kagan; and with Sophie

Berger, who worked for the American Red Cross. Together, these women, all active members of the Social Service Association, decided to establish a small shelter.

They continued to staff and finance the shelter for two years, until the management and funding were assumed by the British government under the supervision of Margaret Nixon, an experienced social worker recently hired as the inspector of female prisoners. Because of the small number of women who were prisoners, her role developed into welfare worker for the women of the country. In this capacity, she supervised prison issues, inspected factory conditions, and acted as a film censor. In addition, she assisted the occasional female slave who escaped from an adjoining territory, female political agitators who went on hunger strikes, unwed mothers, girls and women with matrimonial difficulties, and wives who were in danger from domestic violence.[16]

In the early 1920s, the membership of the Social Service Association remained diverse despite the emerging national movements—Zionism and Arab nationalism—whose rhetoric and actions made cooperation difficult. Working together, the members of the Social Service Association established tentative friendships. Some among them, led by Bentwich, felt the desire to establish a social and cultural club for elite women modeled on similar clubs in London and Paris.

The result was the Jerusalem Ladies' Club, which rented rooms above a restaurant with space for a library, bridge games, and bathing facilities for sportswomen. The sociable Annie Landau was a founding member of the club, which sponsored lectures and teas, providing a place for educated women to meet across religious and national boundaries. Landau lectured at the club on her hobbies, horticulture and needlework. The club held a welcoming party for Lady Beatrice Samuel, the wife of the first high commissioner, Sir Herbert Samuel.[17] Although other multinational women's organizations were founded at the time, only the Social Service Association survived for a significant period. In view of the growing Jewish and Arab nationalism, it is remarkable that a political and social organization of women from different religious communities existed at all.[18]

There was disagreement between General Money and the Social Service Association about prostitution, but they agreed on the need to address the problems of communications and supplies for Jerusalem. The OETA worked to address pressing problems; units of the Royal Engineers built roads, dug drainage systems and wells, restored the railways, and imported food and medical supplies for the needy population. A Palestinian currency was established, pegged to the Egyptian currency. The Ottoman system of closing offices for two to three hours in the afternoon was eliminated.

Perhaps most important, Governor Storrs established the Pro-Jerusalem Society, which brought together the leaders of the different communities to protect the city by maintaining parks, gardens, and open spaces. The society pledged to respect all antiquities and to encourage arts and crafts industries, especially traditional crafts like ceramics. One of the first accomplishments of the society was to repair the citadel at the Jaffa Gate and to establish within its building an annual salon for the visual arts.[19]

At the Evelina School, Landau turned to the critical health problems of her pupils. During the war years, children in Jerusalem had received very little medical or dental attention, and many had suffered from malnutrition. As a result, after the war, many were not physically able to devote themselves to their studies. Landau made arrangements with Hadassah for Dr. Jesse Feinberg and Dr. Louis Ungar to address the dental and medical needs of her students. She gratefully accepted the support of the Nathan Strauss Health Center, which reintroduced the vaccination program established earlier at the school at a minimum cost.

Although dental care and vaccinations were important, in Landau's estimation the most alarming problem was persistent hunger. Julius and Augusta Rosenwald of Chicago, who had begun funding meals for Evelina girls during the war, continued to do so in the years after it. Annie wrote to the Anglo-Jewish Association, "It is not saying too much when I state that the subvention of Mr. and Mrs. Julius Rosenwald has saved hundreds of Evelina School children from certain starvation."[20]

Having secured the continuing support of Hadassah, the Nathan Strauss Health Center, the Rosenwalds, and the Anglo-Jewish Association, who continued to fund most of the operating expenses of the Evelina School, Landau rededicated her efforts to the goal she had established before the war: educating pupils to be firm in faith and modern in outlook. Landau was no longer the young teacher who had arrived in Jerusalem in 1899 with modest experience and big ideas about creating a bilingual program in a girls' school. She had already proved that she could conquer problems posed by hunger, sickness, and the resultant erratic attendance patterns, establishing her school as the premier girls' institution in the area, but she had been forced to abandon her efforts when she went into exile.

Now, with the support of Governor Storrs, who was asked to continue his role in the civil administration formed by High Commissioner Samuel, Landau had the opportunity to build again in a different Jerusalem, a city humbled by the ravages of war but bolstered by the energetic efforts of the British administration to repair the damage and protect the Holy City. During these years, her early vision for the school was fully realized.

During the Ottoman years, the study of English had been looked on with bemusement by many in Jerusalem who thought that other languages—Hebrew, Arabic, French, German, and even Russian—were likely to be more useful to the inhabitants of the city. Zionists demanded that Jewish schools teach only in Hebrew, whereas Arab nationalists advocated teaching only in Arabic. With the arrival of the British, a bifurcated public school system was established: Arab children and Jewish children were instructed separately, each in their national language. Nevertheless, the Evelina School and the other privately funded schools, both Jewish and missionary, remained bilingual.

During the Mandate years, it was clear that proficiency in English was the most important asset in seeking employment in Jerusalem. Landau's pupils, who were not only proficient but had been taught the same English stories and songs and knew the same games and sports as their new employers, were increasingly in demand for jobs that paid well. Their success in working in administrative offices, in banks, and later for the Palestine Broadcasting Service gave the Evelina School and its headmistress an important place in the life of the city. Landau enjoyed the respect of many as she continued to build the reputation of her school through her role as one of the leading hostesses of Jerusalem.

Landau's Salon

At a time when there were few cafés, only one small movie theater, no radio, and few social clubs in Jerusalem, Annie Landau was a celebrated social figure. She reestablished her salon on the top floor of the Abyssinian Palace, which once again served as the Evelina School building. The spacious grandeur of the palace—built for the Abyssinian royal family when it stayed in Jerusalem—with its beautiful tiled floors, its warmth, and its comfort, enabled

Landau to entertain in style. In this period, she favored costume balls, which were attended by British and consular officials, by leaders of the Jewish and Christian communities, and occasionally by Muslim leaders as well.

Helen Bentwich was a frequent guest. She was sometimes critical of Landau's expenditure on parties and once questioned the use of funds provided by the Anglo-Jewish Association; nevertheless, she was soon convinced that Landau's social standing was of great benefit to the Evelina School. Her letters home often contained enthusiastic descriptions of balls hosted by Landau, beginning with one in March 1919 where Landau dressed as a Dutch peasant, the Meyuhas girls came as Bukharan and Yemenite Jews, and one of the Hadassah nurses came as Anna Pavlova, "scantily dressed, beyond the limit."[21] The ball was decorated in Japanese style; the food, imported from Cairo, was excellent.

Rachel Eliacher, a daughter of an old Sephardi family and a graduate of the Evelina School, remembered Landau's parties fondly. She noted that her family was frequently invited to the homes of Mayor Ragheb Bey Nashashibi and other prominent Arab families, but she remembered Landau's events in particular because it was there that she tasted her first strawberries, delivered from Cairo for the occasion. She also remembered that Landau sent printed invitations to her parties written in English. When the Zionist leader Menachem Ussishkin received one, he wrote back provocatively, "I don't understand English, write it in Hebrew." She replied spiritedly, "If you don't understand English, you are not invited."[22]

In addition to hosting her famous costume balls, Landau entertained diplomatic visitors to Jerusalem like His Excellency Dedjazmatch Gabre Selassie, the commandant of the Tigre Troops and the president of the Ethiopian delegation to Jerusalem. These afternoon parties were typically smaller events; the guests were invited to attend from 4 to 6:30.[23] Helen Bentwich observed that Landau's social events were more interesting than the frequent "harem parties" where wives of British officials met wives and daughters of Arab notables.[24]

Landau's strong personality and the support of British Jews and Christians, including titled lords and ladies, gave her undisputed prominence despite her relatively humble position as the headmistress of a girls' school. Most of the time, Landau skillfully navigated the political shoals of Jerusalem politics. However, there were incidents in which she was forced to take a stand that resulted in opprobrium from one of the factions.

Bentwich reported on one such incident that took place at a celebration to mark the opening of the new music school in Jerusalem in March 1919. At the end of the evening, the audience stood as the performers started to play what the British anticipated would be "God Save the King." When General Money realized that they were actually playing the banned Zionist anthem "Hatikvah," he signaled to Storrs and the others to sit down. Landau joined the British in sitting down. Her act was denounced by many Zionists and was often cited by those who charged her with anti-Zionism.[25] Fortunately for Landau, the tempest over this event soon died down, and she retained her role as an admired city leader whose home was graced by a wide range of visitors. Her balls and her famous Friday night and holiday dinners were occasions to see "everyone" in the city.

Landau was at the center of the circle of those Jerusalemites who adopted an inclusive approach to all communities in the early years of the Mandate. The great Hebrew linguist Eliezer Ben-Yehuda, who lived nearby, was another member of that circle. Ben-Yehuda (who died in 1922) and his wife, Hemda, who taught at the Evelina School, hosted an eclectic group of linguists and archaeologists—Christians, Muslims, and Jews, speaking French, German, English, Hebrew and Arabic—on Friday nights. Dr. Ticho, the ophthalmologist who contributed to the health care of the Evelina pupils, was also known for treating Arab leaders. He and his wife, Anna, an artist, conducted their parties in German with a cosmopolitan guest list. George Antonius, a Christian Arab who served in the British administration and later was a member of the Palestinian Arab delegation to London, and his wife, Katy, hosted their sophisticated parties in French.

Some of Landau's circle thought of her as a wise counselor, perhaps because of her role as an educator or simply by virtue of her talent for friendship. One who sought her advice about a delicate personal matter was Dr. Tawfiq Canaan, the first Arab physician in Jerusalem. Dr. Canaan lived in Musrara and worked at Shaare Tzedek Hospital, where he became friendly with Dr. Ticho. When Dr. Canaan believed that he had accumulated enough money to marry, the Protestant Arab turned to the Orthodox, single Annie Landau for advice. Decades later his daughter, Leila Mantoura, recalled the family story. "He said: Look, Miss Landau, you are a good friend. I want a wife."[26] Landau, who knew all the educated women in Jerusalem, made a list of eight suitable young women, four Europeans and four Arabs. She invited each one with her parents to meet Dr. Canaan in her home. Although Canaan did not marry any of the candidates, he and Landau remained close friends.

Meaningful friendships among this elite and cosmopolitan group of Jerusalemites continued until the sustained Arab boycott that began in 1936. The Tichos, the Antoniuses, the Bentwiches, and Judah and Beatrice Magnes shared Landau's belief in the importance of working together to improve Jerusalem. They viewed Storrs's Pro-Jerusalem Society as an important British initiative to restore the city, which was rich in history and culture and capable of becoming a cosmopolitan center once again. Their social events were part of this endeavor to reimagine Jerusalem.

Landau, who had no family in Jerusalem, also developed a small inner circle of special friends. Ethel Ofstein, who like Landau had been trained at the Graystoke Teachers' Training College and had taught for several years in London, was quickly accepted into the inner circle. She arrived in Jerusalem in February 1921 to marry Moss Levy, another friend of Landau's, and was invited to stay with Landau and several other teachers in the Abyssinian Palace until the wedding was arranged. Ofstein's impressions of her first night in Jerusalem illustrate both the cordiality of Landau's welcome and the underlying sense of danger felt by the young Englishwoman:

> We stayed up and chatted that first night of mine and then retired to bed soon after 10 p.m., but the emotion and excitement of my journey and impressions made it difficult to sleep. At midnight, just as I was dozing, a blood-curdling yell split the silence of the night. I gripped the sides of the bed with fright. This yell was followed by a second, reverberating through the night, and a third and a fourth. I could not understand why silence in the house persisted. Somebody was obviously being murdered and not a soul to take the slightest interest. I was too terrified to move. In any case, the house was so big and there were so many doors that I had already lost my way each time I ventured from my room. How then could I expect to find Miss Landau's or any teacher's room to raise the alarm? I lay there; an hour later the blood-curdling yells again rent the air. I fell asleep from sheer exhaustion after the third spell of yells, wondering whether it was in Jerusalem's practice to murder inhabitants every night and whether its inhabitants were too accustomed to murder to bother about it.
>
> Next morning everybody trooped into breakfast looking thoroughly normal and cheerful. Timidly, I asked: "Did you hear those dreadful yells last night?"

"Yells?" they asked uncertainly. "Oh," responded another, "she means the prison guards." I then found out that the central prison was housed opposite the school. Four guards stood at four corners of the flat roof; at every hour each yelled to the other: "Wahed. Tenein. Telate. Arba'a" [one, two, three, four], to be sure that each was awake. You cannot imagine the effect in the still night of these murderous-sounding yells.[27]

Ofstein's fears were calmed by the elegant wedding party hosted by Landau for the young couple on the roof of the Abyssinian Palace. The ceremony was performed by Abraham Isaac Kook, the newly appointed Ashkenazi chief rabbi of Palestine. Rabbi Kook, born in Lithuania, had spent a decade serving agricultural settlements in Palestine before returning to Europe, where he served an Orthodox immigrant community in London. Two couples, Max and Bertha Nurock and Chaim and Hana Salomon, were very close friends and witnesses at the ceremony. Bertha Nurock played bridge with Landau and Hana Salomon taught singing in the school; both families had daughters who attended the school for many years. Storrs, Edwin Samuel (the son of the high commissioner), and many other officials attended. The party was long remembered by Ethel and Moss Levy as an example of Landau's generosity and friendship.[28]

The Ofstein-Levy wedding was not the only one that Landau organized at the Abyssinian Palace. In June 1922, Sarah Jaholom Sapir, a teacher at the Evelina School, was married by Rabbi Kook to Major Alexander Epstein in an event attended by the "elite of Jerusalem."[29] Landau continued to reach out to the many communities of Jerusalem, but she felt most comfortable with British Jews who were religiously observant. She was one of the first members of Yeshurun Synagogue, founded by Rabbi Kook in 1923. She later had a central seat next to Rabbanit Sara Herzog— the wife of the next chief Ashkenazi rabbi of British Mandate Palestine, Isaac Herzog, and in her own right a major contributor to the welfare of women and children in Jerusalem—in the women's section in the iconic building inaugurated on King George Street in 1936.

British officials became accustomed to Landau's need for kosher food at official functions and were aware that she would not attend events that would interfere with Sabbath observance. Most, like Governor Storrs, appreciated her commitment to religious practice. Storrs commented with approval that the phone in her house was never answered on the Sabbath, not even by a servant.[30] Some, like Bentwich, were bemused by Landau's strict observance of Jewish law.

An Expanding Curriculum and New Opportunities

Although they disagreed about religious practice, Helen Bentwich and Annie Landau had many shared interests, perhaps the most important being their support for Girl Guides in Jerusalem. The Girl Guides, a precursor to the Girl Scouts, originated in England in 1911 and were immediately very popular. Bentwich opened enrollment for the first Girl Guide group in Palestine in March 1919 at the Evelina School with strong support from Landau. In 1920, the Evelina School central hall was used to train Girl Guide officers for all of Jerusalem. The movement received a great boost when Monica Storrs, the sister of Jerusalem's governor, came out from London on a long visit and brought with her an encouraging message from the movement's founder, Lady Olive Baden-Powell.

The Evelina School Girl Guides worked with great enthusiasm, learning gardening and first aid, hiking, and engaging in nature study.[31] Girl Guides were taught to be self-reliant, earning the money to pay for their uniforms, boots, belts, and badges. The material for the uniforms was specially woven on the looms of the Alliance Technical School, providing income to the boys of Jerusalem.[32] At a 1921 Girl Guide rally at the home of the Jerusalem governor, presided over by Lady Samuel, a silver challenge cup was presented to the Girl Guides of the Evelina School. A new trophy case was placed at the entrance to the school to showcase the valued prize.

The following year, the Jerusalem Girl Guide companies were inspected by Lady Baden-Powell during her visit to the city. Shortly thereafter, three members of the Evelina staff attended a Girl Guides' camp at Ramallah for two weeks under the direction of Commandant Janson Potts, who came to Jerusalem on her way home from the Malay Straits at the request of Lady Baden-Powell to provide an intensive course of guiding to the leaders. Throughout the years of the Mandate, the Girl Guides program was an important extracurricular activity through which teachers and Landau trained the girls of Jerusalem to be leaders.

Bentwich's influence on Landau's pupils can be discerned beyond the Girl

Guides program. In November 1919, the pupils participated in a bazaar hosted by the Young Women's Christian Association (YWCA) to raise money, in part for the women's shelter organized by the Social Service Association. Bentwich played an active role in the event, procuring fresh fruit, vegetables, plants, and honey to sell at the event, which was held on the grounds of the new sporting club on Jaffa Road. Friends and acquaintances sent contributions from Jaffa, Jericho, Damascus, Hebron, and Beersheba. One large table was laid with grapes from Damascus, another with bananas, a third with dates and nuts, a fourth with dry goods of all sorts. Bertha Spafford Vester's small son drove a cart filled with oranges, coconuts, a basket of fresh fish, and a cage full of goldfinches. Landau shared responsibility for the tea, which featured service by girls of every creed and nationality dressed in tea caps and aprons. Bentwich wrote to her mother, "Miss Landau's girls gave a performance of a Turkish harem play and were frightfully popular."[33]

Landau took advantage of the presence in Jerusalem of a new group of talented women, the wives of several British officials whom she met socially. With their help, she was able to offer new classes in eurhythmics and ballet. Instrumental and choral music followed, as did drawing and art appreciation, aided by the purchase of a slide projector and slides. Landau's school was the first to seize the opportunity to include the latest in modern European education, which had been impossible in previous years because of a lack of adequate teachers.

In a letter to her mother, Bentwich commented on the positive influence of the eurhythmics class. Her letter, which reveals some snobbery and racism, also shows both her enthusiasm for the program and her recognition of the benefits of health and hygiene for the poor pupils of Jerusalem:

> Firstly, it's excellent musical training. Secondly, it's wonderful physical training—the actual movement is healthy and graceful. Thirdly, it's good hygienically. The girls all wear little white muslin dresses and loose underclothes, bare arms and legs and loose hair done Greek style. They have to be clean and well kept for it and everyone is amazed at their appearance. They are so very pretty dressed like that, and the newcomers here wouldn't believe that they were just Jerusalem slum children. They thought they were English educated children....
> It is a great thing to have something clean and new here, among all this fuggy mass of dusty traditionalism.[34]

Landau's friendship with Edith Eder, the wife of Dr. David Eder, a noted psychoanalyst and a member of the Zionist Commission, led to new opportunities for her pupils to experience civic engagement. At a lecture held at Eder's home, Landau heard Professor Patrick Geddes, a Scotsman and town planner, speak about a creative way to teach local governance. She soon adapted it for her ten- and eleven-year-old girls. They were instructed to imagine that their classroom was a city and to identify boroughs, houses, a bank, a library, and gardens, plus ministers of public health, instruction, and finance. The class held a weekly court to decide cases among themselves. Landau encouraged these young girls to think of themselves as participants in the civic life of modern Jerusalem.[35]

Landau was also respectful of the historic importance of the city and sought to make her pupils aware of new archaeological discoveries. She arranged for a series of lectures by Elijah Meyers of the American Colony devoted to a model of the Temple constructed decades earlier by Conrad Schick. Meyers also acted as a guide to the teachers and older girls on a number of walks inside the Old City and on its historic walls; these walks were a supplement to a classroom curriculum on the history of Jerusalem. Landau saw her pupils as future participants in the life of Jerusalem and wanted them to be knowledgeable about the city's history so that they could make informed decisions about its future.

The British official who had the most influence on education in Palestine during the years of the Mandate was Humphrey Bowman, the director of the Department of Education, who was charged with encouraging the development of Arab schools and Jewish schools as well as with setting standards for general educational requirements.[36] Since many Jewish schools received funding from abroad, Bowman devoted most of his time and scarce resources to the needs of Arab towns and villages.[37]

Nevertheless, he was well-informed about the Evelina School and admired its unique program. In recognition of the civic-mindedness of the Evelina pupils who contributed regularly to the Palestine SPCA, Bowman provided an annual subsidy of three hundred pounds to the school.[38] The Public Health Department also assisted the school by sending a nurse to visit daily and a doctor weekly. As a result of these measures, cases of malaria, trachoma, and ringworm were significantly decreased, and the entire student body was vaccinated for smallpox.[39]

In 1922 Landau revised the school curriculum to reflect the establishment of norms for elementary and secondary education set up by Bowman for government schools. Landau acknowledged that the Evelina School exceeded government standards for elementary schools but did not reach the standard for secondary education in several areas. Ever alert to meeting the changing needs of her pupils, Landau revised the syllabi for several classes to bring them in line with government standards.

Now that the war was over and the city was under civilian administration, distinguished Europeans resumed visiting Jerusalem, and many of them stopped to see the Evelina School and marvel at the pupils. The visitors came as a result of the school's strong connection with the British Mandate and the British elite. They included leaders of the Anglo-Jewish Association, like Mrs. Leopold de Rothschild and her sister, Mrs. Arthur Sassoon,* Lucy Franklin,† and Osmond d'Avigdor-Goldsmid; local notables like Bowman, Lady Samuel, the bishop of Jerusalem, and Sir Wyndham Deedes and his wife; and English travelers like Sir Hugh Bell and his daughter, Gertrude, the suffragist Millicent Fawcett and her sister, Miss Garrett, and Mrs. George Joseph.

These guests were pleased to see that the teaching methods of the Parents' National Education Union, recently adopted in England, had already been introduced in Landau's classes, and they commented favorably on the activities of the Girl Guides. Visitors were also suitably impressed by the growing and more credentialed teaching staff: in the early 1920s, Hilda Burstein of Cleveland, Ohio, joined the staff as a domestic science teacher; Sarah Yoffey of Manchester University, England, also joined the staff that year; and Ethel Levy, who was already in Jerusalem, was hired to teach and to assist Landau.[40]

Despite encouraging signs of peace and progress, there were persistent indications that the goal of the Mandate, to prepare the local communities for self-rule, was not being met. The surface calm was punctured by repeated incidents of violence beginning in the spring of 1920, when the Greek Orthodox Easter coincided with the Muslim holiday of Nebi Musa and just a few days separated the Gregorian Easter and Passover. Then in May 1921, Arab riots broke out in Jaffa against continued Jewish immigration to Palestine.

---

* Née Louise Perugia.

† Lucy Franklin was married to Frederick Samuel Franklin.

These riots led to widespread looting and the temporary cessation of Jewish immigration.[41]

British Jews who were newcomers to the city were shaken by these riots, but most were determined to persist in the efforts to build a homeland for the Jewish people. Landau, one of the British old-timers in the city, shared their determination. Sir Herbert Samuel, the Jewish high commissioner, issued a public statement on the occasion of the king's birthday, shortly after the riots, reaffirming his belief in the justice of the Balfour Declaration:

> The Jews, a people who are scattered throughout the world, but whose hearts are turned to Palestine, should be enabled to find here their home, and that some among them, within the limits that are fixed by numbers and interests of the present population, should come to Palestine in order to help by their resources and efforts to develop the country, is to the advantage of all its inhabitants.[42]

Zionists meeting outside Palestine were no longer willing to speak of a *home*. They repudiated Samuel's speech in a meeting in the European spa town, Carlsbad, in September 1921, calling for a Jewish *state* in Palestine. At the same time, a delegation of Palestinian Arabs went to London to protest the Balfour Declaration.[43] Despite the heated rhetoric coming from abroad that was reported in Jerusalem in Zionist and Arab nationalist newspapers, some Jewish and Arab leaders in Jerusalem remained committed to building bridges between their communities, hopeful that the presence of the British would indeed lead to improved conditions for all.

Dr. Helena Kagan emerged as one of the leaders speaking for mutual respect and tolerance. Because she had treated Jewish and Arab patients since her arrival in Palestine, her home had become a social setting for teas with the leading women of all the communities. In the autumn of 1921, she introduced Mme Moussa Kazim, the wife of the former mayor of Jerusalem who became one of the leaders of the Palestinian Arab nationalist movement, to the Jewish women in her circle. The common language at the afternoon tea was not English, Arabic, or Hebrew; instead, the women spoke French.

Kazim referred to the delicate politics of the city as "a family quarrel." She recounted the biblical tale of Sarah and Hagar to illustrate that such quarrels were not new to the area. Kazim viewed the story as a parable of oppression: strong Sarah wronged weak Hagar. Helen Bentwich, one of the guests at the tea, challenged her interpretation. She offered the view that the old, barren Sarah was understandably jealous of the beautiful, young Hagar.[44] This genteel sparring over a biblical narrative didn't obscure the passionate feelings of both sides.

Despite the underlying tension, the women of the various communities in Jerusalem continued to work together to promote the health and education of the girls in the city. One of the projects they supported was the construction of a school building for the Jerusalem Girls' College, a Christian school with students of all religions. Although Annie Landau remonstrated with Jewish parents who sent their daughters to missionary schools, she recognized that the Evelina School and the college shared a commitment to providing an English education for girls. To that end, Landau attended the opening of a new hostel for the college in 1922, continued to participate in ceremonial events at the college throughout the Mandate, and supported friendly competition between the Girl Guide groups at the two schools.[45]

Having thought about secondary education for years, Landau decided that it was time to expand the Evelina curriculum further to ensure opportunities for future employment for her graduates. She resolved to develop a secondary program for the Evelina School so that the Jerusalem Girls' College would not be the only English-language secondary school for girls in the city. In this endeavor she moved further away from the objectives of both Orthodox and Zionist groups: the former were suspicious of the increased attention given to secular subjects in the secondary curriculum, and the latter were opposed to the fact that these subjects would be taught in English. Throughout the 1920s, Landau continued to be criticized by both groups.

Criticism by the Orthodox community resulted in bans charging Landau with immodest behavior because she engaged in social dancing at her balls and her pupils participated in sports. The Zionists demanded that Hebrew be the only language of instruction for Jewish pupils in Palestine. Landau reasoned that even though much progress had been made by the Hebrew School Board, there was still a dearth of suitable Hebrew school books, and those that were available were far more costly than English books.

Therefore, she agreed to teach exclusively in Hebrew only in the kinder-garten, where few books were used. In the years beyond kindergarten, sub-jects were taken in either Hebrew or English. The Hebrew subjects were the Bible, the Jewish religion, postbiblical Jewish history, Hebrew literature and language, arithmetic, and the geography and history of Palestine. The English subjects were general history and geography, English language and literature, domestic science, and nature study. The subjects of manual instruction—drill, sports, needlework, drawing, and painting—were taught in the language of instruction favored by the teacher.[46]

When Landau visited London in the summer of 1922, she met once again with the leaders of the Anglo-Jewish Association to review the financial needs of the school. At the meeting, Claude Montefiore, who had recently returned from Jerusalem, announced that he had been personally impressed by the achievements of the school. He also reported, in an article in the *Jewish Chronicle*, on tributes to the school from two sources who rarely agreed with each other: Sir Wyndham Deedes, the chief secretary of the Mandatory government, and Dr. David Eder, a member of the Zionist Commission. Deedes had asserted that the school provided the highest moral and cultural tone in Palestine. Eder, responding to an unfounded newspaper rumor that the school was going to be closed, had written, "What a disgrace it is that this school, which stands for the cultural upbringing of the women of Jerusalem, should have to close down because the very small sum that is needed for its upkeep cannot be found."[47]

In response to the accolades, the Anglo-Jewish Association continued to meet the growing needs of the Evelina de Rothschild School while funding other schools at a much lower level. The 1923–24 annual report of the Anglo-Jewish Association announced the donation of a total of 5,136 pounds to fifteen schools, ranging from 27 pounds to the school in Tehran to 3,889 pounds to the school in Jerusalem. The following year, the grants totaled 6,277 pounds, with 4,808 pounds going to the Evelina de Rothschild School. The cost of operating the Evelina School that year was 5,967 pounds with the difference made up by rent payments from Frutiger House, school fees, needlework sales, and a grant of 114 pounds from the British administration of Jerusalem.[48]

The growing support of the Anglo-Jewish Association was still insufficient to meet Landau's plans for development, and she sought additional funds from numerous quarters. She thought of going to the United States to raise funds, since she had received a letter from Jacob Schiff, the former head of the Joint Distribution Committee (who was now deceased). He had written to her that the Evelina School should receive funds from the committee, which had been founded in 1914 by wealthy German Jewish families to help struggling Jews in Palestine who were cut off from other European aid during World War I.

Landau wrote to her supporter Sir Elly Kadoorie, proposing that he take over the operating expenses of the kindergarten that would be named the Laura Kadoorie Kindergarten for his wife. Despite Landau's efforts to secure additional foreign donations, however, the largest source of new income came from school fees. Landau and members of the Anglo-Jewish Association were troubled by relying on fees to balance the school budget, since they knew that many of the students, including those younger than fourteen, were employed as part-time housemaids to earn the money because their parents were unable and in some cases unwilling to pay for school.[49]

Landau returned to Jerusalem with funds for the coming year but with no decision on capital funds for the previously approved plan to renovate Frutiger House and no decisions about the future of the school. Shortly after her return, she was presented with an opportunity to showcase her pupils' talents in one of the major social events of the year, a celebration in honor of the twenty-fifth wedding anniversary of Lord and Lady Samuel that took place on a Saturday night in late November at Government House.

The highlight of the evening was a performance of *A Midsummer Night's Dream* by many of Landau's friends who were members of a new drama club. After weeks of rehearsal at the temporary Young Men's Christian Association (YMCA) and the Zion Theatre, Helen Bentwich appeared as Hermia, Max Nurock played Lysander, Aylmer Harris appeared as Bottom, and Harris's wife played Oberon. The fairies were English and Jewish children, including eighteen girls from Landau's school who sang and danced. Boys from the Cathedral Choir also sang. Landau did not hesitate to involve her pupils in this rare opportunity to take part in festivities with British society, many of whom were her friends and supporters. As on many occasions, she wished to prove that her Jerusalem girls were as accomplished as English girls.

The performance of Landau's pupils was the product of weeks of preparation, beginning with a session in the private apartment of the headmistress. There, in the "holy of holies," as the girls called her rooms on the top floor of the school building, she informed them that they had been selected to perform in *A Midsummer Night's Dream* in the palatial Augusta Victoria, the home of the high commissioner. The little girls, eight- and nine-year-olds, were delighted at the chance to perform for local notables in a place that they had never visited.

They practiced for weeks, changing into their special ballet costumes and shoes as they rehearsed the dance numbers with the choreographer. They practiced arm movements and jumped to songs played on the piano under the watchful eyes of their teacher. Finally they were ready. Before the evening of the performance, Landau addressed her young troops: "It is fitting that you represent the Evelina de Rothschild School on this important occasion. I hope that you will not discredit your school."[50]

On the evening of the event, the participants and their parents gathered from every corner of the city, holding their costumes and ballet slippers as they waited for the buses hired to shuttle them from the center of the city to Augusta Victoria. As rain began to fall, the performers and their parents rushed to get on the bus to avoid ruining the carefully set curls of the performers. Some of the parents attended with pride; others were skeptical but attended out of respect for Landau. Finally, at 7:30 the buses arrived at the gates of the "castle." Hannah Meiroff, one of the young performers, remembered her feelings forty years after the event:

> [I saw] with my own eyes a castle, surrounded by a huge garden illuminated with colorful gas lights and emitting the fragrant scent of roses and other flowers. At the gate we were received by a uniformed guard who directed us to the main entrance. Sir Herbert Samuel, of blessed memory, clad in official dress with gold medals and military ribbons, stood tall at the entrance. Next to him was Lady Samuel in a long blue evening gown decorated with jewels. They looked to us like a royal couple we read about in story books. After shaking hands and curtsying, we were shown to the stage entrance. The choreographer, Mrs. Harris, and her assistants were already on stage and helped to dress us for the performance. We each removed a white or green dress from our bags along with a pair of shoes and a pair of wings. We looked and felt like angels.[51]

Hannah described the costume with its fitted bodice and short gathered skirts, revealing bare arms and legs. The girls lined up to have their curls put in place, and each received a sparkling crown to complete the costume. After waiting in utter silence as the sound of the orchestra commenced and the curtain was raised, the girls floated to their places, listening to the music and watching the conductor's baton to know when to sing and dance. Feet and hands swayed to the music of Felix Mendelssohn as the girls searched in vain for their parents in the audience. At the end of the performance, the sound of clapping was thunderous and the girls flew backstage.

The performance was a great triumph for Landau; she beamed as her girls were presented for the second time to Lord and Lady Samuel, who congratulated the "fairies," told them they were beautiful, and offered them drinks and a variety of cakes. In response to the lovely performance, Lord Samuel announced that he would sponsor a second showing of the event for a larger gathering in the Zion Theatre. The public performance of Evelina girls, demonstrating the capacity of Jewish Jerusalemites to learn classical music and song and dance, was a great event in the eyes of the high commissioner and other British officials and their wives. Landau was thrilled with the triumph of her girls. However, the parents of some girls were not pleased with the public display.

Hannah Meiroff recalled how bitterly disappointed she was after the performance when her father and mother ignored her success and refused to speak to her all the way home. Finally, her father, horrified by Hannah's costume and dance, declared, "Shame on the eyes that see girls of Israel as singers and modest girls in dresses above their knees with skin bared, hopping and jumping as though in the grip of Satan."[52] He forbade her to ever appear in a similar production. All of Hannah's pleas and tears to be allowed to perform with her classmates again at the Zion Theatre were to no avail. Her parents tactfully informed Landau that Hannah was "sick." Hannah carried her disappointment with her for forty years. Since she didn't share her father's views, she remembered the day of the performance at Augusta Victoria "as a great day in my life, an experience that I have not forgotten until this day."[53]

The struggle within the Meiroff family between tradition and modernity was repeated in the homes of many Evelina pupils. Rivka Weingarten lamented that her father did not allow her to join her classmates on class trips, which he saw as frivolous, and Rachel Levin campaigned to be permitted to continue to study ballet to no avail, since her father was afraid of what the neighbors would say. It wasn't only the parents who questioned some of the practices at the Evelina School. A pupil from a traditional family, Michal Harrison, noted her disapproval of the "low-cut dresses" worn by Landau during school prayer services.[54]

Despite the criticism, Landau's confidence in her vision for the future of Jewish girls in Jerusalem was unshaken. The triumph of her pupils onstage at Augusta Victoria was proof that she was on the right track. In the months after the performance, Landau, suffering from the recent loss of her mother, redoubled her efforts to build her school.[55] She soon turned her attention to the London University matriculation examination introduced by the Palestine Department of Education as the standard for the secondary school certificate. This standard, she knew, was above the achievement level of Evelina's top class. In the absence of a decision from the Anglo-Jewish Association about the future direction of the school, she decided to add a class or two to the existing program in order to prepare her students properly for the matriculation exam.

Since her arrival in Jerusalem, Landau had developed relationships with the parents of her pupils, trying to involve them in her project to change the values of the girls. Having grudgingly accepted her removal of amulets and her requirements for cleanliness, the parents showed their hard-won enthusiasm for Landau and her school by enrolling whole families of girls and in many cases generations of them.

Landau now enlisted their support in arguing her case to the Anglo-Jewish Association. Those who were more traditional might lament classes in ballet or commercial skills; those who were Zionist regretted the lack of Jewish National Fund boxes in each classroom. However, most were convinced that it was the only school where their daughters would receive both a traditional Jewish education and modern instruction in English, and they supported Landau's plan to supplement the existing course of instruction with new classes to meet the level of the matriculation exam. Landau noted their support in her appeal to the Anglo-Jewish Association for funds to hire additional teachers.[56]

Landau Celebrates Twenty-Five Years in Jerusalem

While Annie Landau thought about ways to implement the new secondary program, her friends and supporters arranged a major celebration to mark the twenty-fifty anniversary of her arrival in Jerusalem. A lavish dinner for 140 guests at the Amdursky Hotel chaired by Governor Storrs began the festivities. High Commissioner Samuel offered a tribute in her honor and announced that in recognition of her services to the city, King George had invested Landau with the Membership of the Order of the British Empire. This was a significant recognition for a girls' school headmistress. The dinner was followed by a fancy-dress ball for five hundred people. The menu for the evening, written in French, was full of humorous references. One copy was recently discovered in the papers saved by Bertha Spafford Vester. It reads as follows:

> *Hors d'oeuvres varies aux trios langues officielles*
> *Consommee Evelyn de Rothschild*
> *Mayonnaise a l'Annie Landau*
> *Dinde a la Lausanne*
> *Chouxfleur au Mont Ophel*
> *Asperges au bal costume*
> *Pouding au quart de siecle*
> *Dessert politique*
> *Café au Palais Abyssinien*[57]

The food, imported from Cairo, included an unusual delicacy, strawberries and cream. At this party, the elite of the city were joined by the stationmaster and tradespeople. Landau, who educated girls from all sectors of the Jewish community, was feted by representatives of the whole city.[58]

The *Jewish Chronicle* interviewed her on that occasion, noting that "a quarter century spent in the Holy City has not diminished her vigour, and her natural force of personality is not abated."[59] Her passionate commitment to Jerusalem and to her pupils is clear in the interview:

> Jerusalem has certainly changed since I have been there. . . . When I first went to Jerusalem one saw wide stretches of field and olive groves. Now these open spaces are filled up with red-tiled houses, much to the disgust of Sir Ronald Storrs, who is endeavoring to restore the oriental character of the city. His Pro-Jerusalem Society is doing valuable work in this direction, and deserves more support than it has so far received from the Jewish community. . . . Jerusalem is, however, still Jerusalem . . . and it has far more modern amenities than when I first went out. . . . When I went out in 1899 there were less than 200 pupils. Before the war there were as many as 700. Unfortunately, during the war period 200 of my little ones died of starvation and disease, and financial exigencies have prevented the Anglo-Jewish Association from taking more than the 500 with which we resumed work soon after the British occupation. It is unquestionable that I could have over 2,000 pupils tomorrow, did finances and the accommodation permit.[60]

Landau commented on the mixed nature of the school community. She noted that some of the pupils were natives of Palestine, whereas others came from eastern Europe, the Caucasus, Persia, Yemen, South Africa, the United States, and England. The most difficult to integrate were the orphans from the Ukraine, who knew no Hebrew or English when they started. Nevertheless, they soon learned. She also tried to clarify her continuing commitment to bilingual education:

> When I first went to the school, Hebrew was only taught for three hours per week, but since 1901 Hebrew has been the sole method of instruction in the lower part of the school, and is used together with English in the higher classes. I should like to make it clear, however, that while I recognize the value of Hebrew in Palestine as the common vernacular of the Jewish population, my prime interest in the language is a religious one, and I always impress upon my children, to whom Hebrew has become their mother-tongue, that the importance of Hebrew is that it is the language of the *Torah*. The English side of the work of the Evelina School is of almost equal importance, especially since the British occupation. The pupils of the school find no difficulty in obtaining posts under the Government and in commercial houses.[61]

Landau's feisty personality is evident in her concluding remarks:

> I know it has often been suggested that I am a strong anti-Zionist. In reality I am not "anti" anything. I am, however, very much "pro" Judaism, and I will always fight to maintain the religious character of the school. One of our most delightful sessions in the week is the gathering we hold on Thursday afternoons . . . when one of the children gives an account in Hebrew of the *Sedrah* [Torah portion] of the week, and I deliver an address in English on its religious lessons. We sing a hymn or two, and part with mutual good wishes for the Sabbath.[62]

Landau continued to build her school and her social network. In late December 1924, as most of the British in the city were involved with Christmas celebrations, she attended a "Jewish Christmas" dinner at the Bentwiches, an annual event that brought together leaders of the Anglo-Jewish community. On this occasion, Dr. Judah Magnes, the president of Hebrew University, and his wife, Beatrice; Max Nurock; and British Zionist lawyer Harry Sacher and his wife, Miriam, and others enjoyed dinner followed by some raucous games. Helen Bentwich was amazed to watch the fifty-one-year-old Landau jumping rope in her shimmery evening dress. She noted that Landau enjoyed it thoroughly.[63]

Despite her energy and enthusiasm, in February 1925, Landau was taken ill with pneumonia. She required hospitalization and an extended recovery period in northern Italy. The normally indefatigable Annie Landau was faced with serious physical weakness. The Anglo-Jewish Association granted her a year's leave of absence, during which time Ethel Levy, her assistant, assumed her duties. Levy successfully negotiated a renewal of the lease on the Abyssinian Palace for five years, since the plans to renovate and expand Frutiger House were still under discussion in London.

Landau's absence coincided with a major cultural event in Jerusalem: the opening of Hebrew University. A large number of visitors from all over the world came to the opening. In recognition of the growing reputation of the Evelina School, many stopped by to visit, including Joseph Hertz, the chief rabbi of the British Empire, whose portrait was donated to the school and hung in the central hall.

Lord Samuel completed his term as high commissioner and left Jerusalem in 1925. He was replaced by Lord Herbert Plumer, who visited the school with his wife, Lady Plumer,* shortly after their arrival in Jerusalem. They were greeted by the guard of honor of the Girl Guides. The school log book recorded, "His Excellency asked that the School should be given a holiday on the following day to commemorate his visit and was greatly amused to learn that the idea of a school holiday in the middle of the term, hailed with delight in English schools, met with but grudging enthusiasm from the eager Palestinian children, to whom the School is in itself one long holiday."[64]

The arrival of the Plumers engendered more socializing for the British establishment and leading members of the Jewish and Arab communities in Palestine. Edwin Samuel, the son of the former high commissioner, and his wife Hadassah; Ragheb Bey and Laila Nashashibi, leading members of the Arab community; Judah and Beatrice Magnes; and Norman and Helen Bentwich were frequent guests of the Plumers. Helen Bentwich noted the presence of several Jewish performers at a reception at Government House,

* Née Annie Constance Goss

an imbalance that was obvious to her but may well have been lost on the Plumers, who were new to Jerusalem:

> It was most amusing, so much more Jewish than Uncle Herbert [Lord Samuel] would ever have dared to make it. The music was the orchestra of the police band [all Jews], Thelma [Bentwich], and two opera singers who sang in Hebrew! I can't think what the Mufti, the Latin priests and bishops, Mussa Kazim, etc., thought of the Hebrew songs![65]

New Advances, New Pupils

Upon her return from Italy, Landau was eager to join the social circle at Government House, but she was soon required to turn her attention to the president of the Anglo-Jewish Association, Osmond d'Avigdor-Goldsmid, who arrived to inspect the school.[66] His impressions, reproduced in the next annual report, were, like those of Lord Plumer, very favorable:

> The children, who number 510, make an excellent impression. They are alert, friendly, and obviously happy. In the week I came, 10 out of 12 classes had 100% for punctuality. There were only three or four absences per class. The children pay 1 s[hilling] per week school fee, this improves attendance.[67]

Landau's efforts to instill new habits like punctuality and regular attendance were clearly working. The president noted that the children looked healthy; presumably they benefited from the permanent presence of a school nurse and the regular visits of a dentist. Their clothing, however, and their boots he found to be substandard. D'Avigdor-Goldsmid continued his report with a review of the teaching staff, which he found impressive. There were now fifteen full-time teachers: six had received training in England or Canada; five were trained in Palestine, including some graduates of the Evelina School; and four were from other European countries. Unlike previous reports about the teaching staff, this one concluded, "This strangely assorted team, happily, forms a very harmonious whole. Taken all together, they are a staff of teachers of whom any school-governing body could well be proud."[68]

D'Avigdor-Goldsmid gathered information about the proposal to create a full-fledged secondary school whose students would take the London matriculation exam. He noted a new problem not discussed by Landau. In previous years there had been no leave-taking exam, but now there were two: the London matriculation and the Bagrut, a Hebrew-language examination favored by Hebrew University. Since classes at Hebrew University were officially taught in Hebrew, it was reasonable to expect students to be fluent in subject areas like chemistry and geography in Hebrew, but the Evelina School taught those subjects in English.[69]

Conversely, d'Avigdor-Goldsmid knew that Evelina graduates could use their scores on the London matriculation exam to obtain jobs with the Mandatory government and that some might wish to attend college in England, so the London matriculation was not irrelevant. He concluded that the school might need to establish two matriculation classes, which would be costly. In any event, he noted, the school needed a new laboratory and additional scientific equipment.

Given the limitations of the budget of the Anglo-Jewish Association, it is not surprising that d'Avigdor-Goldsmid did not offer a solution to the problem he raised. He concluded his report with a long tribute to Landau, pointing out her extraordinary abilities as an administrator responsible for collecting school fees and paying teachers' salaries, for managing the operating budget of the school, for supervising the teaching and nonteaching staff, for negotiating with landlords and tenants, and for hiring local teachers. He was aware of her great burden: "The constant struggle to enforce European standards of discipline, cleanliness, and order among children who are utterly unaccustomed to such standards at home is a burden from which she is never free."[70]

While the Anglo-Jewish Association continued to deliberate the future structure of the school, life in Jerusalem was disrupted by a major earthquake in 1927 that damaged many buildings, including Augusta Victoria, forcing Lord and Lady Plumer to seek a new residence. The Mandatory authorities requested that Frutiger House, which had continued to be used as a rental property after Landau's return to Jerusalem in 1918, be vacated and put at the disposal of the government. Despite considerable resistance on the part of those living in the house, an agreement to vacate was concluded. Extensive alterations and renovations were made by the government before Lord and Lady Plumer moved to the house and became Landau's neighbors.[71]

After the earthquake, as in the immediate postwar years, the diverse communities of Jerusalem rallied to help the needy. A committee was established to plan an exhibition of Palestine's arts and handicrafts; the proceeds from the sale of goods would be donated to the Palestine Earthquake Fund. The committee members were: Lady Plumer; Viola Symes, wife of the chief secretary; Helen Bentwich; Bertha Vester; Ruth Kisch, wife of the head of the Palestine Zionist committee; Reverend C. Steer; Humphrey Bowman; Ernest Richmond; Edward Keith-Roach; Edward Blatchford, director of the Near East Relief Fund; and Ragheb Bey Nashashibi. Evelina girls contributed handiwork to the exhibition, which was attended by ten thousand people, and which raised 1,100 pounds as a result of sales. Bentwich declared it a great success and noted that the previous exhibition, organized in 1922, had raised only 270 pounds.[72]

While Jerusalemites were recovering from the earthquake, interviews for admission to the Evelina de Rothschild School continued. Perla Aryieh Astruc, whose ancestors had lived in Hebron for generations, brought her daughter, Yvonne, to be considered. Like many of her future classmates, Yvonne had already spent a year or two at school learning how to read and write; she had attended the Alliance School in Rishon, where she studied Hebrew and French. Now, back home on Jaffa Street, Yvonne's parents wanted her to attend the Evelina School, unlike her older sister, who had attended the Jerusalem Girls' College. When Perla Astruc approached Landau with a request to admit Yvonne, Landau replied, "I'll have to find room for her, as I will not allow her to go to the mission school."[73] As a consequence of this decision, Yvonne was added to the small group of girls who gained admission to the exclusive girls' school in Jerusalem.

Another student who entered that year was Rachel Harris, the daughter of Minnie Cohen, born in England and herself a graduate of the Evelina School. Rachel remembered that Landau had asked the young Cohen to accompany her into exile in Alexandria during World War I, fearful that the girl was starving in Jerusalem. There was no question in the Harris family about which school Rachel would attend. Indeed, Rachel always felt somewhat special, since her mother was a favorite of Landau's.

Most of the time that Rachel attended the Evelina School, her family lived near the Italian Hospital across the street from Frutiger House. Like most of the homes in Jerusalem at that time, there was neither electricity nor a telephone. Rachel was one of six children sharing a bedroom; the children were expected to be punctual for meals and to eat everything they were served. Rachel's father, a successful and generous businessman, quietly paid the tuition of several pupils from needy families.[74]

Rivka Weingarten, the eldest daughter of the *mukhtar* (headman) of the Jews in the Old City and the first of five remarkable Weingarten girls to attend the Evelina, was a classmate and friend of Rachel's and Yvonne's. Rivka started school at the age of four. Her mother decided that this was the best school for her daughter since it was Orthodox as well as open to ideas of the world. Rivka's mother, whose family had lived for generations in the Old City, stood in line with the other mothers who were waiting to secure a seat for their daughters at the Evelina. Once admitted, Rivka walked the half hour to school each day with her mother and later with her sisters, through the Jaffa Gate and into the new city.[75]

Rachel Harris and Rivka Weingarten developed a strong friendship. Rachel remembered sitting with Rivka in the deep window well of the Weingarten home to study chemistry.

Another new classmate that year was Rachel Levin, whose family lived in the center of town. Like her two older sisters, Rachel attended the Lamel School, where she learned to read and write. When she was eight years old, her father, a widower who later remarried, wanted to transfer her to the Evelina School. To ensure admission, Rachel was told to pretend to be the sister of her cousins, who were already Evelina pupils. Years later, when these cousins emigrated to Brazil, Rachel's classmates teased her about being abandoned by her family. Rachel's older sisters, like Yvonne's older sister, attended the Jerusalem Girls' College. Although the education in that program had previously been valued by some Jewish families, by the time Rachel was ready for elementary school, the Evelina program was considered superior.[76]

These four girls, who commenced their studies in 1927, were different from those who had attended the school before the First World War. They came to class cleaner and were more ready to learn than those whose regular attendance was prevented by poverty and illness. The poorest Jewish parents in the city remained attracted by missionary education, since it provided more material assistance for pupils. Nevertheless, the classes at the Evelina School continued to be composed of a variety of socioeconomic levels, because Jewish families in the city were subject to sharp changes in fortune throughout the years of the Mandate.

In April 1928, Princess Mary visited Jerusalem and was the guest of Lord and Lady Plumer at Frutiger House. In recognition of the close ties between Landau and British government officials, the only school selected by the princess for a visit during her stay in Jerusalem was the Evelina School. Unfortunately, the visit coincided with the school's Passover vacation, and there was no advance notice of the princess's request. Landau was notified at 9 p.m. that the princess would like to see the school the next morning. The headmistress, who was delighted by the honor of being selected for this visit, immediately mobilized her staff to get word to the girls to return to school the next day.

By 9 a.m., four hundred uniformed girls were in their classrooms awaiting the visit of a member of the British royal family. Imagine the excitement of the little girls like Yvonne, the two Rachels, and Rivka, who had only recently begun to read about princes and princesses in their schoolbooks. A guard of honor of Girl Guides lined the entrance to the school when the princess, Viscount and Viscountess Lascelles, Viscount and Viscountess Boyne, Lady Plumer, deputy district commissioner, and others arrived. Six-year-old Ruth Levy, the daughter of Ethel Levy, presented the princess with a bouquet of flowers.

With her entourage, Princess Mary proceeded to visit each class, including that of the four girls admitted just a few months earlier. She admired the achievements and manners of all the pupils, but she favored the top grade with an extra long visit. These students were asked to recite some Shakespeare and to answer questions about English literature. The princess was so impressed with the girls' performance that she urged Landau to compensate them for the extra day's work with an extra day's vacation. Landau reported the details of the visit to the Anglo-Jewish Association with pride.[77]

The visit of Princess Mary was one of many vivid memories shared by the four classmates mentioned above. Other memories open a window onto the girls' feelings about the school culture created by Landau and the teachers. Yvonne remembered Landau watching as each class marched into the building every morning; she thought that the headmistress loved each of her pupils so much that she wanted to see them every day. Yvonne remembered one day when she was responsible for reciting the weekly Torah reading in front of all the assembled students. Her reading fell on a day that Aubrey Eban, an important official of the Jewish Agency and a relative of Landau's, was visiting the school. Landau made a point of explaining that Yvonne came from a home in which the weekly reading of the Torah was not practiced, and thus her excellent performance was particularly commendable. Yvonne's recollection of her stage fright and the subsequent relief was palpable seventy-five years later. She explained that the school set very high standards and encouraged each pupil to strive for excellence.[78]

Similarly, Rachel Harris remembered a day when she was marching in line with the whole school under the watchful gaze of Landau. Suddenly she heard, in horror, the headmistress call out, "Rachel Harris, stand on the stage." Rachel, who was always exacting about her school uniform, remembered feeling terrified of having unknowingly committed an infraction of the rules, only to have Landau look at her freshly ironed pinafore and neat appearance with approval and announce to the assembled girls, "This is how an Evelina girl should look!" Rachel was exceedingly proud of having been singled out for this recognition. She remembered being happy to dress like all the other girls in her school; wearing the same clothing reduced the differences among them.[79]

Rivka Weingarten remembered a day when she was called out of class, handed notebooks, and asked to copy a book in Hebrew and one in English. She copied and copied until classes were over, and she did not return to her home in the Old City that night. She completed the assignment at the home of Rachel Harris, since she lived near the school. At first, the punctilious student feared that she had been given the task as a punishment. The next day it became clear that Rivka's work would be given to a Jewish delegation from Buenos Aires that had requested an example of the handwriting of a Jewish Palestinian girl to take home to their children. Since Rivka was acknowledged to have the best handwriting and the neatest notebooks in the school, she was selected.

She also remembered being singled out by Landau for excellence in leading prayers. On one occasion, when the high commissioner visited during a service, Rivka chanted the prayers perfectly. Landau asked the commissioner, "What can I do? Rivka already has so many red stars." The commissioner replied, "Give her a gold one." As a result, Rivka received the first gold star ever to be awarded at the Evelina School.[80]

Rachel Levin remembered being selected to take a practice London matriculation exam that would be graded and returned to the school so that the teachers could learn how to better prepare the girls for the exam. Rachel was given a small corner of a room with a desk and shelves for her use while preparing for the exam. She felt honored to have been singled out for this work. After the test and the successful results, she was given a beautiful volume of the complete works of Shakespeare, bound in green leather with gilt lettering, inscribed to Rachel for "accepting extra work cheerfully." Rachel remembered that she loved doing this work and being recognized for the way in which it was done. She also recalled an afternoon when Landau placed her hands on Rachel's shoulders as a sign of approval for her recital of the weekly Torah reading, which Rachel could still recite from memory decades later.[81]

Annie Landau was indeed transforming the world of her pupils. The four girls discussed above came from different socioeconomic and cultural-linguistic backgrounds. Yvonne Astruc's more sophisticated family was Sephardi. She spoke Hebrew with her siblings, Ladino with her grandmother, French with her parents, and Arabic with a maid. Her father subscribed to the Librairie Rose for Yvonne. She treasured this series of French children's books and continued to read French and be influenced by French culture throughout her years at Evelina. Despite her father's involvement with the Alliance schools, Yvonne's parents were very supportive of Landau and the Evelina program.

Rachel Harris's Ashkenazi family spoke Yiddish and Hebrew at home. They too provided Rachel with a small library; she especially loved *Gone with the Wind*, *The Picture of Dorian Gray*, *A Tale of Two Cities*, and *Little Women*. Rachel's parents were equally supportive of Landau and her program of education. Rivka Weingarten's family was the most traditionally observant of the four, speaking both Hebrew and Yiddish at home. Rivka was required to wear a hat and gloves whenever she walked to town, and she was not permitted to join her classmates on school trips. Rachel Levin lost her mother as a young girl and grew up in a household that remained deeply saddened by the loss.[82]

At the Evelina School, these four girls joined the Girl Guides, contributed their stories to *School* magazine, and became monitors and prefects. They learned the skills that would enable them to fulfill Landau's vision of strong Jewish women as leaders.

With each passing month, Landau was more determined to develop the secondary school courses offered by the school to prepare students for the London matriculation exam. The *Jewish Chronicle* interviewed Landau and described her struggle with the Jerusalem Girls' College and her desire to have a full-fledged high school:

They [at the Evelina School] were carrying on a continual silent defensive battle with the proselytizing Christian missionaries. If they [Jews] were to have a real Jewish National Home, she [Landau] could not see why there should be room in Palestine for people who were sent out to tell the Jews that their religion was the wrong one. . . . They [at the Evelina School] had opened this high school largely for the purpose of fighting missionaries who had their own British High School in Jerusalem staffed with university-trained women. It was avowedly a school to promote Christianity, and of its 100 students, 33 percent were Jewish. The reason for that was a need for higher education, which was necessary to obtain government posts. That avenue would be closed to Jewishly educated children if they [at the Evelina School] did not carry on [with plans for their own] High School.[83]

The Riots of 1929

As the Anglo-Jewish Association continued to debate the wisdom of a full-fledged high school program, Landau was forced to respond to a new crisis. In August 1929, while she was in England, serious riots sparked by disagreements over Jewish worship at the Western Wall took the lives of thirty-one Jews in Jerusalem and sixty-seven Jews in Hebron, about 10 percent of the Jewish population of that city. Landau hurried home as the remnants of the Hebron community fled to Jerusalem. Hostilities continued, ultimately resulting in the deaths of 133 Jews and 110 Arabs.[84] In November there was an attempt on the life of Attorney General Norman Bentwich, and in December Dr. Ticho was attacked and wounded in front of his clinic after having been warned by Arab nationalists not to treat Arabs.

Life in Jerusalem was disrupted by these events and by the presence of the Hebron refugees. Helen Bentwich visited the hospitals and reported the following:

All of the children have fractured skulls from clubs. . . . One woman had her child killed on her lap and her husband killed in front of her; her skull is fractured and her fingers cut off. She was quite out of her mind. Another who had lain under a heap of dead bodies with her baby for hours and then escaped is also mad.[85]

Landau rallied her teachers and pupils to welcome the pupils who had fled Hebron. The riots resulted in periodic curfews and boycotts of Jewish shops that affected some Jerusalemites, who then, like the refugees, were unable to pay school fees. Reductions and remissions of fees for many pupils were therefore made. Additional expenses were incurred to provide free meals for the increased number of poor students. Donations from Mina Weil of Goldsboro, North Carolina, and from Mrs. M. H. Gold of New York were especially welcomed to meet the emergency needs of 1929. Dr. Kachechian, the school doctor provided by the government, pointed out several cases of severe anemia that year in children who were apparently malnourished. These children were given an egg beaten in milk and a dose of cod liver oil daily.

The British government agreed to assist in feeding refugees throughout Palestine—five thousand in all—and to give them the generous ration allowed to a hospital patient. Rationing commenced on September 11 and ended on November 6, 1929. In Jerusalem, volunteers, headed by Marie Rose Hyamson, the wife of the chief immigration officer, offered to undertake the distribution, aided by Mrs. Leopold Harris, the wife of another official, and Helen Bentwich. All these women had longstanding connections to Landau and her school. Together these women distributed thirty-two hundred rations daily for ten days. Later the government decided to feed only those in bona fide hostels, so the number was reduced to between fifteen hundred and two thousand daily.[86]

Having dealt with the question of food, the next most important item was housing. In the first rush of the riots, the refugees were housed and fed in the Nathan Strauss Health Center, which was filled with people evacuated from Hebron, Motza, and other small towns as well as those living in unsafe parts of Jerusalem, including Musrara, the Damascus Gate, and Siloam. A few days later, many Jerusalem schools responded to the needs of the refugees. The Alliance Boys' School took in 500; the Alliance Girls' School, 100; the Lamel School, 240; the Spitzer School, 90; Old Tachkemoni, 50; New Tachkemoni, 200; the Sephardic Orphanage, 50; and Beit Sefer Levanim, 160. The Evelina School did not appear on this list of schools offering refuge; it bordered on Musrara and was not considered a safe neighborhood in 1929. Officials from the Health Department inspected the arrangements and suggested improvements. The Hadassah Medical Unit undertook the day-to-day health care of the refugees.

Because some of the refugees from Hebron were still wearing bloodstained garments in early September, Helen Bentwich put an appeal for old clothes in the *Palestine Bulletin*, and there was a generous response from the British community. Lady McDonnell, the wife of the chief justice, organized a sewing party, and for six weeks women met to make women's and children's clothing for the refugees. In October, Bertha Nurock secured a gift of nearly eleven hundred yards of Donegal tweed from the manufacturers, which was immediately made into winter overcoats by the unemployed tailors of Hebron. Nurock and Ethel Levy took charge of the clothing arriving from England; working twelve-hour days, these women distributed clothing to those in need.

The final challenge was to find permanent housing and jobs for the Hebron refugees, a task accomplished by Passover of the next year, when all who were able to work had found employment or had started small businesses. The women celebrated the conclusion of their efforts with a large party for all the children of Hebron, Motza, and Migdal Eder. "It was a merry, if noisy party, entertainment; and despite the horrors of only five months before, the children seemed normal and stabilized."[87]

Most of the women involved in rescue efforts for the Hebron refugees were British Jews connected to the Evelina School, often as the result of social relationships with Landau and sometimes through their daughters who were enrolled in the school. These women embodied the spirit of service to the community that Landau practiced and that she was keen to teach to the girls of Jerusalem. Some of the women also volunteered to teach at the school or to lead groups of Girl Guides. Their spirit of enterprise in the face of crisis, learned in English girls' schools and practiced during World War I, inspired the activities of the Girl Guides, who practiced first aid and experienced serving their people.

Jerusalem families were familiar with charity, since they had sometimes been recipients of *chaluka* from abroad, but they were not practiced in organizing wide-scale efforts to solve community problems. Local charitable efforts that existed before the arrival of the British were limited to close neighbors and didn't involve the wider community. Landau encouraged her pupils to participate in communitywide endeavors to help others. This training served them well in the as-yet-unanticipated transition to statehood.

Helen Bentwich, whose life and work was devoted to others, participated in all these activities, but she was increasingly skeptical about the ability of the British to restore order. This reflective woman had expressed her ecumenical views in a letter to her to her husband in 1926: "I am an assimilationist—I want to assimilate to myself the best of every nation and every people and every religion. . . . I feel so happy at being above being Jewish or English anymore."[88] After the Hebron riots she felt differently. She explained the situation in another letter to her mother:

> You ask if we shall ever settle down to pleasant conditions again . . . the answer
> is no. I don't know what will happen or how long we shall be able to stick it,
> or they us . . . the danger and hostility we've been through gives one rather the
> feeling we had during the war. The danger seems over now. I think there are too
> many soldiers for further outbreaks, but the hostility on all sides still exists. . . .
> Mostly we go from day to day, not talking of it except to each other.[89]

The school, like the rest of Palestine, was still feeling the effects of the 1929 riots when the threat of a typhoid epidemic in the summer of 1930 briefly eclipsed the concerns about politics. All the pupils in the school were inoculated in July after a case was diagnosed. Despite the recurrent political and public health emergencies, Landau continued to imagine a wider world for her pupils. She entered the girls of the elementary school in a wild flower competition organized by the newly founded Jerusalem Horticultural Society, of which she was a founding member. Points were awarded for the number of varieties entered, for correct naming, and for a knowledge of habitat. Landau was delighted that the Evelina School won a silver cup for its trophy case; it was presented by the minister of education, Humphrey Bowman, for the girls' school showing the best exhibit.[90]

Landau struggled to meet the needs of the victims of the 1929 riots as she continued to fight for funding for a proper high school. All the while, she used the established structure of her school to provide pupils with a sense of stability and order that was frequently missing from their young lives. In late May 1930, Landau was in London meeting with the Anglo-Jewish Association. There she received a letter from her assistant, Lea Goodman, referring to demands by Zionist groups that the school close in solidarity with their protest and strike aimed at promoting the adoption of Hebrew as the only language of instruction in Jewish schools.

Goodman, knowing Landau's commitment to bilingual education, had refused. Some pupils who lived at a great distance were sent home early because the bus drivers had joined the strike; the other pupils were told to carry on as usual. Levy arrived at the school and was of enormous service in quieting the pupils. When stones were tossed into some classrooms, frightening the pupils, Goodman did not relent; she had the pupils moved to the interior hallways.[91]

In her own letter to Landau, Levy described the fervor of some of the Evelina pupils for the strike. She witnessed two girls "fomenting revolution" during recess.[92] As a result, Levy instructed all the girls to line up and told them that the school had always had their interests at heart, that when they were older they could make their own decisions and act on them, but that while they were at school the headmistress and teachers would decide for them. It had been decided that they would stay in school that afternoon. Levy continued:

> But no child would be forced to stay if she conscientiously felt she could not. Any girl who felt so was to be honest and come forward and say so. But since her opinions were so divergent from ours, she would not be able to return. Now, is there any girl who wants to go?

None came forward, but Levy was aware that there was continued agitation among the pupils. She called them together again and this time specifically called on the agitators, Mina Shester and Bina Edelstein, to ask if they wanted to go home. They said no. Levy told the others that if these girls continued to "make trouble" after having been given a chance to leave, they should be known as "cowards and sneaks." She added:

> I may tell you that the children were on the verge of revolt and it was touch-and-go with the morale of the School. I can never remember being faced with such a predicament.... When I came home to lunch I almost collapsed with the tax on me made by holding those girls with just my voice and my face set like thunder. It would have been easier to just expel Bina and Mina as examples, but I thought it advisable to avoid making "martyrs in a holy cause."[93]

Levy explained that the bad behavior wasn't entirely the children's fault, since they had been influenced by family and friends.

Despite these difficult moments, the administration convinced the students to remain in class and continue their studies. Landau, supported by her loyal staff, continued to be successful in providing a place of tranquillity for learning. Decades after these events, a former pupil recalled her school days in the Abyssinian Palace as an idyllic chapter in her life:

The vast many-winged building on the corner of Melissanda Lane and St. Paul's Rd., which was officially called the Evelina de Rothschild School, was best known as "Miss Landau's School," in tribute to the strong personality that headed it. The building now houses the Israel Broadcasting Station, but there was a time when other sounds resounded within its thick walls.

There was the sound of the school's choir, for instance, as morning after morning it accompanied with gay songs the march of hundreds of pupils clad in pink pinafores to their classrooms. The ungainly pinafores were later changed to smart blue uniforms, and the choir's zestful songs to swift marches, played on a wonderful instrument called "the gramophone." . . .

Now many schools have adopted "the school uniform," but in those days ours was the only school in the country having a special school uniform. Most of us came from large families, and the long hours under school supervision took a great load off our parents' shoulders and kept us out of a good deal of mischief. . . .

Then there was the sound of children playing in games in the asphalt-covered schoolyard during recess, with "monitors" and "prefects" forever present to see that none of us dare overstep the school's strict set of rules, in the excitement of youthful vigour. How I longed to become one of this privileged sect, but this was never to be, for although excelling in studies, I was, alas, so very very naughty in behavior, and to become a "prefect" or "monitor" one had to be so good, so very good. . . .

I remember our teachers, the good ones, and the ones whom in our childish imagination we called "bad."

There was Miss Goldstein (now Moed) . . . it was said that she had been a pupil of the school herself. It was she who instilled in me a love of dramatics by making us act out all the stories we read in our precious *Chisholm Readers*. Later on I was to wait with the same excitement for the recitation of unforgettable chapters in the Bible, which I can to this day repeat by heart. . . .

I remember graceful Miss Schechter and the excitement she caused when we heard that she was getting married. To us she appeared as beautiful as a Greek Goddess with her dreamy eyes and flash of white teeth. I was young enough to imagine then that teachers had a magic eye and could see us every minute of our day, and how I longed to be worthy of Miss Schechter's approval!

I also remember sad-eyed and weary Mr. Wachman, as he tried year after year to bring home to us the importance of studying Hebrew and Hebrew literature well in a school where almost all subjects were taught in English. Burdened for years with a sick wife at home, we girls made his lot all the more unbearable by disregarding his good-natured words of admonition. . . .

And then there was dear Dr. Reider. May he enjoy many many happy and good years for all the trouble we gave him. He had left Germany at a time when Jews still felt free and secure there, in order to teach an unruly lot of little barbarians in a land of strife and trouble. The fact that he did not give up and stayed on to civilize many more generations of barbarians is proof enough that in his heart of hearts he knew all along that there was no malice or disrespect in our pranks. Will he ever forgive us?

And dear Sylvia Appelbaum, of blessed memory, will we ever forget her? She had come all the way from Liverpool to open up new vistas of knowledge in our wisdom-hungry hearts, and she soon identified herself so completely with the country and our little problems that we went out of our way to show her how much we loved and appreciated her. . . .

And above all, I remember Miss Landau, of blessed memory, who to us seemed like a big overshadowing Buddha before whom we all trembled in fear. It took a great deal of courage on our part to peep occasionally into the realm of this Queen of the Rothschild School and note with relief that she like other mortals was able to munch an apple and enjoy a steaming dish of food prepared by her own private cook, Mrs. Cohen.[94]

During the years of turmoil caused by sporadic Arab violence, periodic Zionist agitation, and recurrent outbreaks of disease, Landau maintained an oasis for her pupils within the walls of the Abyssinian Palace. Landau's girls respected their headmistress, but they also loved her. She made them feel special, cherished, and capable of greatness. She inspired them to live ethical and meaningful lives. She urged them to excel in their studies so that they could be self-sufficient and of service to others.

Landau's pupils continued to be hired by the Mandatory Government and were soon working at Barclays and other banks and at businesses that opened offices in Jerusalem, such as Singer Sewing Machines and Prudential

Insurance. Some parents were pleased with the new opportunities for their daughters to earn a living, whereas others were fearful of the increased contact with the English. Landau believed that her girls would remain firm in their faith. She applauded their increasing economic independence and enjoyed meeting with them after graduation.

In the 1920s, Landau's role expanded in Jerusalem. The graduates of her school assumed useful and important roles in the British government and in local businesses, enhancing her reputation as a modern headmistress. She was faced with a range of challenging issues, some familiar and some new: Should Hebrew be the sole language of instruction in Jewish schools? Should Jewish girls study English and commercial skills in order to qualify for employment with the British government? To what extent should Jewish, Christian, and Muslim women continue to cooperate to create social services for women and children in view of the growing tension among the communities?

In the coming years, Landau continued to devote her life to building her school and answering these questions. She possessed extraordinary emotional intelligence, which made her sensitive to the feelings of her pupils, teachers, supporters, and friends. Her personal warmth and her capacity for friendship made her the center of an eclectic group of Jewish, British, and some Muslim friends.

If she thought of marriage, she didn't commit her ideas about the subject to paper. It is possible that her desires did not tend in that direction. It is also possible that she experienced love for a man at some time in her life, but that like her contemporary, Henrietta Szold, her love was unrequited. Perhaps, like Dr. Helena Kagan—whose secret romance with Sigmund Freud's cousin, an X-ray technician at the Rothschild Hospital, ended with his early death[95]—Landau lost someone to illness. She may have thought that she needed personal freedom without the obligations of family life to realize her ambitious goals. Her needs for companionship and emotional closeness may have been satisfied through her close friendships and active social life. Whatever the case, the lion's share of her focus, energy, and devotion were given to her students, her school, and the city of Jerusalem.

[4]

RETURN TO

FRUTIGER HOUSE

In 1930, Annie Landau began her fourth decade at the helm of the Evelina de Rothschild School. The disruption caused in previous years by malnutrition and health crises no longer threatened regular school attendance. Ethel Levy and a team of dedicated teachers attended to the daily program of the school. Landau, as energetic as ever, turned her attention to her long-harbored dream of building a secondary school. As early as 1904, Boyd Carpenter of the Anglo-Jewish Association had recommended the creation of a distinct secondary program. Landau had returned to this plan in her reports to the association after the reopening of the Evelina School in 1918, but budget limitations had precluded the fulfillment of this dream. Although financial conditions had not improved, new considerations gave Landau hope that she would be successful in realizing her goal.

Educational opportunities in Jerusalem for Jewish youngsters had changed since Carpenter had written his report. In the early days the Evelina kindergarten program had been the only modern one in the city, but by 1930 both the Lamel and Alliance Schools had established modern kindergarten programs. Landau reasoned that the Evelina School could close its kindergarten program, certain that the other schools would be happy to accept additional pupils to their kindergartens.

Yet even as there were new opportunities at the kindergarten level, the only school to have a complete secondary program for girls in the city was the missionary Jerusalem Girls' College. Landau did not want to lose her best students to the college. The story of Simha Valero illustrates that Landau's fears were well-founded. Simha attended the Evelina School from kindergarten through the end of primary school and then transferred to the Jerusalem Girls' College, where she was a star athlete and a good student. In 1938, she enrolled at Oxford University and studied English language and literature.[1]

No Evelina student had been accepted at Oxford before. Landau wanted the same opportunities for academic advancement for the students who remained at the Evelina School, so she proposed a three-step action plan to the Anglo-Jewish Association: first, close the kindergarten; second, open the secondary school; and third, since the secondary program would be smaller than the kindergarten, move the entire school back to Frutiger House. The association debated the wisdom of the plan but ultimately agreed to support the headmistress. Landau triumphantly announced that the school would return to Frutiger House after a "temporary absence" of twenty years.[2]

The decision to return to Frutiger House was propitious, because the building, which had served as the residence of the high commissioner since the earthquake in 1927, benefited from improvements made by the British authorities. A new drainage system had been installed, and electricity, modern plumbing, and a water supply had been added. While occupying Frutiger House, the British had begun construction of a grand government house on the Hill of Evil Counsel that was now ready for occupancy. The improvements to the infrastructure at Frutiger House made additional alterations more affordable. At Landau's request, the Anglo-Jewish Association built a large assembly hall connected to the main building, a change that had been recommended long ago by Carpenter. Above the hall, a private apartment was built for Landau.[3] This new apartment put an end to the communal living arrangements of earlier years. It was to be Landau's final home.

While the plans for the secondary school classes were taking shape, Landau continued to develop the commercial and vocational offerings of the school. The curriculum of the commercial class was designed to meet the criteria of the Pitman Speed Test in shorthand and typing. In the early 1930s, each graduating commercial class took the test, and the pass rate was near 100 percent. These graduates received certificates and were soon offered jobs in government service, at Barclays Bank, and in several private offices. Students in the higher elementary grades were offered classes in sewing, taught on new Singer sewing machines by an instructor provided by the company, and classes in nutrition and cooking in a demonstration kitchen modeled after the modern Nathan Strauss Health Center. Thus, the opportunities for commercial and vocational training remained as the new secondary classes were offered to students who prepared for the London matriculation examination.[4]

In 1931, the Evelina de Rothschild School moved desks, chairs, musical instruments, typewriters, gym equipment, and books across the street to Frutiger House. There were no longer any kindergarten classes. From this point on, children were admitted at the age of seven, having already learned how to read. For the next few years, the school was organized as follows: two years, called preparatory A and B; six years of elementary school classes (class 1 through class 6); and two years of commercial classes. In addition, two secondary school classes were created to prepare students for the London matriculation examination. Landau was extremely keen to improve the chances for her students to excel on the exam, and to this end, the recruitment of qualified teachers for the secondary school became a priority.

To prepare the pupils for their leave-taking exams and also to increase the visibility of her students in the city, Landau encouraged them to participate in a variety of local competitions in Hebrew and in English. Girls from the two upper classes entered drawings, charts, and essays for inclusion in the Food and Dietetics Exhibition at the Strauss Health Center in 1931. Batia Blumenfeld won the prize for the best essay, while the essays of Malca Many and Simha Valero were highly commended. All three essays were published in Hebrew newspapers, and an English translation appeared in the *Palestine Bulletin*. Malca Many was also highly commended for her drawings, one of which was kept on permanent display.

The next year, the Strauss Center exhibit was dedicated to the idea of healthy living. Pupils contributed posters, drawings, models, and essays. The best was a large clock face showing the healthy ways of spending hours on one side and unhealthy ways on the other side. This poster was awarded first prize.[5] The Evelina students were thus increasingly identified with civic institutions devoted to modernization.

In the mid-1930s, the school curriculum achieved the form that Landau had been planning for many years. At this point, all pupils were expected to complete eight years of classes and to take the matriculation exam; only then were they offered the opportunity to take a revised one-year commercial course. Thus, girls starting at age seven were likely to complete the course of study at age sixteen or seventeen, qualified to work in an office requiring bilingual assistants or to continue their education at the university level. In 1931, two girls took the matriculation exam, but only one passed. By 1938, the test was required for all those in the graduating class, and the pass rate was very high.[6]

Not all the girls were happy with this change. Some, like Rachel Harris, were eager to start working and wished to graduate without taking the exam. Rachel was so angry about the change in the course of study that she wanted to leave the Evelina School to finish her education at the Jerusalem Girls' College, where she would not be required to take a matriculation exam. However, Rachel's parents, influenced by the climate of growing strife between Arabs and Jews, were firmly opposed to sending her to the college.

A neighbor acting on their behalf confronted the teenager with questions reflecting their concerns. He asked Rachel rhetorically, "Wouldn't you be embarrassed to learn with Christians and Arabs together? With murderers? Would it be pleasant for you to sit with the daughters of murderers on one bench while there is a good Jewish school to attend?" After days of discussion, Rachel's mother offered her daughter a choice: enroll in sewing classes or return to the Evelina School. Her mother knew that Rachel hated sewing and correctly predicted that she would decide to return to the Evelina School.[7]

While Rachel Harris was opposed to the additional academic classes, some of the more traditional parents were opposed to the commercial class. Rabbi Weingarten, Rivka's father, supported expanding his daughter's academic horizons, but he rejected the notion that she should learn skills to enable her to be employed in British offices. He insisted that Rivka leave the Evelina School after she took the London matriculation exam and continue her education in the Teachers' Seminary for Girls in Jerusalem; teaching was perceived as an acceptable occupation by Rabbi Weingarten.[8] After several months of studies, Rivka convinced her father that the level of education at the seminary was low and that discipline was lax. He finally acceded to her request to join her classmates Rachel Harris, Yvonne Astruc, and Rachel Levin in the commercial class at the Evelina School, where instruction was at a high level and discipline was maintained.

With continuing challenges from some parents and students, Landau renewed her efforts to create a distinctive school spirit at Frutiger House. School rules were strict and were taken to heart by the girls. Each morning the entire student body of about four hundred girls in crisply ironed uniforms gathered in the courtyard of their beautiful school building, surrounded by its well-tended garden. Landau, who lived in new quarters on the top floor of the building, often stood on her balcony high above the students to watch the entrance ceremony. Like royalty, she never stood alone; one of her assistants, either Goodman or Levy, accompanied her. Decades later, Rivka Weingarten remarked approvingly that Landau looked like someone from the time of Marie Antoinette, wearing a strands of pearl and a long-sleeved silk dress.[9]

The teacher in charge would appear on a lower balcony overlooking the courtyard and ring the school bell promptly at 7:40 a.m. At the first ring the girls were expected to stand in place. At the second ring they walked quickly to the rows assigned to their respective classes. At the third ring they stood at attention in their places and then proceeded in a long line, without uttering a word, into the school building. The teacher in charge of the procession would instruct, "Right, left, right, left, lift your feet, do not shuffle."[10] Most girls who participated in this processional with their class every year for eight or nine years remembered the entrance ceremony fondly.

For example, Rachel Levin, whose home life was austere, recalled with pleasure the exquisitely choreographed entrance to school. The first class to mount the highly polished linoleum-covered stairs with brass railings, reflecting the highly polished shoes of the girls, was the most advanced, followed by classes in descending order. The first stop was the new cloakroom, where each girl entered in silence and quickly placed her coat on a numbered peg reserved for her use. The students left the cloakroom and marched around the beautifully appointed main hall under the watchful gaze of one of the older girls who had been selected to be a prefect. Another prefect was responsible for playing John Philip Sousa marches on the school gramophone; the Evelina School boasted one of the first gramophones in the city. Other prefects were designated to maintain order as students moved to different activities throughout the day.[11]

Once they arrived in their classroom, the students were expected to stand silently at their seats until the teacher greeted them with "good morning" and the students returned the greeting, referring to their teachers as, for example, "Miss Goodman," "Mrs. Chaikin," or "Dr. Reider." Informality of greeting, common in Zionist schools, was not the Evelina School's way.

As was true of most English schools of the period, the first activity of the day was communal prayer. The younger girls prayed in their classrooms; the older girls deposited their school bags, picked up their prayer books, and returned silently to the assembly hall for a half hour of prayer. The prayer book used by all the girls was the *Authorized Daily Prayer Book of the United Hebrew Congregations of the British Empire* in an edition printed specially for the school. It included standard prayers in Hebrew and English and a prayer for the government that was addressed to "Our Sovereign Lord, King George, Our Gracious Queen Elizabeth, Mary the Queen Mother, The Princess Elizabeth and all the Royal Family."[12]

In the hall, Landau and a student leader selected to begin the prayers were already on the stage. Most of the prayers were said in silence, but some were sung collectively. Girls with good voices, like Rachel Levin and Menuha Eden, were selected to lead the singing. Praying in common was another way to build school spirit and accustom the students to the idea that they were part of the larger world of the British Empire.

Unlike the other British schools in Palestine, the Evelina School held classes on Sunday through Thursday. No classes were held on Friday so that girls from religious families could learn from their mothers to prepare for the Sabbath in keeping with the responsibilities of an observant wife. The highlight of the school week was the Kabbalat Shabbat (Sabbath Welcome) program on Thursday afternoons, when a pupil recited a portion of the weekly Torah reading and Landau offered interpretations of the reading.

This school practice broke with traditional Judaism, because it put girls in roles usually reserved for boys. Landau, who attended Orthodox services throughout her life, nevertheless organized this departure from tradition to encourage knowledge and love of the Torah readings. Landau's Kabbalat Shabbat program, begun before World War I, remained an important feature of the school throughout her tenure and was continued by her successor, Ethel Levy. Graduates of the school fondly remembered these programs as a special time of the week for the entire school to gather with Landau, their revered headmistress, who spoke with her pupils about Jewish law and lore.

Many students were awed by Landau and tried to live up to her high expectations. For example, the headmistress, who held to a British standard of punctuality, believed that her pupils should never be late. Rivka Weingarten remembered a school maxim: "If you can come two minutes late, you can also come two minutes early." Rivka remained punctual all of her life. Girls who arrived just as the bell was ringing were rushed to their places in line by Diab, the Arab gardener, who helped enforce school rules. Girls who were too late to enter the hall with their class were escorted to the front of the room and made to wear a sign that read I AM LATE throughout the morning prayers.

Typically punctual, Rachel Levin remembered being humiliated one day when she arrived late. Ruth Lask, who attended the Evelina School in the 1940s, walked two miles to school. On rainy days she sometimes stopped to seek shelter en route to school, causing her to arrive late. She too remembered the sting of humiliation associated with lateness; she sometimes turned around and went home rather than go in and have to wear the sign.[13]

It was not only individuals who were affected by lateness; there was a collective reward for punctuality. There were two school flags made of velvet and embroidered with gold thread. One was blue and the other was red. Each month a class with no latecomers would be allowed to march with one of these flags, and the other was given to a class with no absences. The flags were borne with pride during the parade that initiated Kabbalat Shabbat.[14]

Landau's firmness regarding punctuality and attendance was the product of her own schooling and the result of a desire to instill in her charges different manners from the ones found in the other institutions of the city. Her efforts were rewarded by the devotion of her pupils, who saw in her demands a demonstration of love rather than the exercise of arbitrary authority. They were honored that she wished to share with them the English culture of precision that she valued.

All the graduates recognized the difference between the culture of familiarity in other schools and the correct tone to be taken with the teachers in the Evelina School. Punctuality, cleanliness, and modulated voices, all hallmarks of British civility, were associated with being an Evelina girl. Some graduates added that good manners might have put them at a disadvantage in the rough-and-tumble first years of the state of Israel, but rather than criticize Landau's rules, they lamented the lack of such training in other schools and homes.[15]

Landau's students were easily recognized in the city not only because of their modest demeanor but also because of their distinctive uniforms. By the time Yvonne Astruc and her classmates entered the Evelina School, the uniform had achieved its final form. The girls were no longer dressed in fabric remnants sent from London to make serviceable pinafores for the bedraggled girls of Jerusalem. In a city where different communities were identified by their dress, the Evelina style was an icon for modern Jewish girls. It incorporated some of the strictures of dress observed by Orthodox girls and women while adding the smart touches of European fashion.

FIGURE 4.1 Evelina girls in their summer uniforms, 1942

The week after Passover vacation, the pupils began to wear the summer uniform. Young girls wore white short-sleeved blouses, while older girls wore long sleeves; all the girls wore blue tunics with three pleats in front and three in back. Young girls wore short white socks, while long socks were required for the older girls; all the girls wore white shoes. A stylish white straw hat with a black band and the Rothschild crest completed the summer outfit.

In winter, the white blouses were replaced with white sweaters, white shoes and socks were replaced with brown ones, straw hats were replaced with blue berets, and a dark blue blazer with the Rothschild crest embroidered in red completed the outfit. The winter uniform was worn from the beginning of classes in October until the Passover vacation. To minimize the differences among them, the girls were not permitted to wear jewelry, although some hid necklaces under their uniforms and showed them to special friends.

Most pupils were proud to wear the distinctive school uniform. Michal Harrison, who started attending the Evelina School in the late 1930s, chose the school because she loved the uniform.[16] No deviations were permitted in the dress code. Girls who were found walking to and from school without the complete uniform on were written up in the school's notorious black book.[17]

Rivka Weingarten remembered when there was a torrential rainfall the day after Passover vacation, which posed a dilemma for her and her sisters: Should they follow the school rules and wear their summer uniforms, or should they dress more prudently in view of the weather? Rivka's mother arrived at a solution that protected the girls' health yet allowed them to comply with the rules. Rivka and her sisters, Yehudit and Masha, wore their winter clothes and carried their summer clothes in a bag from the Old City to school. When they arrived at the school, they quickly changed into their summer uniforms.

As Rivka remembered the event, that day only the three Weingarten girls were properly attired according to the school rules. The Weingarten girls were called to the school secretary to explain their behavior. Rivka explained that it was their duty and that of their parents to uphold the school's rules. That day, all three Weingarten girls were singled out in the hall, called to stand on the stage, and awarded prizes for their diligence.[18]

Although there were many rules governing the girls' behavior, Landau was not rigid. She made exceptions for girls who demonstrated an understanding of the rules but who faced unusual circumstances. Victoria Netzer remembered an event from the late 1930s when she was forbidden by her four older sisters to wear her summer uniform on a particularly rainy day. Victoria remembered that most of the girls lining up in the courtyard that day wore their winter uniforms. Landau nevertheless praised the girls who came properly attired and took them to her office, where they received gifts of books. Victoria mustered up all her courage and went to Landau's office to explain that she had really wanted to come in the summer uniform but had been forbidden to do so by her older sisters. Landau, impressed with Victoria's self-confidence, smiled, forgave her for the infraction, and gave her a book as well. Victoria, remembering the incident thirty years later, noted, "The book is kept among my books until today."[19]

The uniforms, marching, prayer sessions, and other school traditions and rules helped to create the culture of an English girls' school in Jerusalem. Parents and children alike valued the ladylike atmosphere of the Evelina School. The new dining hut, opened in 1935 and named in memory of Lady Waley Cohen, a long-serving member of the Ladies' Committee, provided another opportunity to inculcate gracious manners. Set among the pine trees, the hut was light, airy, and spacious. Long tables covered with white linen and gleaming cutlery exposed the girls to a way of life that was rare in Jerusalem.

At lunch each day, the girls were taught proper manners and were instructed not to be "aggressive at table."[20]

Girls who attended the neighboring schools, where the discipline was more relaxed, where school often let out earlier, and where there were no school uniforms, routinely teased the Evelina girls: "The girls in uniform are prisoners of Miss Landau."[21] The Evelina pupils didn't experience the uniform and formal manners of the school as an effort to humiliate them or to create distance between them and their European teachers. On the contrary, the girls felt loved by their teachers and encouraged by them to perform at the highest level. Rachel Levin expressed a view held by many: "We felt as if we came from a royal family—Miss Landau's girls."[22]

It is not surprising that every year the Evelina School was inundated with applicants; hundreds were turned away because of a lack of space. Landau was especially receptive to new immigrants from Germany, some of whom moved to Jerusalem just so their daughters could attend the Evelina School. If the general conditions of the city had been stable, Landau might have suggested opening another school, but periodic outbreaks of violence in Jerusalem as well as the soaring needs of Jewish communities in other places made further investment by the Anglo-Jewish Association unrealistic. It was only in 1942 that Hadassah opened a vocational high school for Jewish girls in Jerusalem, the Alice Seligsburg School, named for the social worker who had worked with Landau in the early 1920s.

Many of the teachers at the Evelina School hailed from England and from other parts of Europe, and some came from the United States and South Africa. They created an atmosphere in which order and good manners were expected. The girls were taught to speak softly, not to shout; they were taught to walk in pairs rather than in large groups, impeding the passage of others. One girl remembered walking with a book on her head to improve her posture so that she could walk like Ethel Levy.[23] Neatness and cleanliness as well as punctuality were repeatedly stressed. Each infraction of the rules resulted in a notation in the black book kept in the school's office. Once a student had gotten three marks in the black book, she received a white card inviting her parents for a conference to discuss her behavior. Three additional infractions merited a yellow warning card. Finally, another three infractions resulted in expulsion. Few students were expelled from the Evelina School, but there were some; banishment from the school wasn't an empty threat.[24]

With the closing of the kindergarten and the hiring of new teachers, many of whom were native English speakers, the primary language of instruction at the Evelina School became English. Mathematics, world history and geography, world literature, and chemistry were all taught in English. In addition, there were classes devoted to English language and literature. Hebrew grammar and vocabulary was taught in Hebrew, which was increasingly the mother tongue of many pupils. In addition, the girls read Hebrew literature and studied the Jewish religion and the history of the Jewish people in Hebrew, which was offered as a field of study on the London matriculation exam.

Landau addressed her pupils in both Hebrew and English. The girls were encouraged to excel in all their studies. Their report cards gave them individual grades in each subject but also included their class ranking for English studies and for Hebrew studies, plus an overall ranking. Those who excelled received prizes and tuition stipends. The social ranking of a girl in the school was influenced by her rank in class.

By the end of their first year at the Evelina School, most of the pupils were able to conduct a simple conversation in English. Marta Zayonce, who started at the school in 1935, remembered that by the end of her first year at school, her English was already good enough to allow her to play with an English girl, Shulamit Hyamson, the daughter of a government official.[25] There were two American girls in the class of 1938, Sarah Lederberg and Naomi Teitelbaum, who contributed to the speaking of English. Rachel Levin, who spoke Hebrew at home, remembered thinking about one of these girls, "She's such a little girl, and look how well she speaks English!"[26]

The girls were encouraged to read children's books in English, available in the Evelina School library. One favorite was Edwin Chisholm's *The Jolly Book for Girls.* The stories in this book extolled initiative, self-confidence, problem solving, and perseverance. The girls were taught to stand up to bullies; to use the skills that they learned as Girl Guides to save themselves and others from danger, whether in the form of wild animals or gun-toting smugglers; and to respond with alacrity to help others. Although the stories often involved European settings replete with snow and avalanches, the girls understood the underlying messages and were able to adapt them to their lives in Jerusalem. Landau wanted to prepare Jewish women for leadership roles in their families, their communities, and their homeland. Her assumption that they would be able to use the morals in Chisholm's stories to great benefit was proven to be correct.

Since the Evelina School held no classes on Friday, for those who had few home responsibilities, Friday morning became a time for club meetings. There was a music club in which a teacher played the piano and taught students to play a variety of simple instruments: drums, castanets, and triangles. Sheet music was distributed, and the girls who joined this club learned to read music. The older girls formed a choir and were taught to sing and project their voices to a large audience. There were also sewing and cooking clubs.[27] The use of Friday morning for club meetings is another example of Landau's innovative ideas.

In addition to the Friday morning clubs, the Girl Guide groups started by Helen Bentwich in 1919 continued to flourish. These groups typically met after classes and during school holidays. In 1932, the Girl Guides made several interesting trips to the Galilee and acted as hostesses at a Girl Guide afternoon that was held in the Evelina School hall; two patrols of the first company won the choral badge in July. Landau took pride in these achievements and in the fact that a former pupil and Girl Guide, Devorah Goldberg, living in Petah Tikvah, had started a Hebrew Guide company there that showed considerable promise.[28] The following year at the Girl Guide rally at the Jerusalem Girls' College, Evelina's first company won the Lady Plumer Shield, which was carried back to the school to be placed next to the sports shield and the horticultural silver cup in the trophy case in the entrance hall.

A few years later, Landau reported that the Girl Guide movement continued to grow with the addition of a new company, along with a Ranger company. Girls who were interested started as Brownies, graduated to Girl Guides, and were promoted to Rangers. In the 1930s, Yvonne Astruc, Rachel Harris, Rivka Weingarten, and Rachel Levin joined the Girl Guides. They wore their special uniforms, learned to tie knots, practiced first aid, learned Morse code, engaged in nature study, and danced English country dances. On a trip to England thirty years after her graduation, Marta Zayonce remembered dancing the English country dances she learned as a Girl Guide. Like their English counterparts, Evelina girls liked organization, strenuous group activities, the appearance of self-government, and group spirit.[29]

The Girl Guides volunteered for service with the Jewish Municipal Com-

FIGURE 4.2 Rangers, ca. 1938

mittee, helping to care for young refugee children and to distribute clothing among them. The Evelina School, demonstrating that its students had learned valuable lessons from the months of helping the refugees from the Hebron riots, was the first to take the initiative to collect money and clothing for refugees fleeing from Jaffa to Tel Aviv in the wake of the Arab boycott and strike of 1936. The Tel Aviv municipality wrote to thank the students and to encourage others to follow their example. During the years of the Arab boycott and of the Second World War, Rangers, Girl Guides, and Brownies made warm clothing for the destitute of Palestine in response to an appeal from headquarters for Girl Guide service.[30]

The Evelina Girl Guides participated in the annual fund drive to support hospital services for sick children by taking tickets at the annual Jerusalem Bazaar held at the new residence of the high commissioner. One guide, Chava Weinberg, recalled being stationed at the entrance to the tennis courts and charged with checking people as they entered to ascertain whether they had bought a ticket for the event. She remembered a tall, well-dressed man approaching and trying to enter without showing his ticket. She asked him for the ticket; he said he didn't have one and quickly paid the price of entry. As he entered, another man exclaimed, "I bless you on your success; you received money from the high commissioner to enter his own house." Chava recalled, "I blushed of course, but the Commissioner had already gone, and his ten *grush* were used for the good of children in Jerusalem hospitals."[31]

Just as the spirit of community service was a key component of Girl Guide activities, service to the school community was the core of the prefect system. Prefects had been introduced to the Evelina School in the mid-1920s, but the system reached its full potential after the return to Frutiger House. Now that the school had ample courtyard and hall space for schoolwide activities, there were opportunities for the prefects to perform their duties.

The coveted role of prefect was given to the best-behaved and most accomplished students in the upper grades; each wore an enamel pin engraved with the Evelina de Rothschild School shield and the title *prefect* in Hebrew and English. The prefect system was an English import not found in religious or Zionist schools in Jerusalem. Both the prefect system and the Girl Guide program used badges and pins to convey membership in an elite group.[32] By showing her respect for the prefects and assigning them special duties that placed them in leadership roles, Landau hoped to give them the confidence they would need to assume leadership roles in the future. Landau prohibited her students from joining Zionist youth groups, which were coed and, in her view, not appropriate for schoolgirls. Nevertheless, it is clear from the comments of Yvonne Astruc, the head prefect of 1938, that nationalist and military ideas had become part of the girls' vocabulary:

> A prefect is an "officer" of the Evelina de Rothschild "troops." The order is given and the troops are ranged in rows. It is not enough for the "captain" to give the order from the "tower," whence she reviews the whole camp; we must aid her by marshalling the "troops" into lines. Though dressed like the rest of the "soldiers," we wear a small distinguishing badge. Many a girl regards our approach as that of the "enemy." The prefects can inflict disgrace or bestow praise. Many of the "troops" think of us as very severe, hard-hearted individuals, for each "battalion" possesses its mischief-makers who have good cause to know the prefects. Our job is difficult, but interesting. When a wrongdoer falls into our hands we are prepared to listen to explanations, but not to plausible excuses. We are divided into prefects and sub-prefects, each performing her duties to the best of her ability. We are proud of being chosen as prefects and we hope that our "commanders" are glad to have us as their helpers.[33]

FIGURE 4.3 Students drinking milk

The next year, Naomi Teitelbaum, an American immigrant to Jerusalem and the new head prefect, offered a more functional view of the prefect system at the Evelina School. The school had six prefects and four subprefects. The head prefect was responsible for drawing up a list of tasks to be performed. There was a weekly rotation of duties, so that every prefect had a chance to do them all in turn. The subprefects were girls who were scheduled to take the London matriculation exam in June; they were not given tasks that might make them late for class, such as the duties of the gramophone, the bell, or the lines.

At least two prefects were stationed in the cloakroom on warm days, and more in wet weather. During lunch hour, a prefect was on duty near the entrance to see that no one reentered the building without permission. During recess, they ensured that none of the younger girls strayed into the part of the playground known as Hyde Park, which was reserved for the upper classes. A new task was added in 1938, the distribution of a cup of milk to each pupil at morning recess. The milk was provided to schools by the Tnuva Dairy Cooperative in conjunction with Hadassah; the pupils paid a small sum for it each week. At 3 p.m. a prefect rang the bell for dismissal, while another turned on the gramophone as the girls marched out. Naomi observed that the main lesson the prefects learned was the value of working together in harmony.[34]

Old Girls' Club members, the school's alumnae, were encouraged to continue to affiliate with the school. In 1932, the club was formally registered with the district commissioner's office. The officers were Landau, president;

Levy and Goodman, vicechairwomen; Esther Porush Shani, secretary; and Rachel Kokia Eliaschar, treasurer. The group had 200 members and met monthly. There were also weekly classes in gymnastics and cooking. Hebrew and English libraries were established for the Old Girls, who reported that all who wanted jobs were employed.[35]

Landau was eager to reinforce the modern Jewish educational values that had been inculcated in the girls as students when they were graduates who were developing careers and families. She also wanted to build a network of support for the current students among the graduates. The Old Girls' Club met three times each year, held an annual dance, and had weekly netball games. Members were charged a modest one hundred mils per year. Regular meetings were held in the late afternoon, often preceded by tea and followed by a lecture. In 1936, for instance, the postmaster general spoke about the internal procedures of the post office and the development of the telegraph and telephone. Thus, the Old Girls kept up with modernizing trends in Jerusalem.

As Landau had hoped, the Old Girls took an interest in the advanced students and included them in their volunteer activities, such as their work at the Jewish Institute for the Blind. The Old Girls took current students with them in order to create meaningful Sabbath afternoon experiences for the girls and to teach through experience the importance of community service. Rachel Harris was one of the three girls invited to participate in weekly Sabbath visits to the home for the blind in 1937. She recorded the following in her diary:

> Yesterday our group's turn to go arrived. And as my fate would have it, I had to sit and read stories. I was very frightened when one entered with a pitiful face ... I had never seen anything like it in my life. It was sad that he didn't have a normal organ in his body, but after a little while I came to realize that he had sublime talents and wisdom. After I tired from reading to the children, this boy sang Purim songs and though he made a few mistakes his singing lifted the spirits of all. After awhile a blind girl entered and entertained the others with jokes. Later, they took us on a tour of the school ... in the library we saw how they learned to read with their fingers. They read faster than those who read with their eyes. From there we went to the workshop and saw the beautiful handmade items made by the children.[36]

Rachel and her friends continued to visit the blind children and raised funds to support the home.

The annual dances held by the Old Girls' Club were special events in the increasingly nervous city. Old Girls attended in evening gowns accompanied by their brothers and their brothers' friends. Dancing was to live band music; refreshments were ample. Some Old Girls came from traditional families that frowned on social dancing, while others came from Zionist families that looked askance at evening gowns and preferred the hora to social dancing. As always, Landau marched to the beat of her own drummer. Alarmed by interfaith friendships, which sometimes grew into romance and marriage, she organized these social occasions to foster meetings between Old Girls and young Jewish men.[37]

Landau was supported by an unusually talented and devoted group of teachers; some were English and others were German. These teachers were deeply involved in both the curriculum and the extracurricular activities of the girls. Since many spent their entire careers in the school, the pupils knew them for many years.

One of the teachers who was greatly admired and loved was Esme Aaronson, who had arrived from London in 1935 engaged to be married and ready to join the staff at the Evelina School. She spent nearly four decades lovingly teaching English, music, and geography to the girls in her classes. Her husband, who was often obliged to tend to a family wine business in Petah Tikvah, and her two children were her only family in Palestine. Aaronson became very close to Frieda Brandes, David Reider, and especially Helena Schonberg, all teachers at the Evelina School who became her extended family. Aaronson's pupils remembered that she was a disciplinarian but that she always wore a smile and had a cheerful disposition. She expected them to strive hard to achieve excellence. One of her former pupils recognized that this expectation of excellence was what spurred her on to achievements she had not been aware were possible.[38]

Mrs. Hetzroni, the new gym teacher, was also a favorite. Under her direction, the sports program was expanded, and new games called flying ball, boundary ball, and *mahanaim*, a local version of dodgeball, were added to the popular netball. Hetzroni organized a sports team that met every Thursday afternoon to practice high jumps, long jumps, running, and games. Interschool competitive matches were held with the Jerusalem Girls' College and later with several other Jewish schools. The Evelina girls were keen to bring home flags to add to the trophy chest in the front hall of the school. Interest in sports, fitness, and competitive games continued to grow during the 1930s.[39]

Helena Schonberg joined the faculty in this period, arriving from Down Lane Central School in Tottenham, north of London. She was a favorite teacher from her arrival until her retirement more than twenty years later. Adaya Hochberg explained, "Miss Schonberg was present." Adaya thought that Schonberg focused intently on each student; she knew her class. Adina Shoshani remembered her breadth of knowledge: "She taught all of English literature, including Chaucer." Many graduates remembered poems by William Wordsworth and Percy Bysshe Shelley that they learned in her class. Miriam Ochana and Shulamit Lilienfeld remembered that Schonberg taught them Latin during their last year. When she first arrived, Schonberg shared an apartment on King George Street with Miss Sayre, another beloved teacher, who hailed from Ireland and taught mathematics. Rachel Levin was invited to visit by Sayre and was shocked to discover that the teacher she so admired had a home like other mortals—with a bed and a dresser, a table and chairs, and cups and saucers.[40]

Another favorite teacher, who taught chemistry for decades, was the diminutive and gentle David Reider. Reider and his wife arrived from Frankfurt before the rise of the Nazis, imbued with the desire to live in Jerusalem. They lived modestly in Rehavia. Having no children of their own, they befriended the young Marta Zayonce and often brought her gifts when they returned from trips abroad. When Esther Cailingold joined the faculty in 1946, she rented a room from the Reiders and enjoyed their frequent hospitality. When Rivka Weingarten and Rachel Harris asked Reider to pose for a graduation picture with them, he agreed only if they would allow him to stand on a step.

Joseph Goldschmidt of the Universities of Frankfurt and Munich, who held a teachers' training certificate from the Institute of Education at the University of London, joined the faculty of the Evelina School in 1939, replacing Sayre, the mathematics teacher, who left in the middle of the school year to attend her ailing mother.[41] Goldschmidt suggested creating Sabbath afternoon walking tours for girls in class 7. Schonberg joined him in this endeavor. He recalled a class trip to walk around the wall of the Old City:

In those days there was no fence and the girls walked at a height of five to ten meters [about sixteen to thirty-three feet] above the ground. I almost passed out when some of the cheerful girls called to me "bravo" from the other side of the wall. I counted every second until they came down in peace.[42]

On another trip the class walked to the Monastery of San Simeon in southern Jerusalem. It took a full hour to get there, and upon their arrival the guards of the monastery, fearful of damage, were reluctant to allow them in to wander on the trails. The trip chaperones promised that the class would be careful, so the guards finally relented and let them in to see the beautiful views. These trips were a natural development of the earlier trips initiated by Landau to provide informal instruction to her pupils, a practice not adopted in other schools until many years later.

Since Jerusalem was a small city, pupils often saw their teachers outside class and related to them as people as well as teachers. Walter Reis, a handsome young teacher of mathematics, was a great favorite of many pupils, who admitted to having a crush on him. Elhanan Wachman, on the other hand, was a seasoned veteran, whose Bible classes were popular for decades. Batia Salasnik, a history teacher, was remembered fondly for not abandoning her pupils, since she returned to the Evelina School after marrying and having children. Liselotte Levy, a beloved art teacher from Italy, gave Rivka Zweig's graduating class a painting, urging them to meet annually as Old Girls in order to circulate the painting among members of the class. Varda Heinemann, who fled Germany, was appreciated for her music classes and for riding her bicycle to school, an uncommon practice among married women at the time.

Jerusalem in the 1930s: Growth and a Return to Violence

By the 1930s, Annie Landau's efforts to transform her pupils' lives had developed in ways that she could only have imagined in her early years in Jerusalem when filth, malnutrition, and illness were primary concerns. Jerusalem was beginning to look very different. Roads were widened, railroad connections grew, and gas lighting made getting around at night safer. Mail service improved greatly, and telephone service was installed. In recognition of the importance of the school, Landau was awarded one of the first hundred telephones; her number was 88. Shops carrying a greater variety of goods began to open on Jaffa Road.

Adding to the more cosmopolitan feel of the city were two new luxury hotels built on King David Street: the Palace, opened in 1929, and the King David, which welcomed its first guests in 1931. The Zion Cinema, which had opened in 1920 with six hundred seats, was eclipsed in 1932 by the Edison Cinema, which accommodated two thousand. Attendance at lectures became popular as new concert halls, like the grand one at the Y M C A inaugurated in 1933, opened their doors. The Y M C A also boasted an indoor swimming pool and outdoor tennis courts. Classical music was played in the new concert halls and on the radio through the Palestine Broadcasting Service.

In 1939, the Palestine Broadcasting Service, which had rented office and recording space in the Palace Hotel, moved to the Abyssinian Palace. Since the assembly hall of the nearby Evelina School was suitable for rehearsals and broadcasts, a relationship between the Palestine Broadcasting Service and the Evelina School developed. Karl Salomon and his wife, Esther, were accomplished musicians who conducted the Evelina School choir; they also worked for the Palestine Broadcasting Service and facilitated its ongoing relationship with the school. Some concerts were performed in the school hall, which was wired for broadcast, permitting students an unusual opportunity to hear classical music. On October 14, 1938, the operetta *Shulamith* by Abraham Goldfaden was aired. The publication *Jerusalem Radio* commented as follows:

> This program was relayed from the Evelina de Rothschild School and for the first time in local radio history an operetta was performed with adequate musical accompaniment. The voices were those of Miriam Segall, Arieh Megido, Yehuda Harmelach, Benjamin Ernstein, and Karl Salomon. Listeners who would appreciate being present at such productions are advised to book their places early.[43]

The school choir frequently performed on the radio, enhancing the radio's popularity with Evelina pupils. In addition, the girls participated in two popular radio programs: the English Children's Hour and the Hebrew Children's Hour. Some of these programs were written by Evelina graduates. Ziona Caspi, who joined the Palestine Broadcasting Service staff in 1938, wrote a five-part radio play, *The Magic Sea-Shell*, that commenced its broadcast on November 1, 1938. She later contributed a second multipart play, *When the Clock Strikes Thirteen*. Menuha Eden, an Old Girl who had a beautiful voice, played Bastienne in Mozart's operetta *Bastien et Bastienne* on the radio in January 1940. In September, a current pupil, Ruth Karpf, contributed a play, *The Air Raid Warden: A Thrilling Adventure of the Blackout.*[44]

The years 1936–1939 were marked by Arab boycotts of Jewish businesses, strikes, and sporadic violence. Fifteen-year-old Rachel Harris wrote about the events of the day in a secret diary. She wanted a private place to record her complicated feelings of anguish about the rioting and deaths she saw in Jerusalem. She wrote the following:

> Right now it is as if I received a sort of strong push and I heard the voice of Rachel. . . . In my heart I knew that there was nothing standing in the face of my desire. . . . What I feel, this paper feels. Days will come when this paper will be covered in tears.

She inscribed the Hebrew date, 27 Tamuz 5696 (1936, in the Christian calendar), and added:

> Rioters on every side and from every corner hurt us, and despite everything our pride in Israel remains eternal and strong. . . . The air is saturated with poison and the land is saturated with innocent blood, the blood of young brothers who fell dead without warning. . . . These youth who wish to create from the ruins of this land the country of Israel. These poor men who went to their work and planned to return in time for Shabbat with their families, but were stopped by a bullet. . . . No and no . . . I do not agree with this. . . . And now the worms eat this young flesh until they are full. I cannot accept that these young, blameless men fell dead. . . . I want only to die. What value does my life have, now that I know that brothers protecting me and our nation have fallen? And, yet, I sit on the balcony and watch those coming and going.[45]

A few days later she continued:

> I heard something that I cannot believe. It is like an arrow tipped with poison that has pierced my heart. . . . Yosef Katz, a 17-year-old boy, finished school only three years ago and went to work, work for the good of his nation. This young Yosef was nice; blue eyes, blond hair, and always wearing a blue shirt to bring out the color of his eyes. . . . Yosef went to work every day and returned in the evening to his parents, his brothers and his sisters, and his friends. But he will return no more. Last night as he walked home, three bullets hit him in

the head. The poor boy didn't even manage to say a word; he just fell in a pool of blood. Here, God did not think. Yosef had only begun to taste life, but his aspiration was to grow up and to be able to work for the good of his nation; he did not live to fulfill his aspiration in full, only in part.[46]

Rachel's diary continued with descriptions of riots and death: bombs exploded periodically, and there were shootings near the Schneller orphanage in which two people were hit and a sixty-two-year-old Jewish man was seriously wounded. At the end of August she reported that the newspaper was printed with a black border for two Jewish sisters who were killed on their way home from work. She asked rhetorically, "Until when will these sorrows continue? Until when will innocent blood be spilled?"

Rachel was also aware of violence in other parts of Palestine. A few days later, she copied into her diary a long letter to the editor she had read in a newspaper from "Ella Lipschitz, an unfortunate grandmother." The letter was from Safed and was addressed to the high commissioner. Lipschitz was seventy years old and had a broken heart and bitter soul after her son-in-law and his three small children were murdered in their sleep—shot to death in front of the children's mother, who had begged the murderers to leave at least one child alive. The grandmother, who had lost seven other children, was now left with one daughter; as a result of these violent events, her daughter had become deranged. The grandmother asked, "For what were the quiet man, writer of Torah books, and his three small children murdered? Were they killed because of the lack of strength of the government of their city? . . . Yes, they fell as sacrifices to the mistakes of the government." Lipschitz demanded that the Mandatory government of Britain end the murder of innocent people and bring peace to the land. Rachel agreed with her demands.[47]

Rachel's diary included typical teenage concerns: light-hearted references to boys, anger at her snooping brother, and frustrated efforts to buy a birthday present for her mother. But there were also many dark references to her fears of Arabs and anger toward the British. In contrast, Landau's comments on the period convey little anger toward the British. She continued to praise British achievements in Jerusalem, such as the more adequate water supply. She noted that despite the turbulence in the city, school routines were uninterrupted. She even treated lightly a potentially deadly incident: the tossing of a bomb into the school garden just before recess. Landau faced the threat posed by

the bomb with bravado and explained to the children, "It was fortunately discovered by our loyal fellah, who turned his garden hose on it at full strength
and rendered it harmless."[48]

For a few weeks all of Jerusalem was diverted from its troubles by the visit
of noted conductor Arturo Toscanini, whose concern for the danger facing
German Jewish musicians led him to support the creation of an orchestra in
Palestine. Toscanini visited Tel Aviv and Jerusalem to conduct the first concerts of the newly formed Palestine Orchestra in December 1936. In Jerusalem
there were not enough tickets to meet the demand. Since the final rehearsals
were held in the Evelina School hall, the girls in the top classes—including
Yvonne Astruc, Rachel Harris, Rachel Levin, and Rivka Weingarten—were
privileged to attend the rehearsal of Franz Schubert's "Unfinished Symphony,"
followed by Felix Mendelssohn's "Midsummer Night's Dream," Carl Weber's
"Overture to Oberon," and a piece by Gioacchino Rossini.[49]

Landau's belief in the dignity of all human beings, a value she learned at
home and in her English school, did not change as a result of her years in
Jerusalem, where growing Jewish and Arab nationalism caused many to alter
their views. Landau's vision of the Holy City as a place important to all three
Abrahamic religions remained steadfast in the face of losses that were hard
to understand. On October 21, 1937, Avinoam Yellin, the chief inspector of
Jewish schools for the British administration, was shot and died after two
days of suffering in Hadassah Hospital. Thousands of Jerusalemites accompanied his coffin to pay their last respects.[50] Landau mourned his loss but
continued to socialize with educated Arabs and to treat her Arab employees
with respect. Her home remained a center of hospitality for all Jerusalemites
who shared her views.

Life at the Evelina de Rothschild School continued to be an oasis. Landau
believed that the British would allow no harm to come to her school or her
pupils. She remained a loyal Englishwoman, mourning the passing of King
George V, whose efforts for peace and progress she praised, and celebrating
the coronation of George VI. The students at the Evelina School shared in
the joyous celebrations hosted by the high commissioner in honor of the
coronation. Several students whose parents were British subjects were invited
to a coronation tea party given by the Sports Club. All pupils wore buttons
with pictures of the king and queen with attached red, white, and blue rib-
bons, provided by the school. The coronation parade, with airplanes flying in

formation overhead, was attended by 180 Rangers, Girl Guides, and Brownies. The high sprits accompanying the coronation temporarily deflected Landau's growing concern about the precarious position of German Jews.

Through the late 1930s, Landau continued to refuse to support political Zionism, viewing it as disloyal to the British government. Nevertheless, she energetically supported the immigration of German Jews to Palestine. While the United States and most European countries closed their doors to fleeing Jewish refugees, the number that reached Palestine continued to grow. Starting in 1925, the immigration of Jews to Palestine outnumbered the immigration of Jews to any other country. In 1933, thirty thousand Jewish immigrants arrived in Palestine. In 1934, the number of immigrants soared to forty-two thousand, and in 1935 it reached sixty-two thousand.[51]

Landau hoped that their arrival would result in fulfilling the vision of a national home for the Jewish people in Palestine. In previous years, Landau's school had accepted refugees from Hebron and from missionary schools. Now she turned her attention to German refugees. She continued to view her endeavors at the Evelina School as central to the effort to regenerate the Jewish people.

Refugee Pupils

Special efforts were made to accept refugee girls at the Evelina School through-out the 1930s. Some entered without sufficient skills in English; others lacked preparation in Hebrew. Many of their families experienced difficult financial conditions as their parents, previously able to earn a good living in Vienna or Berlin, were now desperately searching for a way to earn a modest living while adjusting to life in Jerusalem.

Daisy Ticho, a niece of the famous ophthalmologist Albert Ticho, arrived with her parents from Vienna in 1938 to face just such a situation. Her father, a lawyer, was unable to find work, even as a clerk, and her mother, a dentist, was given various part-time jobs, since there were many dentists arriving in Jerusalem at this time.[52]

Shulamit Lilienfeld, another refugee from Vienna, arrived in Jerusalem in 1940. Shulamit and her older sister Miriam had been sent to London with the *kindertransporten* in 1939. She arrived at the Evelina School with one arm in a cast, resting in a sling, as the result of a shipboard fall. Some of her classmates envied her cast and sling. Nevertheless, Miriam's European boots, her mother's absence for several months, and her father's unemployment made her feel like an outsider.[53]

Nine months before Kristallnacht, Ella Schwartzstein, now the headmistress of the Girls' Jewish Orphanage of Frankfurt, traveled to Jerusalem to ask her friend Annie Landau for help. The friendship of these two headmistresses was part of an international network of female educators, social activists, and philanthropists that sustained Landau. Upon notification of Schwartzstein's arrival, many of her former pupils, scattered throughout Palestine, rushed to Jerusalem to greet her. Despite the 5 p.m. curfew, the Old Girls were eager to pay their respects to a beloved teacher.

Amid the brief merrymaking, Schwartzstein explained her troubles to Landau.[54] Fearing for the continued safety of the girls under her supervision in Frankfurt, Schwartzstein asked Landau to accept some of them into the Evelina School. Schwartzstein was already ailing with the cancer that would lead to her demise a few years later; Landau, then sixty-five years old, was no longer the spry woman who had jumped rope in the Bentwich home. Nevertheless, they agreed to work together to save the lives of Jewish girls. Landau contacted her colleague and friend Henrietta Szold, who was planning the large-scale rescue effort for European children that became Youth Aliyah. Together the three women devised a rescue plan.[55]

Landau offered to accept fourteen girls from the orphanage and to pay for their tuition, uniforms, books, and private instruction. To that end she quickly raised 350 pounds from her friends. Szold secured an additional 3,000 pounds from Brazilian Jews who offered to assist children displaced by the war. All the other children rescued by Youth Aliyah were sent to rural villages, but Szold arranged for this unique urban school experience because she had no doubt that her friend would provide an excellent program for the girls.[56]

Landau did not disappoint. She was involved with every aspect of the rescue project, personally ensuring the comfort of the girls in a residence that would carry Schwartzstein's name and providing seats for the orphaned girls for Sabbath and holiday services at the Yeshurun Synagogue, where she was a founding member. Because they were all bereft of parents and family and now country and language, she wanted them to feel at home in Jerusalem.

At first, Landau tried to obtain a visa for Schwartzstein to accompany the girls to Jerusalem. She presented a strong case to the British authorities for a visa on the grounds that the orphaned girls needed their housemother, but the authorities were unmoved. When the girls finally left Frankfurt in the spring of 1940, they were chaperoned by Louise Heineman, who at seventeen was the oldest of the fortunate girls who were granted visas. They left Frankfurt and traveled by train to Trieste.

Nine-year-old Shoshana Heineman and ten-year-old Lea Steinhardt were among them. In Trieste they waited a few days for the departure of the *Marco Polo*, and while waiting they learned to reply to the boys who tried to speak with them with "*Non capisco Italiano*" (I don't understand Italian). The *Marco Polo* landed in Haifa on April 14, 1940. It was to be the last trip for this ship, which sank in the Mediterranean on its return voyage. Shoshana arrived with a case of the measles and was taken straight to Rambam Hospital. The rest of the girls were met by Hans Bayit, a senior Youth Aliyah official, who took them to Jerusalem. When Shoshana recovered, Bayit returned to Haifa to ferry her to Jerusalem as well.[57]

The Schwartzstein House, as the residence for the orphans was called, was located at 5 St. George Street, less than a mile from Frutiger House, on the second floor of a large Arab dwelling. Youth Aliyah funds paid the rent. Lea Steinhardt remembered how relieved she was when the girls arrived at their new house in Jerusalem, which looked like a family home, not an impersonal institution. The new girls were accustomed to living together in the Girls' Jewish Orphanage in Frankfurt, supported by the Rothschild family. Lea had arrived there in 1936 and Shoshana in 1938. Lea's mother had died in childbirth, and her father had escaped alone to the United States. Shoshana's father was sent to a concentration camp after Kristallnacht; her Christian mother abandoned Shoshana and her siblings at the Jewish Orphanage.[58]

Sensitive to the needs of the young girls, Landau searched for a housemother who would be familiar to the new arrivals. She hired Marta Lange, who had arrived in Jerusalem a few months earlier from Frankfurt, to fill that important role. Marta was assisted by her mother, Hermina Lange, who lived in the home as well, and by Mrs. Friedman, who was the housekeeper and cook. These three women, aided by Landau and the teachers, worked together to make the house into a home. Lea remembered the first Yom Kippur services she attended at the Evelina School with the teachers and other students; she learned to recite Yizkor, the prayer for the dead, at that service. She also remembered the joyous meal to break the fast at the conclusion of the day.[59]

Schwartzstein House had three bedrooms, a central room, a dining hall, a kitchen, and two rooms for the staff. Marta and Hermina Lange shared one bedroom. Friedman shared a room with her husband and their baby. The two seventeen-year-old girls who arrived with the group were sent to a religious kibbutz, since they were too old to start learning the Evelina curriculum. The remaining fourteen shared a large bedroom. When they arrived, they found each of their cots covered by a handmade colorful patchwork quilt, made by Evelina students to welcome them.

A Christian Arab family lived on the bottom floor of the house. Despite the volatile political situation, relations between the family and the girls were excellent during the years they shared the house. The girls got to know their young neighbors, three boys who enjoyed playing in the house's courtyard. The Jewish girls visited their Arab neighbors on Christmas and brought them special foods for Passover.

The home bore the traces of the bourgeois European world the girls had lost—a handsome library with English books and classical art reproductions on the walls were designed to make the transition to their new life less abrupt. Lea remembered reading several books by the Brontë sisters, as well as *The Grapes of Wrath, Gone with the Wind*, and *The Count of Monte Cristo*. Shoshana said that she learned to value friendship at the Evelina School and has remained close to the girls who shared the residence. An inspector from Youth Aliyah found the lack of Zionist books and the artwork lamentable and recommended replacing the artwork with paintings of tractors and kibbutz life. Landau and Marta Lange, in contrast, tried to provide continuity for these young uprooted girls in at least some aspects of their lives.[60] They believed that the girls would integrate more fully into their new environment if they were allowed to maintain vestiges of their past.

Lange and her mother proved to be excellent guides for the girls. They filled their after-school hours with supplemental education imbued with spirituality, humor, strictness, and affection. The Sabbath and holidays were observed with traditional meals, and birthdays were celebrated. The girls often sat around the large dining table and told of their studies, shared their artwork, and even spoke of problems in school. Varda Heinemann, Lange's sister, who taught music and gym and rode a bicycle to school, was a frequent visitor. Other teachers dropped in to offer extra lessons, and each girl was assigned a student mentor from among the older Evelina girls, who also helped the newcomers to improve their skills in English and Hebrew.

Landau recognized that some of the older girls would not have enough time to master English sufficiently to pass the London matriculation exam, so she counseled them to transfer to programs where they would have more success. Some attended the nearby Strauss Center to learn health and nutrition; others moved to the Bikur Holim hospital to study nursing. Those who stayed at the Evelina School made good progress. As the cost of living in Jerusalem increased during the war years, Szold supported Landau's request for extra Youth Aliyah funds to meet the growing expenses. Letters between the two women show their concern for the well-being of the girls in their care.

When officials of Youth Aliyah declined to purchase an extra stove to heat the Schwartzstein facility, urging the school to adopt a more pioneering approach, Landau bought the stove with her own funds. She believed that the physical and emotional warmth of the school and the home would help the girls to adjust to their new homeland. One sign of their adapting to the new environment was the adoption of Hebrew names: Loni Karola became Ariela, Erika became Esther, and Ilse became Yudit.[61]

Landau and the teachers worked to integrate not only the orphans from the Schwartzstein House but all the new arrivals, by assisting those who needed extra lessons to reach the level of English and Hebrew required for their grade level. Extracurricular activities were also used to bridge the gap between recent arrivals and girls who had been in the school for many years. Landau reassured her new students that their school routines would continue in Jerusalem and that they would be protected from the outside world. She also helped their parents to find jobs that enabled them to qualify for visas. Ethel Levy later observed the following:

> Nobody was more helpful in bringing Jews out of Hitler's hell after 1933 than Miss Landau. She was so generous and gave so freely that all, Jew and non-Jew, were anxious to serve her on the few occasions that she ever asked for help of them. She was thus able to find jobs in government and businesses for those who came and who had to adapt their lives anew.[62]

Despite the efforts of Landau, the teachers, and the pupils, some of the newcomers were unable to adjust. From the outward signs it seemed that Ruth Karpf, who arrived in Jerusalem knowing little English and no Hebrew, learned rapidly. It appeared that she was beginning to get used to her new surroundings and friends, but notes taken by Levy labeled "confidential" attest to Ruth's struggle with finding her place in school and in the city:

> Almost from the beginning Ruth was a difficult child. In spite of the circumstances which forced her family among so many thousands of others to leave Germany, she retained a love of Germany and its language and had no desire to learn Hebrew and did so most unwillingly. During the breaks she would gather around her other German children and talk German and create a "little Germany" within the School. Time after time we remonstrated with her on this subject and told her that as she was now an inhabitant of the country, she must learn the language of the country and unless she learned to play in that language she would never really be a child of the land.[63]

As this passage suggests, Ruth was not alone in clinging to German language and culture. However, the Evelina School, which promoted bilingual and bicultural studies despite opposition from Zionists, was keen on limiting the school to two languages in order to foster community.

Levy then explained that Ruth's family circumstances added to her problems. Ruth, her siblings, and their mother had arrived in Jerusalem first, opening a laundry to make a living. Her father, a lawyer, arrived later. The mother was extremely observant; the father was not. Ruth admitted that she found it impossible not to quarrel with her mother. Beginning in 1937, when Ruth was fifteen, she rebelled. Jerusalem was a small town. Teachers and parents of her classmates reported seeing her at night with older male companions. She was warned that her conduct was compromising her and the reputation of the school.

For several months Ruth's behavior both inside and outside school improved, but in 1938 she was reported in unfrequented parts of the city in the company of British policemen. At about that time her mother left for the United States. At the beginning of 1939, Diab, the gatekeeper, reported that all the Arab shopkeepers opposite the school were gossiping about Ruth, who was seen walking in Musrara, an area not frequented by Jewish women, with a British policeman.

Ruth was warned, but she did not heed the school rules. She was again found walking in dangerous quarters with a British policeman. Her father was called in and advised that if one more incident took place, he would be asked to remove his daughter from the school at once. He replied by stating that he could see no harm in his daughter's behavior, but he promised that she would do nothing more to cause the school anxiety. In March there was another incident, and she was expelled a few months shy of taking the matriculation exam. After she left school she was seen consorting with a man known only as Captain Mason, who was married and the father of three children. When it was discovered that Mason was in great debt, he was transferred out of the country. Soon after, Ruth followed her mother to America.[64]

Landau continued to be concerned with the safety of her pupils as they walked to school through the increasingly dangerous neighborhood of Musrara, which bordered the school. Musrara was built at the beginning of the twentieth century, and its original inhabitants were mainly well-to-do Muslims, but during the years of the Mandate, Christians, Armenians, Greeks, and a few Jews moved to the neighborhood. In the late 1930s, many government officials lived there, and their homes became a target for the rioters.

In light of the unrest, Landau opened the front entrance to the school on St. Paul's Street. This entrance, previously restricted to guests, was safer than the side entrance on the Street of the Prophets, which faced Musrara and was subsequently closed. In addition, three *ghaffirs*, part of a special British police force established during the 1930s, were stationed at the school, guarding the grounds day and night. Landau appreciated the courage of her students and their parents; school attendance remained normal throughout the late 1930s. She was also grateful to the British authorities for protecting her school and for exempting her students from the frequent curfews imposed in the neighborhood of Frutiger House.[65]

Despite the increasing violence in Jerusalem, Landau remained convinced that the British soldiers and police would protect her students. She was more concerned with the danger faced by Jews in Europe. Having always believed that Jews could live meaningful lives in western Europe, the United States, and Palestine, Landau now began to express new thoughts. Reflecting on the Nuremberg Laws, Landau reasoned that in countries where limitations were placed on freedom for Jews, the ability of Jews to participate in modern life was compromised. She began to believe that the opportunity to develop modern Jewish life would best be accomplished in Palestine.[66]

Her vision for the expansion of modern Jewish life encountered an unexpected obstacle in Jerusalem. During the late 1930s, graduates of the Evelina

School, who had previously been assured of government and business jobs, faced shrinking employment opportunities. Landau responded to this challenge by expanding the instructional opportunities to prepare Evelina students for advanced education and new career paths. Plans were drawn up to create a designated classroom for the students of the top academic class to prepare for the matriculation exam, which had become compulsory. Passing the exam was the prerequisite for further study that was now required for degrees in teaching, social work, nursing, law, and liberal arts.

Simultaneously, Landau made plans for a new building to house a music room and an indoor playroom. This construction was the last addition to the Frutiger House site. The music room had space for choir practice and music education, which facilitated the ties between the school and the Palestine Broadcasting Service, another new source of jobs for graduates. The new building reduced the size of the garden, but the playroom provided accommodation to students during inclement weather.

In 1937, Rachel Harris, Rachel Levin, Rivka Weingarten, and Yvonne Astruc, who had previously passed the matriculation exam, completed the commercial class and passed the Pitman tests with high grades. Rachel Harris's father, a businessman, wanted his daughter to have experience working. Concerned that she might not find a job, he arranged with a friend at the Prudential Company to hire her but agreed to pay her first year's salary himself secretly. Rachel worked at Prudential a short time; she married young and stayed home to raise her children, honoring her husband's wish.

At the age of forty, she gained his approval to return to the workforce. Rachel recalled that her Evelina School experience continued to serve her well. She refreshed her skills and soon found a job working for the Israel Scientific Translation Company. She worked there for thirty-five years. When she retired at age seventy-five, she went to work for Keren Kayemet, the Israel affiliate of the Jewish National Fund. Her language and organizational abilities, skills learned decades earlier in the Evelina School, remained sharp and useful.[67]

Rachel Levin loved ballet and wanted to continue to study dance after graduation. She had hoped to win a scholarship, but she was foiled by one poor grade, in history. Rachel's father, fearful of his neighbors' disapproval of ballet dancing, forbade her further study. She resented his decision for many years, but she did not challenge his authority. She found a clerical position with the Palestine Corporation (now the Union Bank). Rachel was hired by a British Jew and worked for him for ten years. During that time she joined the new YMCA on King David Street, where she attended concerts and lectures and used the swimming pool and the library.

In 1949, Rachel married an American rabbi and returned to New York with him. In New York, Rachel worked for a short time for El Al Airlines and was later hired by the Yeshiva of Central Queens, a modern Orthodox school, where she taught second grade pupils for thirty years. After retirement, Rachel and her husband returned to Jerusalem, where their children had settled.[68]

Rivka Weingarten's first job after finishing her studies was in the office of the governor of Jerusalem. Rivka, who had been an outstanding student, became an outstanding employee. She learned about accounting and taxes and was promoted regularly. Ultimately, after the foundation of the state, she became the head of a department of seventy-eight employees and later the commissioner of income tax, the most senior position in the Treasury Department filled by a woman at that time.

In 1967, Rivka gave up her position in order to fulfill a promise she had made to her mother in 1948. Just before the fall of the Old City, Rivka's mother, whose family had lived in the same house on Rehov Or HaChaim for seven generations, insisted that Rivka, a new bride, leave the city with her husband before it fell to the Jordanians. Her mother asked her to promise to return to the house and rebuild it when that became possible. In 1967, Rivka returned to the house and fulfilled her promise in a creative way. She rebuilt the house as a museum, the Courtyard of the Old Yishuv, so that visitors could see how Jews lived in the Old City before 1948. She built a modest apartment for herself above the museum.[69]

Yvonne Astruc found a job as a secretary for the British Medical Services right after graduation. Unlike her three classmates, Yvonne encountered anti-Jewish prejudice at her job. The head of her unit was an Arab who expressed antisemitic views. Another Arab who worked in the unit made trouble for her and for three other Jews who worked there. Not long after she started, all the Jewish employees were told to report to work on Yom Kippur, a day when no Jews in Palestine were expected to work. The head of the unit was adamant.

Yvonne, the youngest of the Jewish employees, was selected as the spokeswoman to present their case to General Pritchie, who held the ultimate authority for the unit. She explained that Jews were not allowed to work on

Yom Kippur. Pritchie, assuming that the attractive blonde, blue-eyed Yvonne was Catholic and French, asked, "Why do you care about those Jews?" She informed him that she was Jewish. Although he still refused to countermand the order to report to work, none of the four Jews came to their offices on Yom Kippur. When they returned, nothing was said about their absence. Yvonne remained at her post until she married at the age of twenty-four.[70]

The Eve of War

The crisis facing European Jews occasioned by the steady rise of Nazism remained the major concern of Annie Landau in the last years of her life. She had come of age when Anglo-Jewry was in the midst of its greatest era. The Jewish Board of Guardians, established in 1859, provided medical aid, vocational education, and housing support for poor Jewish immigrants. The Anglo-Jewish Association, founded in 1870, addressed civil and religious freedom for Jews in the Balkans and the Middle East.

Landau grew up as a proud Jewish Englishwoman. Although it bothered her that Jews in eastern Europe faced discrimination and poverty, propelling many to seek asylum in the West and to a lesser extent in Palestine, she shared the belief of emancipated Jews that they could live full Jewish lives in London or Frankfurt, where she had studied, or Paris, where her mother had been a student.

Landau had immigrated to Palestine to address the lamentable situation of Jews in the Holy City. She sought to raise the standard of living through education so that Jewish life could again flourish in the historic homeland, but she expected most Western Jews to continue to live comfortably in the European cities where they had established synagogues, schools, and a strong network of communal organizations. In the 1930s, with the growing threat to Jewish life in Europe, Landau questioned the belief that had been central to her life.

These doubts gradually led to changes in her thinking about the role of the Evelina de Rothschild School. In previous decades, Landau had supported the goal of the Anglo-Jewish Association that was adopted at its annual meeting in 1885: to educate the Jewish girls of the East. The reason for devoting funds to the vocational education of girls was stated clearly: "The Jewish community will never be able to raise its social status or make any substantial progress unless girls receive education in schools."[71]

Landau was selected to represent the interests of the Anglo-Jewish Association precisely because she had experience working in London with poor Jewish girls and was therefore prepared to offer the same type of education to the girls of Jerusalem. She had fulfilled this mission since her arrival in the city in 1899. However, the underlying principle of the school, that Jews from the West had something vital to teach to Jews in the East, was eroded with the rise of Hitler.

The premise of modern Jewish life in western Europe was built on the assumption of a quid pro quo: Jews would adopt new skills and values, enabling them to participate in all areas of modern life, and as a result, antisemitic hostility would cease. Jews would be able to enter higher education and the professions; they would enjoy civil rights, including the right to vote and to run for office. In return, the right of Jews as individuals to follow their religion would be guaranteed.

English, French, and German Jews urged their coreligionists in the towns and cities of the Ottoman Empire, the Levant, and eastern Europe to follow their path of successful integration into modern life. Thus, Jewish girls and boys in Baghdad and Damascus were urged to master the local language and to learn technical skills so that they would become part of the productive life of their cities and suffer less social and economic discrimination. Their efforts were only partly successful. Emerging nationalism and the outbreak of World War II proved the premise to be deeply flawed.

The Evelina de Rothschild School had become one of the most successful of the Anglo-Jewish schools, largely because of the superior leadership skills of Annie Landau. Cautiously, Landau questioned the principle on which she had developed her school. She began to believe that it was in Palestine, the historic homeland of the Jewish people, and not in Europe that the future of the Jewish people would be written.

Nevertheless, she remained wary of political Zionists and stayed loyal to the British despite their growing opposition to Jewish immigration to Palestine. She approved of British efforts to improve civic and cultural life in Jerusalem, and she was grateful that the Mandatory government provided professional employment for her graduates, giving young Jewish women opportunities to be self-sufficient and to assist their families. She continued to invite British officers to her social functions because they protected the school and assisted Evelina pupils in attending classes even when most of the city was under curfew.[72]

Landau remained deeply concerned with her students' physical welfare, but she simultaneously endeavored to encourage their commitment to community service. In 1938, she asked all her pupils—both longtime residents of Jerusalem and newcomers who had fled Germany—to contribute to a local relief fund established by Judah Magnes, the president of Hebrew University. The money went to aid the children of an Arab driver who had been shot on the road between Tel Aviv and Jerusalem.[73]

Whereas in earlier years Landau had sought to protect her pupils from the stress resulting from periodic violence in Jerusalem, in the late 1930s she placed her subscription copy of the *Palestine Post*, a Zionist newspaper widely read by the British community in Jerusalem, in the playroom for the girls to read and discuss with their friends and teachers. Some students heard about Arab attacks and German treachery against Jews at home, but it was in the playroom that they could confide their fears to their fellow students and seek guidance from the teachers about how to understand what was happening. Articles in the *Palestine Post* covered violence against Jews in Germany as well as stories about Jewish defiance of the restrictive immigration policies of the British.

An article on the front page of the May 18, 1939, issue proclaimed, "Britain's Blow Will Not Subdue Jews." The article asserted that the new policy for Palestine, known as the White Paper, violated the Balfour Declaration by denying to the Jewish people the right to reconstitute a national home in its ancestral land, since it decreed an end to immigration as soon as the Jewish inhabitants of the country became one-third of the population. The article concluded:

> The Jewish people regard this breach of faith as a surrender to Arab terrorism, a delivery of England's friends into the hands of its enemies. It widens the gulf between Jews and Arabs and destroys any prospect of peace in the country.
>
> The Jewish people will not acquiesce in such a policy. The new regime envisaged in the White Paper will be a regime of mere coercion devoid of any moral basis and contrary to international law.[74]

Landau was concerned that the growing violence against German Jews and the continued hostility of Arabs contributed to a pervasive sense of doom among her pupils. Having fought so hard to imbue her students with the feeling that they were capable and that they could contribute to solving the problems of their community, she responded to this new challenge by revising the school's celebration of Jewish holidays to focus on the national content of these festivals.[75]

Thus, Chanukah was still celebrated at school with candlelighting and prayers, but it was the story of the ancient struggle against foreign oppressors in Jerusalem that was now featured in song and dramatic presentations. Similarly, on Tu B'Shvat, the tree-planting holiday, fruit from the newly settled Jewish villages were distributed and blessings were recited on eating them, but now the importance of these villages as part of the national story gained prominence. Finally, Purim, always celebrated with costumes and joyful songs and dances, now focused on the heroism of Esther, a young Persian Jewish woman who saved her people. Through these celebrations, Landau built morale and slowly encouraged her students' commitment to a nation-centered Judaism.[76]

On September 4, 1939, the students reading the *Palestine Post* in the play-room read a statement by King George VI to the British Empire:

> For the second time in the lives of most of us, we are at war. Over and over again we have tried to find a peaceful way out of the differences between ourselves and those who are now our enemies, but it has been in vain. We have been forced into a conflict . . . to meet the challenge which, if it were to prevail, would be fatal to any civilized order in the world. It is the principle which permits a state in selfish pursuit of power to disregard treaties and solemn pledges, which sanctions the use of force or the threat of force against the sovereignty and independence of other States. Such a principle, stripped of all disguise, is merely the primitive doctrine that might makes right. . . . It is for this high purpose that I now call on my people at home and my people across the seas who will make our cause their own. I ask them to stand firm and calm, and unite in this time of trial . . . with God's help we shall prevail.[77]

The leadership of the Jewish community of Palestine quickly responded to the new challenge of war, pledging to aid Britain in its fight against Nazi Germany while continuing to protest British restrictions on Jewish immigration to Palestine. In June 1940, Landau was invited to participate in a ceremony at the Jerusalem Girls' College. Despite her preoccupations with the needs of German refugees and her hostility to the enrollment of Jewish girls at the college, Landau joined other dignitaries at Diploma Day, the first presentation of diplomas by the college since 1937.

High Commissioner Harold MacMichael and his wife presented the diplomas and addressed the pupils. The ceremony began with prayers led by Reverend George Herbert Martin. The Anglican bishop, Dr. Graham Brown, spoke on truth in all its aspects as the highest aim of education. The mayor of Jerusalem, Mustapha Bey Khalidi, proposed a vote of thanks to the college in Arabic. Winifred Coate, the principal, addressed the group in English; she reviewed the past three years, in which the demand for places in the college had grown despite the disturbances. She explained that to meet the demand, a separate kindergarten and elementary school had been opened in the German Colony in January 1940, and students in the teachers' training class of the college were able to practice there. After her talk, there was a display of folk dancing, a drill, and some singing games by the younger pupils.[78] Despite the deepening divisions in Jerusalem, Landau continued to believe in the possibility of intercommunal cooperation and exhibited this belief by attending the missionary school's ceremonial function.

A few months later, the sixty-seven-year-old Landau addressed her pupils. She had battled disease, poverty, and ignorance in the years leading to the First World War; she had worked with the British to build a model school for girls only to watch the country and her city be torn apart by riots; and she had worked with Ella Schwartzstein and Henrietta Szold to rescue orphans from Frankfurt. Now she commended the Girl Guides for working to aid the Social Service Association and for supporting Air Ambulances and Motor Life Boat Funds, inaugurated by the Girl Guide Association of England. Finally, she summoned the students' faith and courage:

> We hoped that the catastrophe of War would be averted, and that the oppressor would be turned from his evil ways. That was not to be, and today we pray that, although the full tide of War is let loose upon the world, God's mercy will ordain that Hatred and Persecution will give way to Love, Justice, and Toleration. We are grateful that the harsher side of War has not yet come to the Holy Land, but should the time ever come when sacrifice is demanded of us, we shall not, I am sure, be found lacking in the desire to give generously of all that is required of us. . . . The best contribution that you can make to the well-being and happiness of this country is to go about your work normally, with heads held high, faith in your hearts, and courage in every endeavor.[79]

[5]

SCHOOL MAGAZINE
The Girls Speak Out

The Evelina students were deeply influenced by the enduring British values of their headmistress, but their lives were also affected by the growing nationalism of their families and friends. They went about their schoolwork with resolve, offering friendship to the new students from Germany and expressing both pride in their own accomplishments and rousing school spirit.

The students—natives and newcomers—left a remarkable record of their feelings and ideas about their school, their city, their country, and the larger world in a unique publication, *School* magazine. Launched in 1935, when nearly all of Landau's dreams for the school had been realized, the magazine continued for six annual issues, ceasing publication in 1940 in response to wartime paper shortages. It was the last important innovation introduced by Landau.

School magazine was printed on high-quality paper, with a bright red cover featuring the Evelina de Rothschild School crest and motto: *Concordia, Integritas, Industria* (Harmony, Integrity, Industry). Like the curriculum of the school, the magazine was bilingual. It included stories and poems, puzzles and riddles, essays and games in Hebrew and English, written by pupils from prep A through the commercial class. Landau, who had taught her students to be self-confident, now encouraged them to give voice to their thoughts and feelings.

The magazine captures the essence of the Evelina students as they struggled to define themselves. The model of Landau, proper British and Orthodox Jewish, provided a framework for their identity building, but it was not a perfect fit for girls born in Jerusalem or for recent refugees from Nazi brutality. These young women addressed the conflicting values learned at home, from friends, and in school. Most became more clearly Zionist than their headmistress and teachers, believing that the Balfour Declaration would be fulfilled by the creation of a Jewish state in Palestine. However, like Landau, they were comfortable with complex identities. They maintained Jewish practices and worked for Zionist goals in Jerusalem. Simultaneously, they became English-speaking citizens of the world and Hebrew-speaking members of the founding generation of the state of Israel.

The issues of *School* magazine open a rare window into the interior world of these girls during the difficult years of Arab strikes and boycotts in Palestine and of the growing persecution of European Jews. Their writing allows us to read the feelings, hopes, and concerns of the Jewish girls of Jerusalem as they developed into young adults. Their essays, organized thematically below, speak eloquently about the memories of refugee students, the growing nationalism of all students, and the unique spirit of the Evelina de Rothschild School.

Refugee Memories

At the Evelina School there were many girls who had arrived with their families from English-speaking countries, some of whom continued to think fondly of their home countries while developing an appreciation for Palestine. One such girl, Honour Levine, a student in the commercial class, wrote about her feelings for Australia:

> The notes of the bellbird
> Are heard in the breeze,
> Mingled with the fragrance,
> From wattle-trees,
> And away in the west,
> Where the sunbeams show
> And the creek is a-gurgling,
> Where bulrushes grow,
> Where the gum-trees are waving,
> And wild violets blow,
> I can see the old home,
> I love and I know. . . .
> The crickets come out,

When the frogs 'gin to sing,
And the wild dingoes' howl
Makes the forest depths ring.
But amidst the quiet farm,
Where a sound is not heard,
Save the movement of cattle,
Or the cry of some bird,
Is peace, perfect peace,
Til the homestead is stirred,
By the call of the cock . . .
"Home's" a wonderful word.[1]

Unlike this unambiguously sunny memory of home, the memories of the daughters of recent refugees from Europe included conflicted feelings about their former homelands. These young girls had both happy and sad memories of their early years spent in German, Hungarian, Romanian, and Greek schools. In many Zionist schools, refugee children were advised to forget the past in order to become just like their Palestinian-born classmates. In contrast, at the Evelina School, refugee girls were encouraged to share their emotions as they struggled to adapt to life in their new land. They were provided ample opportunity to record their feelings in *School* magazine.

Ruth Karpf demonstrated considerable talent as a writer, but she had difficulty integrating into the Evelina School. She contributed two essays about Nuremberg, her former home, which provide insight into her dilemma. Ruth and her family arrived in Jerusalem sometime in 1934, the year after the burning of the Reichstag building in Berlin in February 1933. Ruth's pieces did not refer directly to the events that precipitated her family's flight, but it is clear that the abrupt changes accompanying their departure led to serious identity issues for the young girl. She was thirteen years old when she chronicled her journey.

FROM EUROPE TO ASIA

It was a dark and rainy day, when I left my native town of Nuremberg. After four hours in the overfilled compartment of the train, we reached the first town, which was Munich. Munich is the capital of Bavaria. It is a very nice town, and its church is famous all over the world. Now began the nice part of our journey;

our way went through the Alps. We saw high, high mountains covered all over with snow. Later on we saw what a great difference there was between these mountains and the rocks of Greece. Both ranges show the character of their country and its inhabitants.

On and on we went. Through the monotonous plains of Jugoslavia. At 8 o'clock in the evening we reached Italy . . . the port of Trieste. Before us lay houses and roads; we heard the noise and sounds of a big town; and behind all that lay the sea, dim and deep.

The next morning found us on deck of the big steamer "Pilsna." What a swarm of people! We saw yellow Chinese, black niggers [sic], white Europeans, and also a red Indian.

The Chaluzim on deck began to sing the "Hatikvah"; the last we saw on shore was a rabbi who blessed the ship. Slowly, slowly the shore disappeared, and an hour later, there was nothing more to be seen than the heavens and the water.

One day afterwards we reached Brindisi. . . . The ship stopped a second time at Larnaca, the capital of Cyprus. There we saw the first Arabs.

The next morning we reached Jaffa. Here was the end of our journey. We had arrived in Palestine—Eretz-Israel.[2]

Ruth's description of leaving Germany provides several clues to her high level of anxiety. First, she was crowded onto a train leaving Nuremberg, her "very nice town," on a "dark and rainy day" and settling into an "overfilled compartment." Her spirits picked up by the time the train reached Munich: "It is a very nice town, and its church is famous all over the world." This description might have been written for a travel brochure. In sightseeing mode, she continued to describe the scenic snow-covered Alps and the rocky landscape of Greece.

However, Ruth and her family were refugees, not tourists. Once they embarked on the *Pilsna*, they left the European world they knew for the Asian world with its unfamiliar people of many races and colors. Ruth's description of "yellow Chinese, black niggers, white Europeans, and red Indians" is an indication of the education in racial supremacy she had received in Nuremberg. Racial tension is also evident in Ruth's apprehension about the "swarm" of unfamiliar-looking passengers.

Ruth and her family were unsure of what awaited them in Palestine. The essay has a foreboding tone, moving from warm recollections of Europe to seeing her first Arabs and the arrival in Jaffa.

In the next issue of *School* magazine, Ruth contributed a second essay; this time she wrote specifically about the two cities that she called home. Her descriptive lines indicate that she was trying to feel more at home in Jerusalem.

NUREMBERG AND JERUSALEM

It is night! I stand on the balcony with my eyes turned to the East, where the Old City lies, and into my mind flash pictures of this old, interesting place which I visited this afternoon.

I think of those old, narrow alleys in which I strolled about for nearly four hours, of those mysterious dark bazaars with all the interesting oriental things in them.

Ruth's description was influenced by her European education, which portrayed Jerusalem as a place of Oriental mystery and interest. However, Ruth was beginning to see beyond the bazaars; she was trying to understand the unfamiliar people:

The strangest and most interesting things in the Old City are the people there. I remember that when I came here first, I felt as though I were in the Cinema. It was all so different, so odd and strange that I could not believe it was true. The sight of the first Jew with his "kaftan and shtrimel" made me think of a Purim fancy dress . . . what surprised me most of all was the Beduin. When I saw him in his dirty rags, sitting on the ground, I got so excited that I grasped the camera from my brother's hand to take a picture of him, because I thought that never again in my life would I see anybody like him.

Ruth was struggling to find a place for herself in this new environment. In Nuremberg she had developed her identity as a European child. In Jerusalem her sense of self began to change. However, she felt as distant from Jews in traditional eastern European garb as from the Bedouin in their flowing robes. Intrigued by her new surroundings, she believed that having lived in Palestine for eighteen months, she should be used to these sights; nevertheless, each time she visited the Old City she was astonished anew. Ruth was representative of the girls whose identities were formed in Europe before they arrived in Jerusalem.

Conversely, her remarks about the Western Wall signal her emerging Jewish identity:

> The time I first visited the Wailing Wall will always stay in my memory. I saw Jews from all the world standing and praying to God. There were Europeans and natives, Jews from all parts of Asia and Africa. But there was one spirit among them all, mourning for their lost country and Temple.

Ruth's struggle to define herself as a member of the Jewish family was conflicted because of her remaining positive memories of Nuremberg:

> My thoughts sometimes fly back to Nuremberg and her Old City, which is so different from the one here. Her alleys are also narrow and stony, but there is sun and light in them; instead of the dark, mysterious bazaars, there are small, old houses built in baroque or renaissance style with high, red, slate roofs. Everything is quiet and still, because the people who once lived there are dead long ago and no one lives there nowadays.
>
> But although nobody is present, there is some sort of atmosphere pervading which causes one to think of the past and picture imaginary people walking in the streets—ladies with wide silk frocks and whole gardens on their hair and men with wigs all covered with powder. And then the famous people who once may have walked through those streets: Gustavus Adolfus, the mighty conqueror; Albrecht Durer, the famous painter; and Johann Uhland, the wonderful poet.

Living in Jerusalem, Ruth found it increasingly difficult to identify with the city of her birth and its current inhabitants. Her memory of the city was more like a fairy tale than the Nuremberg of recent years, where racial laws were enacted against the Jews. Ruth's rather simplistic conclusion in this article betrays her inability to comprehend the changed circumstances of her life: "Cities are so different," she wrote. "The one is Orient and the other Occident, yet they have one thing in common, a wonderful, mysterious and interesting past."[3]

Leah Schoenberger, a newcomer from Frankfurt, also revealed her struggle with identity in *School* magazine. She wrote an essay presenting Frankfurt to her fellow students. She started with geography, noting that Frankfurt lies in the center of Germany, with the Main River flowing through the fertile fields surrounding the city. Historically, Leah pointed out, Frankfurt was the town in which kings and emperors were crowned in great coronation festivals. The old city of Frankfurt had such narrow streets with houses so close together that two people on opposite sides of the street could reach out through their windows to shake hands. In the center of the old city stood the Cathedral, the "Dom," the guardian of the town.

MY NATIVE TOWN

Formerly there were great walls surrounding the whole town. They have been demolished, however, and instead of the walls there are today lovely prom-enades.... There is the Palmgarten with its exotic plants, the Zoo which is said to be one of the largest in Europe, [and] many interesting museums. Goethe, the great German poet, was born in Frankfurt, and today we can still see the house in which he was born.[4]

Leah's historical overview omits the *judengasse*, the narrow and fetid streets of the Jewish ghetto that confined Jews for five hundred years. She didn't mention that the walls of the city were torn down as a result of the Napole-onic invasion and that the exotic plants in the Palmgarten were planted and maintained by one of Frankfurt's leading Jews, Amschel Rothschild.[5] Later in her essay she referred to the fact that within the past few years many Jews had emigrated because it was practically impossible for them to carry on their professions and businesses. However, she continued to feel loyalty to her city, proudly describing the building of the Frankfurt aerodrome and the completion of the Frankfurt terminus of the Reichsautobahn that ran throughout Germany. Leah felt a continuing connection to her natal city, concluding, "I liked living in Frankfurt and I hope I shall one day see again the town where I was born."[6]

A year later, Leah Schoenberger contributed a second article about Frankfurt; this one conveyed tragic news of the destruction of the Frankfurt synagogue.

IN MEMORY OF THE FRANKFURT SYNAGOGUE

The magnificent synagogue no longer exists! I could not believe it. My first feeling was as if a dear friend had suddenly died in the prime of life. But this holy building meant even more than a friend to me; it was the symbol of Jewish life in our town.

Like the friend "in the prime of life," the synagogue was not old; it had been erected about thirty years before, at a time of peace and prosperity for the Jews of Frankfurt.

It stood there surrounded by lovely promenades like a king's palace, and even the non-Jews could not but admire it. The majestic building kept the splendor of its first years, and during the recent persecutions it still radiated much of its former glory and inspired every one of us with hope. How imposing was the aspect of the hall on the Sabbath and festivals! The Ark containing many Torah scrolls, the richly embroidered curtain, the broad marble steps covered with carpets, and the hanging lamps with their radiant light—all made a profound impression on us. Children saw only the light, and enjoyed it, but grown-ups understood the deeper meaning of the light in the house of God. When, on the Day of Atonement, we fasted and prayed in it, we became united like a big family; and during the Concluding Service, when the sun casts its lasts rays upon the large square stones, every one of us felt God's presence.[7]

With the destruction of the Frankfurt Synagogue, Leah's idyllic memories of Frankfurt ended. Her goal was now to help the Jews of her city. The destroyed synagogue reminded Leah and others who had fled the city of the suffering of Frankfurt's Jews. Following the example set by Landau, she concluded, "We tried to help them as much as we could."

One of Leah's classmates, Zipporah Rosenblut, had very fond memories of her natal city, Budapest. She eagerly anticipated her visit there in 1937. However, she was soon made aware that the city was no longer her home. Her essay begins with a frenzy of emotion.

I REVISIT HUNGARY

The train was fast nearing the border, swallowing up kilometer after kilometer. The passengers prepared their luggage for inspection. Men playing cards stopped their game, and ladies glanced into the mirror for the last time. The slowness with which the luggage was examined made me so impatient that angry tears came into my eyes. My heart was too full of emotion at the thought of seeing Hungary again to tolerate the delay. At last, the rushing train stopped with a great screech, and the noise and bustle of the people descending from the train made my head whirl.[8]

Soon Zipporah was lost in a world of memories; she imagined her nurse playing hide-and-seek with her little brother in the garden, her white poodle running after her into the kitchen, and a "wonderful gypsy wedding!" She remembered the peasant boys wearing big hats trimmed with "Orphan Roses," knitted shirts that buttoned all the way down, and trousers that reached to their boots. The girls wore white dresses with aprons and kerchiefs on their heads. The boys played drums and fiddles and danced around with the girls.

Zipporah's happy reverie was shattered by the sound of people whispering: "More unpleasant Jews!" "Confounded Jews!" The words made her shudder. Hungarians who had been kindly disposed to the Jews when she was a child were now hostile. Disappointed, her thoughts turned to Palestine. She wrote:

Till recently Palestine was (and we hope it will be again) a land of peaceful toil and study. The pleasant chant of the Torah is heard in the early dawn and little boys recite from Isaiah:

For out of Zion shall go forth the law, And the word of the Lord from Jerusalem. . . .

Hungary is a land where metals are turned into ammunition; a country where iron becomes a gun and steel a sword. The words heard at daybreak are the commands of soldiers at Reveille.[9]

Thus, Zipporah juxtaposed the vision of peaceful Palestine with that of warlike Hungary. She continued to describe the Jews of Hungary, who were occupied with their own troubles and could not attend to anybody's affairs but their own, while the Jews of Palestine, in her view, felt the joys as well as the sorrows of their brethren in faraway lands. The words *Israel* and *Jerusalem* filled young Zipporah's heart with longing. It was now clear to her that Eretz Israel was the land for all the Jews. She ended her essay with a reference to a Jewish prayer: "If I forget thee, O Jerusalem, let my right hand forget its cunning."

The essays written by European refugees were instructive to all the Evelina students. Those who hailed from different cities, such as Nuremberg, Frankfurt, and Budapest, learned of their shared disappointment. Those who were born in Jerusalem understood the importance of helping new arrivals; they saw their task as an opportunity to serve the Jewish world, a value taught by their headmistress. The Evelina School was unique in giving refugee girls a place in their new country that did not ask them to denounce their past.[10]

Emerging Nationalism

Palestine is frequently called Eretz Israel, a name that emphasizes the Jewish people's connection to the land, in *School* magazine, which is replete with Zionist tropes such as blooming oranges, nutritious milk, and thriving pioneers. There are few references to the Arab inhabitants of the land, while there are many descriptions of the heroic Jewish farmer. When Arabs appear, the images are for the most part fearsome or stereotypically exotic. These stories and essays exhibit the strong attachment to the land, expressed though a variety of loving images, felt by the young Evelina girls as they developed their identities in a politically charged climate.

The appreciation for Zionist agriculture reached its peak with love for oranges. Ruth Karpf, the refugee from Nuremberg, explained that the ground on which the orange trees stood was not very long ago a stony desolate wilderness. Jewish pioneers armed with bravery, idealism, and a strong will to struggle against the sand and the stone had fought one of the hardest and noblest battles in history. They succeeded wonderfully in planting little seeds that had grown into trees, with blossoms, leaves, and fruit. Ruth declared her love for the taste of the oranges; she believed that the fruit built strong bodies, and she was happy to support the orange industry. She explained, "I like to do my tiny share in helping my country. Sentimentally, I drink the juice because for me it stands as the symbol of rejuvenated Palestine." In a lyrical vein she searched for additional reasons to love orange juice:

WHY I DRINK FRESH ORANGE JUICE

Or is it the beauty of an orange grove? At night the moon shines on their dark green foliage and makes the heavy, golden fruit glitter under its light. Their strong, sweet scent fills the air like incense and makes one dizzy and dreamy.

Did you ever lie down beneath those trees and breathe this air, till you fell asleep, only to dream of their beauty again?

Her poetic reflections link the ancient history of the Jews with the pioneering spirit of Zionist planters:

Or is it their history or their beauty? Is it both? Or is there still something else around this fruit that makes me love it so? Is it the idealism of its planters that has made it so sweet, or the holiness of our forefathers' earth that had made it so luscious? I don't know. But I do know that for me and my brothers and sisters here and in all of Palestine, it stands as a symbol of our work, our fight, and our success.[11]

Ruth ended her essay with a call to all Jews in Palestine to drink orange juice for their health and to help the development of their country. This essay was selected by Landau to represent the school in a competition sponsored by the Citrus Juice Advertising Committee and judged by the Department of Education. Ruth won second prize. Although she was a troubled girl who was later dismissed from school for fraternizing with British officers, her youthful essay shows that she had absorbed Zionist ideas about the majesty of the land and its produce.

Ziona Caspi, a native Jerusalemite, wrote about the daily distribution of milk to Evelina pupils that helped to build strong bodies and provided the vitality and energy the girls needed to study for exams. In her view, milk consumption also became a way to help the development of the nation. The title of her essay exhibits some knowledge of astronomy and a fine sense of humor.

"THE MILKY WAY!"

The first lesson has barely ended when the pupils of the Evelina de Rothschild School stream into the playground to receive their daily milk. . . . The Commercial Class girls look very important as they keep a watchful eye on the little ones and supervise the distribution. . . .

I taste one sip of milk, "How delicious!" With the second sip I think, "How refreshing!" With the third, "How splendid and nourishing!" . . . I think how milk helps to build up our body, giving us energy, vitality, and health, and oh dear! how we need these three, especially the bigger girls who have to spend long hours in difficult studies.... I think of all the good that this consumption of milk will do for the country. Why, even we, mere children, can help in the material part of building up Palestine. With thousands of children drinking milk every day, many a hitherto unemployed man will be engaged in work.... I think how slowly, but surely, Palestine is showing herself in her true colours, as a fertile country with a rich soil, "a land flowing with milk and honey."[12]

Leah Azulay shared the Zionist sentiments of Ziona Caspi and Ruth Karpf. Her essay lauded the accomplishments of the agricultural pioneers who worked the land. She wrote the following on a trip to visit the northern settlement overlooking the countryside from Afuleh.

A TRIP TO THE EMEK

Fields full of crops extended on all sides. The corn moved with the wind, whispered to me and said, "Stretch out beneath my shade and I will tell you the story of the Emek."... The wind caressed me and the corn said, "Do you see all these wonders? They have only been in existence for fifty years. Before that this place was no more than a wild desert. Not a human being was to be seen here, save only the Beduin who wandered about pasturing their flocks. Then came an "Aliyah" of Jewish youths who made it their aim to redeem the land and prepare it for Jewish settlements.... Many of those pioneers fell, victims to malaria and fever, and many of those who escaped were killed by the Beduin.... But ... they would not forsake their ideal. For every one who fell, ten others came to take his place.

Leah's description echoes those of several classmates in recreating the nationalist mythology of a barren land settled by heroic young pioneers and turned into a paradise. She continued her trip to Ein-Harod, where she saw the peaks of the Gilboa Mountains, remembered the prophet Deborah, and saw the new school of agriculture built by the British government with funds donated by Sir Ellis Kadoorie. She ended her trip brimming with pride in the accomplishments of Jewish pioneers, identifying with them, and vowing to continue their work: "I, too, will be among the builders of the land, among those who can proudly say, 'Our hands did these wonders; we created all this.'"[13]

Some students wrote about the beauty of rural kibbutz life as well as the need to guard the settlements from Arab intruders. These stories often associate physical bravery with boys and men. Sarah Lorberbaum, class3, wrote a playlet titled "Courage." The story takes place on a kibbutz consisting of ten huts surrounded by a cactus hedge. At the opening of the story, the father and the older son of a family go off to help build a new kibbutz farther north. While they are gone, their kibbutz is attacked. Young David, eight years old, saves the kibbutz by stealthily going out to find help. David's mother and baby sister are saved. The play ends with a toast to the young hero.[14]

In another story, "A Week on Kfar Saba" by Chana Loshinksy, class 4, we witness the influence of nationalist sentiment in her visit to the settlement and her appreciation for her uncle, to whom she referred as a real "halutz," a pioneer. She made these observations:

> At six o'clock, before we went to bed, the young men of the colony were sent in all directions to keep guard. I saw them move off, their guns slung across their shoulders. These guns were their only protection. How I wished I were one of them. Oh, how I longed to be a boy and go with them!

Chana recognized the gender roles at Kfar Saba, but, tellingly, in her dream she is the one with a gun:

> I dreamt I was on guard and heard someone say in broken Hebrew, "Who's there?" . . . I felt in my right pocket and found a Mauser pistol, took it out, and just as I had my hand on the trigger, the alarm clock went off and I awoke.

On her last day, she said good-bye to her new friends: the two red cows, the leader of the goats, the dog, and all the poultry. She concluded, "How I love life on the farm! What good fortune to have had the opportunity of spending some time there during the holidays."[15]

Chana's visit to the kibbutz confirmed her predisposition to believe in the beauty of rural life, but she also became aware of the privileging of men's roles as defenders of Jewish settlement life in an area surrounded by hostile neighbors.

Rolande Valero class 3, was also influenced by the nationalist sentiment of the period, but she saw a different aspect of rural life. Her description of a visit to Givat Brenner included cows and hens but also referred to the communal dining room and the communal reading and music room. She noted the kibbutz rest house built by Jessie Sampter, an American children's writer whose books were read at the Evelina School. She mentioned that there was a children's orchestra that were planning songs for Tu B'Shvat.[16] This Evelina student focused on the communal aspects of kibbutz life rather than on the dangers of living in remote areas of the country.

It is clear that many Evelina pupils visited agricultural settlements during school holidays as a result of growing nationalist sentiment, which encouraged love for the land. One of them, Miriam Indik, class 7, wrote a paean to Palestine, emphasizing its rural nature.

MY HOMELAND

"Ah, my homeland, how beautiful you are!" burst from my lips. I stood gazing at the wonderful scene before me. The glittering dew-drops on the green grass and on the trees looked like so many sparkling diamonds. The sweet smell of the flowers filled the warm air with fragrance, while here and there a butterfly fluttered in and out of the flowers. Yonder the corn-fields looked like an ocean rippling in the breeze. . . . I gazed on at the fields and the hazy mountains which stood silent and watchful. . . .

Ah, what a wonderful smell comes from the orange groves! Over there walks the land-worker behind his plough, the sweat pouring from his brow. His song fills the air with music and the birds seem to accompany him.

Palestine, my homeland! I love thee in days of great heat, when the sand burns under the feet and all the world is parched with thirst. I love thee on moonlit nights, when the world is covered with a blanket of lights and shadows. I love thee in happy days when I wish to sing and dance without a stop, and in sad days when tears roll down and the heart aches—I always love thee. I wish I had arms big enough to embrace thee, my homeland, from Dan to Beersheba, and hold thee tight in my heart.[17]

Whereas Miriam saw only Jewish dwellers from Dan to Beersheba, a few others, like Elka Eden, saw Jews and Arabs living side by side in peace. Elka described her town, Romema, a new neighborhood that stood alone on a hill outside Jerusalem, with ten big houses surrounded by gardens. Romema was important to modern Jerusalem because it housed two reservoirs that supplied water to the city. It had historic importance as well, since the prophet

Samuel's tomb was visible to the north of the town. At night the residents of Romema could see the lights of Jerusalem and Ramallah.

Elka explained that not far from Romema was the Arab village of Lifta. It was here that she became familiar with the beauty of traditional Arab village life. She especially appreciated the weddings in Lifta, which were preceded by a week of celebrations. A marriage ceremony always took place on a Friday, and the villagers would walk around Romema singing and dancing. Adolescent literature of the time often included lavish descriptions of Bedouin weddings; perhaps Elka saw the Arabs of Lifta through some of these dramatic images. However, Elka also knew the Arabs of Lifta as farmers who kept cows, hens, and geese and grew vegetables, providing fresh eggs, milk, and produce to the residents of Romema every day. Elka's description of the relations between the Arabs of Lifta and the Jews in Romema contained no hint of disapproval or hostility.[18]

Elka's appreciation for her Arab neighbors who continued to provide for the Jewish families of Romema was a refutation of the Zionist view of the importance of Jewish self-sufficiency. Her sympathetic view of Jews and Arabs living side by side in cooperation is highly unusual. Several of her classmates wrote about their love of their homeland in ways that ignored the presence of Arabs. Others wrote in exotic language about Arabs, and still others expressed hostility to Arabs for their cruelty. The next two stories exemplify these last two approaches.

Twelve-year-old Hannah Saltzman saw her Arab neighbors as exotic but laudable men and women. She wrote in the voice of a *piastre*, a small coin, telling the story of a traditional Arab woman.

A DAY IN THE LIFE OF A PIASTRE

I was found by an Arab who gave me as a present to his wife on the day of their marriage.

She made a chain of piastres, placed me in the centre, and then tied the chain around her head. When I first came I was bright, my face shone and looked as if I always smiled at those who saw me. But alas! Now I am old, have no more luster, and am worn out. Very seldom do I see the sun shine, because my lady goes out very little. . . .

Even though I am old, my lady still loves me very much because every time she looks at me she is reminded of her wedding day.[19]

Whereas Hannah imagined the beloved existence of a small coin in the possession of an Arab woman, Margalit Rubovitz adopted a harsh tone in her depiction of the voice of a camel to paint Arab behavior in a brutish and cruel manner:

A DAY IN THE LIFE OF A CAMEL

Early in the morning, before the sun rises and shines in all its glory upon the earth, I am awakened by a kick from my master and given about five minutes in which to eat as much, or, as my master would rather have it, as little, as possible. When the five minutes are over, I am commanded to lie down and a saddle is fastened upon my back. My master then gets into it and my day's work begins.

Slowly I walk through the hot desert. My feet burn as if they are on fire. I become thirsty and look about me for a drop of water. . . . Oh, to have a rest! To be able to sit down beneath the shade of a tree, with a spring of water on one side . . . all of a sudden my dream comes to an abrupt end, for my master has given a shout. "Eeou, eeou! Go faster! Hurry up! . . .

It is now noon and the hot sun shines down upon my back as if it cannot find any greater pleasure than burning a hole through my skin. My wish for a drink of water has not been fulfilled. . . . Suddenly I feel my master lurch forward. "Thank God!" I say to myself, for I realize that he has fallen asleep. I can now go at any speed I please, for I need not fear his kicks or shouts.

Twilight changes into evening. A heaven full of twinkling stars is above us. I am again at peace with the world. . . . We camp in a cool spot. . . . I dream of a stream of water that goes along with me and never dries up.[20]

In another essay, Margalith developed her negative image of Arabs along familiar Zionist lines. She saw Palestine as a backward wasteland that had responded to development by Jewish immigrants. She explained that less than a century ago, Palestine had been a desert, but it had since become one of the most prosperous countries and the most civilized in the Near East. In her view, this was a result of the immigration of Jews from the four corners of the earth who "left their riches or their misery" and came to the Holy Land to cultivate and revive it.

These immigrants had achieved a great deal despite the many challenges they faced, building the new city of Tel Aviv, the seaport of Haifa, the agricultural colonies, and the new quarters of Jerusalem. Margalit looked askance at Arab culture, ignored British support, and recognized only the successful efforts of Jewish immigrants to Palestine. She concluded with fervor, "Palestine has grown, is growing, and will continue to grow and become the most important spot in the universe."[21]

The Holy City, witness to periodic violence in the 1930s, was also the subject of many stories and essays featured in *School* magazine. Whereas some Zionist schools taught that urban life was a deviation from the ideal of kibbutz life, the Evelina School encouraged pupils to love Jerusalem for its historic significance and to appreciate the modernization of the city during the British Mandate. The students' stories reflect daily life in the Old City and in the new quarters, and they capture the unique juxtaposition of ancient stones existing side by side with gaslit streets and electrified homes. Some stories echo the fear caused by the strikes and boycotts.

Jehudith Hurwitz, thirteen years old, wrote humorously about the annual custom of renegotiating the rent at Muharram, the Muslim New Year (which she calls "Muharim"). In Jerusalem, many Jews rented apartments from Muslim landlords who owned apartments in both the Old City and outside the walls. The tenants were obliged to agree on a new price or to seek a new dwelling. In 1935, there were few trucks available for moving; poor families made do with the services of a *sabal*, a man who hauled household goods on his back. Jehudith described this in her story.

THE TRIALS AND TRIBULATIONS OF "MUHARIM"

All the furniture of five rooms was crowded before me in my once charming bedroom. The new tenants had already moved into our flat, but we could not get out because our flat-to-be was still occupied. What mean things they said about our being there! As if we could help it! Piles of dishes to the right of me! Unbelievable heaps of furniture to the left of me! Sauce-pans and frying pans volleying and thundering at intervals to the floor!

Jehudith was sent by her mother to find a *sabal*. She looked in Meah Shearim, in the Old City, and in Mahane Yehuda, the outdoor marketplace, all to no avail. Finally, she was directed to the Bukharan quarter and found a *sabal*, a little thin wiry man about five feet tall, who agreed to do the job. She continued:

I took him home. My father was waiting for us. Beds, chairs, boxes gradually found themselves tied to the man's back. He was no longer human—but some huge, gigantic creature who kept, of his original form, only his feet. Would he break in half? He seemed so bent over! I kept looking at him in dismay though I knew right well that he would return very shortly to get three or four more similar loads.

Muharim, how glad I was when it was over![22]

Although the dramatic moves associated with Muharram happened only once a year, there were daily street sounds that affected thirteen-year-old Hadassah Margalit. Her humorous piece captured the familiar sounds of Jerusalem in 1939.

NOISES IN MY STREET

"Gaaaaaz! Gaaaaaaz!" This one word is the first thing that strikes my ears when I awaken. The petrol seller must be a very musically inclined fellow, for he begins the word "gaaaaaz" on low Doh and ends up on high Doh. As if his delightful voice is not enough, his donkey accompanies him with a loud hee-haw.

Hadassah continued with a description of the cars and buses with their grinding brakes and the sound of church bells. Then she heard a loud bang, which she first thought was gunfire and later recognized to be the opening of window shutters. Workmen appeared on the scaffolding of the new houses being built nearby, and their planks falling to the ground added to the cacophony. Soon after, the "opera singers" arrived—Mr. Buyer of Old Clothes and Mr. Primus Mender. They kept up their arias for a long time. The housewives then entered the musical discourse. The thwacking of carpets was accompanied by songs to pass the day. These sounds were joined by those of the newspaper boys trying to sell their papers by outshouting each other. Hadassah concluded this musical visit to her neighborhood as follows:

As if all this noise is not enough, the radio shop turns on one of the sets as loudly as possible; the piano teacher in the next house is giving a lesson to a pupil who plays without a scrap of feeling; the dogs begin to bark, motorists toot their horns, and I resolve to put cotton-wool into my ears to rest my aching head.[23]

Some students, like Hasidah Rakover, class 4, were aware of the variety of people they saw around them in Jerusalem:

It is possible to see in Jerusalem people from nearly all the nations of the world, each with his own habits and customs.

On feast days we see Orthodox Jews going through the Old City to the Wailing Wall, some of them wearing a "shtreimel" [a velvet hat with a fur brim], and most of them with beards and side-curls.

We also see Christian priests, wearing long flowing garments and sandals on their feet, hurrying to church.

We come across Moslems who have quite a different form of worship. During their prayers, they turn in the direction of Mecca and kiss the earth three times.

There are also Orthodox Christian Arabs who wear European clothes, and who previously wore a "tarbush" or red fez on their heads, but now that the fez is forbidden they wear a "kefiyeh" instead with an "agal" of cord.

There are also Ethiopians with their special customs and Yemenites too.[24]

Hasidah believed that all these nationalities made Jerusalem a very cosmopolitan city.

For the Evelina students, Jerusalem was both home with its funny quirks and the Holy City with deep meaning embedded in every stone. They were young girls, carefree and full of joyful youth, and simultaneously members of the Jewish people, whose history in Jerusalem intruded into their daily thoughts and helped to form their identities. Their school curriculum taught them about the history of the city: its role as a Jewish capital as well as the disasters of destruction and exile.

For the most part they were shielded from violence and curfews by virtue of the fact that they were Evelina students, protected by the British administration when they were in the vicinity of the school. However, during the years of the Arab Revolt (1936–1939), years of boycotts, strikes, and violence, Jerusalem was also a source of fear for some students. Whereas Jehudith and Hadassah responded to the trials of Jerusalem life with humor, sixteen-year-old Rachel Harris wrote about her fear of the Old City and its Arab inhabitants.

LOST IN THE OLD CITY

It was a dark and desolate night, when I found myself in the Old City, looking for our neighbour's boy, who had been missing all day.

I kept shouting Yosef, Y-o-s-e-f, but got no answer, except weird echoes which disturbed the silence. It was bitterly cold. I kept moving on, trembling with fear. I looked at the sky and suddenly saw a star falling. This made me feel much more frightened. The lamps on the corners shook in the wind, making alarming and mysterious shadows on the wall. I tumbled over a peasant who was fast asleep on the ground. He began shouting, but I ran away as fast as I could, only to bump into a man, who was wearing spectacles, which broke with a crash on my head. . . .

You can imagine the trials and tribulations I went through, but worst of all was to see my shadow on the wall, which made me think someone was following me. . . .

At last, dizzy and dirty, I found myself outside the Old City. To my great surprise, I saw that horrible Yosef standing with his hands in his pockets, near Jaffa Gate. I shall never forget that awful night.[25]

Rachel's story described terror in the Old City. Her classmate Miriam Cohen, on the other hand, described her feeling of security near the Western Wall, the most important place to Jews in the Old City:

THE WESTERN WALL

The Wall seems to be receiving . . . all the prayers of the Jews who have been coming thousands of years. . . . One day it will . . . tell all its memories and all the events it saw since it was part of the Temple. . . . It still remembers how King Solomon's slaves worked so hard, brought stones from the quarries, cut them by making holes, and in them put pieces of wood and poured water on them. The wood expanded and thus the big stones broke into pieces and from that they easily made the shapes they needed. They arranged them one on top of the other and got the present wall. . . . It remembers too when it was crowded in Shavuoth with thousands of people carrying baskets full of the first fruits on their shoulders. . . . How joyful did the wall look then and how beautiful this place was!

But from that terrible day, the day of destruction, it seems to have fallen into a deep dream, and to think a great deal about what, I wonder? I hope it is about the Redemption of the Jews.[26]

Naomi Teitelbaum, an American student, in an essay written to celebrate the fortieth anniversary of Annie Landau's arrival in Jerusalem, used the

FIGURE 5.1 Photograph of Annie Landau from
School magazine *Courtesy of the Jerusalem Municipal Archive*

rhetoric of Zionism as a vehicle to praise Landau, who was sometimes accused of being anti-Zionist and criticized for being "too British." Here she is lauded for being a "special kind of pioneer." Naomi declared that not all pioneering involved cows and hens. She pointed to the significant contributions made by her headmistress in the field of girls' education at a pivotal moment in the foundation of Zionism.

She explained, "Forty years ago when our movement was still in diapers and our country was empty and neglected, without the necessary means of daily life, Miss Landau came to our country." Teitelbaum, referring to Zionism as "our movement," noted that Landau left a cultured, sophisticated European life that was comfortable in every way to contribute to a gloomy wasteland. She asked rhetorically, "Is there a higher form of pioneering?"

Naomi repeated the often-told apocryphal story of the little school Landau had found on her arrival, with a small number of girls sitting on the ground around a *maestra*, using the walls as blackboards. In four decades, Naomi wrote, Landau built a formidable institution whose graduates take the London matriculation exam, and later, as Old Girls, remain connected to the school.

> What do we wish Miss Landau to celebrate her fortieth year? To learn more Torah—she already had Torah learning. To achieve greatness—she already achieved greatness. To be accorded respect—she already had respect. So we wish that her pupils will be like her.[27]

Naomi Teitelbaum's encomium to Landau revealed her understanding of the historic mission of the school and of the pivotal moment of Jewish history in which she lived. Her identification with Landau's mission was clear in her appreciation. Teitelbaum lifted Landau to the highest pinnacle she could imagine by promising to follow in her footsteps. This was the Evelina spirit cultivated by the formidable headmistress.

The Evelina Spirit

Annie Landau admired the British for their confidence in their ability to get things done well, despite obstacles. Nevertheless, during the 1930s her vision of the future for the Jewish people began to change. In her introduction to the first issue of *School* magazine, she voiced both her loyalty to King George V and her belief that the opportunity to serve the Jewish people might be greater in Eretz Israel than elsewhere. Her enthusiasm for Jewish life in Palestine continued to be influenced by love for her pupils, whose affection for the country was unfiltered by memories of a peaceful European childhood.

Landau's dual sympathies to England and to Eretz Israel were evident in the curriculum and in after-school activities of the Evelina de Rothschild School. Despite growing Jewish nationalism, Evelina girls remained deeply respectful of English tradition and culture. They saw no conflict between the Jewish national ideal and their love and respect for England. Their essays reflect this unique Evelina spirit.

For some, like Miffy Nurock and Shulamit Hyamson, daughters of British officials, loyalty to England was something they learned from their parents and on visits home to England as well as in school. For others, it was an identity they learned from their schoolbooks and in their Girl Guide activities, and it was reinforced by their affection for the headmistress and the teachers, most of whom were English. It was solidified in their celebrations of the monarchy, British holidays, and special events. In 1936, students in the commercial class were required to write essays in appreciation of King George V.

Mary Hanbridge, the former headmistress of the Central Foundation School in London, visited Jerusalem that year and was asked to select the best essay for a prize. She gave the award to Gerda Kaplowitz for her work, "The King Is Dead, Long Live the King." Gerda's appreciation of King George was tied to his support for Jews who wished to return to Palestine. She noted that the king had earned a special place in Jewish history for declaring, "It is written in the Bible that the Jews will return to Palestine, and I am happy that my country will help to this end." Gerda added, "Today, when Jews in other countries are being driven out of the places in which they were born, they look to Palestine in confidence, to the land and the government, to find a new home." She continued:

> A peace-loving King was King George V. Although the World War broke out during his reign and England had to take part in it, it was not his will that soldiers should be shot; even the thought of a victory did not lessen his sadness for the price he paid.
>
> An uncommon veneration and love of the English subjects for their sovereign was shown at the Silver Jubilee last year.[28]

FIGURE 5.2 Frutiger House, decorated for the coronation, 1937

When Hanbridge returned to London, she sent the essay to the royal family. Landau was thrilled to learn that she had received a reply indicating that His Majesty expressed pleasure and interest in reading it.

Following the death of George V, Evelina pupils followed the news about the abdication of Edward VIII and the coronation of George VI. Jerusalem was festooned with lights and flags for the occasion. *School* magazine included several pieces about the big celebration.

Rachel Frankel contributed a Hebrew essay, "Jerusalem on the Night of the Coronation." She described the great joy of the people who marveled at the illuminated streets and the English and Hebrew flags flying from the buildings of the Jewish Agency and the Jewish National Fund. The King David Hotel "drowns in a sea of colors and lights. Its decorations are done with wisdom and taste; the whole building is like the image of a crown, symbolizing the crown of the King."

Rachel was proud of the role played by the Evelina School: "In the midst of the decorated buildings our school excels, flying hundreds of flags and pictures of the King." She concluded, "Sounds of music and singing come from every direction ... this is the first time in Jerusalem's existence since the destruction that she takes part in such great happiness."[29]

In another essay, Ziona Caspi described the participation of Evelina students in honor of the occasion:

THE CORONATION IN JERUSALEM

For us, the girls of the Evelina de Rothschild School, the celebration of the Coronation began on Tuesday, May 11, when after an inspiring talk by Miss Landau, we were given adorable coronation buttons which we proudly pinned on. Later in the day we received yellow mugs with the portraits of Their Majesties on them. How lovely they were! I shall treasure mine forever! And our School! Oh, it was beautifully decorated with innumerable gay flags and electric lights! There was a huge sign, "Long May He Reign!" ...

Jerusalem looked a thousand times more beautiful than usual on Coronation Eve. As seen from my house in Talpiot, it was ablaze with myriads of coloured lights. Driving through the town, one felt the excitement in the air. It seemed as if the whole population was out in the streets. The wall of the Old City, floodlit in glory, did not look its ancient self, but [like] a beautiful painting. Government House, on its hill, seemed to float in the air. King David Hotel was framed in dazzling light. Our school was magically transformed into a dream fantasy....

As a Guide, together with 180 Rangers, Guides, and Brownies of the School, I was to see the Military Parade which was to be held at the Talavera Barracks.... It was magnificent! Yes it was. After His Excellency took the salute, a short inspection was made by General Dill. Then the soldiers marched in full swing, to the rhythm of the military band. Aeroplanes droned overhead. The High Commissioner then distributed decorations to a few people—and how thrilled we were to learn from our teachers that our own dear Headmistress was to receive a coronation medal, too....

At 11 a.m. the whole Coronation Service was broadcast.... We felt as though we were actually there, for the description of the whole ceremony was so colourful and vivid that when I closed my eyes I could just picture everything in my mind. The gilded carriage rolling along the streets followed by the military parade amidst a crowd of cheering people; their Majesties in Westminster Abbey, in their magnificent robes and sparkling crowns; the Royal family, Peers, and other great men who made up the audience.

Ziona's celebration of the coronation, like Gerda's appreciation of George V, explicitly linked the students' loyalty to England to British support for building a Jewish homeland in Palestine. Ziona ended her essay with a prayer: "Dear God in Heaven, King of Kings, let us, the Jews, who are trying to build up a home under His Majesty's Mandate, let us find favour in his eyes and let us find in him a true friend as we found in his late father."[30]

Appreciation for the monarchy and for English culture did not exist at the expense of appreciation for Jerusalem and for developing Jewish culture. Ruth Klonsky contributed a fanciful story that compared the environs of her city to the lake districts of England and Switzerland. Clearly influenced by the schoolbooks and teachers at the Evelina School, Ruth had learned to revere these European locations and the poets associated with them. Understanding these faraway sites as the inspiration for great poetry, she imagined a lake district in Jerusalem as the source of future poetic brilliance:

JERUSALEM'S LAKE DISTRICT

Not only in Switzerland are there beautiful lakes among the high, snow-covered mountain peaks; and not only in England is there a Lake District where famous poets such as Wordsworth lived; but here in Palestine, in Jerusalem, we also have a "Lake District."

She explained that on the way to Ein-Kerem, when you pass the Blind Institute, a lovely view comes into sight. There the bare white rocks emerge from the velvety green grass sprinkled with hundreds of red poppies. Between the rocks, deep holes have formed. During the winter, when heavy rains fall, the water gathers in them and forms little pools. When there is continuous rain for some days, the water rises high, and only the tops of the rocks are seen above it, taking on all kinds of shapes. Ruth continued:

Even in the winter when we get sunny days, it is very pleasant to go out, sit and play by the side of these crystalline waters; we throw stones and watch the splashes and ripples. . . . Perhaps as in England where the Lake Poets were famous, there might be amongst us a Wordsworth or a Keats or some still "mute inglorious Milton." Who knows?[31]

Haya Lieder, in the matriculation class, contributed an equally imaginative story that expressed awe at the advances made by her city. Lieder captured the modernizing changes brought by the British, linking loyalty to England and love for Jerusalem through an appreciation of the progress brought to the city during the Mandate. She described the Jerusalem of her day, both as she imagined it and as she actually experienced it, as "supereducated and fantastically scientific."

FALLING ASLEEP IN 1850 AND AWAKING IN 1937

Black and white machines called motor-cars . . . ran without being pushed or pulled, up and down the streets which had been rough and cobbled before, and were now smooth and neatly paved. These cars seem to have supplanted camels and donkeys as means of locomotion. . . . My amazement was increased when I saw the most beautiful buildings, many stories high, and I wondered how it was that they had not yet toppled over in the severe Jerusalem storms. . . . Even the appearance of the women was different; the voluminous skirts and tight bodices were now nowhere to be seen; short, light, loosely fitting gowns were the order of the 20th century. . . .

The two things which surprised me next were the telephone and the radio. To speak to someone many miles away! All you have to do is turn a handle, take off the instrument, say a certain number, and in a moment some person answers. . . . With the radio all you have to do is press a knob and you hear some beautiful music; another, and you hear a speech or lecture from far away, far over seas and oceans, in any language you prefer.[32]

Haya, who lived among sellers of "gaaaz" and witnessed the *sabal* loaded with furniture and household items struggling through the narrow streets of the city, was keenly aware and appreciative of the role of the British in modernizing Jerusalem. Although none of the pupils had home telephones at this point, they were proud of the telephone in their British school. Likewise, few students had radios at home, but they were already familiar with the art of broadcasting, since many had participated in the recordings for the Palestine Broadcasting Service. They were keen to hear themselves perform on the radio and gathered to listen at the homes of fortunate neighbors who had sets.

A radio station, a clock, a bus, and mail delivery all appeared as evidence of modern life in Jerusalem in a story about summer vacation written by Tova Cohen.

MY FIRST APPEARANCE ON THE RADIO

I waited impatiently for Thursday at 10 in the morning when I had to meet my friends at the radio station. . . .

Father went to work. Mother was busy in the house. . . . I looked at the ticking clock frequently and it seemed to me that it wasn't moving. . . . Finally, the clock chimed ten. I left the house and flew like a bird to the number 3 bus station and asked the driver to take me to the radio station. Tens of eyes looked at me as if they wanted me to explain this thing. I arrived at my destination. I went up to the second floor and knocked on the door of the appointed room, my heart beating inside me. I heard a voice call, "Come!" I entered the room, and one thousand electrical wires greeted me. I was frightened by this sight, but when I saw the rest of my friends my spirit calmed down. The broadcaster told us that she wanted us to learn a play and if it went well she would broadcast it one day.

I was scared during the first rehearsal, but afterwards I got used to rehearsals. A few weeks later, on the eve of Yom Kippur, while I was selecting the white chickens for atonements, the mailman appeared and called out, "Tova Cohen!" At first I didn't know who he was talking about. I was not accustomed to receiving letters addressed to me personally. When I looked at the envelope I found that it was for me. It was an invitation to return to the radio station on Tuesday to broadcast the performance. The broadcast was a great success.[33]

These two stories about modernization indicate that Landau's pupils thought of themselves as residents in a city that had both historic importance and the benefits of Western life. They saw themselves as participants in the modernization of Jerusalem. Their smart British-style uniforms, their command of English, and their role with the Palestine Broadcasting Service all contributed to their modern identity.[34]

Margalith Havilio felt so comfortable with the concept of radio broadcasting that she compared her classroom to a broadcasting studio:

Hello! This is the Evelina de Rothschild School Broadcasting Station Class V calling!

We start our programme this year by telling you about our "studio" and the "workers" who belong to it. It is situated on the second floor and has room for forty. . . . We are now taking you to the Science lesson. You hear excited exclamations from the girls who are doing an experiment. No! The noise you hear was not a bomb! We must apologise for a technical hitch in the machinery.

We go on to the demonstration kitchen for a Cookery lesson. With white aprons and clean white kerchiefs, we look exactly like little women. We learn how to make soups, salads, puddings, and many other delightful dishes.

On now to Geography. We learn the geography of the other countries in English, but the geography of Palestine is taught to us in Hebrew, our own language.

"I must down to the seas again." You are now listening to Class V reciting. We sometimes dramatise our poems and hope that one of our verse-speaking group will give a special broadcast before the end of the year.

We regret that there is no time to take you over to our History, Reading, Mathematics, and Bible lessons. We shall, however, be broadcasting again next year as Class VI, so don't forget to order your copy of the School Magazine in good time.[35]

Landau established pen pals for Evelina students to increase their proficiency in English and to help the girls of Jerusalem feel like world citizens. The poem below by Zipporah Levy demonstrates that Evelina students used Landau's idea to celebrate their school and their city. They were proud of their identity as Evelina girls and as Jerusalemites.

From far off lands they want to know
What Evelina girls can show,
Letters, welcome, big and small
Daily arrive from all to all.
America, Italy and Erin,
Fill post bags to the brim,
And everyone doth snatch the chance
Even little girls from France.
Says Miss America: "Please,
Won't you write to me?"
Miss Erin, "Me too," chimes in,

"If you will you'll help me fill
My cup of knowledge to the brim."
And Signorina Italiana,
"Come on," says she, "and write to me too,
Compositions by the score,"
On the Wailing Wall and Friday night,
Tel-Aviv, Shabbat, Galilee by moonlight.[36]

The girlish exuberance and pride in the above poem is an example of the esprit de corps of the Evelina School. In the 1930s, the Evelina School maintained a welcoming attitude toward newcomers. This was in sharp contrast to Zionist schools, which often looked down on diaspora Jews, stressing their weaknesses, while lauding the new Israeli-born Jew, the Sabra.[37] Nevertheless, the influx of refugees brought change to the culture of the school.

A different expression of pride in the culture of the school can be seen in the work of ten-year-old Shoshana Drosdovsky. She provided insight into the change in status of European and American schools compared to the Evelina School. In her short play she used a Palestinian Jewish girl as the moderator in a discussion between a German Jewish girl and an American Jewish girl. The girls, unfamiliar with one another's customs, started to quarrel, but soon they recognized how lucky they were. Landau's influence and the stirring of a new nationalistic spirit are both evident.

OUR CLASS

GERMAN GIRL: When I was in Germany I was not in a school like this.

AMERICAN GIRL: Of course you were not. I was not either.

PALESTINIAN GIRL: Do not quarrel, girls. Now you are here in the lovely Evelina de Rothschild School in Palestine.

GERMAN GIRL: Yes, I'm very glad to be away from Germany.

AMERICAN GIRL: [in an angry tone to the German girl] Yes, but some German girls like to speak German even here.

PALESTINIAN GIRL: I am very happy that you have come here, and that we are in the same class. Aren't you happy to learn two languages?

GERMAN AND AMERICAN GIRLS TOGETHER: Of course.

PALESTINIAN GIRL: And our class-teacher is very kind to all the girls in the class.

AMERICAN GIRL: I do like our classroom. The pictures on the wall are very interesting and some of them are beautiful.

GERMAN GIRL: [to both of the others] I like the room because it is very clean and airy.

PALESTINIAN GIRL: What about our playground and garden? There are not many schools in Palestine where girls are as lucky as we are.[38]

In the first decades of the twentieth century, from the point of view of Jewish girls living in Palestine, the lucky girls were European. They were featured in the books imported from London and Paris; they wore beautiful clothes, lived in elegant homes, and rode ponies. By 1936, the pendulum had swung: the German girl felt out of place, the American girl understood her feeling of dislocation, and the Palestinian girl was welcoming and reassuring. The lucky girls in the play are students at the Evelina School in Jerusalem. Shoshana was aware of the importance of the classroom and the playground in integrating the newcomers to life in Jerusalem. She wanted them to join her in appreciation of the advantages afforded to Evelina students, to feel lucky to be in their new homeland, Palestine.

Hava Etlinger, a newcomer to Jerusalem, began her studies at the Evelina School at the age of twelve. She found in the Evelina School some elements that were familiar from her old school and some that were new. She concluded that the Evelina School was an ideal place to become part of the new nation.

Hava noticed the diversity of pupils. "In our class there are 55 girls from different countries: Germany, America, Russia, Poland, Rumania, Turkey, and Palestine." She described the physical surroundings: "We have a very nice, large classroom. Every two or three girls share one desk. Our classrooms look out on the beautiful school garden, with many trees and beautiful flowers." She explained that in the beginning she found the lessons very difficult and the school tradition of communal prayer unfamiliar, but she immediately liked the uniforms and lining up to go to class.

Hava confided that she had difficulty doing the work: "I was very unhappy because I saw how the other girls worked, and I could not do anything. I had private lessons.... At the end of the term I was afraid to get my report. I knew that it would not be good, but I hoped that I would pass." She reported happily that she did better than expected and soon began to understand all the lessons and to do what her teachers asked. She concluded, "I like the school very much because of the great order that prevails in it and the respect and love among all the girls and their teachers."[39]

For Hava Etlinger, the welcoming spirit of the Evelina girls provided a unique pathway to integration into her new city and new country. She was grateful to the teachers for their tutoring and to her fellow students for providing informal guidance about how to become part of her new school.

Although the refugees struggled to learn English and Hebrew, the atmosphere of the Evelina School—the emphasis on decorum, the use of uniforms, and the opportunity to participate in sports or to sing in a choir—was often similar to their experience in European schools, making their transition less difficult. Regina Havilio created a humorous acrostic to describe the essential features of the school.

THE EVELINA DE ROTHSCHILD ALPHABET

A is for asphalt, where netball is played;
B is for blazers in which we're arrayed.
C is for classrooms where long hours are spent;
D is for detentions, on which we're not bent.
E is for Evelina, the school we are in;
F is for fame, which we hope to win.
G is for games, which we play with zest;
H is for our holidays, oh joy for the rest!
I is for ink, sometimes spilt in the school;
J is for juniors, not quiet as a rule.
K is for kitchen, where lunch is prepared;
L is for laughter, throughout the school shared.
M is for math, which is turning us gray;
N is for netball, which in winter we play.
O is for obedience to our teachers' warnings;
P is for prayers said every morning.
Q is for quiet, which we strive to be;
R is for reading, so dear to me.
S is for Sabbath, when everyone rests;
T is for our teachers, who love to give tests.
U is for our uniform, known far and wide;
V is for vehicles—some to school ride.

W is for work, which we do with a will;

X is for exams—oft a bitter pill.

Y is for yells which at matches are heard!

Z is for zeal—and that's my last word![40]

Ruth Karpf, like many pupils, worried about exams. Following a school tradition of making up new lines to famous poems, Ruth's verse expressed the heroism of the entire student body of four hundred girls. Her poem was based on one loved by many of her classmates, Alfred Lord Tennyson's "Charge of the Light Brigade."

EXAMINATION TIME

Half a day, half a day,

Half a day onward,

Into the terrors of tests

Went the four hundred.

"Be calm and don't faint with fright,

Don't be dismayed when you write.

Then it will be all right."

Into the terrors of tests

Went the four hundred . . .

Papers to the right of us,

Papers to the left of us,

Papers in front of us

At which we wondered.

Stormed at with problems fell,

Boldly we worked and well,

Into the jaws of tests,

Into the mouth of Hell,

Went the four hundred.

Notes to the right of us,

Notes to the left of us,

Notes in front of us,

Not many blundered!

Stopped by the ringing bell,

Ended that awful spell,

How we rejoiced,
All the four hundred.
When can our glory fade,
Oh, the fine marks we made,
All the staff wondered.
Honour the fight we made,
Honour each struggling grade,
Noble four hundred.[41]

Each issue of *School* magazine reported on the Girl Guides, the Rangers, and the Brownies. The weekly activities of the Girl Guides were an integral part of the character formation of Evelina students. A typical meeting is described here:

We usually open the meeting with a jolly country dance, especially on wet and cold days, and proceed to Roll Call, Drill, and Inspection.

Since we hold our meetings after school we provide a canteen. Every guide contributes something towards it. It is one of the jolliest times of the company. We sell everything cheaply, and every guide takes out her last mil, comes to buy something, and eats it with great appetite . . . now ready for badge work. We take our corners and work away busily for 15–20 minutes. Then we learn a new dance and play various morse games [based on Morse code]. On fine days we go out hiking, then there is much fun. We make a fire, cook a meal, and make tea. The patrol who arranges the nicest table in the open wins a prize. We play games and sing around the fire.

We hope to keep increasing our number (from 32) and to be healthy and useful citizens.[42]

Most girls wrote about their studies and their classmates with purposeful affection, whereas others were more inclined to write humorously about the different types of students in their classes: those who were not too smart, those who were too shy, those who took interest only in easy classes, those who were very smart but conceited, those who were interested only in sports, those who studied too much, and those who were both modest and witty. Bella Leider and Hava Weinberg imagined their classmates as members of an orchestra:

The orchestra contains a few "drums" which are easily recognisable by their loud voices that seldom have any wit. The emptier the drum, the more noise does it make! Such girls are advised to take to heart the proverb—"There is wisdom in silence."

Then there are the "lutes" that sound very finely by themselves but are easily drowned in a multitude of instruments, unless special attention is paid to them. These are the girls who are full of knowledge but are too shy to play a big part in the concert.

There are also several "trumpets" . . . agreeable as long as they keep within their pitch. These are our young ladies "who have a short reach of understanding" and are specialists in drawing, cookery and sewing. . . . Trumpets, you need to acquire much more knowledge before you venture to sit for the London Matriculation Examination.

"The violins are the dominant instruments in every concert." They have a great deal of knowledge and intelligence, which they are quick to display. . . . If less conceited they would be perfect.

Then there are the "bass-viols" of which there are quite a number in our concert. . . . These are the unassuming girls who do not like to draw attention to themselves "but sometimes break out with extraordinary wit."

The girls who take an interest only in high-jump, netball, basketball, and tennis are mere ornaments to our class . . . we can entrust them with no instrument than the "sports whistle."

Finally, there are the "passing-bells" who are much too serious and melancholy. They are the girls who study on and on without a break. They ought to know that work without play will not do.[43]

Bella and Hava did not fear social ostracism for their critique of their fellow students. *School* magazine provided room for satire. "Social Concert" was not about growing nationalism or the integration of refugee pupils; it was a lighthearted, girlish assessment of the strengths and weaknesses of fellow classmates regardless of where they had been born. This could have been written by schoolgirls in London or Manchester, but girls at Zionist or Orthodox schools in Palestine were not educated in this spirit.

Ziona Caspi's essay here stresses the feeling of unity in her class, the desire for her classmates to excel, and her pride in their accomplishments.

Although we have 34 girls in our class, we are one in spirit and friendship. We delight in helping each other in our work and joining each other in our play. Every one considers us a hardworking, jolly class. Outside school we often arrange class trips and picnics. Our class is brimful of talents. There are girls who can draw and paint beautifully. Some girls write with marvelous skill and style. We have several graceful dancers and a great number of actors who would shine on any stage. Last but not least we have ever so many real scholars. I love my class and hope I shall never have to leave it until I finish School. I have been in it since babyhood. No class can be so dear to me as my own. I want it to be the pride and example of the School.[44]

Ziona's generosity and optimism are reflected in all her essays. She was typical of the girls who attended the Evelina School from the age of seven and shared experiences with their fellow pupils for ten years.

Humor was another tool used by Evelina girls to facilitate camaraderie. All the students were encouraged to work hard, none more so than the matriculation class. Despite the need to study, these girls made time to contribute a spoof modeled on the Passover song "Who Knows One?" Using the tropes of a religious song to demonstrate their feelings about their rigorous studies would have been considered blasphemy by some, but this original and humorous ditty was considered creative in the Evelina de Rothschild School.

WHO KNOWS ONE?

Who knoweth one? I, saith Class VII, I know one:
One is Matriculation, that ruleth over us.
Who knoweth two? I, saith Class VII, I know two:
Two are the languages we are studying: Hebrew and English;
But, One is Matriculation that ruleth over us.
Who knoweth three? I, saith Class VII, I know three:
Three are our new lessons this year: Chemistry, Translation,
    and Logarithms;
Two are the languages;
But, One is Matriculation that ruleth over us.
Who knoweth four? I, saith Class VII, I know four:
Four are the lessons that were taken from us this year:
    Music, Art, Cooking, and Sewing;

Three are the new lessons;

Two are the languages;

But, One is Matriculation that ruleth over us.

Who knoweth five? I, saith Class VII, I know five:

Five are the subjects for Matriculation: Hebrew, English,
        History, Chemistry, and Mathematics;

Four are the lessons that were taken from us;

Three are our new lessons;

Two are the languages;

But, One is Matriculation that ruleth over us.

Who knoweth six? I, saith Class VII, I know six:

Six is the time we rise in the morning;

Five are the subjects;

Four are the lessons that were taken from us;

Three are our new lessons;

Two are the languages;

But, One is Matricuation that ruleth over us.

Who knoweth seven? I, saith Class VII, I know seven.

Seven are our teachers: Miss Sayers, Miss Kramer, Miss Salasnik,
        Mrs. Levin, Dr. Reider, Mr. Wachman, and Mr. Many.

Six is the time we rise;

Five are the subjects;

Four are the lessons that were taken from us;

Three are our new lessons;

Two are the languages;

But, One is Matriculation that ruleth over us.

Who knoweth eight: I, saith Class VII, I know eight:

Eight is the time we begin prayers every morning.

Seven are our teachers;

Six is the time we rise;

Five are the subjects;

Four are the lessons that were taken from us;

Three are our new lessons;

Two are the languages;

But, One is Matriculation that ruleth over us.[45]

Whereas the matriculation exam was the focus of class7, Rachel Levy, in the commercial class, wrote an essay about preparing for the Pitman tests by studying bookkeeping, shorthand, and typing. Her class planned for careers in business and government offices by reading the latest *Palestine Official Gazette*, in order to be up-to-date with ordinances, tariffs, and procedures, and by writing summaries of business reports. Landau also ensured that the girls in the commercial class had lessons in cooking and baking, since many would soon have homes of their own. They continued to prepare for an active cultural life as well, learning songs and listening to music.

With all of this multifaceted stimulation, Rachel concluded, "We are becoming Domesticated Philosophical Businesswomen!" Her description of her classmates provides unusual testimony to the textured identity developing under Landau's tutelage. The girls didn't have to choose between family life and careers, nor did they have to choose between careers and community service. They could do it all. Rachel ended her essay with rhetorical flair:

> This is the last time we appear in the *School Magazine* as a class. I wanted to say good-bye, but it sounded Victorian and sentimental, so—Cheerio, and some day, perhaps, you will see us again in the *Magazine* as Old Girls.[46]

Rachel's "cheerio" sums up the common feeling of the Evelina students of this period: self-confidence and optimism. Miriam Titkin and Lilian Shapiro shared this feeling. They "burned with enthusiasm" and "waited impatiently for the time to come when [they] may take an active part in the economic and industrial development of the country."[47] These young women maintained their connection to the school through membership in the Old Girls' Club, where the values of their alma mater were reinforced.

The essays, stories, and poems contained in *School* magazine give voice to the girls' struggle to balance their competing identities and loyalties. They also reveal the quintessential Evelina esprit de corps, developed in their uniquely British and Jewish school, a spirit that molded adolescent girls to develop confidence in themselves and in their resolve to carry on despite challenges. The 1930s were times of trial and tribulation for Landau and her students, who were affected by the threatened destruction of European Jews and by seemingly random acts of violence in Jerusalem.

The Evelina School continued to remain an oasis of civility as it had been since 1900, but it was never impermeable to the struggles of the outside world. The essays in *School* magazine reveal Landau's success in teaching the girls of Jerusalem to assume important roles in the city. The education her pupils imbibed with their daily glass of milk helped them to persevere in tough times. There would be no shortage of opportunities in the years ahead to test their resolve.

[6]

TRANSITIONS

1940–1960

In 1940, the school year began a week late; Annie Landau and others were delayed in returning to Jerusalem because the war created difficulties in securing transport for civilians. A few weeks after classes resumed, the girls were summoned into the hall corridor to be fitted for gas masks by Major Sparks, who was in charge of Air Raid Precaution (ARP) in Palestine. Despite these events, life went on as usual in Jerusalem, for the most part.[1] Landau continued to write annual reports describing the special challenges faced by her school in wartime:

> In spite of war conditions School work has continued to function smoothly. When Italy entered the war and France collapsed and air raids on Haifa and Tel Aviv began, we had, of course, to adapt certain aspects of School life to war conditions. In the first place ARP drill was instituted. Within one and a half minutes every child had left the classroom and taken up her position in her own particular Shelter Room (furnished with a first aid outfit and certain essential equipment), the teacher in charge taking roll call. There was a great influx into Jerusalem from Tel Aviv and Haifa, and we were inundated with requests to admit children into our School. As we were already over-full we could take a very limited number.[2]

The next year, Landau added the St. John Ambulance First Aid Course for the top two classes and noted that the entire student body was sewing garments for the Red Cross. Sixty girls were awarded Red Cross worker badges in recognition of their effort. Because of the disruptions of the war, the

January 1941 matriculation examinations did not arrive, and the June exams arrived a month late. The Pitman shorthand test arrived four months late. Despite these difficulties, the pass rate at the Evelina School remained very high.[3]

In September 1941, Bertha Spafford Vester hosted a party to celebrate the sixtieth anniversary of the founding of the American Colony, inviting leading members of the British, Arab, and Jewish communities. Although social events that brought together the various communities in the city had been commonplace in the 1920s and 1930s, Vester's party was one of the last such attempts to bridge the divide. There were now three distinct communities in Jerusalem.

The British, who had come to Palestine to foster the establishment of a national home for the Jewish people while simultaneously protecting the civil and religious rights of existing non-Jewish communities, no longer had faith in their mission. They were engaged in a bloody fight against fascism that strained their resources and caused them to close ranks against enemies, real and imagined.

The Arabs were united in their anger at the British and the Zionists, whom they saw as colonial interlopers in their ancestral region. The Mufti of Jerusalem, Amin al-Husseini, was charged with inciting violence, had evaded British arrest, and fled Palestine in 1937. He pledged support to Hitler and worked with Nazi propagandists to win Arab support during the war years.

The Zionists, who joined British forces to fight the Nazis, simultaneously fought the British policy in Palestine that limited immigration to a thin trickle. They planned for the future of a Jewish state in Palestine.

During the Second World War, pupils in the Evelina de Rothschild School saved the silver foil that wrapped their chocolate candies, rolled it into balls, and donated it to the war effort; they practiced air raid drills and blackout procedures. They added lines to their notebooks in order to conserve precious paper. In June 1942, as the school struggled with wartime shortages, Landau received news of the death of Lionel de Rothschild, whose father, Leopold, was a former vice president of the Anglo-Jewish Association, and whose mother was the long-serving leader of the Ladies' Committee.

Rothschild family members informed the Anglo-Jewish Association that they would no longer be able to support the Evelina School budget. The annual Rothschild contribution dated to the middle of the previous century, when the family had paid for the entire budget of the school. In 1942, this contribution was about fifteen hundred pounds, or 25 percent of the annual expenditures. Inheritance taxes and pressing wartime needs led to the family's decision.[4]

Landau, almost seventy years old, responded to the unexpected financial dilemma with the determination that had seen her through many crises. She decided to raise school fees to cover the budget shortfall. Her decision was based on several factors: first, Evelina School fees were low compared to other schools; second, wartime salaries had risen and Jerusalemites had more disposable income; and third, the alternative was to close several classes, which would force two hundred children to find new schools. Landau's calculations were correct, and she was pleased that only three pupils failed to return after the fees were raised. She expected the new fees to yield thirty-five hundred pounds in 1943.[5]

This effort to balance the budget was Landau's last heroic act. In her last years, her health declined; she ventured out less and less, maintaining command of her school from her apartment atop Frutiger House. Suffering chronic weakness and rarely leaving the school grounds, she managed to provide an island of calm for her pupils during tough times, as she had done so often in the past. Her physical presence in the garden or on her balcony was reassuring to older girls, who remembered her fondly from their early years, and to younger girls, who learned to respect and love the now gentle-looking Landau. Former teachers, pupils, and scores of friends visited with the headmistress, who was often ensconced at her great desk, surrounded by her many horticultural awards and looking out at the troubled city below. Gradually, as she was less able to fulfill her duties, her assistant, Ethel Levy, took over the burden of daily operations.

Annie Landau, headmistress of the school for nearly half a century, benefactress, and a leading figure in the life of the capital, died on January 23, 1945. Despite heavy rain and biting wind, two thousand Jerusalem residents and friends from all over Palestine gathered at the Evelina de Rothschild School the next day at noon to pay their respects. The mourners, among them pupils of the school and a number of Old Girls with their families as well as the representative of the high commissioner and members of the government and the Jewish and British communities, filed past the body, which lay in state in the school hall, and later they accompanied the bier to the cemetery on

FIGURE 6.1 Annie Landau (left)
and Ethel Levy, ca. 1942

the Mount of Olives. A service was held before the cortege left the school at which tributes were paid by Chief Rabbis Isaac Herzog and Ben Zion Uziel and by a senior member of the school staff, Elhanan Wachman. All praised Landau's devotion to Judaism and her pioneering spirit in education and good works. A cantor recited Kaddish.[6]

The bier was borne out of the building by friends and members of the school staff and proceeded along St. Paul's Street and St. George's Street to the Schwartzstein House, where Kaddish was recited again. The pallbearers were Landau's nephew, Major Aubrey Eban, and three teachers: David Reider, Walter Reis, and Elhanan Wachman. Norman Bentwich, a friend of many decades, spoke at the graveside. Members of nearly every community came to pay their respects: British officials, Jewish and Christian religious leaders, Zionist officials, academic leaders of Hebrew University, Arab notables, and volunteers with the Red Cross and the Girl Guides.[7]

Levy closed the school for seven days to mourn Landau's death. A month after her funeral, the *Palestine Post* reported the following:

> Tribute to a great citizen of Jerusalem was paid yesterday when several hundred friends gathered at the Evelina de Rothschild School in Jerusalem to commemorate Miss Annie Landau, on the thirtieth day after her death, in accordance with Jewish tradition.
>
> Speaking first in Hebrew and then in English, Mr. N. Bentwich, a former Attorney General of Palestine, stressed Miss Landau's triple loyalty to Judaism and Jerusalem, to the school of which she had been headmistress for 45 years, and to England, the land of her birth.
>
> Annie Landau, declared Sir William Fitzgerald, the Chief Justice, lived her life in truth, justice, and righteousness. Her intensified devotion to her own religion had made her the more appreciative of the best that the English tradition could offer, and this was the heritage she had left behind her. . . .
>
> Her devotion to Jerusalem, and the contribution that she brought with her to the land of her fathers, had entitled Annie Landau to be hailed as a "daughter of Jerusalem," said Mr. M. Eliash in his tribute.
>
> Dr. J. Magnes, President of the Hebrew University, then read Psalm xc in Hebrew and English, and Major Eban read Ch. xxxi of the Book of Proverbs, also in both languages. The Memorial Prayer and Kaddish were chanted by the Cantor.[8]

Levy, the vice principal who had been at the helm of the school during Landau's illness, addressed the young pupils attending the memorial in an effort to help them understand the important decisions made by their late headmistress that had influenced the school and Jerusalem:

My dear children:

Thirty days have passed since the passing of our dear Miss Landau. We have none of us forgotten the grief we felt and still feel as we realize she will no longer grace our morning assemblies and rejoice with us at festivals, guide us, advise us, and give us the pleasure of seeing her vivid, generous, and most gracious personality among us.

Other speakers will tell you about different phases of our dear Miss Landau, but I would like to tell you of how she first came here, which will show you something of the courage and resolution she had then and which always stayed with her. . . .

She left Mother and Father and a large number of sisters and brothers to come here where she knew nobody, where there was nothing of the comfort and excitement she knew in her own home and big town. However, she knew she could help Jewish girls in the Holy City and that was to be her reward for any hardship she was likely to suffer. . . .

She worked not only at giving the girls the best teaching but at training their characters so that she might carry out her aim in life—To make her girls fine Jewesses, a pride to their parents, their country, and to themselves. . . . If you remain true to your religion . . . no harm can come either to you or to our people.

When government officials asked her once to allow her girls to work on Shabbat as there was a great rush of work which had to be done, her reply was, "Not only does the Sabbath not belong to me to give my girls to give to you, but I will do all in my power to prevent my girls doing what you ask. The Sabbath is our most precious possession and cannot be given to anybody for any consideration whatever." . . .

She had hard and difficult days here; days full of ill-health—malaria, rheumatic fever, pleurisy, pneumonia, other bad spells. She suffered the sorrow of intrigue against her. She bore with slander. But against that she had the appreciation, the love and respect of the thousands of girls who passed through her hands. She had the love and devotion of her friends.[9]

Rachel Harris remembered attending the memorial service for Landau with her husband and hundreds of students, teachers, and Old Girls at the Evelina School. After the speeches and prayers, the crowd walked from St. Paul Street to the burial site on the Mount of Olives, where a memorial stone was erected in Landau's memory. Nearby was the freshly dug grave of Henrietta Szold, who had died three weeks after her colleague and friend Annie Landau.

For those unable to attend the service in Jerusalem, the Palestine Broadcasting Service in conjunction with the BBC broadcast a memorial service, with messages recorded by Sir Herbert Samuel, the first high commissioner of Palestine; Leonard Stein, the president of the Anglo-Jewish Society; and Sir Arthur Wauchope, the high commissioner from 1931–1938. Each captured a different facet of her life and work in Jerusalem.

Lord Samuel focused on her outreach to all the communities of the city:

During the five years that I was High Commissioner in Palestine, from 1920–25, Miss Landau was one of the best known, and one of the best loved, personalities in Jerusalem. It had been so for some years before that, and has so continued ever since—till now, when her life has ended.

In a community much troubled by divisions—racial, religious, political—she made her house a meeting-place for all. It was a center for friendly intercourse and goodwill. Miss Landau never tired in her kindly work of reconciling differences and promoting understanding. Thereby she contributed not a little to the better atmosphere which gradually came to prevail in those years.

As an educationist she won a great reputation; especially for her success in developing in her pupils those qualities of character without which the acquirement of knowledge is of little avail.

Stein stressed her commitment to religious observance:

Above and beyond all else, she believed in and loved the Torah. Nothing—nothing whatever—was allowed to interfere with her observance of its precepts. Truly, to her the Law was a delight and shone in its radiance upon her in all her ways.

It is hard to think of that eager spirit, that vivid personality, that active mind at rest, but in a greater degree than is granted to most of us, she saw her life's work crowned with success and her wishes fulfilled.

Sir Wauchope noted her strong beliefs and her equally strong commitment to tolerance:

> I am proud to think that I was a friend of Miss Landau throughout the seven years when I was High Commissioner in Palestine.
>
> Miss Landau was a woman of the highest principles, and held strong convictions; but she was entirely free from all bitterness of thought towards those whose aims and views were different from her own.[10]

A New Headmistress

Within a few weeks, Ethel Levy was appointed headmistress by the Anglo-Jewish Association. She had lost a close friend as well as a professional mentor. She wrote to the members of the association, who had supported her predecessor for more than four decades, referring to the great and almost overwhelming loss sustained as a result of Landau's passing:

> The Anglo-Jewish Association and the School lost a great headmistress and I personally lost a dear and valued friend. We had lived in harmony and friendship both in our private lives and in our work and we are all left the poorer by her passing. Her influence extended beyond the walls of the School and many tributes were paid to her; but the greatest of all tributes is the School itself. With your help she laid the foundations well and truly and thousands of Jerusalem's young women have reason to rise up and call her blessed.[11]

Levy thoroughly understood and supported Landau's vision, and she contributed immeasurably to its fulfillment by adapting the school program to meet the challenges of the postwar period. In addition, Levy explicated the ideas she shared with Landau in countless speeches and articles. Her narration of the history and program of the school provided a record of the school's development. In an address to the summer school of the educational and cultural organization the British Council in July 1946, Levy discussed the early days of the school and its graduates; she was the first to point out that Landau's work had a direct effect on the economic and social infrastructure of Jerusalem. Others had noted that Landau built a school that influenced the lives of thousands of young women, but Levy recognized that by teaching the girls skills and encouraging them to become productive participants she also helped to build the city and the country.

Levy reviewed the history of efforts to provide employment for the graduates, enabling the girls to work in dressmaking, millinery, lace making, and gold and silver embroidery. With the development of the country and the addition of a secondary course of studies, a wider scope of careers opened to the graduates, who were hired as teachers and who worked in government and Jewish Agency offices, business offices, law and accounting firms, and banks. Finally, in the 1940s, graduates with matriculation certificates enrolled in Hebrew University, the Hadassah School of Nursing, the Bezalel School of Arts, the Vaad Hakhilah courses for social services, and the Government Law School.[12]

None of this, Levy explained, would have been possible without Landau's determination in the 1930s to create a secondary school program in which students were encouraged to think of themselves as capable of high levels of achievement.

Levy took over the helm of the Evelina School just a few months after the arrival of Yona Scharf, a remarkable young girl from Czernowitz, who had arrived at the Schwartzstein House along with three Greek girls in late 1944. Yona, like Levy, chronicled her experiences. Her letters and essays provide a student's perspective on the years after Landau's death and testify to the continuing importance of the Evelina School to Jewish girls in Jerusalem. Yona, who had lost her parents and her home in the Holocaust, compared her new experiences in the Schwartzstein House to life in a family with many daughters who all attended the same school.[13]

Yona had been an excellent pupil in her hometown before the Russians invaded and expelled her from school at age twelve for being a "capitalist Jew." When the Germans occupied Czernowitz in 1941, her situation went from bad to worse. She experienced starvation, a forced march, imprisonment, and the death of her parents and her grandmother. Yona was spared the same fate because the Germans agreed to repatriate children under age fifteen. A few months shy of fifteen, Yona was placed in an orphanage in her hometown but was helped by relatives to immigrate to Palestine in August 1944.

There, her family urged her to find work, thinking that it was pointless for her to return to school, since she knew no Hebrew. Yona persevered, determined to find a school that would admit her. After being turned away from many schools during her first five months in the country, her older brother, Yoel, who had studied with Marta Lange's father in Frankfurt, contacted Marta at the Schwartzstein House. Informed of Yona's desire to learn, Marta and her mother, Hermina, approached Levy, who convinced Youth Aliyah officials to give Yona a chance.

Years later, when her eldest son started school, Yona wrote a long piece about her recollections of her first days at the Evelina School and of Levy, the headmistress who encouraged her:

> A beautiful building, towering over an array of smaller ones and bearing the legend, "The Evelina de Rothschild Secondary School for Girls," stood in the midst of a big and flowering garden. As I meandered in and stopped hesitatingly at the entrance, a secretary beckoned me inside. I mumbled a few words in my own language and presently she ushered me into the Headmistress's room. My tongue clove to the roof of my mouth as I beheld the beauty of it all. The Headmistress, tall and upright, with that remarkable reserve so typical of the English, did not ask any questions. She just looked me over and said: "You'll have to try hard, dear, very hard."[14]

Yona did try very hard, but the obstacles were great. In the beginning, she knew neither English nor Hebrew, and she was already fifteen. However, returning to school gave her a second chance to complete her childhood and her education:

> It would be hard to express . . . the excitement I felt when first I faced a black-board again. Here was the plaything of my imagination, verily real and tangible at last. But my excitement was short-lived and the troubles, for the moment dispersed, came back in torrents. I understood little of the thousands of questions that were hurled at me by my new classmates and was not very sure that I was welcome among them. The school discipline to which I was no longer accustomed, the subjects taught, which befitted my age but not my educational level and the two languages I did not know, left me prey to constant apprehension. I could not partake in any lessons, I could not even join in the fun; I just sat there, a miserable, crestfallen and desolate creature, thriving on the bitter seeds of disillusionment so deeply implanted in my heart.

Yona's determination to learn and the kind assistance of the teachers proved to be stronger than her despair:

"The new girl over there, would you try to answer my question?" asked the kind voice of a teacher every now and then. Sometimes I thought I even knew the answer, but for fear I might give it the wrong expression, I just faced the ground and shrugged my shoulders unknowingly. But the teachers were kind and helpful and went to no end of trouble to pull me through. They hovered over me with unusual care, they praised my conduct to make me feel good at something at least, they sat with me after school, they taught me the language in their spare time, they worked my maths with me late at night, they spurred me to make a first attempt, and when I did, they credited it with a praise I often thought I did not earn. But even so, I dwelt on such praise and on every good word I heard for hours on end. I thought I could not possibly let these good people down, and I had to prove the skeptic wrong—so I worked hard. "Who is that up already?" rang a cheerful voice quite early in the morning, and "Who is that up yet?" chided the same voice late at night, but though I often thought that voice would soon give way to a bitter reprimand, it was always followed by an extra cup of tea.

Yona's hard work continued, and soon she was hearing soothing words from her teachers:

"Your work is very satisfactory," I heard and heard again, but this work was still returned to me unmarked, because no mark was low enough to do it justice. But the time came when the menacing red pencil, thitherto kept in arrest for want of room to go about, made its debut on my work as well and marked it busily with ever so much zeal. That was an improvement and the improvement gradually grew. Slowly I acquired a fair command of the two languages and by the time I had read my first English book, I knew that my hardest times were well behind.[15]

One of Yona's classmates, Adaya Hochberg, befriended the newcomer. Adaya, a very good student, was an only child whose mother had a full-time job. She experienced loneliness and empathized with Yona, who had lost her parents. Adaya invited Yona to her home in Talpiyot and decades later remembered that Yona taught her to say "I love you" in Hungarian.[16]

After a few painful months, Yona made significant progress. By the end of the year she was able to skip two grades. In subsequent years, she was always at the top of her class. Yona attributed her success not to her talent or perseverance but rather to Levy and her teachers:

But for the Headmistress's unusual good will and the teachers' boundless patience, all my endeavors would have come to naught. My teachers often spoke to me in later years about my futile first attempts, praised by them to give me courage, about the doubts they had and did not show, about the marks they gave me I did not earn, until the day they pulled me through. I was the recipient of every kindness, enjoyed every privilege, and was the exception to many a harsh rule.[17]

Yona corresponded with Levy for decades, confiding her hopes and dreams for further education and for a professional career as a writer and seeking the assistance of her former headmistress. She introduced Levy to her fiancé and invited her to the wedding. Several teachers sent Yona booties when her first child was born, and Hermina Lange, her former housemother, helped her with the baby.

In 1980, Yad Vashem published Yona's diary of the war years. Yona donated a copy of the book to the Evelina School library and dedicated it "to the School that saved my life."[18] In later years, Yona was an active member of the Old Girls' Club. Every year before Rosh Hashanah, she donated a book to the school library. When she received reparations money from Germany, she donated 10 percent to the school; her older sister did the same.[19]

Yona's description of her safe haven at the Evelina School stands in sharp contrast to the reality of the threat of violence in the years after the war. Beginning in December 1945, terrorist activities in the city culminated in an attack on the police station followed by the imposition of a curfew in Jerusalem. Levy announced that school would open half an hour after the lifting of the curfew, and those who could not reach school on time were permitted to drop quietly into their places in the hall where prayers were said at the beginning of each day. At the beginning of January 1946, there was an attack on the Central Prisons and the Palestine Broadcasting Service, both located very near Frutiger House. Levy reported the incident in detail to the Anglo-Jewish Association:

Explosions and shooting began at 8:10 p.m. and continued until after 11 p.m.....
Something had gone wrong. The attack had failed. It was a Saturday night and we were just getting ready to go out to the local Dramatic Society's performance when the attack began. Mr. Zayonce, the School Superintendent, who lives

in the lodge at the gate, was worried about his daughter who was out and he came up to ask if Mrs. Zayonce could stay with us while he went out to find his daughter. We pointed out that he would surely be arrested once he set foot outside the School as the road was by then full of troops, police, and armoured cars, searching for attackers. So he and his wife stayed with us until the attack was over. Next day there was curfew all day; it was lifted at 10 a.m. on Monday; school started at 10:30. Rumor started that the attack on the PBS [Palestine Broadcasting System] had failed because the attackers had applied to the School for help and not only had it been denied, but the School had called the police and given them away.[20]

Levy reported that rumors spread like wildfire that she was responsible for turning in the purportedly Jewish terrorists. Some thought that she had been flown out of the country by the British. Others said that she had been placed on a death list by the Irgun, the underground militant group. Levy categorically denied the rumors again and again; the perpetrators were never identified.[21]

Like her predecessor Landau, Levy did not permit the political events of the day to distract her from her focus on educating the girls of Jerusalem. One of her most successful initiatives of these years was an expanded music program. The school now had two choirs, one led by Varda Heinemann and the other by Esther Salomon. Both teachers were asked to prepare music for broadcasts for the Palestine Broadcasting System. Heinemann arranged a Chanukah program and later created additional holiday programs. Salomon created a program about rhythm for the English Children's Hour that was later translated and aired on the Hebrew Children's Hour, too. The two choirs performed twenty-five concerts for the Palestine Broadcasting Service in 1946 and 1947.[22] The girls' appreciation for music grew as a result of their performance of both classical and Jewish music in these programs.

The English Children's Hour sometimes brought together Arab, Jewish, and British children to broadcast plays, but intercommunity cooperation was the exception in this period. Even the Social Service Association—the organization of Christian, Muslim, and Jewish women that Landau had helped to establish in the early 1920s—experienced difficulties. Levy attended a meeting of the Social Service Association, called by the wife of Chief Secretary John Shaw in May 1946, to find ways to augment the funds of the association. At the meeting, Arab women recommended that the group host a film performance at either the Rex Cinema or the YMCA as a fundraiser. A lengthy discussion ensued on the work involved and whether the results would merit the effort.

Levy offered an alternative: using the grounds of the Evelina de Rothschild School at no cost to host an open-air concert. Many of the members were enthusiastic about this suggestion, since there would be a rental fee at the cinema and at the YMCA. However, the Arab women said that they would not be able to sell tickets if the event were held in a Jewish place. The atmosphere of the meeting became contentious. Shaw suggested a compromise: having a concert first and then a film event. Later, she phoned to say that the Arab women thought it was a mistake to introduce something as controversial as a concert at the Evelina School. Levy noted that it did not occur to them that Jews might be reluctant to attend the Rex Cinema (which was attended primarily by the Arab community) or the YMCA.[23]

In view of the continuing unrest in the city, Levy canceled her plans to return to London and remained in Jerusalem during the summer of 1946. She judged that the situation was calm enough to send her daughter Ruth with two of the Weingarten sisters to attend the Girl Guide Camp in Ramallah in July. The three Evelina girls won several awards, but a week after they arrived in camp, Ruth received a phone call from her mother telling the girls to come straight home. The King David Hotel, which had served as British administrative headquarters in Jerusalem, had been bombed by Jewish nationalists, killing 92. Levy feared there would be reprisals.

Yvonne Astruc, who had recently been hired to work at one of the offices in the King David Hotel, was scheduled to report to work that day. At the last moment she was asked to go to another office for some training before reporting to her boss, a decision that spared her life. A change of plans also saved the life of Marta Zayonce, who had been scheduled to work at the King David that day.[24]

The Jewish Agency denounced the bombing. The day after the explosion, all work and traffic stopped in the Jewish areas of Jerusalem to mourn the dead.[25] Although the Haganah, under the command of the Jewish Agency, denounced the violence, two smaller groups, the Irgun and its splinter group, the Stern Gang, continued to target the British. Soon the British erected barbed-wire barriers all over Jerusalem, and as a result the area around Frutiger House was cut off from other parts of the city. Levy appealed to the British authorities to assist the pupils in making their way to school on roads blocked by army trucks and barbed wire. Constables were assigned to help the children cross the streets in the early morning and again when school was let out, and the school prefects aided the constables by directing the younger pupils to safe crossings. Levy noted, in a report to the Anglo-Jewish Association, "We were very appreciative of this consideration on the part of the police at a time when they were harassed and hard-put to find sufficient police for essential duties."[26]

Despite the proximity of the police, increasing lawlessness in Jerusalem resulted in another problem for Levy. In late October, the school safe was destroyed by a bomb, and seventeen hundred pounds was stolen. The police were called; fingerprints were removed, but the burglars were never found. Levy reported this unfortunate incident to the Anglo-Jewish Association with a heavy heart. The theft led to new procedures for the immediate deposit of all funds—including school fees, lunch money, staff savings, and funds for salaries.[27]

On December 5, 1946, loud explosions were again heard near the school, after which an alarm was sounded by the British authorities. A truck full of explosives had been abandoned on the road adjoining the school. The authorities detonated the bomb, with disastrous results. Damage to the school buildings was estimated at three thousand pounds. The dining hut and the adjoining kitchen were destroyed and not repaired for six months. The carefully nurtured oasis was no longer secure. Levy stoically recorded the pupils' response to the damage:

> Our children could not believe that anything could happen to their beautiful school buildings, and when they arrived on Sunday morning (we had all worked at a terrific pace on Friday cleaning up glass and debris) they were appalled at the extent of the damage; but when told that their share towards the repair of the damage done was to continue to work as though nothing had happened, they lifted their heads, marched in to the gramophone, proud to be giving what was asked of them; their response was magnificent.[28]

In response to the continuing violence, martial law was imposed on parts of Palestine, including sections of Jerusalem. More than a quarter of the pupils lived inside the area cordoned off, and only one part-time teacher, Varda Heinemann, lived in that area. With the help of Old Girls who were unable to get to their jobs, an effort was made to teach the pupils in the affected area.

Martial law was soon lifted, but the school maintained supplies in readiness in several areas of the city.

Despite the continuing threat of violence, the pupils at the Evelina School pursued their studies and their extracurricular activities. In April 1947 the British government officially informed the United Nations that it wished to give up its responsibilities in Palestine. That summer, Levy returned to London to meet with the Anglo-Jewish Association. In view of the volatile situation in Palestine, she appealed to the association to establish a provident fund (retirement benefits) for the long-serving teachers of the Evelina School. Unfortunately, the coffers of the association had not recovered since the war; the four-thousand-pound annual subsidy it allocated to the Evelina School remained by far the lion's share of its distributions.[29]

Just before leaving Palestine, the British administration announced its final annual grant to the Evelina School, increasing it from 120 to 1,000 pounds in recognition of the superior achievements noted by the McNair Commission, which had inspected the schools of Palestine in the early months of 1947.

In June, the United Nations Special Committee on Palestine (UNSCOP) arrived in Jerusalem to review the situation and to make proposals for the future of the country. UNSCOP published its report on August 31, 1947, recommending that Palestine be divided into two sovereign states, one Jewish and one Arab, with Jerusalem designated a demilitarized city under an international trusteeship and a UN-appointed governor. The plan was to take effect on September 1, 1948. The Jewish Agency accepted the plan despite the loss of Jerusalem. The Arab Higher Committee rejected the plan.[30]

While waiting for the United Nations to vote on this proposal for partition, the British established three security zones in Jerusalem. The pupils and teachers of the Evelina School found additional barbed wire and barricades in front of Frutiger House, which faced one of the security zones. The neighborhood of the school became increasingly dangerous as the Jewish residents left and moved to the western part of the city. As Jews left their homes in neighboring Musrara, Arab fighters used the vacant buildings as hideouts.

On November 29, 1947, the United Nations voted to accept the resolution of UNSCOP. Because of the time difference, news of the decision reached Jerusalem after midnight that night. Throughout the early hours of the morning of November 30, Jewish Jerusalem celebrated. However, the revelry was cut short as Arabs attacked a bus traveling to Jerusalem. Six Jews were killed that day. On December 2, about two hundred Arab youths looted the commercial center of Jerusalem near the Jaffa Gate, setting several textile stores on fire. Jews responded by attacking Arab stores on Queen Mary's Avenue and setting fire to an Arab garage. The British imposed a curfew on Jerusalem's Arab neighborhoods.[31]

Amid this continuing violence, Levy urged her pupils to come to school as usual. As on so many previous occasions when violence had erupted in the city, the headmistress urged the girls to carry on. Parents, fearful for the safety of their children, insisted that the school close its doors until the rioting stopped. Levy was steadfast, however; she relied on the support of the Royal Air Force, which had quarters near the school, to provide a safe corridor around the school entrance for her pupils. Even during times of curfew, Evelina students and teachers were conducted safely through the British security zone that bordered the school. Nevertheless, repeated threats to the nearby Palestine Broadcasting Service increased the climate of fear around the school.

Fear was not limited to the parents of Evelina pupils. Zvi Zayonce, the superintendent of the school, had developed relationships over the years with neighboring Arabs. They confessed to him that they were fearful of the milk cans that were used to deliver milk to the school. He understood that they were thinking of the milk cans that had been used to hide explosives in the King David Hotel bombing. Zayonce, knowing that the school had no weapons for self-defense, encouraged this erroneous belief.[32]

While the parents of Evelina girls pressed Levy to close the school, the Haganah pressed her to keep it open to prevent a further ceding of Jerusalem neighborhoods to Arabs. Zayonce, who had been working secretly with the Haganah for many years, now revealed his previously clandestine role. He proceeded to surround the school with even more barbed wire and added bars on the windows facing the restive neighborhood of Musrara. These actions quieted parental concerns for a short while.

In response to increased violence, on December 28, 1947, worried parents called a meeting to demand that Levy close the school. After permitting the parents to air their views, she informed them that the Defense Ministry of the Jewish Agency had requested the school to keep its doors open and had promised to send Jewish guards to protect the children. She noted that the Royal Air Force continued to be of immense help in protecting the school.

Finally, she assured the parents that she was at work on a contingency plan for the school that would go into effect when necessary.

In recognition of the seriousness of the danger, she distributed new safety protocols designed to address their concerns:

1. All breaks were shortened.
2. Half the staff would be on duty at each break to see that children kept to the hall side of the playground and that noise was kept to a minimum.
3. Seventh-period lessons and after-school activities were suspended to allow all children to go home together.
4. Staff members would be on duty to watch the girls coming to school and going home.
5. As of January 1, 1948, the school day would be reorganized to allow children to go home as early as possible. There would be no lunch hour. The younger pupils would have five lessons daily, finishing at 12:45 p.m. The rest of the school would finish at 1:30 p.m. almost every day, and the top classes would finish at 2:15 p.m. one day a week. Group lessons and Girl Guide meetings would be suspended for the time being.[33]

The Move to Rehavia

One day after issuing these guidelines, an explosion at the Damascus Gate shook the whole area. This time, fearing reprisals, Levy decided to dismiss the pupils immediately.[34] The Evelina girls never returned to Frutiger House. For months, Levy had been secretly working on a plan using her long experience in solving problems in Jerusalem to establish the Evelina School in a new home in the Jewish neighborhood of Rehavia. The Jerusalem Girls' College, built near the Ratisbonne Monastery in Rehavia, had vacated its premises in February 1947 when British women and children were ordered to evacuate Palestine. The district commissioner of Jerusalem had given the buildings to the Jewish authorities to house Jews who had been forced to leave their homes when parts of the city were zoned for British troops. A handful of pupils and teachers of the Jerusalem Girls' College who had not yet left Palestine were living at the American Colony.[35]

While keeping up a brave front with the parents and her pupils, Levy had quietly approached Archdeacon Campbell MacInnes, the son of the former bishop who had befriended Landau many years earlier, to suggest an exchange of premises. Her suggestion was received with enthusiasm; since Frutiger House was adjacent to St. George's School and to St. Paul's Church, it was a more convenient neighborhood for the college. However, before the plan could be put into effect, those who had been temporarily housed in the college buildings would have to leave, and the Anglo-Jewish Association would have to agree to the exchange. At the same time that these discussions were occurring, the administration of Hebrew University on Mount Scopus announced that the university would close and classes be suspended.[36]

The tension in the city had reached new levels when the Evelina School began to move into one of the buildings of the Jerusalem Girls' College in mid-January 1948. In the two weeks that it remained empty, Frutiger House, a symbol of British-Jewish cooperation, became the target of violence. Bullet holes were found in Levy's office, just above her desk, and in many classrooms. Jewish porters were reluctant to work on the transfer and to use their trucks for transporting desks and chairs. Zayonce negotiated with the neighboring Arabs, who gave him one of their trucks and even helped to load the furniture and supplies. This truck carried the goods to the border of the Jewish section, where it was unloaded and reloaded by a Jewish driver.[37]

The Evelina School reopened on January 13 in Rehavia. There were as many parents as pupils on the first morning. Levy reported, "The happy faces of the parents and pupils were reward for the difficulties of the prior two weeks."[38] The headmistress was forced to make several changes in response to the new circumstances. Since the new facilities had no large assembly hall, the morning assembly for prayer was discontinued; prayers were held instead in each classroom. Communal school lunches were also abandoned, since there was no place to establish a kitchen, nor was there space for schoolwide dining. Children ate at their desks and made do with what they could bring from home. For several weeks the limited space was shared with one remaining tenant and with the Fire Brigade, whose fire engines, parked on the doorstep of the school, the children soon started using as a playground. Finally, in March the tenant moved out, and soon after the Fire Brigade found other quarters. The school now had more room.

Levy and the teachers tried to continue regular classes for a little while longer. Despite their efforts, there was little gaiety as the school struggled to maintain normalcy amid the chaos around it. On February 1, there was an explosion in central Jerusalem in the building that housed the offices of the *Palestine Post*. In response to the growing violence, the Jewish Agency approached Levy with a request to free the girls in the upper two classes one day a week for training and national service in the Haganah. In view of the deteriorating situation of the previous two months, she decided that she could not refuse. She explained as follows:

> In any case, almost every girl of those classes has during those two months volunteered for some service or other, but it has been "underground," as they know that until now we have not allowed these activities among our pupils. Should we now persist in this attitude we would engender resentment of pupils and parents alike, for most of the latter are in the Civil Guard … and we would not prevent the girls from doing what they feel is their duty.[39]

To protect the girls as much as possible, she arranged for the gym mistress to accompany those who volunteered for training. Training sessions were held on Thursday, and classes normally held on that day were moved to Friday.

The Road to Independence

The students who were scheduled to graduate in 1948 and 1949 had unique experiences shaped by the shortages of World War II, by the siege of Jerusalem that followed the UN vote on the partition of Palestine, and by their experiences in youth groups and the Haganah. These girls belonged to various youth groups despite the school ban on such activities. Several girls in the class of 1948 joined Maccabi Hatzair, among them Miriam Ochana, Adaya Hochberg, and Adina Shoshani. Others, like Michal Harrison, joined Bnei Akivah. Marta Zayonce, a few years older, joined the socialist Hashomer Hatzair.

Membership in youth groups was attractive to the young teenagers because it was an opportunity to socialize with boys as well as a way to express their growing Zionist feelings. The youth groups were training grounds for membership in the Haganah. The German refugee girls were the only ones officially permitted to belong to Ezra, an Orthodox youth group, to which they had belonged before coming to Jerusalem. Although the school formally continued to forbid all other girls to join youth groups, none of those who joined were dismissed because of their membership.[40]

Throughout the early months of 1948, violence continued unabated. On

February 22 three trucks exploded on nearby Ben Yehuda Street, killing 52 Jews, among them Adaya Hochberg's mother. On March 11 a car bomb destroyed a section of the Jewish Agency building, killing thirteen. Unpredictable killings and repeated attacks on food convoys left Jerusalem hobbled. Levy reported that by March the food supply had diminished alarmingly. Shops were empty. There was nothing to be bought but a ration of bread. There was no milk; no fresh fruit or vegetables; indeed, no fresh food of any kind. People lived on their stores of preserved food.

As abundant spring flowers returned to the hills of Jerusalem, the violence escalated. On April 9 the Arab village of Deir Yassin was attacked by the Irgun and the Stern Gang, killing more than a hundred, including women and children. Hala Sakakini, a twenty-four-year-old Christian Arab teacher living in Katamon, wrote, "The most terrible stories have reached us from eyewitnesses who escaped this unbelievable massacre. I never thought Jews could be so cruel."[41] In retaliation, on April 14 a convoy of ambulances, buses, and trucks carrying doctors, nurses, and hospital supplies was attacked by Arabs en route to Hadassah Hospital, killing seventy-seven. Zipporah Borowsky, an American student whose studies at Hebrew University had ceased, was working as a medical volunteer. She wrote home, "So many friends, so many doctors, nurses, patients, university scientists, administrative staff, such a heavy loss.... All Jerusalem is walking around asking itself:'Is there no end?'"[42]

After the move to Rehavia, the refugee girls living in the Schwartzstein House were cut off from classes for security reasons. Teachers periodically came to visit and to tutor the girls. The Haganah asked the Schwartzstein girls to assist its efforts by keeping a lookout from their bathroom window, which had a view of the Damascus Gate, and by reporting any suspicious activities. Later they were asked to learn first aid; they practiced at the Schneller Center, built as an orphanage and now serving as a Haganah staging ground. The Schwartzstein girls joined Zipporah Borowsky and many others at filling sacks with sand to protect homes in the neighborhood. Because of the increasing vulnerability of their own home to attack, many of the girls moved in with family members in safer parts of the city. By the time the Haganah closed the Schwartzstein House, in May 1948, it had been abandoned by the refugee orphans for whom it had once served as a haven.[43]

At the end of April, the attention of the city was focused on the availability of food. Thanks to the extraordinary effort of the water engineers of

Jerusalem, who saw to it that reservoirs, tanks, and cisterns were filled and sealed to await the coming of more difficult times, water rationing worked well. When the water supply was cut, people could count on one pail of water per person per day. However, food was a bigger problem, since convoys to Jerusalem were repeatedly attacked and turned back.

Finally, just before Passover, two convoys were successful in reaching the starved city. Jerusalemites rushed to buy food for the holidays, but the festivities were brief. A third convoy was ambushed and the road closed again. The entire civilian population contributed to the defense of the city. Men up to forty-five years old and women up to forty years old were called up for military duty, and men and women over those respective ages joined the Civil Guard. They helped with fortifications and took over the distribution of water. Teachers and older pupils at the Evelina School participated in part-time defense work.

Despite the country's rapid descent into anarchy, the British announced their intention to leave several months before their anticipated withdrawal in September 1948. On the morning of May 14, the last high commissioner, Sir Alan Cunningham, left Palestine. In Tel Aviv that afternoon, David Ben-Gurion, the chairman of the Jewish Agency, read a declaration of independence and announced the establishment of the Jewish state, to be called Israel. Celebratory singing and dancing broke out all over the country, but by nightfall the Arab Legion had amassed at the Allenby Bridge, the entrance to Jerusalem from Jordan. King Abdullah commanded them to cross.

In Jerusalem, shelling began immediately. Levy reported the following:

> The first shell to fall in Rehavia fell in the School grounds. An order came to close all schools on May 17. On May 23 all school heads met to determine future action. I shall never forget that meeting—the room rocked with the explosion of shells. We heard that Abdullah, at the head of his troops, had reached the Old City, the Egyptians had reached Bethlehem, indeed the fate of the Old City was so insecure that it seemed unreal to discuss whether or not to reopen School when at any minute the city might fall. We decided to meet in a few days but the meeting was not resumed as shelling was so continuous that parents were unwilling to send their children to school.[44]

For a month children stayed huddled at home; nobody went anywhere unless it was absolutely necessary. Essential services such as bakeries, water distribution, and newspapers were maintained, but all other shops remained closed. In Levy's opinion, this was the most trying period of all. It was terribly unsafe to be outside and not particularly safe to be indoors. There was no communication with the outside world, no postal service, no light, and no fuel, and bread rations were reduced from a quarter of a loaf per person to a sixth; no one knew how long this state of affairs would last.

Levy put into practice the ideals she had taught her students. After the Hadassah convoy was attacked in April, when so many doctors and nurses were killed, the hospital moved into town, taking over the English Mission Hospital and St. Joseph Convent. With primitive equipment and no medical supplies, the medical personnel began to work. Levy volunteered to help them:

> It was tragic to see the victims of the shelling of Jerusalem. I must confess that most of us were less frightened than indignant and angry that the Nations of the world should stand by and see Jerusalem, the Holy City, become the scene of the worst and most savage fighting of all. So many victims were old men and women and small children—this small boy without a leg, this girl of 15 delivering a letter for the Civil Guard finds herself without a hand, which has been completely blown off at the wrist. She cried pitifully when she was brought in—"Where is my hand? Give me back my hand."[45]

The Jews remaining in the Old City suffered from lack of information, random violence, and privations of food and water. Their worst period was mid-May, when shelling of the Jewish Quarter began. The daughters of the *mukhtar*, Rabbi Weingarten, were all either former pupils or presently attending the school. The older ones worked in the hospital opened by their father.

One of the wounded was Esther Cailingold, a teacher who had arrived at the Evelina School from England in November 1946, when she was twenty-one. She asked for leave in December 1947 in order to join the defense forces. Levy explained that teachers were exempt from full-time service and urged her to follow the example of the other teachers who taught during the day and did volunteer defense work after classes. Despite Levy's advice, Cailingold stopped teaching in order to give herself completely to the defense effort.

Nevertheless, whenever she was able, she came to visit the school. The pupils admired her youth and beauty; they saw her as a heroine bravely fighting for the future of the Jewish people. After the school moved to Rehavia, Cailingold, who had worked with refugee girls in London during the war, visited the girls who remained at Schwartzstein House, encouraging them to continue studying at home. She also supported them in their efforts to aid in defense work.[46]

In late May 1948, Cailingold waited in line for a whole week so that she could be one of ten volunteers who were permitted to enter the Old City each day. It was the most dangerous period of all. Levy recalled, "We prayed for her." Later Levy learned that Cailingold was wounded a week after entering the Old City. She was in the hospital when conditions became so desperate that all the patients who were ambulatory left to help in the defense. The doctor begged her to remain to assist him, since his only assistant was the young nurse Masha Weingarten. Cailingold refused; she returned to her post and was hit again by a shell. She was paralyzed below the waist when she was brought back to the hospital. She died on May 28, the day the Old City surrendered.[47]

The schools in Jerusalem remained closed for a month, until a truce came into effect in mid-June. The girls in the top three classes had been working for the Haganah, which became the Israel Defense Forces (IDF) on May 15, 1948. Some who returned to school in June had suffered personal injuries; many had lost family members and friends. The school atmosphere was one of bereavement. The truce ended in mid-July; again all schools closed, and they stayed closed until early September, when a second truce was declared that lasted several weeks.

There was an exodus from Jerusalem during the truce period. The seat of the government moved to Tel Aviv, and most government offices moved at this time. Lawyers and businessmen followed them. In Jerusalem, Levy reflected, "On the Ninth of Av when we read Lamentations in the synagogue, the picture of Jerusalem described therein was not very different from conditions prevailing in the Holy City."[48]

Matriculation Exams Canceled

Despite the disruptions caused by civil strife and the shortages caused by the siege, the students in the matriculation class studied for their exams. However, the exam that was scheduled to arrive in June 1948 did not come. Some girls, like Shulamit Lilienfeld, were deeply disappointed when the London matriculation exam was canceled. Shulamit had hoped to study medicine, but without a school-leaving examination she could not continue her education. Her father used his connections to enroll his daughter in Ma'aleh, a Hebrew-language high school, where she studied for the Bagrut, the leave-taking exam created for Zionist schools.

Shulamit passed the test, but the disruption to her education took a severe toll. Her science grades were not high enough for her to enter medical school. In 1950 she was drafted and served as an army nurse. Later she studied physical therapy and was employed in that field for many years. After marrying and raising four children, Shulamit, ever a serious student, returned to school, where she was awarded both a bachelor's degree and a master's degree. She became a leader in developing an academic curriculum for the field of physical therapy, serving for many years as head of the Physical Therapy Department at Tel Aviv University. She continues to consult in this area.[49]

Miriam Ochana was also deprived of the opportunity to take the London matriculation exam. Unlike Shulamit, she didn't enroll in another high school and attempt to pass the Bagrut. In 1952, after army service, she returned to Jerusalem and was hired to work in the prime minister's office, where her knowledge of Hebrew and English as well as her strong work ethic made her a valued member of the staff. She set up protocols for the offices of David Ben-Gurion and later of Levi Eshkol. In 1968, she was recruited to work at Hebrew University, where she set up the International Students' Office. She worked at the university for thirty years until retirement. Like most of her contemporaries, Miriam also married and raised a family.[50]

Adina Shoshani also took no school-leaving test. However, the love of gardening developed during her years at school prompted her to seek fulfillment working on the land. After army service, Adina settled with members of her youth group, Maccabi Hatzair, in the Jezreel Valley, where they started Kibbutz HaSolelim. In the beginning, she worked moving large stones to create roads and to clear the land for farming. She participated in every aspect of kibbutz life and raised a family. Adina affirmed that her thriving garden in the kibbutz today is the result of the love for gardening inspired by the beautiful garden surrounding Frutiger House. Adina also married and raised a family.[51]

Another member of the class who did not take a school-leaving exam was Michal Harrison. After her graduation from Evelina, she attended the David Yellin Teachers' Training College and later served in the IDF. Michal worked as a kindergarten teacher at an immigrant camp, and in 1951 she represented

Israel in the Miss Universe pageant held in London. Arriving in London, she reported, was like a homecoming. The city felt familiar from the illustrations in the schoolbooks used in the Evelina School, and of course she spoke fluent English.

Michal returned to Israel and married Yitzchak Modai, a long-serving member of the Knesset and the minister of finance. She began her volunteer career at the Women's International Zionist Organization (wizo), at first focusing her attention on the absorption of new immigrants. Michal, who came from a poor family in Meah Shearim that was used to accepting charity, explained that she learned to give to others as a student in the Evelina School. She became the chairwoman of wizo Israel in 1979; in 1996 she was elected president of World wizo, and in 2000 she was reelected. Michal, who died in 2012, had two children and seven grandchildren.[52]

Elisheva Shifman was also deprived of the chance to take the London matriculation exam. Like Miriam Ochana, Elisheva's first position after army service was in government. She served for two years in the office of Foreign Minister Moshe Sharett and for four years in London as secretary to Ambassador Eliahu Eilat. In Israel, she worked as a secretary to Abba Eban when he was the president of the Weizmann Institute and later as secretary to Professor Ephraim Katzir, the head of the institute's Department of Biophysics. Elisheva returned to Jerusalem in 1973 when Professor Katzir became president of Israel, and she became his personal assistant.[53]

Elisheva retired from government service in 1979 and worked part-time in documentation of the president's archive. She later created a business for office services and word processing in English and Hebrew. Elisheva is married with three children and nine grandchildren. She explained her success and that of her fellow classmates as follows:

> The "Landau girls" were integrated into high positions in the new institutions that were created after the establishment of the State, and contributed a great deal to the integration of Israel in the world community—in Foreign Service, in the Israel Broadcasting Authority, and to a large extent in academia too.... For those who majored in studies that required knowledge of English, this was especially a great blessing—in the fields of medicine, law, English literature, and the like.[54]

The disruption caused when the 1948 London matriculation exam failed to arrive was only one of several pressing concerns for Ethel Levy when the school reopened in September. Enrollment was reduced to 323 when 30 percent of the Evelina pupils did not return. Some were serving in the IDF and others, like Adaya Hochberg, left Jerusalem with their families. There was little reason to believe that the exam sponsored by the British Mandatory government would ever be sent again. As a result, Levy offered students the opportunity to study the same material in Hebrew so that they could take the Bagrut, the exam given by the Jewish Education Department, soon to become the Ministry of Education.[55] Eleven members of the class, including Rivka Zweig, spent an extra year learning chemistry and math in Hebrew from David Reider and Walter Reis, neither of whom had ever taught their subjects in Hebrew before.[56]

Resolutely, Levy issued a booklet reformulating the purpose of the Evelina de Rothschild School in the following way: "The aim of the School is to give its pupils an education fitting them to become good Jewish women, able to take their place in the country as loyal Self-Supporting citizens."[57]

Israel Ministry of Education: New Policies

The challenges for Levy, severe during the end of the Mandate and the War of Independence, did not abate as the cease-fire was deliberated. In January 1949, Wachman, the senior Hebrew teacher, died suddenly. Mr. Itzchaki, who normally would have taken on much of Wachman's work, was still in the army. Reis, the mathematics teacher, was also mobilized until March. The shortage of teachers caused serious problems, but the decision of the Ministry of Education, which announced free and compulsory elementary education for all children up to the age of twelve, excluding bilingual programs, caused many to defect from the Evelina School. Levy recognized that many parents would send their children to free public elementary schools to avoid paying school fees. Simultaneously, the Anglo-Jewish Association decreased its subsidy. In view of their limited funds, the association's leaders decided to give their support to individual students from Israel who were admitted to advanced studies in Britain.[58]

Levy held several meetings to try to save the elementary division of the school, but she was unable to create an exemption from the new rules for the Evelina School. The goal of elementary school education funded by the state was to unify through the national language, Hebrew. Thus, the bilingual character of the Evelina School, which had come under attack throughout its history, was dealt a fatal blow. In May 1950, Levy, following the example set by the Alliance schools, reached an agreement with the Ministry of Education whereby the elementary classes of the Evelina de Rothschild School were turned over to the municipality of Jerusalem. In a concession to the head-mistress, the two top elementary classes were given some English instruction, paid for by the Anglo-Jewish Association.

Secondary education, which was not yet compulsory or free, continued to operate as an independent program, dependent on funds from school fees and a small grant from the Anglo-Jewish Association. The Bagrut replaced the London matriculation exam as the school-leaving examination.[59] Mrs. Levy remained the headmistress of the secondary school and the guiding spirit of the entire program, which retained the Evelina de Rothschild name.

At this critical moment in the school's history, Levy shared her reflections with the school's supporters in London. Noting that the school, in common with almost every other institution, had entered a new phase, Levy reviewed its history:

> The first phase was from its founding in 1867 by the Rothschild family until 1893, when it was taken over by the Anglo-Jewish Association; its second— from 1893 till the First World War, when Miss Landau began her great work of making it a modern School of the first order; the foundations were firmly laid in the practice of orthodox Judaism. By this she won the confidence of parents who had been disinclined to give their daughters a secular education, and many of them in sending their daughters to the School risked ostracism and even loss of "chaluka," the subsidy paid by the different committees to their nationals. When parents found that the School strengthened their children in the knowledge and appreciation of Judaism taught in the home, they had neither fear nor doubt, and the number rose. Later, the excellent secular education was to attract orthodox and non-orthodox alike.

She continued her review with the third phase, which began when Britain received the Mandate for Palestine. During this period the school had extended its activities to become a secondary school, with the London matriculation exam as its final test, and had continued its commercial class. Levy stressed that the work of the school could be judged by what its Old Girls contributed to the life of Jerusalem and the country. The earlier generations of pupils had married, and their children and grandchildren became pupils of the school.

In their day, she explained, they found useful and profitable work with little difficulty and often supported the whole family with their earnings. During the period of the Mandate, Evelina girls were to be found in every government office, in the banks, and in important businesses.

The school, Levy concluded, had entered its fourth phase:

> Most people thought it was because of their extremely good knowledge of English, but this was only half the reason, for were that all, our girls today would have difficulty in finding jobs, with Hebrew of such supreme importance in the new State. Yet they are now to be found in most important Government offices—in the Prime Minister's Office—in the Treasury, the Legal Department, and every other office. Banks and businesses, etc., and they are highly thought of and given responsible work requiring trust. Why is it then that with these new conditions that exist since Israel developed out of Palestine that our girls are much sought after, and why were so many of our girls given commissions and positions of trust in the Army during the dark days of the war two years ago? The Old Girls themselves have told me the reason. Our employers, they say, tell us that we know how to start a job and how to finish it, and we also know how to behave while the job is in progress. They feel they can rely upon us and trust us and are glad to work with us.

Levy concluded her overview and analysis with a rhetorical question: In the new conditions now prevailing in the country, is the school still necessary? Her answer was passionate:

> It was necessary in the past for the particular reasons and conditions that existed then, it is no less important today in fulfilling the needs created by the new conditions. The most important public schools of England have long and interesting histories and have made their tremendous contribution to the life and history of England, but almost every one of them—Charterhouse, the Guild Schools, etc.—began centuries ago as Charity or Poor Law Schools. Conditions have changed with them, but their *value* has not changed. The Evelina made its great contribution in the past and it has its contribution to make in the future.

Finally, Levy included a view of the larger situation of the new state:

> These are most interesting days in Israel; one is conscious of living in the midst of momentous happenings. The new State has shown remarkable courage in

undertaking tasks that would have overwhelmed older and more stable states; it has also shown remarkable political maturity in some aspects of its political life. Many mistakes have been made and many more will no doubt be made. It is not always comfortable to live in times of great change, however interesting they may be, and the change that has come to Israel is enormous. One hears criticism and grumbling from time to time—nevertheless the overall achievement is so remarkable and so great that one feels one must do everything to maintain this great opportunity and extraordinary achievement. The School has made its great contribution in the past; its contribution is as necessary today as it was then. The AJA gave willingly then and I am sure it will continue to support the School and thus make its contribution in the future welfare of Israel. [60]

Levy had modified the school curriculum in order to guarantee its survival. She also decided that the future of the school would be more secure in Rehavia. When the Child Welfare Department asked if it could rent the now abandoned Frutiger House for five years, she began a series of negotiations that resulted in a five-year rental of the building in Rehavia, paid for by the rent on Frutiger House. When the badly damaged Frutiger House was ready for occupancy, the Department of Education arranged to take over the rental from Child Welfare. Today, the office that was Landau's and later Levy's is used by the minister of education.

The strong tradition of service, begun in the early years of the school, continued in the 1950s. The Evelina School was one of the first to offer help to new immigrants in the *ma'abarot* (temporary housing) in the Jerusalem Corridor. Pupils of the top three classes, accompanied by their teachers, took turns spending the Sabbath with the new arrivals. Levy reported that this was a satisfying experience for the girls and for those whom they helped. In addition, every girl in the school provided toys for the general collection made at Chanukah; eleven Evelina girls, in school uniform, carried the gifts to the offices of the *Jerusalem Post* (the renamed *Palestine Post*), which organized the collection.[61] These activities followed the school tradition of community service started so many decades earlier under Landau's leadership.

In 1951, the country was suffering from shortages of all sorts; food, clothing, and building supplies were rationed. Even so, a large group of Old Girls from Tel Aviv, Jaffa, Lydda, and various army camps gathered in January, eager to attend the first Old Girls' meeting since the siege of Jerusalem. They shared their wartime experiences and their plans for the future. Many planned careers as teachers and nurses.[62] The Old Girls also continued to report their successes to their former teachers. Shulamit Braun was one of sixteen students selected from a pool of eight hundred applicants for scholarships at American universities. She followed several other Old Girls who were already studying abroad on university scholarships. Rachel Tokatly, who had graduated in 1947, was training the Knesset stenographers and had recently produced the first Hebrew shorthand textbook.

The next few years were difficult economic times for the country, for the city, and for the school. Levy reported in June 1952 that for the first time in many years the school was unable to provide milk for the children at midday. The Jerusalem municipality, which had assumed the schools' milk service, made the *ma'abarot* their priority; as a result, the children of the Jerusalem schools were no longer served. Therefore, Evelina pupils were given nothing to drink from 7:30 a.m. until they got home at 3 p.m.

In addition, the rationing regulations made it impossible for the school to distribute textbooks and stationery. Shortages and rationing also affected the needlework and handiwork lessons. Despite these disadvantages, the pupils enjoyed some new opportunities. The Department of Education introduced swimming lessons at the YMCA; this was viewed very positively by the pupils. Also, a School Children Traffic Police was established in Jerusalem. The girls selected as "police" were given special berets and white sleeves; they led a citywide campaign for "safety first."[63]

The economic crisis in Jerusalem continued. In 1953 only ninety-eight girls remained in the secondary division of the school. Since no children had been admitted during the siege years, it was not surprising that the overall number of girls was affected. The decline also reflected the difficulty faced by parents who were asked to pay climbing school fees. The state continued to cover the costs of elementary education and to provide grants to Hebrew University and to the Technion, but secondary schools were forced to rely on fees and contributions from abroad. The burden for some parents was alleviated by the introduction of scholarships for twelve students.

At the same time, the Old Girls continued to record successes in a wide range of endeavors. Dvorah Rackover, a student in her last year at Hebrew University, was selected by her professor to assist him on a piece of scientific research that was published in the *Biochemical Journal of Great Britain* under both their names. In recognition of her work, she was awarded a scholarship by the Massachusetts Institute of Technology. Another student, Shulamith Burstein, was employed by the Foreign Office; she was the only woman and the youngest contributor to an anthology of poetry by young Israeli poets. Rachel Tokatly's Hebrew shorthand book was adopted as a textbook at the Evelina School. Despite the disruptions caused by turbulent times, the girls possessed the self-confidence and skills to develop professional lives, using both Hebrew and English to further their careers.[64]

In June 1955, Levy visited England and reported on a successful year to the Anglo-Jewish Association. She noted that in addition to classroom studies, literature and Latin circles were held. These after-school clubs, run by teachers, were remembered fondly by the participants. In addition, many of the pupils were members of the Bezalel Museum Association, and a number continued to provide social services to the ma'abarot. Tzipora Sharett, the wife of the prime minister, appealed to schoolchildren to help entertain new immigrants during the Purim celebrations. In response, a party of Evelina girls went to the Yemenite settlement of Yishi, where they performed plays and entertained with music and dancing; they enjoyed a memorable evening. Levy also reported that the Johannesburg Festival of the Universe had a competition for Queen of the Air, in which twelve airlines participated. The winner of the crown was Aliza Flasher, an El Al hostess, an Evelina graduate, and the daughter of an Evelina graduate.[65]

The next year, the school was visited by forty students from Hebrew University, accompanied by Dr. Adar, their lecturer in education. The students observed the prayer assembly that had been part of the school since early in Landau's tenure, attended class lessons, and were given a brief history of the school. They were particularly interested in the daily morning assembly and prayers, which they viewed as something quite exceptional. Adar commented that the morning assembly set the tone for the school and had an influence on the individual characters of the pupils. The Hebrew University students also noted that the dignity of the service was made more memorable by the requirement to wear school uniforms.

This visit was followed by one from Mr. Watkins, the education officer for the British county of Gloucester; Mr. Lake, a British Council representative; and Noah Nardi of the Israeli Ministry of Education and Culture. Watkins spoke to the girls in the matriculation class on aspects of education in England

and recent projects for young people. He was impressed by their command of English and by the books they had read.[66]

In later October 1956, school classes and activities were again interrupted by war. The Sinai Campaign commenced shortly after classes had resumed after the summer recess. Air raid shelters were hurriedly constructed, air raid drills were instituted, and a first-aid course was arranged. Many teachers were called away for military service. By December, school life had returned to normal, but Levy anticipated serious problems that would be caused by a new influx of immigrants from Egypt and other parts of North Africa.

Her instincts were correct. The population surge led to a serious teacher shortage throughout Israel. Inducements were made to pupils at all levels to enter teachers' seminaries to speed up the certification of teachers. Under normal circumstances, pupils were expected to complete secondary schooling before entering a teachers' seminary, but exceptions were made to meet the urgent need. Tuition at the Teachers' Seminary was sixty pounds per year, whereas the typical tuition for secondary schools was six times that much; parents were sometimes forced to make decisions based on their limited budgets.[67]

Although tough times continued, a joyous Purim carnival was held in 1957 in Jerusalem. This carnival was the fruit of weeks of hard work on the part of children, youth leaders, teachers, and the Jerusalem municipality. The Evelina contribution was a historical pageant, a national-religious presentation of Miriam and her maidens dancing before Moses and Aaron after the crossing of the Red Sea. The girls were cheered enthusiastically by the watching crowds.[68]

Levy's report the next year focused on the celebrations for the tenth anniversary of the state of Israel. To mark the occasion, the pupils created an exhibition featuring the history of the Evelina School. The opening event coincided with a parents' meeting and was of great interest to parents and pupils alike. Photos of the old classrooms in which sewing and embroidery were taught, attendance records, sports trophies, and Girl Guide uniforms were displayed along with coronation mugs, Evelina prayer books, and copies of *School* magazine. Pictures of the schoolgirls and their teachers were searched for loved ones. These artifacts of days gone by were deeply appreciated by those in attendance. The exhibition was a catalyst for many of the alumnae to examine their memories and to begin to tell their stories.

As in earlier decades, the school played a role in communal celebrations. On Independence Day, the school grounds were used by the municipality for a campfire with community singing and dancing that went on into the early hours of the morning, and the Evelina Gadna (prearmy) group, which had replaced the Girl Guides of earlier years, took part in the Independence Day torchlight parade. Members of class 6 responded to the municipality's request for young people to help those less fortunate than themselves by forming a chapter of the *noar le-noar* (youth to youth) group that met regularly for talks on psychology and training in youth leadership. The group's activities, which included helping in playgrounds in poor districts on the borders of Jerusalem, visiting sick children, and assisting the blind, had deep roots in the history of the school.[69]

Ethel Levy continued to serve as headmistress until her retirement in 1960. She devoted a considerable amount of time to working out a pension plan for the long-serving teachers and staff of the Evelina School, but she also sought to ensure the future of the school. In view of the continuing economic hardships in Israel and the shrinking resources of the Anglo-Jewish Association, she recommended a merger with the Ephrata Secondary Girls' School. Like the Evelina School, it was a religious school, and it acted as a "feeder" to the Ephrata Teachers' Training College.

In view of the serious teacher shortage in the country and the growing need based on increased immigration to Israel, this merger was welcomed by the Anglo-Jewish Association. Pupils studying at the combined secondary school, which retained the Evelina de Rothschild School name, now had a choice of a general academic curriculum or one that prepared them to enter the Teachers' College.[70] The merger had the immediate result of bolstering flagging enrollment.

Upon her retirement, Levy returned to London, where she never tired of talking about the Evelina School. In 1965, she presented a progress report to the readers of the *Jewish Observer and Middle East Review* in which she disclosed that the Evelina high school enrollment was now 429, with four times as many new immigrants as those born in Israel. Pupils at the Evelina School reflected new immigrant groups arriving from a variety of countries: Iraq, ninety-one; Morocco, fifty-six; Poland, forty-two; Iran, thirty-nine; Yemen, thirty-five; Germany, twenty-eight; Romania, nineteen; Hungary, fourteen; Czechoslovakia, fourteen; India, three; England, three; and the

United States, two. Eighty-three pupils had been born in Israel. Some of the pupils came from outside Jerusalem and were housed in a dormitory in Baka that also housed the Ephrata Teachers' College pupils.[71] One-third of the Evelina graduates went on to university, others trained as lab technicians or nurses, and the majority became teachers.[72]

Levy continued to maintain ties to the Old Girls through letters and visits. She was tireless in giving talks and writing articles encouraging continued support of the school. For these talks and articles, she documented her thoughts on the history and significance of the Evelina de Rothschild School within the larger framework of the history of modern Jerusalem, providing evidence of its robust traditions and continuing vitality.

Nevertheless, after her departure—and the retirement of Pnina Moed, formerly Goldstein and Batia Bromberger, formerly Salasnik, both of whom had entered the school at the age of five and were educated and trained there as teachers, and of David Reider, who taught science, mathematics, and Jewish subjects for more than thirty-five years—the school gradually lost the special character it had taken so long to build. English studies lost importance to all except those who planned to become English teachers or to pursue university studies in English literature.

As a result of the hard work of Levy's successor, Pincas Rosengarten, the student body grew and new areas of study were added. In the 1970s enrollment reached 750 and the pass rate on the Bagrut approached 100 percent. In 1972, after prolonged negotiation with the Anglo-Jewish Association, the upper division of the Evelina de Rothschild School was transferred to the Jerusalem municipality.[73] In subsequent decades, the achievements of Evelina students were eclipsed as new high schools developed programs of excellence that attracted high-performing students. Gradually, the level of performance of the incoming pupils declined, and so did the level of instruction.

Four decades after the school celebrated its centenary, the municipality of Jerusalem began to discuss closing the Evelina high school and maintaining only the elementary school, which had been part of the Orthodox stream of public schools since 1949 and retained the name of the former school. That fate was averted by a court decision resulting from a lawsuit brought by the Anglo-Jewish Association. Today the upper division of the Evelina School continues to operate as a junior and senior high school, part of the religious stream of public girls' schools educating new generations of Jewish girls in Jerusalem.[74]

EPILOGUE

Lessons Learned

When Annie Landau arrived in Jerusalem in 1899, she found it to be in a pitiful state. She believed that the poverty, disease, dirt, and lack of initiative that characterized the Jewish community of the city were a result of the woeful neglect of the education of its girls, and she devoted her life to changing the situation, developing a curriculum focused on Jewish values and modern texts. She was often accused of educating her pupils to be unfit for their surroundings. She happily pleaded guilty to the charge, convinced that her graduates would change the city for the better. Landau, and later Levy, prepared the pupils for leadership roles in their communities and in their professions. The young women who graduated in the 1930s and 1940s were aware that they attended an unusual school that expected much of them. They did not disappoint their headmistresses and their teachers.

As the decades passed, the graduates pursued careers, nurtured families, and built their homeland. Many maintained contact with one another, rejoicing together in their successes and grieving at their losses. Slowly they retired from their professional roles and began to think of the legacy they would leave to their children, their grandchildren, and the nation they had helped to create. All the alumnae contacted for this book appreciated the opportunities they had as citizens of a modern society, opportunities that were denied their parents, who had grown up in more restrictive settings. All expressed disappointment that their children were still fighting for the safety and security of their homeland. Some wondered whether they could have prevented some of the current problems by making different choices. Others wondered what they could do today to facilitate dialogue among hostile groups.

The women profiled in this section were selected from a larger group of women interviewed, all of whose stories enriched this study. Each was selected because she had thought deeply about the influence of the school on her life and because she had contributed to the foundation and the development of the state of Israel. Each expressed appreciation for the unique education she had received that prepared her to act boldly, with confidence, and with skill when called on to respond to a myriad of challenges. Each spoke of role models—Annie Landau, Ethel Levy, and several teachers—as important sources of personal strength and determination. Each, like her mentors, was devoted to educating and caring for others.

Many histories of Israel have been written since the foundation of the state. Few focus on the achievements and contributions of women. Fewer still examine the thinking of women who helped to put into place the building blocks of the state. This epilogue is part of the effort to redress this lamentable lacuna in the historical narrative.

Shulamit Kishik-Cohen

Shulamit Cohen was born in 1919 in Buenos Aires, Argentina, where her father was the chief Sephardi rabbi. She was the third child and eldest daughter of a family of eight children. Her mother, Allegra Harush, had graduated from the Evelina School before World War I. The family returned to Jerusalem in the summer of 1926. Landau agreed to admit three of the Cohen girls because she remembered that Allegra had been a very good student.

Shulamit adjusted rapidly to her new school and classmates. Her school experiences remained vividly alive for her decades after they had taken place. She commented frequently on their importance to her way of thinking. One of her strong memories involved a personal interaction with Landau. Shulamit and her friends were preparing for a test and continued studying during their recreation time in the garden. At the appointed hour, a prefect rang the bell to indicate that the girls should form their lines to return to class. Shulamit, absorbed in her studies, didn't move quickly enough to suit the prefect. Consequently, she was instructed to write "I must obey orders" one thousand times. She asked for a diminution of the punishment in order to complete studying for her test, but the prefect was firm.

Seeking a way out of her dilemma, Shulamit asked five of her friends to share the punishment, suggesting that they each write the sentence two hundred times. When they refused, Shulamit was disappointed, but she soon devised a different approach. She wrote "I must obey orders" once and then added 999 rows of ditto marks. She handed in the punishment assignment to the prefect the next morning and accompanied her class into the hall for morning prayers.

At the end of the service she heard, "Shulamit Cohen, Miss Landau wants you." Shulamit approached the office with trepidation. Landau handed Shulamit her work and asked, "What's this?" Shulamit explained her predicament. Landau, who at that point had been headmistress for more than a quarter century, said that she had never before seen anything like Shulamit's work. She chuckled at the creativity of the response and told Shulamit that she was forgiven because of her admirable ingenuity. Nevertheless, Shulamit was required to write out the statement five hundred times for the next day.

In Shulamit's view, Landau showed concern for each of her pupils. She held them to high standards of performance but was not unreasonable when told the mitigating circumstances of their infractions. Shulamit accepted the fact that she had not obeyed school rules and merited a punishment, but she was pleased that Landau saw the validity of her appeal and adjusted the punishment accordingly.

A few years later, Shulamit faced another case of injustice when the English teacher, Bertha Chaikin, arbitrarily removed her from the post of librarian for the school English library. Chaikin had previously asked for a volunteer to organize all the English books into a library to encourage after-school English reading. Shulamit was happy to take on this responsibility and created a system that gave each class a specific time to withdraw and return books. When one of her classmates asked Shulamit to waive the rules in her case, Shulamit, imbued with the British sense of fair play, declined. The student complained to Chaikin, who summarily replaced Shulamit with the complainant without giving Shulamit a chance to explain why she had refused the request.

Not long after Shulamit had been removed as the librarian for English books, Elhanan Wachman, who remained impressed with her skill as a librarian, asked her to create a Hebrew library. A few weeks later, Chaikin asked Shulamit if she could borrow books for her sons. Shulamit refused, since the books were meant for Evelina girls only. Upon reflection, Chaikin recognized that Shulamit had created a fair system that served the pupils of the school well. She soon reinstated her as English librarian. Years later, Shulamit observed that she had been relieved when the principle of fairness that she perceived as a hallmark of her school was upheld.

Shulamit was frequently ranked first in terms of her grades in her class and was often a leader of morning prayers. In her final years at the school she became a Girl Guide and a prefect, participated in the choir, and took ballet lessons. Unfortunately, the Cohen family faced severe economic difficulties in Jerusalem, so Rabbi Cohen decided to return to Buenos Aires to earn some money. He took his eldest daughter to keep house for him. Although Shulamit would have preferred to remain in school, she left her classmates and studies in 1932 at age thirteen. Neither she nor Landau had any choice in the matter; strict obedience to her parents was expected. Landau presented Shulamit with an English-Hebrew Bible with gold letters on the cover as a parting gift.

Shulamit and her father remained in Buenos Aires for three years. When they returned, she was just shy of her seventeenth birthday. She could have returned to the Evelina School, but her parents decided that it was time for her to be married. They arranged a match for her with Joseph Kishik, a man twice her age, part of an affluent Sephardi family in Beirut. Once again, Shulamit was not consulted about the decision. Her parents and two younger siblings accompanied her to Beirut for the wedding and then returned to Jerusalem.[1]

Shulamit moved into her husband's family home in Wadi Yahud, the Jewish quarter of Beirut. The house was large, with eleven rooms, and the family employed several servants. Shulamit brought with her the expectations of her family, her experiences keeping house for her father in Buenos Aires, and the knowledge and values she had learned in her years as an Evelina girl. She began to adjust to her new life and to her role as a wife and soon a mother, but she chafed under the supervision of her mother-in-law. Each Sabbath evening she heard youthful singing coming from a building just across from her home, where the Jewish scouts met. Shulamit was attracted to their enthusiasm but was disappointed that they sang only French and Arabic songs. Years later she reflected on this moment in her memoirs:

I remembered Miss Landau, the principal of the Evelina de Rothschild School, who used to say that if something is not in order one should examine oneself first before blaming others. Am I guilty perhaps of not going downstairs to teach them to sing? I contemplated. If I did not live in such a restrictive environment,

I would have done it gladly, but here it is forbidden. Unthinkable! Here no one can do anything out of the ordinary without the whole Jewish quarter fermenting like a concoction. Whispers soon develop into offensive and hurtful gossip. If I, a young married woman, from a respected family, a mother of a little girl, break social norms and run to teach the youngsters to sing—what will they say about me? Such an act would be seen as insanity, social suicide.[2]

Nevertheless, after a few weeks of soul-searching, Shulamit made the decision to act. She ventured outside and began to teach the group Hebrew songs she had learned at the Evelina School. The reaction from her husband's family was swift and negative. Joseph withdrew to his room and remained silent. She was grateful that he didn't participate in the criticism but disappointed that he didn't defend her. Shulamit waited for the feelings to cool down, but they didn't. Her new family interpreted her silence as an admission of guilt. Finally, she found her voice:

I have my wants, too. I didn't do anything wrong or hurt anyone. I know how to keep my respect, and no one can tell me that I didn't keep my respect as a loyal married woman. From here, from this window, you can see everything that I do down there in the club with your own eyes. I want to see one soul in all of *Wadi Yahud* who will teach me, Shula, the daughter of Meir and Allegra Arazi from Jerusalem, how to maintain family honor! So I taught some Jews to sing Zionist songs—what is so terrible about that?![3]

Shulamit reported that from the moment she declared her independence from the traditional role expected of her, she was happy. She began to be more independent, attending club meetings each week and teaching Hebrew songs. She had found a purpose in life: contributing to the education of Jewish youth in Beirut. In time, she asked the club members if they would like to learn folk dances, which were popular in Palestine. The club was enthusiastic, and a second night a week was selected for Shulamit to instruct them in folk dancing. After a while, Shulamit had another idea. She was concerned that these young men and women prayed and sang in Hebrew but had no idea of the meaning of the words. She suggested getting together for an evening of Hebrew conversation. Finally, she added an evening for Hebrew reading and writing.

Shulamit's ability to teach Hebrew reading and writing was limited by the lack of appropriate textbooks in Beirut. During a trip home to visit her parents in Jerusalem, she bought several books and took them back to Beirut, where she removed the Zionist content so as not to anger the Lebanese authorities and had them reprinted. Joseph, who was increasingly proud of his wife's growing role in the local Jewish community, volunteered to pay for this printing. Shulamit used these texts to teach Hebrew to a growing number of Jewish students. At first, she taught only one hour each week; later the classes became daily sessions. As the result of Shulamit's persistence, the Lebanese matriculation examination, which had recognized only three languages—Arabic, French, and English—added a fourth, Hebrew.

During the years after Shulamit's arrival in Beirut, the Jewish population of Lebanon began to feel threatened and sought refuge elsewhere. Most went to Brazil and Argentina, and some to Italy. Few went to Palestine. Shulamit continued to work with the Talmud Torah, the Alliance School, and with the Jewish scouts. Like Annie Landau in Jerusalem, Shulamit Cohen in Beirut became known as an important person with whom it was useful to have connections. People began to ask her advice on different issues, and some even asked her to settle disputes. Increasingly, she was invited to various celebrations, she visited the sick, and she consoled mourners. The respected people of the Wadi Yahud invited Shulamit and Joseph to their homes. After many years, at Shulamit's insistence, her husband agreed to move the family into their own home, which soon bustled with life.

During World War II, Jews in Beirut faced new difficulties. Those with Palestinian passports were arrested and held in detention. Shulamit was not affected by these measures, since she had traveled to Beirut on her father's passport and thus had no independent legal identity as a Palestinian. She continued her work at the Alliance School, where every year a representative of the school requested permission from the prime minister's office to hold an awards ceremony. Because of the tense situation, none of the other teachers was willing to request permission, so Shulamit stepped into the breach. When she met with Prime Minister Riad al Sohl, Shulamit recalled, she felt "like Annie Landau, like Hercules, powerful."[4]

Sohl granted the necessary permission, beginning a relationship that continued for a decade. During these years, Shulamit became interested in the battles between Arabs and Jews and between the British and the Jews in

Palestine. Members of her family were actively involved in fighting for the Jewish people. Like other Jews in Lebanon, especially the youth, she felt solidarity with those who fought for Jewish freedom in Palestine. Shulamit asked herself what she could contribute to the cause. She didn't exempt herself from the imperative to act because she was far from the scene of battle. Again thinking of her beloved Miss Landau, she asked, "Surely, I am not brave, but in a situation like this there is no place for cowardice. What right do I have to sit down and do nothing?"[5]

During the siege of Jerusalem, Shulamit thought about her struggling family deprived of food while she attended lavish parties in Beirut given by the prime minister. At these social gatherings, Shulamit began to pick up bits of intelligence that she thought might be of use to the Haganah, but she didn't know how she could send the information. She remembered stories of the ingenuity of Girl Guides who solved similar problems by using invisible ink that was made with readily available household materials; the message would remain invisible until it was subjected to a special process. Shulamit wrote down everything she had overheard from the political and military personnel in the prime minister's circle. She signed the letter with her name and address and sealed it; on the envelope she wrote in English, "To Jerusalem."

One of her Arab acquaintances who had connections with smugglers agreed to pass her letter to a Jew whom he frequently met at the border. Many days later Shulamit found the following letter slipped under her door:

> Well done, thank you very much. We would have liked to know more details about you. By the way, we would like you to do us a favor. We have an officer in our underground organization whose name is Winkler; the British sentenced him to expulsion. Tonight he is going to board the ship Transylvania in Haifa. It will dock for a few hours in Beirut. Will you be able to take him out of the ship and smuggle him to Metula? We'll wait there until 4 a.m. Thank you very much.[6]

Shulamit struggled to fulfill her first mission and every subsequent one, often involving great risks to herself and ultimately to her family. She navigated the treacherous waters of the rival tribal leaders in Beirut, becoming more vulnerable after her protector, Prime Minister Sohl, was assassinated while on a trip to Amman in 1951, accused of being a friend of Israel. (King Abdullah had been assassinated not long before that for the same reason.) Shulamit worked clandestinely for the Israeli government, bringing thousands of Lebanese Jews safely to Israel, until her arrest in 1961. She spent the next six years in a Syrian jail, explaining that she survived by singing the same Hebrew songs with which she had begun her public life in Beirut. She returned to Israel as part of a prisoner exchange after the Six-Day War. After reuniting with her family, Shulamit wrote her memoirs and lectured before many high school groups, always seeking to inspire the young to serve their people. In reflecting back on her life she stated, "I gave everything for my country."[7]

Masha Weingarten Kaplan

Like Shulamit Cohen, Masha Weingarten was one of several sisters, all of whom attended the Evelina School. Unlike the peripatetic Shulamit, Masha grew up in the Old City in a house that had been in her mother's family for generations. Landau awarded a special dispensation to allow Masha to begin her studies at the Evelina School at the age of three. Masha's mother had explained to Landau that Masha was continually infested with lice from her attendance at a *cheder* in the Old City. Since her two older sisters, Rivka and Yehudit, were already outstanding students at the Evelina School, the exception was granted. A few years later, Masha's younger sisters, Rachel and Karena, were enrolled as well. Masha proved to be an excellent student, graduating with distinction in 1941. That year, eight hundred students in Palestine took the London matriculation exam. Two hundred passed, and four received first-class marks. Masha was one of those four.

Masha was influenced by her mother, who gathered her daughters every Friday morning to distribute food and clothing to the poor of the Old City; by Landau, who provided an atmosphere of respect and calm and beauty in the Evelina School; and by her teachers, who introduced her to the wider world through reading Robert Louis Stevenson, Alfred Lord Tennyson, William Blake, John Keats, and Henry Wadsworth Longfellow. All these influences were evident in the choices she made as an adult.[8]

Masha contributed several articles to *School* magazine. In one she reviewed a film, *From Haifa to Baghdad and the Near East*. She was keenly interested in the customs of a nomadic tribe portrayed in its tents with separate compartments for women and children. The future pediatric nurse noted that babies were wrapped in animal skins and suspended from the top of the tent.[9]

An essay about Jerusalem illustrates Masha's emerging identity. She described rising early after a few hours of rest, "full of energy and . . . the desire to do spiritual and physical work." She explained that the air of Jerusalem is fresh and invigorating and that the sight of the old "holy" stones put her in a good mood, giving her the desire to act. The panorama of the city enchanted her: to the north, Mount Scopus with the Hebrew University and Hadassah Hospital; to the east, Mount Moriah, with the Western Wall and the Mount of Olives with its thousands of old graves; to the south, the houses of Yemenites; further south, the palace of the high commissioner with its British flag. She concluded with fervor, "Oh how beautiful and amazing our holy Jerusalem is that every stone in her is full of holy memories from our lofty past. And from them, a basis also for our future in our holy land."[10]

Masha's love of her city and her people are evident in the decisions she made after her graduation from the Evelina School. Masha continued her studies at Hebrew University for one year and then transferred to the Hadassah School of Nursing. She had wanted to become a physician, but since there was no medical school program available during the war and since nurses were in high demand, she changed her plans. In 1945, Masha returned to her family home in the Old City to assist her father, the *mukhtar* of the Jews of the Old City, who had opened a clinic. These were lean years in the Old City as the Jewish population continued to decline and hostilities between communities that had lived in relative peace increased. Masha worked in the clinic, where operations often took place by candlelight. When the Old City fell in May 1948, she accompanied wounded prisoners of war to Jordan and remained there until the cease-fire.

When Masha returned to Jerusalem, she began to work at Hadassah Hospital. Within a few months she was asked to go to Aden to organize a hospital for Yemenite Jews who had left their homes with the intention of emigrating to Israel. When she arrived, she found a camp constructed for four hundred people surrounded by fourteen thousand sick and hungry men, women, and children. Relying on her practical experience and her knowledge of Arabic, Masha began to work with the refugees. She stayed in Aden for many months, until the last of fifty thousand Yemenites were evacuated to Israel in the rescue mission called Operation Magic Carpet.

Masha had the necessary inner strength, vision, and leadership to transform a camp built for four hundred to a staging ground for fifty thousand immigrants—skills that had been prized at the Evelina de Rothschild School.

After this assignment, she returned to Hadassah Hospital, where she became the head nurse of the pediatrics department. Exhibiting another characteristic of the Evelina girls, Masha expressed a desire for continuing professional development. She was sent to England, where she studied the treatment of premature babies and simultaneously renewed her ties with former Evelina teachers and students who lived in London and Manchester. When she returned to Hadassah, she started the first modern unit for premature babies.

It was at this juncture that she met and married Dr. Isaac Kaplan, a recently divorced immigrant from South Africa working as a plastic surgeon at Hadassah. Isaac was an atheist, whereas Masha had remained faithful to the religious Orthodoxy of her home and of the Evelina School. Nonetheless, Masha had learned to respect different views while attending school and had developed friendships with girls whose families were secular. Throughout their marriage, Masha and Isaac remained true to their individual beliefs. A year after their wedding, Carmi, a daughter, was born.[11]

A few years later, Isaac was offered the chance to create a plastic surgery department at Beilinson Hospital, so he and Masha moved to the Tel Aviv area. In 1967, Isaac was invited to Saigon to operate a burn unit for children. Masha accompanied him and once again used her prodigious organizing skills to convert a residence into a hospital. Using her experience in Aden, she went to the port area where the medical supplies of the U.S. Agency for International Development (USAID) were located to arrange for beds, cutlery, dishes, and other essentials. When she found that there was no transport available, she went in search of trucks, hired drivers, and arranged for them to bring the equipment to the new hospital building. Some of the apartments on the ground floor of the building were occupied by USAID employees. Masha arranged to have them moved, but only after they had agreed to help move the beds and equipment from the trucks.[12]

When the family returned to Israel, Isaac set up the first fully equipped burn unit in Israel at Beilinson, a unit that became particularly important during the Yom Kippur War in 1973. Masha was an avowed pacifist but nevertheless volunteered her nursing skills in every war. In view of her service, she was named the honorary "mother" of an armored corps division.[13] Masha's complex ideas about peace and war as well as her ideas about the compatibility of people of different religious beliefs are examples of Annie Landau's enduring legacy.

Marta Zayonce Shamir

Another Evelina graduate who thought deeply about her role in the early years of the state of Israel is Marta Zayonce Shamir, the daughter of the superintendant of the Evelina School grounds. Marta recently printed her memoirs, a 146-page illustrated book, to provide her children and grandchildren with a picture of her life at the time of the struggle for independence and beyond. Titled *Daughter of the Generation of 1948*, it describes her commitment to public service, an important aspect of Israeli life that had been neglected in the first histories of Israel. Marta recorded her actions so that future generations would recognize the importance of her work and that of other women in building the nation.

Marta's parents, unlike the Orthodox families of Shulamit Cohen and Masha Weingarten, were members of Hashomer Hatzair, the socialist-Zionist youth group. They arrived in Palestine from their native Poland to work the land in 1920. By the time Marta was born in 1929, the family had moved to Jerusalem and was living in a small flat in Nahalat Shiva where there was no running water or electricity. Marta's father struggled to make ends meet working on various construction jobs. Her mother, who was sickly, was unable to work. When Marta was a baby, her father was offered the job of superintendant of the Evelina School grounds. Although Zayonce knew that Landau was an Orthodox Jew and he remained a socialist Zionist, he took the job because it offered a good salary and a small house on the school property.

Marta grew up in this house and was soon registered at the Evelina School. She was aware that there were differences of opinion between her parents and her headmistress. Marta's mother believed that toys would stifle a child's imagination, but she allowed Marta to play with the dolls brought back from England by Landau and with the train puzzles and coloring books brought back from Germany by David Reider.

As a youngster, Marta asked her mother, "Why do we pray in school and not at home? Why do we eat kosher in school and not at home?" Her mother explained that some people believe one way and others in other ways and that when Marta was an adult she could decide for herself. The principle that there were different ways to believe and that people with different beliefs should be respected was taught in school and reinforced at home. Marta remained aware of the beliefs of others throughout her life.

Like many children who were raised in nonobservant households, Marta was appreciative of Landau's holiday celebrations, describing them as a positive feature of the school. She remembered the Passover seder, with sixty to ninety guests seated at tables set with fine china and utensils, and the tall Sudanese waiters dressed in white tunics and red belts. Important rabbis led the service; there were always guests from England. She also loved Sukkot, when her father erected a glorious sukkah big enough for many guests. The decorations, lights, and fruits that hung from the roof were admired by all who came to dine there each year. As an adult, Marta maintained some of these rituals as the religious holidays of her youth became the national holidays of Israel. Likewise, she described the innovative music classes and sewing classes as important character-building experiences.

Marta also identified the shortcomings of her education. She noted that most of the teaching was rote memorization rather than creative or intellectual work and that a lot of time, perhaps too much, was devoted to discipline: showing respect to elders, speaking quietly without shouting, obeying parents and teachers, working hard in school, studying hard after school, and being considerate of others. Despite these limitations, Marta loved her classes and excelled. She took prizes home year after year, all documented in her memoir.

Another character-building activity Marta noted was the Girl Guides. She joined and remembered vividly the activities of her group. Decades later she still knew all the lyrics to several Girl Guide songs, such as the following:

> We are the Girl Guides marching on the broad highway
> With a step that's light and a heart that's gay
> There is room for me and there's room for you
> And there's work in the world for a guide to do.
> As the stars that shine overhead to cheer
> We try to learn how to shine down here.
> Lend a hand, comrade mine,
> Lend a hand, lend a hand.
> Up girls, wake girls, there is no time for sleeping
> Out in the open where the air is fresh and free
> Up girls, wake girls, comrade time still keeping
> Set the windows of your soul as wide as they can be.

When Marta was twelve years old, her parents decided that she should also have the experience of a Zionist youth group. They ignored the school ban on such activities and quietly helped her to join Hashomer Hatzair. The youth group experience played a key role in Marta's developing sense of self. In contrast to the decorum of the Evelina School, Hashomer Hatzair encouraged lively discussions about politics, shouting and debating were part of the culture, there were hiking trips all over the country, and boys and girls sang and danced together. Marta was thrilled by the feeling of becoming a pioneer and by the ideal of self-sacrifice to build a Jewish homeland.

Marta struggled to reconcile the socialist-Zionist ethos of Hashomer Hatzair with the British individualism of the Girl Guides. Although both programs encouraged dedication and having goals larger than oneself, Marta noted one significant difference: the Girl Guides encouraged girls to take leadership roles, whereas those roles went to the boys in Hashomer circles.

In 1945, Marta passed the London matriculation exam and continued in school to complete the commercial course. When she graduated, she was offered a job working for the Mandatory authority. In this job she learned the limitations of the British sense of fair play. She discovered that the Mandate hiring and salary system treated Palestinians as colonial subjects; it gave less qualified British expatriates higher salaries than more qualified locals. Years later, when she worked at Hebrew University, she learned the limitations of the Zionist system when she was encouraged to join the Labor Party in order to get ahead in her job. Marta was sustained by a saying of Landau's: "Every Jewish girl has a halo around her head." She interpreted this to mean that no matter what the system, she had abilities and she could have pride in her accomplishments. Landau's school was the source of this self-assurance.

Like many of her classmates, Marta was dedicated to Haganah activities throughout the months of the siege of Jerusalem. She carried grenades and disassembled weapons hidden under her blouse, traveling from one end of the city to another. She also worked for the intelligence unit of the Haganah, using the Morse code she learned as a Girl Guide. When the war ended, Marta married Shmuel Shamir in the Evelina de Rothschild School Hall in Rehavia on January 12, 1949.[14]

In 1954, Marta submitted an essay to a competition sponsored by the United Nations. Titled, "The Role of Education in Developing International Understanding," this eleven-page essay is a clear indication that Marta saw herself as a full participant in the larger world, able to assess issues and to recommend solutions to difficult problems. In the essay Marta wrote the following:

> More than half of those now alive have had no primary education of any sort. Apart from the fact that conscience must revolt against such iniquity, mere prudence warns us that so tremendous a host of backward people would endanger the advance of humanity as a whole, indeed the very spread of human rights. Ignorance is part of a vicious circle of insufficient production, undernourishment, and disease.

These observations were influenced by the socialist rhetoric of Hashomer Hatzair. Her next statement shows that she had also learned the pluralistic values of the Evelina School:

> It is a grave mistake too to permit half humanity to remain bereft of the benefits of culture; this implies that mankind as a whole is deprived of the co-operation of people who, if their abilities were cultivated instead of lying fallow, might make a contribution towards human progress. Ignorance hinders the development of the human personality.

Marta continued with the observation that special stress should be put on the study of geography, history, languages, the development of a sense of solidarity, respect for life, and, of course, a study of the efforts made toward international understanding and peace, especially by the League of Nations and the United Nations. She explained as follows:

> Geography brings out particularly clearly the common interests of all men in their endeavors to adapt themselves to their natural environment.... Economic geography shows up the interdependence and complementary nature of the various nations and countries. It indicates what each country gives to and receives from the others, and this again is a powerful factor making for international understanding.

Marta continued her essay with observations about teaching history that were astute when she wrote them more than fifty years ago and that remain important in the continuing conflict over the content of history textbooks in Israel and neighboring Arab countries:

School textbooks have, as a rule, been written with so little objectivity, that the teaching of history has been rather an obstacle to international understanding up to now. The reader has been led to believe that perfidy and oppression are always and solely the characteristics of the enemy. Another weakness is over-emphasis on military and political factors, which tend to divide nations from each other, and too little attention to the history of science, technology, and the arts, which tend to unite nations. . . . Only by means of a revision of the textbooks can the development of international understanding by means of the teaching of history be pursued. . . . Attention should be drawn to the constructive activities which help advance civilization materially and spiritually, great discoveries, inventions making life more secure and happier, methods for putting the resources of the globe at the disposal of all. These make the reader feel that he belongs to humanity as a whole, and impel him to discharge his debt to the past by working with all his might towards a better life.[15]

Since this was written in 1954, one may assume that Marta intended the *he* and other masculine pronouns in her sentences to include all of humanity. Her emphasis on "humanity as a whole" rather than on nationalism was no doubt appreciated by the reviewers. Her thoughtful essay was awarded a prize, a trip to the United Nations in New York, but when Israeli authorities realized that the writer was a student and a "housewife," the travel award was given to a university professor instead.[16]

Marta was too busy to protest. She gave birth in 1955 to Irit, who was stricken by infantile paralysis that left her with a limp and affected her ability to speak. Irit's continuing medical needs prompted Marta to spend more time at home. Six years later, Yael was born, and then Zviki after another six years. When Zviki started school at Beit Ha-Yeled, Marta began to commit a lot of her time to volunteer work. She was selected to represent her school on the citywide parents' committee and later to represent the city committee at national meetings. She encouraged parents to lobby for better textbooks and for audiovisual and sports equipment, and she worked to create a school esprit de corps. Marta's volunteer work continued for six years, involving citywide and later regional meetings with parents and school administrators.

In 1981, Marta was hired by Dov Shilansky, the deputy minister responsible for maintaining ties between the prime minister's office and the Knesset.[17] This was the beginning of Marta's work in the Knesset, first as office manager for Shilansky, later in a similar position for diplomat and politician Uri Savir, and finally as advisor to Shilansky, who was elected speaker of the Knesset in 1988. During these years, Marta worked on Nativ, an outreach program to young Jews from the Soviet Union; she lobbied for funds to continue Yiddish and Ladino studies, and she helped to establish a ceremony for Holocaust Memorial Day in the Knesset. These activities brought her into contact with major issues facing the state. When she retired in 1994, she began to write her memoir.[18]

At the end of her book she asked: "Was the Zionist dream realized?" Her answer was as follows:

My generation, the generation of 1948, realized the 2000-year-old dream of the Jewish people, experienced the wars of occupation, the war of liberation, and the establishment of the State of Israel. We and our parents did not feel that we were conquering the land at the expense of another nation. . . . We were prepared to accept the decision of the United Nations even though we had been promised much more in the Balfour Declaration. . . . We fought back after being attacked. . . . In our blackest dreams we did not imagine that our children and grandchildren would be forced to continue fighting.

I cannot say that we didn't make mistakes. Only he who does nothing makes no mistakes. Is Israel the country we dreamed of in our youth? The answer must be "no." We dreamed of an ideal country, a utopia . . . a land of pleasant evening gatherings; where people care for each other; where moral behavior is the norm; where there is a desire to work and to earn from all sorts of work including manual labor; a land with no thieves, murderers, drunks, or addicts; a secure country where it is pleasant to live. We were certain that we would succeed in living in peace and with honor with the Arabs when the British stopped mediating between us. We didn't want to rule them or to fight them. Reality hit us in the face.[19]

Marta's memoir is testimony to her intelligence, her character, and her Evelina de Rothschild education.

Adaya Hochberg Barkay

Adaya Hochberg was a few years behind Marta Zayonce at the Evelina de Rothschild School. She shared Marta's search for better solutions and her hope for the possibility of finding them. Born in 1932, Adaya started at the Evelina School in 1939 after attending the De Croly kindergarten, a Montessori-style program run by Miriam Ascoli, who had studied in Belgium. Like Marta, Adaya came from a secular family and was often lonely as a child.[20] There the similarities cease.

Adaya's mother, Mina, was a Jerusalemite of many generations whose family left the Old City in the 1920s. Mina was the only one of the girls in the family who went to school. Adaya's aunt lamented the fact that Ashkenazi rabbis forbade their community to send girls to school. She credited Mina with strong determination that eventually overcame her parental opposition and enabled her to attain the skills that procured her a good job as a vice manager of the Savings and Loan Bank, which funded Jewish Agency operations.[21] Adaya's father, Tzvi, was a handsome, multilingual, talented inventor who arrived in Palestine from Odessa at age ten. He worked for many years as the representative of European appliance companies that sold washing machines and radios in Palestine. Tzvi and Mina Hochberg frequented the attractive places to be seen in Jerusalem, such as the Café Europa and Café Vienna.

At the beginning of World War II, Tzvi was approached by Moshe Sharett and asked to serve in the British army. He agreed and was mobilized in March 1940 and stationed with the Auxiliary Military Pioneer Corps in North Africa, supervising the hiding of British arms and ammunition in the western desert. He often took his leave in Jerusalem, arriving at the Evelina School in the uniform of a British lieutenant. Landau, Levy, the teachers, and the pupils all held him in high esteem.[22]

Adaya's mother was one of the very few mothers of Evelina girls who worked full-time. The fact that the Evelina School had a longer day than most schools and provided lunch for its pupils worked well for the Hochberg family. The curriculum also gave Adaya, who had little religious instruction at home, knowledge of Judaism. Adaya, who was often lonely, appreciated the extra attention she received in school.

Adaya's family was more affluent than Marta's or Shulamit's. It was able to afford private lessons in French, piano, gymnastics, ballet, and tennis.

However, Adaya was not spoiled. She was expected to practice regularly or lose the privilege of these extra lessons. One summer, Adaya attended a day camp in Rehavia. There she met a boy about whom she wrote a poem that revealed a precocious understanding of the European Jewish crisis:

A BLOND BOY, A DIFFERENT BOY

In Jerusalem of the Mandate, in the forties, there were no blond boys.
>Nor girls.
There were browns, blacks, redheads, with and without yarmulkes.
>With or without braids.
One summer, when we were still at the age of one digit, a blond boy
>appeared in the summer-camp in Rechavia.
He rolled his "resh" when he spoke and mostly kept silent.
He was tanned like us but strange—with a part in his combed yellow hair.
He wore sandals like us but differently—with light, short socks.
"I am from Tel Aviv," he answered. But the counselors said he was
>"from there."
He was with us but different. Tanned, handsome, blond and quiet.
My soul cried out to him.
Sometimes I saw children like him in the movies, those from the two-for-one
>matinees at the "Zion" cinema.
And then I knew—those were movies "from there."
And I dared—"I know where you came from, know where you are from."
"You know?" and fell silent.
I explained—"blond boys and girls, happy families, big houses, drink orange
>juice every morning and speak English even with the dog."
He kept silent.
And then added—"in my movie—it is a different 'there.' The families are sad,
>the houses are destroyed, and the dog barks at me in German."
"I'm a blond boy, but I'm a different boy," different ... different ...
>with rolling "resh"
And my soul cries out to him.[23]

Adaya spent several years at the head of her class at the Evelina School, participating in Girl Guides and in the choir, sometimes selected to sing with the school choir on the Palestine Broadcasting Service, and helping the school's Hebrew librarian. Despite this model behavior, Adaya secretly joined a youth group, Maccabi Hatzair, along with several Evelina girls in her class. She was later recruited into the Haganah by an Evelina girl in the class above her. After the massacre of thirty-five young Haganah men in Gush Etzion, Adaya and some of the others were asked by the Haganah to post notices on the walls of the city. Adaya did not go to school the next day; instead she posted the notices. Ethel Levy called her that evening to ask where she had been. Although Haganah membership was forbidden, Adaya told her the truth. Levy, in tacit recognition of the changed situation, merely told her to return to school the next day.[24]

The excitement of belonging to a nation in the making influenced Adaya to ask her mother whether she could transfer to the Rehavia Gymnasia in late 1947. Here, like most children, she would prepare for the Bagrut exam rather than the London matriculation exam. Her mother agreed to take her for an interview with the principal, who told her that she would have to repeat a few classes. Adaya thought that perhaps her mother had prompted the principal to discourage her from transferring. In any event, she stayed on at the Evelina School until the tragedy of her mother's death in the Ben Yehuda Street bombing a few months later.

At the beginning of 1948, the Hochbergs moved to central Jerusalem, seeking safety, since the road to their home in Talpiyot had become a target for snipers. The family moved into a hotel on Ben Yehuda Street that also housed several teachers who worked at the Evelina School, including Esme Aaronson and Nora Miller, both of whom taught English. At 6:30 a.m. on February 22, Adaya heard a loud noise, followed by her mother's voice asking, "What was that?" She heard her father reply, "It's nothing, just a car backfiring."

Nevertheless, her mother got out of bed and went to the balcony to see what had caused the noise. Mina Hochberg's last words were "Why are the British laughing?" She was killed instantly by the second bomb blast from the street below. (Although it has never been proved, it is widely believed that British police were involved in this bombing.) After the blast, Adaya called to her mother. There was no answer. She ran to the balcony to find her. The balcony where Mina Hochberg uttered her last words had collapsed onto the pavement below. Adaya raced downstairs and located her mother's body in the rubble by identifying her blue bathrobe under the debris. Her mother's head was cut in two. She remembered looking into her mother's severed head and thinking that it was not normal to be able to look inside one's mother's head. Her father, wounded, remained in bed.[25]

With remarkable speed, Mina's body was collected for burial, and Tzvi was taken to the hospital; fifteen-year-old Adaya was left alone. Covered with soot from the explosion, disoriented, and not knowing what to do, she put on her mother's fur coat and set off for school. When she entered her classroom, she announced to her teacher, Elhanan Wachman, and to her classmates that her mother had been killed. All her classmates started crying.

Adaya remembered that Wachman took her to Levy's office, where the headmistress held up a mirror so that she could see herself. She saw that she was disheveled and dirty. She said, "I think I better go home, because I am scaring the other students." Adaya spent the next few days with her father's family but found their cries for revenge troubling. She went to Netanya and spent a few weeks there with her mother's family, but then she returned to Jerusalem to be with her father and to fulfill her obligations to the Haganah in the defense of Jerusalem.

Adaya stopped going to school. She and several of her classmates worked as couriers, volunteered to aid the wounded in the hospital, and secured neighborhoods like Katamon after the flight of their Arab inhabitants. Because of the bombing, Adaya and her father had lost all of their belongings and were left with no money. Adaya, acting like one of the fearless Girl Guides she had read about who saved their families from disaster, marched to the bank where her mother had worked and spoke to the manager, requesting the wages that were due her deceased mother.

The manager replied that he could not discuss this with her, since she was not yet eighteen years old. Adaya stood her ground, reminding him that her mother had worked at the bank for twenty-six years. Finally he gave in to her demands and handed her five pounds sterling, a veritable fortune. She raced home and gave the money to her father. During these months, Adaya and her father, like most in Jerusalem, lived with constant hunger. The Haganah gave her cigarettes to dull her hunger pangs. Adaya remembered eating the leftovers of blind soldiers she fed in the hospital and on one occasion disobeying orders by stealing some macaroni.[26]

She wrote a poem, titled "Loot," about hunger in Jerusalem during the siege:

During the siege of Jerusalem I sometimes wondered which made one
hungrier—an empty stomach or an empty larder.

And it's possible the answer is "both."

At times I was very hungry, both in my stomach and in my head.

And we would talk about food. My father would ask what would I most
like to have now? Then we would talk. I would say, "Strawberry." He
would quickly add, "With cream." I would say, "Chicken." "Roasted,"
he would add.

We spoke of full and satisfying meals. Of Sabbath and holiday feasts.

Once, armed with a gun, he forced the grocer, Zalman Dolinsky, to open his
shop, . . . and to give us a ration of bread. "The girl is hungry," he said,
paying. That day we ate bread and talked of sandwiches.

We were children of the Haganah. We were called to work, to carry messages
and assist where possible.

One morning we were asked to fill sand bags in the beautiful Katamon
neighborhood. "There?" I asked. It was explained that the Arab
residents had fled, that their houses were empty, and that it was
necessary to protect them.

We were permitted to enter the houses—"It's permitted just to look. It is
forbidden to take. It is forbidden to loot."

These were beautiful big villas, highly decorated. Everything was left in a
hurry. And I . . . I went immediately to the kitchen.

It was almost like being in a holy room; I looked in all of the cabinets, in the
ice box, everything was full. FOOD, but it was FORBIDDEN.

Opposite a small package of Italian spaghetti, I hesitated and thought: "To
take was forbidden, but, to eat, maybe that was permitted."

And thus, in the kitchen in Katamon, I stood and ate one piece of uncooked
spaghetti at a time. I counted each piece and wondered how I could
include my father in this meal. Slowly I finished the package while
still wondering how to take some of it home.

I couldn't answer the question before I finished the whole package.[27]

During the first truce, in June 1948, Adaya left Jerusalem and went to Tel
Aviv, where she met members of Maccabi Hatzair who were preparing to
establish a kibbutz. She worked with them for several months, but when her
father succeeded in relocating to Tel Aviv, he convinced her to leave the unit

to complete her high school education. She registered at Gymnasia Herzliyah along with several other displaced Jerusalemites. By now she was an addicted smoker. Smoking was forbidden in school, but the principal allowed her to smoke outside the school grounds during recess. He also asked if she would tutor Samaritan students who were having trouble with their studies. She agreed, but she refused payment for her work, explaining that she had received help from others when she was in great need.

After graduation in 1950, Adaya signed up to serve in the IDF on Kibbutz Ma'ayan Baruch near Metula. She spent two years of military service on the kibbutz and an additional year working as the kibbutz economist, which largely meant struggling to find food for the members. Three years later she left for Europe to pursue her goal of becoming a doctor. Adaya received her medical degree in Paris and opened a practice as a pediatrician. She also married a physician and had four children there, later moving with her husband to practice in Brussels.[28]

In 1967, Adaya and her family returned to Israel, where she worked for five years at Tel Hashomer Hospital. Not content to do clinical work only, Adaya studied for a master's degree in public health and later for a law degree so that she could make health policy. For eighteen years, she served as the district medical officer for the Ministry of Health in the Northern District, working to increase services for the poor children of Nazareth, primarily an Arab population. She was also appointed head of the Mother and Child Health Department in the ministry, and in that capacity she was the delegate to the World Health Organization (WHO). Today she continues to volunteer with the human rights division of Médecins sans Frontières (Doctors without Borders).

Adaya credits the Evelina School with giving her the skills and values that have informed her life. She learned from the rituals and ceremonies of the school to appreciate organization and structure, and she praised the school for creating a framework that was inclusive and for inculcating a pluralistic attitude in which people's differences were respected, even welcomed. Her devotion to improving the services for Arab children in Nazareth was Adaya's way of contributing to the civic life of Israel. Her work with WHO and with Médecins sans Frontières brought her contributions to an international level and focused them specifically on the needs of women and children.

Ruth Lask Rasnic

Ruth Lask was one of Adaya's classmates. She credited the Evelina School environment with giving her the opportunity to grow up in two cultures: Zionist and British. Feeling at home in two worlds gave Ruth the inner strength to question policies and practices and ultimately to recognize injustice and fight for change.

Ruth was born in Jerusalem in 1934. Her father was an immigrant from London who worked as a freelance writer and translator. Her mother, who came from a Ukrainian family in Berlin, did not work outside the home. The family left Jerusalem for Tel Aviv in 1938 in search of greater safety. Ruth started school in Tel Aviv. There her classes were co-ed, instruction was in Hebrew, there was a Jewish National Fund (JNF) box in each classroom, and the day began with singing "Hatikvah."

In the winter of 1942, the Lask family returned to Jerusalem, once again for reasons of safety. Ruth's parents were secular Jews but decided to enroll her at the Evelina School. Ruth immediately was aware of the diverse makeup of her class. She observed that her new school knew how to bring girls from different backgrounds together. Her new friends included the daughters of professors and merchants, Sephardi and Ashkenazi, religious and secular.

She was very fond of Ruth Kirsch, whose father was a veterinarian. The Kirsch family was very cosmopolitan, having previously lived in Ethiopia and having a wide range of friends. Other friends were Rina Levy, Hannah Cohen, and Judith Smith. Abigail Marash and Yehudit Atergi, both from Sephardi families, were also new friends.

At school, Ruth Lask developed a passion for reading English stories and later books, which opened a new way of thinking for her. She missed the JNF box and the singing of "Hatikvah" that was familiar to her from her school in Tel Aviv, but she credited the Evelina School with giving her access to the world of English literature and culture. Ruth remembered reading *Little Women* by Louisa May Alcott and discussing the book with her friends in class and at recess. The girls talked about the characters of the girls in the March family and wondered which one of them they were most like. Ruth, whose family was poor, remembered having only one pair of shoes and frequently stuffing cardboard in the shoes to cover the holes in the soles. Since she walked so much, her shoes periodically had to be resoled, and on those occasions she had to stay home, since she couldn't walk around barefoot. The poverty of the March family and the ingenuity of Jo in meeting challenges resonated for Ruth.

Ruth treasured her copy of *Jane Eyre*, a birthday present. However, it was the Evelina library that provided most of her books. A biography of Florence Nightingale had a great deal of influence; Ruth saw nurses tending the wounded British, French, and Australian soldiers in the courtyard of the Italian Hospital just across the street from the Evelina School. She also remembered reading about Emmeline Pankhurst and her daughters, British suffragists, and being very impressed with their activities. Her interest in women who fought for political rights was not surprising, given the strong emphasis at the Evelina School on women's participation in civic life.

In 1946, Ruth reluctantly left the beautiful garden of the Evelina School, which she likened to nirvana, for Tel Aviv. Her parents were not well, and she was needed to help support the family. She did not finish high school and did not become a nurse. Ruth used her bilingual skills to get a job as a secretary and later became an assistant kindergarten teacher. When her parents' condition improved, Ruth went to live on a kibbutz for eighteen months and then joined the Air Force.[29]

Later she went to London to study journalism, where she also married. She returned to Israel after her brother was killed in the 1956 Sinai Campaign, when her parents again needed support. The death of her brother Amittai moved Ruth to write a poem about the loss of young soldiers:

AMITTAI

You are at peace.
With your mate they laid you low
With the volley's last echo
You, to all of us so dear
Never further, yet so near.
Pain and grief have never been
For us here so sharp and keen
Brother mine—but eyes will blur

With those tears that will recur.
O the skies are blue and wide
Does it matter where you died?
You are gone and we are left
Broken hearted and bereft.[30]

Ruth had four children and spent time raising her family and helping her invalid parents. However, beneath the exterior of the housewife and dutiful daughter, Ruth's feelings about the special role of mothers in Israeli society began to stir. Ten years after her brother's death, she wrote another poem more pointedly against war:

TO ALL MOTHERS

We who are mothers
who in our flesh have felt
creation.
We who are mothers
who nine months long have borne
the fruit of love.
We who are mothers
whose bodies writhed
in labour.
We who are mothers
whose nipples taught
the newborn suck.
We who are mothers
who world's delight uncovered
in baby's play.
We who are mothers
the miracle discovered
of baby's speech.
Woe! For we stood in the breach
and kept still.
Woe for we stood aside.
While our children were led

to the slaughter, like cattle
on battlefields.
We who are mothers
are bent
in silent grief.[31]

Not long after writing the poem, Ruth discovered Betty Friedan's *The Feminine Mystique*. She was fascinated by Friedan's analysis of "the problem that has no name" and corresponded with Friedan. Ruth joined one of Israel's first consciousness-raising groups and supported feminist politician Shulamit Aloni and citizens' rights groups. In 1977, Ruth was the second candidate on the Women's Party list. A platform plank was devoted to battered women. When the Women's Party failed to win any seats in the Knesset, Ruth decided to leave politics and devote the rest of her life to protecting battered women and children and to creating educational tools that would prevent future generations form having to deal with this problem. She is the founder and executive director of Lo ("No"), an organization dedicated to combating violence against women. In February 2009, in recognition of her extraordinary commitment to women's rights, Ruth Lask Rasnic was awarded the Israel Prize, the highest civilian distinction given by the State of Israel.[32]

The Legacy of Annie Landau

Shulamit Kishik-Cohen, Masha Weingarten Kaplan, Marta Zayonce Shamir, Adaya Hochberg Barkay, and Ruth Lask Rasnic are representative of the thousands touched by the legacy of Annie Landau. The headmistress would have wondered at some of their decisions, but she would have applauded their self-confidence and their efforts to contribute to their families and their people. Each followed her own path in building the state of Israel.

Shulamit Kishik-Cohen helped thousands of Lebanese Jews escape to Israel; Masha Weingarten Kaplan was instrumental in bringing thousands of Yemenites to Israel; Marta Zayonce Shamir played important roles as a volunteer and as a staff member in the Knesset; Adaya Hochberg Barkay devoted her efforts to underserved people through her work in the Ministry of Health; and Ruth Lask Rasnic pioneered services for battered women and children.

It is conceivable that these women would have made important contributions to society had they gone to different schools. It is clear that they were also influenced by the major events of their lives: the Holocaust, the siege of Jerusalem, and the fight for Israel's independence. It is difficult to assess the precise influence of their Evelina School education. However, one thing is certain. Each of the women profiled believed that Annie Landau and the Evelina de Rothschild School provided them with invaluable life lessons that guided their actions.

It was at school that they were taught in two languages to believe in themselves, that they studied poetry and music and sports and ballet and participated in Girl Guides and prepared for Shabbat, that they learned to feel sure of their abilities to move mountains through persistent effort and high personal expectations. It was at school that they learned to cherish their heritage but simultaneously to value people from different backgrounds. They appreciated that both the religious and the secular subjects they learned enabled them to feel at home in the wider world.

These outstanding women and thousands of other Evelina girls made a reality of Annie Landau's vision to educate the "mothers" of a new nation. Their education prepared them to recognize the needs of others: recent refugees, Arab Israelis, and battered women. Their contributions can be found in every village and town where an Evelina graduate taught school, cared for the sick, worked in offices, participated in parent meetings, or became a member of the government. Many of them remain in Jerusalem, a city whose promise was recognized by the Ladies' Committee of the Anglo-Jewish Association at the turn of the last century. The women described above all agree that a lot of work remains to be done for that promise to be more fully realized.

NOTES

Introduction

1. Mrs. Leopold de Rothschild, ed., *An Appeal to Jewish Women on Behalf of the Anglo-Jewish Association* (London: Jewish Chronicle, 1911), 6.

2. Joseph B. Glass and Ruth Kark, *Sephardi Entrepreneurs in Jerusalem: The Valero Family, 1800–1948* (Jerusalem: Gefen, 2007), 235–94.

3. Margalit Shilo, *Princess or Prisoner? Jewish Women in Jerusalem, 1840–1914* (Waltham, MA: Brandeis University Press, 2005), 143–80; and Liza Slutsky, "The Evelina de Rothschild School during the Yishuv" [in Hebrew], paper presented at the Schecter Center seminar, Jerusalem, 2006, 5.

4. Louis Loewe, ed., *Diaries of Sir Moses and Lady Montefiore* (London: Jewish Historical Society, 1983), 36–43.

5. Jonathan Frankel, *The Damascus Affair: "Ritual Murder," Politics, and the Jews in 1840* (Cambridge, UK: Cambridge University Press, 1997), 109–48, 362–85.

6. Aron Rodrigue, *French Jews, Turkish Jews: The Alliance Israélite Universelle and the Politics of Jewish Schooling in Turkey, 1860–1925* (Bloomington: Indiana University Press, 1990), 80–85.

7. Shilo, *Princess or Prisoner?*, 143–80.

8. Rothschild, *An Appeal to Jewish Women*, 1.

9. Shifra Shvarts, "The Development of Mother and Infant Welfare Centers in Israel, 1854–1954," *Journal of the History of Medicine and Allied Sciences* 55, no. 4:398–39.

10. Margalit Shilo, "A Cross-Cultural Message: The Case of Evelina de Rothschild," in *Jewish Women in Pre-State Israel*, ed. Ruth Kark, Margalit Shilo and Galit Hasan-Rokem (Waltham, MA: Brandeis University Press, 2008), 170–73.

11. Eliezer Manneberg, *The Evolution of Jewish Educational Practices in the Sancak of Jerusalem under Ottoman Rule* (Ann Arbor, MI: University Microfilms, 1976), 149–59; cf. Slutsky, "The Evelina de Rothschild School during the Yishuv," 8. Slutsky says there were only fifteen girls in the original school.

12. Shilo, *Princess or Prisoner?*, 169.

13. Rothschild, *An Appeal to Jewish Women*, 2.

14. Ibid., 4.

15. Annie Landau, "Recollections That Are Past but Not Forgotten," Ethel Levy Collection.

16. Interviews with Rachel Levin Reinitz, Shulamit Kishik-Cohen, Marta Zayonce Shamir, and Elisheva Shifman Baram.

17. Rothschild, *An Appeal to Jewish Women*, 2.

18. Ibid.

19. Interviews with Reinitz, Kishik-Cohen, Shamir, and Baram.

20. Yair Wallach, "Readings in Conflict: Public Texts in Modern Jerusalem, 1858–1948," PhD diss., University of London, 2008, 195. Wallach notes that Jerusalemites often referred to buildings by unofficial names. The German school for orphan girls, Talitha Kumi, was known as "Charlota" after its headmistress, Charlotte Pilz, and the Syrian Orphanage was called "Schneller" after its founding pastor, Johan Schneller.

21. Rodrigue, *French Jews, Turkish Jews*, 84.

1. Annie Landau's Road to Jerusalem

1. Family tree, Landau Family Papers.

2. Ibid.

3. Ibid.

4. Oliver Sacks, *Uncle Tungsten: Memories of a Chemical Boyhood* (New York: Vintage Books, 2001), 17.

5. *Centennial Celebration: Evelina de Rothschild School* [in Hebrew], 1964, 26, Evelina de Rothschild School Collection, Jerusalem Municipal Archives (JMA).

6. Max Nurock, "A Memory of Annie Landau," 1945, Ethel Levy Collection.

7. "To Our Readers," *Jewish Standard*, March 2, 1888, 2.

8. "Jewish Middle Class Education," *Jewish Standard*, 4.

9. Ibid.

10. "Judaism and Art," *Jewish Standard*, March 9, 1888, 3; "The Sabbath," *Jewish Standard*, March 16, 1888, 4.

11. "The Sphere of Woman," *Jewish Standard*, April 27, 1888, 4.

12. "Musical Evening at 20 Highbury Park," June 2, 1907, Landau Family Papers.

13. "Family Record," *Jewish Chronicle*, February 16, 1945, 16.

14. Sacks, *Uncle Tungsten*, 17, 172.

15. Annie Landau to Helena Landau, November 1942, Chester Archives, D6335, box 1.

16. *Endowed Charities*, vols. 4 and 5, London Metropolitan Archives (LMA).

17. Felicity Hunt, ed., *Lessons for Life: The Schooling of Girls and Women 1850–1950* (Oxford, UK: Basil Blackwell, 1987), 6.

18. Sylvia Harrop, *The Merchant Taylors' School for Girls, Crosby* (Liverpool, UK: Liverpool University Press, 1988), 3–8.

19. *Caroline Franklin: Tribute to Her Memory* (London: Frome, Butler and Tanner, 1936).

20. Personal note to author from David Dimson of London, who knew Annie Landau in the 1930s.

21. Noah Rosenbloom, "Religious and Secular Co-Equality in S. R. Hirsch's Educational Theory," *Jewish Social Studies* 24, no. 4 (October 1962): 225.

22. Ibid., 230.

23. Ibid., 231.

24. Annie Landau, letter to the editor, *Jewish Chronicle*, December 7, 1894, 7.

25. "Westminster Jews' Free School," *Jewish Chronicle*, April 5, 1895, 26.

26. Gerry Black, *Living Up West: Jewish Life in London's West End* (London: London Museum of Jewish Life, 1994), 160–61.

27. Dr. Yitzchak Schwartz to Leopold de Rothschild, April 21, 1886, Rothschild Archives London (RAL).

28. Anglo-Jewish Association, *Fifteenth Annual Report, 1885–86*, Appendix B, Hartley Collection (HC).

29. Anglo-Jewish Association, *Twenty-First Annual Report, 1891–92*, 36–37, HC.

30. Anglo-Jewish Association, *Twenty-Third Annual Report, 1893–94*, Appendix C, HC.

31. Ibid.

32. C. Mona Hajjar Halaby, "School Days in Mandate Jerusalem at Dames de Sion," *Jerusalem Quarterly* 31 (Summer 2007): 42.

33. Shilo, *Princess or Prisoner?*, 166.

34. Anglo-Jewish Association, *Twenty-Fifth Annual Report, 1895–96*, 34, HC. The association, founded in London, now had branches in Manchester, Liverpool, and Birmingham. Five vice-presidents of the association were members of Parliament.

35. Ibid., 35.

36. Ibid., 38.

37. Ibid., 36–37.

38. Michael Firestone, *Beit Mahaniim*, Historic Preservation Report (Jerusalem: Israeli Ministry of Education, 1995), 3–5.

39. David Kroyanker, *Jerusalem: The Street of Prophets, the Ethiopian and Musrara Quarters, 1850–2000* [in Hebrew] (Jerusalem: Keter, 2000), 63–71.

40. Compare this with the Alliance Israelite Universelle curriculum. Frances Malino, "The Women Teachers of the AIU, 1872–1940," in *Jewish Women in Historical Perspective*, 2nd ed., ed. Judith Baskin (Detroit, MI: Wayne State University Press, 1998), 257–58.

41. Kevin J. Brehony, "English Revisionist Froebelians and the Schooling of the Urban Poor," in *Practical Visionaries: Women, Education and Social Progress, 1790–1930*, ed. Mary Hilton and Pam Hirsch (New York: Longman, 2000), 183–99.

42. Shilo, *Princess or Prisoner?*, 156.

43. Ibid., 169.

44. Anglo-Jewish Association, *Twenty-Sixth Annual Report, 1896–97*, 28–30, HC.

45. Bertha Spafford Vester, *Our Jerusalem* (Jerusalem: Ariel, 1988), 108–9.

46. Anglo-Jewish Association, *Twenty-Seventh Annual Report, 1897–98*, 35–37, HC.

47. Todd Endelmann, *The Jews of Britain: 1656–2000* (Berkeley: University of California Press, 2002), 266. Endelmann notes that creative and ambitious Jews regularly looked outward to be challenged, to find excitement and to win recognition.

48. Anglo-Jewish Association, *Twenty-Eighth Annual Report, 1898–99*, 28–29, HC.

49. Annie Landau, "Recollections," *Jewish Chronicle*, October 30, 1903, 21.

50. Ibid.

51. Ibid.; see also Wallach, "Readings in Conflict," 241–42.

2. An English Girls' School in Ottoman Jerusalem

1. *Confidential Report on the Evelina de Rothschild School, Jerusalem, December 1899–January 1900*, February 1900, Ethel Levy Collection.

2. Ibid., 1.

3. Ibid., 2.

4. Ibid., 3.

5. Ibid.

6. Ela Greenberg, "Between Hardship and Respect: A Collective Biography of Arab Women Teachers in British-Ruled Palestine," *Hawwa* 6, no. 3 (2008): 287.

7. *Confidential Report*, 5.

8. Ibid., 4.

9. Ibid.

10. Anglo-Jewish Association, *Thirtieth Annual Report, 1900–01*, 34–36, HC.

11. Adela Goodrich-Freer, *Inner Jerusalem* (New York: Dutton, 1904), 60; and S. Y. Agnon, *Only Yesterday* (Princeton, NJ: Princeton University Press, 2000), 312, which refers to these wall posters that denounced schools that taught English.

12. Anglo-Jewish Association, *Thirtieth Annual Report*, 34–36.

13. "Girls' School Jerusalem," *Jewish Chronicle*, October 25, 1901, 13.

14. Ibid., 14.

15. Ibid.

16. Anglo-Jewish Association, *Thirty-First Annual Report, 1901–02*, 28–29, HC.

17. Ibid., 29.

18. Ibid., 30.

19. "Distribution of Prizes, Evelina de Rothschild School, 1902," Evelina de Rothschild School Collection, JMA. Public examination of pupils and the awarding of prizes dated back to 1878; Shilo, *Princess or Prisoner?*, 163.

20. Goodrich-Freer, *Inner Jerusalem*, 53–54.

21. Dr. R. J. Petri, "Precautions against Cholera," October 1902, Evelina de Rothschild School Collection, JMA.

22. Anglo-Jewish Association, *Thirty-First Annual Report*, 29.

23. Anglo-Jewish Association, *Thirty-Second Annual Report, 1902–03*, 36, HC.

24. Ibid.

25. *Centennial Celebration*, 19.

26. Ibid., 20.

27. Ibid., 21.

28. "'The Holy City' and Some of Its Inhabitants," *Jewish Chronicle*, October 30, 1903, 21.

29. Cf. Bernard Wasserstein, *Divided Jerusalem: The Struggle for the Holy City*, 3rd ed. (New Haven, CT: Yale University Press, 2008), 46. He points out the lack of reliable data before 1992. Nevertheless, he provides the following numbers: 45,000 Jews, 12,000 Muslims, and 12,900 Christians, for a total of 69,900.

30. "'The Holy City' and Some of Its Inhabitants," *Jewish Chronicle*, 21.

31. Ibid.

32. H. G. Boyd Carpenter, *Report on the Evelina de Rothschild School in Jerusalem*, 1904, 1, HC.

33. Ibid.

34. Ibid., 2.

35. Ibid., 3–4.

36. Anglo-Jewish Association, *Thirty-Third Annual Report, 1903–04*, 31, HC.

37. Ibid., 32.

38. Ibid., 30, 58.

39. Ibid., 57.

40. Ibid., 57–59.

41. Anglo-Jewish Association, *Thirty-Fourth Annual Report, 1904–05*, 28, HC.

42. Anglo-Jewish Association, *Thirty-Fourth Annual Report*, 32.

43. Vester, *Our Jerusalem*, 313–15; see also S. P. Emery letters, Middle East Collection (MEC).

44. Anglo-Jewish Association, *Thirty-Fourth Annual Report*, 29.

45. Ibid., 32.

46. Anglo-Jewish Association, *Thirty-Fifth Annual Report, 1905–06*, 31, HC.

47. Anglo-Jewish Association, *Thirty-Sixth Annual Report, 1906–07*, 23, HC.

48. Ibid., 22–23.

49. "Anglo-Jewish Association," *Jewish Chronicle*, June 7, 1907, 21. The article erroneously states that Landau had been absent for four years.

50. Ibid., 21–22.

51. Robert Henriques, "Centenary Evelina de Rothschild School: Vision and Fulfillment," *Jewish Chronicle* (Supplement), June 18, 1965.

52. Ibid.

53. Ibid.

54. Anglo-Jewish Association, *Thirty-Seventh Annual Report, 1907–08*, 25–26, HC.

55. *Centennial Celebration*, 5–6.

56. Martin Gilbert, *Jerusalem in the Twentieth Century* (New York: John Wiley & Sons, 1996), 19.

57. Anglo-Jewish Association, *Thirty-Seventh Annual Report*, 26.

58. Anglo-Jewish Association, *Fortieth Annual Report, 1910–11*, 24–25, HC.

59. Ibid., 26–27.

60. Anglo-Jewish Association, *Thirty-Eighth Annual Report, 1908–09*, 27–28, HC.

61. "Jerusalem…in the days of her…Miseries," *Jewish Chronicle*, April 11, 1911, 16; Anglo-Jewish Association, *Fifty-Fifth Annual Report, 1926*, 28–29, HC.

62. Anglo-Jewish Association, *Forty-First Annual Report, 1911–12*, 29, HC.

63. Anglo-Jewish Association, *Fortieth Annual Report*, 24.

64. Ibid.; see also Moshe Hananel, *The Jerusalemites: A Journey through the British Mandate Telephone Book, 1946* [in Hebrew] (Tel Aviv: Eretz, 2007), 188. Hananel claimed that Annie Landau was placed at the head of the Red Crescent with the mayor of Jerusalem.

65. Anglo-Jewish Association, *Forty-First Annual Report*, 28–29.

66. Ibid.

67. Rothschild, *An Appeal to Jewish Women*; reprinted in *Jewish Chronicle*, June 11, 1911. For details of this publication, see the introduction.

68. "The Palestine Exhibition ad Bazaar," *Jewish Chronicle*, May 12, 1912, 16–17.

69. Committee of the Palestine Exhibition and Bazaar, *Awakening Palestine* (London: Committee of the Palestine Exhibition and Bazaar, 1912), 3.

70. Ibid., 4.

71. Hemda Ben-Yehuda, "Palestine before the War," in *Jerusalem: Its Redemption and Future* (New York: Christian Herald, 1918), 3–4.

72. Ibid., 4–16; see also Rachel Elboim-Dror, "Israeli Education: Changing Perspectives," *Israel Studies* 6, no. 1:84.

73. Anglo-Jewish Association, *Forty-Second Annual Report, 1912–13*, 28–29, HC.

74. Anglo-Jewish Association, *Forty-Third Annual Report, 1913–14*, 26, HC.

75. Helena Kagan, *The Voice That Called* (Jerusalem: n.p., 1978), 44–46.

76. Abigail Jacobson, *From Empire to Empire: Jerusalem between Ottoman and British Rule, 1912–1920* (Syracuse, NY: Syracuse University Press, 2011), 5–6.

77. Anglo-Jewish Association, *Forty-Third Annual Report*, 29.

78. Jacobson, *From Empire to Empire*, 26–27.

79. "The Death of a Hadassah Head Nurse," *Macabaean*, August 1917, Hadassah Archives (HA).

80. Jacobson, *From Empire to Empire*, 40–48. Ben-Yehuda, "Palestine before the War," 26.

81. *Centennial Celebration*, 5–6.

82. Albert Montefiore Hyamson, *Palestine: The Rebirth of an Ancient People* (London: Sidgwick & Jackson, 1917), 230.

83. Ben-Yehuda, "Palestine before the War," 38–40.

84. "The Death of a Hadassah Head Nurse."

85. Nellie Nissim to Annie Landau, September 6, 1915, Ethel Levy Collection.

86. Anglo-Jewish Association, *Forty-Fourth Annual Report, 1914–15*, 17, HC; and Anglo-Jewish Association, *Forty-Fifth Annual Report, 1915–16*, 16, HC.

87. *Centennial Celebration*, 6.

88. Vester, *Our Jerusalem*, 264; Margalit Shilo, "Women as Victims of War: The British Conquest (1917) and the Blight of Prostitution in the Holy City," *Nashim: A Journal of Jewish Women's Studies and Gender Issues* 6 (Fall 2003): 74.

89. Central Zionist Archives, (CZA) S2774.

90. Nissim to Landau.

3. Rebuilding in British Jerusalem

1. Wasserstein, *Divided Jerusalem*, 78–80.

2. Ronald Storrs, *The Memoirs of Sir Ronald Storrs* (New York: G. P. Putnam and Sons, 1937), 301–7.

3. S. Horowitz to Deputy District Commission, Jerusalem, March 30, 1931, HC.

4. Storrs, *Memoirs*, 442.

5. Sir Ronald Storrs Collection, Pembroke College, Cambridge. Copy provided to the author by Dr. Nirit Shaley-Khalifa.

6. *Centennial Celebration*, 19.

7. Helen Bentwich to Caroline Franklin, February 8, 1918, Papers of Helen Bentwich, Women's Library (HB).

8. Anglo-Jewish Association, *Forty-Eighth Annual Report, 1918–19*, 12–13, HC.

9. Rachel Elboim-Dror, "British Educational Policies in Palestine," *Middle Eastern Studies* 36, no. 2 (April 2000): 28-29.

10. See letter from Wyndham Deedes cited in "Jerusalem Girls' College," *New York Times*, April 30, 1922. Warburton was asked by General Allenby to come to Jerusalem to supervise the Schneller Orphanage; she soon accomplished this task and turned her attention to girls' education.

11. Shilo, "Women as Victims of War," 72–73; cf. Ellen L. Fleischmann, *The Nation and Its "New" Women: The Palestinian Women's Movement, 1920–1948* (Berkeley: University of California Press, 2003).

12. Shilo, "Women as Victims of War," 74–75.

13. Storrs, *Memoirs*, 458.

14. Shilo, "Women as Victims of War," 76; see also Ela Greenberg, *Preparing*

the Mothers of Tomorrow: Education and Islam in Mandate Palestine (Austin: University of Texas Press, 2010), 92–95.

15. Helen Bentwich to Caroline Franklin, September 16, 1918, HB.

16. Helen Bentwich Papers, CZA, A255/475.

17. Helen Bentwich to Caroline Franklin, March 12, 1922, HB.

18. Helen Bentwich Papers, CZA, A255/475; see also Vester, *Our Jerusalem*, 314, and Susan Lee Hattis, *The Bi-National Idea in Palestine during Mandatory Times* (Haifa: Shikmona, 1970), 19–38; cf. Fleischmann, *The Nation and Its "New" Women*, 33.

19. Storrs, *Memoirs*, 327–30.

20. Anglo-Jewish Association, *Forty-Eighth Annual Report*, 13.

21. Helen Bentwich to Caroline Franklin, March 26, 1919, HB.

22. Hadara Lazar, *Out of Palestine: The Making of Modern Israel* (New York: Atlas, 2011), 34–35.

23. Faitlovitch Collection, file 116., Sourasky Library, Tel Aviv University.

24. Helen Bentwich Papers, CZA, S2774.

25. Jennifer Glynn, *Tidings from Zion: Helen Bentwich's Letters from Jerusalem, 1919–1931* (London: I. B. Tauris, 2000), 20.

26. Lazar, *Out of Palestine*, 18.

27. Ethel Levy, "I Remember," December 18, 1951, Ethel Levy Collection.

28. Ethel Levy, "Address to League of Jewish Women," 1961, Ethel Levy Collection.

29. Sarah Jaholom Sapir to her family in London, January 29, 1922, Shalva Weil Collection.

30. Storrs, *Memoirs*, 442.

31. Anglo-Jewish Association, *Forty-Eighth Annual Report*, 13.

32. Anglo-Jewish Association, *Forty-Ninth Annual Report, 1919–20*, 10–11, HC.

33. Helen Bentwich to Caroline Franklin, November 15, 1919, HB.

34. Helen Bentwich to Caroline Franklin, July 7, 1921, HB.

35. Bertha Badt-Strauss, *White Fire: The Life and Works of Jesse Sampter* (New York: Arno Press, 1977), 67.

36. Hilda Ridler, the inspector of girl's education under the Mandate government and the principal of the Women's Training College, worked only in government Arab schools; see Government of Palestine, *Department of Education Annual Report, 1926–1927*, Jerusalem, 28.

37. Humphrey Ernest Bowman, *Middle East Window* (London: Longmans, Green, 1942), 251.

38. Anglo-Jewish Association, *Fiftieth Annual Report, 1920–21*, 19, HC.

39. Anglo-Jewish Association, *Fifty-First Annual Report, 1921–22*, 16, HC.

40. Ibid., 17.

41. Bowman, *Middle East Window*, 278–79.

42. Storrs, *Memoirs*, 378.

43. Rashid Khalidi, *Palestinian Identity: The Construction of Modern National Consciousness* (New York: Columbia University), 172–73.

44. Norman and Helen Bentwich, *Mandate Memories 1914–1948: From the Balfour Declaration to the Establishment of Israel* (New York: Schocken Books, 1965), 85.

45. "Diploma Day at Girls' College," *Palestine Post*, June 28, 1940, 1.

46. Anglo-Jewish Association, *Fifty-Second Annual Report, 1922–23*, 13, HC.

47. "The Evelina School," *Jewish Chronicle*, June 30, 1922, 18.

48. Anglo-Jewish Association, *Fifty-Third Annual Report, 1923–24*, 22, HC; and Anglo-Jewish Association, *Fifty-Fourth Annual Report, 1924–25*, 12, 16, HC.

49. See Sara Epstein letter in Daniel Ophir, ed., *The House on Montefiore Street* [in Hebrew] (Petah-Tikvah, Israel: Frumkin, 2010), 43.

50. *Centennial Celebration*, 32.

51. Ibid., 33.

52. Ibid., 34.

53. Ibid.

54. Interviews with Rivka Weingarten, Rachel Levin Reinitz, and Michal Harrison Modai.

55. Helen Bentwich to Caroline Franklin, October 26, 1923, HB.

56. Anglo-Jewish Association, *Fifty-Third Annual Report*, 14.

57. Bertha Spafford Vester papers, 1924, American Colony Archives, given to the author by curator Rachel Lev.

58. Helen Bentwich to Caroline Franklin, February 24, 1924, HB.

59. "A Quarter of a Century in Jerusalem," *Jewish Chronicle*, June 13, 1924, 16.

60. Ibid., 17.

61. Ibid.

62. Ibid.

63. Helen Bentwich to Caroline Franklin, December 26, 1924, HB.

64. Anglo-Jewish Association, *Fifty-Fifth Annual Report*, 15.

65. Helen Bentwich to Caroline Franklin, November 21, 1926, HB.

66. Helen Bentwich to Caroline Franklin, January 8, 1927, HB.

67. Anglo-Jewish Association, *Fifty-Fifth Annual Report*, 28.

68. Ibid., 30.

69. Nina Kheimets and Alek D. Epstein, "Languages of Science in the Era of Nation-State Formation: The Israeli Universities and Their (Non)Participation in the Revival of Hebrew," *Journal of Multilingual and Multicultural Development* 26, no. 1 (2005): 12–14.

70. Anglo-Jewish Association, *Fifty-Fifth Annual Report,*, 31–32.

71. Helen Bentwich to Caroline Franklin, January 14, 1928, HB.

72. Helen Bentwich to Caroline Franklin, February 18, 1928, HB.

73. Interview with Yvonne Astruc Sitton.

74. Interview with Rachel Harris Babad Pirani.

75. Interview with Rivka Weingarten.

76. Interview with Rachel Levin Reinitz.

77. *Centennial Celebration*, 24; and Anglo-Jewish Association, *Fifty-Seventh Annual Report, 1928*, 13, HC.

78. Interview with Sitton.

79. Interview with Pirani.

80. Interview with Weingarten.

81. Interview with Reinitz.

82. Interviews with Sitton, Pirani, Weingarten, and Reinitz.

83. "Christian Missionaries in Palestine," *Jewish Chronicle*, July 13, 1928, 17.

84. "Shaw Commission Report," August 1929, 65.

85. Helen Bentwich to Caroline Franklin, September 14, 1929, HB.

86. The daily ration consisted of about eighteen ounces of bread; one and a quarter ounces of meat; about seven ounces of fresh vegetables; almost two ounces of potatoes; almost three ounces of lentils, rice, beans, or oatmeal; two-thirds of an ounce of fresh butter or two and a half ounces of jam or cheese; one ounce of sugar; half an ounce of salt; one-third of an ounce of tea; one ounce of olives; half a tin of sardines or one-third of a tin of salmon; and one-fifth of a tin of condensed milk. Helen Bentwich Papers, CZA, A255/475.

87. Ibid.

88. Helen Bentwich to Norman Bentwich, September 16, 1926, HB.

89. Helen Bentwich to Caroline Franklin, March 29, 1930, HB.

90. Anglo-Jewish Association, *Fifty-Eighth Annual Report, 1929*, 19, HC.

91. Leah Goodman to Annie Landau, May 22, 1930, HC.

92. Ethel Levy to Annie Landau, May 23, 1930, HC.

93. Ibid.

94. Sarah Kleiman to Centennial Committee, n.d., Evelina de Rothschild School Collection, JMA.

95. Helen Bentwich to Caroline Franklin, November 7, 1925.

4. Return to Frutiger House

1. Glass and Kark, *Sephardi Entrepreneurs*, 71.

2. Anglo-Jewish Association, *Fifty-Ninth Annual Report, 1930*, 17, HC.

3. Ibid., 18.

4. Annie Landau to Claude Montefiore, October 30, 1930, HC.

5. Anglo-Jewish Association, *Sixtieth Annual Report, 1931*, 15, HC; and Anglo-Jewish Association, *Sixty-First Annual Report, 1932*, 16, HC.

6. Anglo-Jewish Association, *Sixty-Eighth Annual Report, 1939–1940*, 19, HC.

7. Rachel Harris Babad Pirani, diary, September 7, 1936, 71. In author's possession.

8. The Teachers' Seminary was part of the Mizrahi (religious) stream. See Noah

Nardi, *Education in Palestine* (Washington, DC: Zionist Organization of America, 1945), 50.

9. Interview with Rivka Weingarten.

10. Interview with Rachel Levin Reinitz.

11. Ibid.

12. United Hebrew Congregations of the British Empire, *Authorized Daily Prayer Book* (Jerusalem: Zuckerman, n.d.).

13. Interviews with Reinitz and Ruth Lask Rasnic.

14. Marta Zayonce Shamir, *Daughter of the Generation of 1948* [in Hebrew] (Jerusalem: privately printed, 2003), 21.

15. Interview with Marta Zayonce Shamir.

16. Interview with Michal Harrison Modai.

17. Interview with Shamir.

18. Interview with Weingarten.

19. *Centennial Celebration*, 37.

20. Interview with Shamir.

21. Ibid.

22. Interview with Reinitz.

23. Sarah Kleiman to Centennial Committee, Evelina de Rothschild School Collection, JMA.

24. "Confidential File," Ethel Levy Collection.

25. Interview with Shamir.

26. Interview with Reinitz.

27. Ibid.

28. Anglo-Jewish Association, *Sixty-First Annual Report*, 16.

29. Gillian Avery, *Childhood's Pattern: A Study of the Heroes and Heroines of Children's Fiction, 1770–1950* (London: Hodder and Stoughton, 1975), 207.

30. Anglo-Jewish Association, *Sixty-Fifth Annual Report, 1936–37*, 20, HC.

31. *Centennial Celebration*, 47.

32. Avery, *Childhood's Pattern*, 225. He points out that many adolescent girls enjoyed belonging to a clique with a particular mystique and badge.

33. Yvonne Astruc, "What Is a Prefect," *School*, 1938, 23–24, National Library of Israel (NLI).

34. Naomi Teitelbaum, "The Life of a Prefect," *School*, 1939, 35–36, NLI.

35. Anglo-Jewish Association, *Sixty-First Annual Report*, 17.

36. Ibid., 29.

37. Esther Shani, "A Few Words on the Old Girls' Association," *School*, 1936, 29, NLI; Esther Shani, "The Old Girls' Association," *School*, 1938, 19, NLI; and Esther Shani, "The Old Girls' Association,"*School*, 1939, 39, NLI. Ziona Caspi married a Christian coworker at the Palestine Broadcasting Service and settled in South Africa. Ahuva Morgenstern married a South African pen pal and settled there, too.

38. Interview with Hannah Aaronson Newman.

39. Miriam Cohen, "Sports Notes,"*School,* 1935, 11–12, NLI.

40. Interviews with Adaya Hochberg Barkay, Adina Shoshani Toklaty, Miriam Ochana Guini, Shulamit Lilienfeld Verner, and Rachel Levin Reinitz.

41. Anglo-Jewish Association, *Sixty-Eighth Annual Report,* 19.

42. *Centennial Celebration,* 14.

43. "Shulamith," *Jerusalem Radio: The Only Radio Publication in Palestine,* October 15, 1938, 3.

44. "The English Children's Hour," *Jerusalem Radio* vol.1, #5, October 28, 1938, 4; "The English Children's Hour," *Jerusalem Radio* vol. 3, #1, December 29, 1939, 4; "The English Children's Hour," *Jerusalem Radio* vol.3, #4, January 22, 1940, 4; "The English Children's Hour," *Jerusalem Radio* vol.3, #7, 4; "The English Children's Hour," *Jerusalem Radio* vol 3, #36, 4.

45. Pirani, diary, July 17, 1936, 2.

46. Ibid., July 18, 1936, 4.

47. Ibid., August 20, 1936, 12–13; see also Anita Shapira, *Land and Power: The Zionist Resort to Force, 1881–1948* (Stanford, CA: Stanford University Press, 1992), 229.

48. Annie Landau, "The Head's Foreward," *School,* 1937, 1, NLI.

49. Dina Ettinger, "Toscanini," *School,* 1937, 24, NLI.

50. Shoshana Prager, "The Death of Avinoam Yellin," *School,* 1938, 20–21, NLI.

51. Bowman, *Middle East Window* 291. In 1925, thirty-five thousand immigrants, mostly from Poland, arrived in Palestine. For the next several years, immigration declined, reflecting the economic crises in Europe.

52. Interview with Daisy Ticho.

53. Interview with Shulamith Lilienfeld Verner.

54. Esther Shani, "The Old Girls' Association," *School,* 1938, 19, NLI.

55. Interview with Lea Steinhardt Keller.

56. Schwartzstein file, CZA.

57. Interviews with Shoshana Heineman Bar Ilan and Keller.

58. Ibid.

59. Ibid.

60. Schwartzstein file, CZA.

61. Ibid.

62. Levy, "I Remember."

63. Ethel Levy, "Special Cases and Incidents," n.d., Ethel Levy Collection.

64. Ibid.

65. Annie Landau, "The Head's Foreward," *School,* 1939, 1, NLI.

66. Ibid.

67. Interview with Rachel Harris Babad Pirani.

68. Interview with Rachel Levin Reinitz.

69. Interview with Rivka Weingarten.

70. Interview with Yvonne Astruc Sitton.

71. Anglo-Jewish Association, *Fifteenth Annual Report*, 53.

72. Rachel Elboim-Dror, *Hebrew Education in Palestine, 1854–1914* [in Hebrew] (Jerusalem: n.p., 1986), 1: 78–82.

73. Ibid., 4.

74. "Britain's Blow Will Not Subdue Jews," *Palestine Post*, May 18, 1939, 1.

75. See also Oz Almog, *The Sabra: The Creation of the New Jew* (Berkeley: University of California Press, 2000), 21.

76. Bina Makofky, "School Notes," *School*, 1938, 3, NLI.

77. *Palestine Post*, September 4, 1939, 1.

78. *Palestine Post*, June 28, 1940, 1.

79. Annie Landau, "The Head's Foreward," *School*, 1940, 1, NLI.

5. School *Magazine: The Girls Speak Out*

1. Honour Levine, "Thoughts of My Native Land: Australia," *School*, 1937, 26–27, NLI.

2. Ruth Karpf, "From Europe to Asia," *School*, 1935, 15, NLI. The British called the territory it administered Palestine; the Arabs called it Filastin; the Jews called it Eretz Israel.

3. Ruth Karpf, "Nuremberg and Jerusalem," *School*, 1936, 28–29, NLI.

4. Leah Schoenberger, "My Native Town," *School*, 1938, 27, NLI.

5. Laura Schor, *The Life and Legacy of Baroness Betty de Rothschild* (New York: Peter Lang, 2006), 9–10.

6. Schoenberger, "My Native Town," *School*, 1938, 28–29.

7. Leah Schoenberger, "In Memory of the Frankfurt Synagogue," *School*, 1939, 20–21, NLI.

8. Zipporah Rosenblut, "I Revisit Hungary," *School*, 1938, 31, 32, NLI.

9. Ibid.

10. See Almog, *The Sabra*, 86–90.

11. Ruth Karpf, "Why I Drink Fresh Orange Juice," *School*, 1936, 29–30, NLI. See also the story of a youngster who wrote about brushing his teeth as service to the nation in Almog, *The Sabra*, 30.

12. Ziona Caspi, "'The Milky Way!,'" *School*, 1938, 32–33, NLI.

13. Leah Azulay, "A Trip to the Emek," *School*, 1938, 21–22, NLI.

14. Sarah Lorberbaum, "Courage," *School*, 1939, 24–26, NLI.

15. Chana Loshinksy, "A Week on Kfar Saba," *School*, 1939, 27–28, NLI.

16. Rolande Valero, "A Visit to Givat Brenner during the Tu B'Shvat Holiday," *School*, 1940, 19–20, NLI.

17. Miriam Indik, "My Homeland," *School*, 1940, 17–18, NLI.

18. Elka Eden, "Our Quarter and Its Surroundings," *School*, 1935, 16–17, NLI.

19. Hannah Saltzman, "A Day in the Life of a Piastre," *School*, 1935, 25–26, NLI.

20. Margalit Rubovitz, "A Day in the Life of a Camel," *School*, 1938, 29, NLI.

21. Margalit Rubovitz, "Palestine," *School*, 1935, 18, NLI; see also Almog, *The Sabra*, 146–48.

22. Jehudith Hurwitz, "The Trials and and Tribulations of 'Muharim,'" *School*, 1935, 12–13, NLI.

23. Hadassah Margalit, "Noises in My Street," *School*, 1939, 29, NLI.

24. Hasidah Rakover, "Jerusalem," *School*, 1939, 28, NLI.

25. Rachel Harris, "Lost in the Old City," *School*, 1936, 24, NLI.

26. Miriam Cohen, "The Western Wall," *School*, 1936, 13–14, NLI.

27. Naomi Teitelbaum, "A Special Kind of Pioneering" [in Hebrew], *School*, 1939, 23–24, NLI.

28. Gerda Kaplowitz, "The King Is Dead, Long Live the King," *School*, 1936, 19–20, NLI.

29. Rachel Frankel, "Jerusalem on the Night of the Coronation" [in Hebrew], *School*, 1937, 25, NLI; see also "The Coronation in Jerusalem," *Jewish Chronicle*, May 21, 1937, 16. Reviewing the coronation celebrations in Jerusalem, it noted, "A fine show was provided by the veteran educator Miss Annie Landau, Principal of the Evelina de Rothschild. The school was so covered in bunting and decorations that very little masonry could be seen. Colored lights added to the picture at night."

30. Ziona Caspi, "The Coronation in Jerusalem," *School*, 1937, 25–26, NLI.

31. Ruth Klonsky, "Jerusalem's Lake District," *School*, 1937, 31, NLI.

32. Haya Lieder, "Falling Asleep in 1850 and Awaking in 1937," *School*, 1937, 28–29, NLI.

33. Tova Cohen, "My First Appearance on the Radio," *School*, 1938, 11, NLI.

34. The same was not true for Carmel Halabi, a Greek Orthodox student at the Jerusalem Girls' College, who wrote an essay, "The Present Is a Period of Change: What Values in Eastern Life Should Be Carefully Safeguarded?", in the *Jerusalem Girls' College* magazine, 1938, 66–67.

35. Margalith Havilio, "Class V," *School*, 1939, 10, NLI.

36. Zipporah Levy, "Class VI's Stop Press," *School*, 1935, 5–6, NLI.

37. Almog, *The Sabra*, 77–78.

38. Shoshana Drosdovsky, "Our Class," *School*, 1936, 12–13, NLI.

39. Hava Etlinger, "Class III," *School*, 1937, 16–17, NLI.

40. Regina Havilio, "The Evelina de Rothschild Alphabet," *School*, 1937, 12–13, NLI.

41. Ruth Karpf, "Examination Time," *School*, 1936, 26–27, NLI.

42. Ahuva Vinkler, "Third Company," *School*, 1935, 10, NLI.

43. Bella Leider and Hava Weinberg, "Social Concert," *School*, 1939, 37–38, NLI.

44. Ziona Caspi, "Class IV," *School*, 1935, 7, NLI.

45. "Portions of the Hagada as Applied to Class VII," *School*, 1937, 11–12, NLI.

46. Rachel Levy, "Senior Commercial," *School*, 1936, 6–7, NLI.

47. Miriam Titkin and Lilian Shapiro, "Junior Commercial," *School*, 1936, 7–8, NLI.

6. Transitions: 1940–1960

1. Shulamit Patt, "School Notes," *School*, 1940, 2, NLI.
2. Anglo-Jewish Association, *Sixty-Ninth Annual Report, 1940–1941*, 7, HC.
3. Anglo-Jewish Association, *Seventieth Annual Report, 1941–1942*, 3–4, HC.
4. Anglo-Jewish Association, *Seventy-First Annual Report, 1942–1943*, 2, HC.
5. Ibid., 3–4.
6. "Last Tribute to Annie Landau," *Palestine Post*, January 25, 1945, 3.
7. Ibid.
8. "Tribute to Citizen of Jerusalem," *Palestine Post*, February 23, 1945, 3.
9. Ethel Levy, "Talk to Evelina Girls," February 1945, Ethel Levy Collection.
10. Ethel Levy, "Talk to Anglo-Jewish Association," July 7, 1947, Ethel Levy Collection.
11. Ethel Levy to the Anglo-Jewish Association, n.d., Ethel Levy Collection.
12. Ethel Levy, "An Address to the Summer School," Hebrew University, July 1946, Ethel Levy Collection.
13. Yona Scharf Malleyron, "On Taking My Son to School," Ethel Levy Collection.
14. Ibid.
15. Ibid.
16. Interview with Adaya Hochberg Barkay.
17. Malleyron, "On Taking My Son to School."
18. Yona Malleyron, *You Will Get Out of Here* [in Hebrew] (Jerusalem: Yad Vashem, 1980).
19. Yona Scharf Malleyron to Ethel Levy, November 3, 1969, Ethel Levy Collection.
20. Levy, "Talk to Anglo-Jewish Association."
21. Edith Levy to Leonard Stein, secretary of the Anglo-Jewish Association, February 1, 1946, HC.
22. Ethel Levy to Anglo-Jewish Association, May 20, 1945, HC; and Anglo-Jewish Association, *Seventy-Fifth Annual Report, 1946–47*, 19, HC.
23. Ethel Levy, office diary, May 1946, Ethel Levy Collection.
24. Interviews with Yvonne Astruc Sitton and Marta Zayonce Shamir.
25. Gilbert, *Jerusalem in the Twentieth Century*, 172.
26. Levy, "Talk to Anglo-Jewish Association."
27. Ethel Levy to Leonard Stein, October 27, 1946, Ethel Levy Collection.
28. Anglo-Jewish Association, *Seventy-Fifth Annual Report*, 19, HC.
29. Anglo-Jewish Association, *Seventy-Sixth Annual Report, 1947–48*, 40, HC.
30. Gilbert, *Jerusalem in the Twentieth Century*, 174–75.
31. Ibid., 176–79.
32. Interview with Shamir.
33. Ethel Levy, "Talk to Parents," December 28, 1947, Ethel Levy Collection.

34. Ethel Levy, "Notes on Rehavia Transfer," n.d., Ethel Levy Collection.

35. Inger Marie Okkenhaug, *The Quality of Heroic Living, of High Endeavor and Adventure: Anglican Mission, Women and Education in Palestine, 1888–1948* (Leiden, Netherlands: Brill, 2002), 181.

36. Gilbert, *Jerusalem in the Twentieth Century*, 189.

37. Interview with Shamir.

38. Levy, "Notes on Rehavia Transfer."

39. Ethel Levy to L. C. Beber, February 12, 1948, HC.

40. Interviews with Miriam Ochana Guini, Adina Shoshani Toklaty, Michal Harrison Modai, Adaya Hochberg Barkay, and Marta Zayonce Shamir.

41. Hala Sakakini, *Jerusalem and I: A Personal Record* (Amman, Jordan: Economic Press, 1990), 118.

42. Gilbert, *Jerusalem in the Twentieth Century*, 190, 196, 199, 203–4.

43. Schwartzstein file, May 1948, CZA.

44. Ethel Levy, "Jerusalem under Siege," May 1948, Ethel Levy Collection.

45. Ibid.

46. Interviews with Shoshana Heineman Bar Ilan and Lea Steinhardt Keller.

47. Asher Cailingold, *An Unlikely Heroine: Esther Cailingold's Fight for Jerusalem* (London: Vallentine Mitchell, 2000), 223–38.

48. Levy, "Talk to Anglo-Jewish Association."

49. Interview with Shulamit Lilienfeld Verner.

50. Interview with Miriam Ochana Guini.

51. Interview with Adina Shoshani Toklaty.

52. Interview with Michal Harrison Modai.

53. Interview with Elisheva Shifman Baram.

54. Elisheva Shifman Baram, "Brief Biography," n.d., unpublished manuscript in author's possession.

55. Ibid.

56. Interview with Rivka Zweig Winograd.

57. "Evelina de Rothschild School for Girls," n.d., 1, Evelina de Rothschild School Collection, JMA.

58. Anglo-Jewish Association, "Memorandum on the Evelina de Rothschild School," 1952, HC.

59. Ethel Levy, notes for article in the *Jewish Review*, n.d., Ethel Levy Collection; see also Sefton Temkin (secretary of Anglo-Jewish Association) to Daniel Auster (mayor of Jerusalem), July 17, 1950, HC.

60. Levy, notes for article.

61. Anglo-Jewish Association, *Seventy-Ninth Annual Report, 1950–51*, 19, HC.

62. Ibid., 20.

63. Anglo-Jewish Association, *Eightieth Annual Report, 1951–52*, 23–24, HC.

64. Anglo-Jewish Association, *Eighty-Second Annual Report, 1953–54*, 21–22, HC.

65. Anglo-Jewish Association, *Eighty-Third Annual Report, 1954–55*, 24–25, HC.

66. Anglo-Jewish Association, *Eighty-Fourth Annual Report, 1955–56*, 26–27, HC.

67. Ethel Levy, "Report for 1956–57," May 28, 1957, 1, Ethel Levy Collection.

68. Ibid., 2.

69. Ethel Levy, "Report for 1957–58," October 24, 1958, 1–2, Ethel Levy Collection.

70. Norman De Mattos Bentwich, *The Evelina de Rothschild School, Jerusalem, 1864–1964* (London: Anglo-Jewish Association, 1964), 22.

71. Ethel Levy, "One Hundred Years of the Evelina School," *Jewish Observer and Middle East Review*, June 25, 1965.

72. Robert Henriques, "Centenary Evelina de Rothschild School: Vision and Fulfillment," *Jewish Chronicle* (Supplement), June 18, 1965, 1.

73. Anglo-Jewish Association, "Minutes, Charitable Trusts and Education Committee," May 20, 1971, HC.

74. Anglo-Jewish Association, "Evelina de Rothschild School," press release, June 19, 2009, HC; see Peggy Cidor, "The Odd Couple," *Jerusalem Post*, June 21, 2007, for background.

Epilogue

1. Interview with Shulamit Kishik-Cohen.

2. Ezra Elnakam Yachin, *The Song of Shulamit* [in Hebrew] (Jerusalem: Ezri, 2000), 14.

3. Ibid., 20.

4. Interview with Kishik-Cohen.

5. Yachin, *The Song of Shulamit*, 30.

6. Ibid., 41.

7. Interview with Kishik-Cohen.

8. Interview with Masha Weingarten Kaplan.

9. Masha Weingarten, "Educational Films," *School*, 1939, 34–35, NLI.

10. Masha Weingarten, "Dawn in Old Jerusalem" [in Hebrew], *School*, 1940, 15, NLI.

11. Interview with Kaplan.

12. Isaac Kaplan, *The Wandering Jew* (Jerusalem: Teper, 2004), 61–64.

13. Interview with Kaplan.

14. Interview with Marta Zayonce Shamir.

15. Marta Zayonce Shamir, "The Role of Education in Developing International Understanding," 1954, unpublished essay in author's possession.

16. Shamir, *Daughter of the Generation of 1948*, 83.

17. Shilansky was arrested in October 1952 while attempting to bring a suitcase bomb into the Israeli Foreign Ministry in an apparent plot to assassinate Moshe

Sharett. An Auschwitz survivor, he was accused of being a member of an underground organization opposed to Israeli-German reparations negotiations. He was sentenced to two years in prison.

18. Shamir, *Daughter of the Generation of 1948*, 102, 109, 117, 122–24.

19. Ibid., 145.

20. Interview with Adaya Hochberg Barkay.

21. Esther Roth, "Memoirs from My Life" [in Hebrew], n.d., unpublished manuscript in author's possession.

22. Interview with Barkay.

23. Adaya Hochberg Barkay, "A Blond Boy, a Different Boy," n.d., unpublished manuscript in author's possession.

24. Interview with Barkay.

25. Ibid.

26. Ibid.

27. Adaya Hochberg Barkay, "Loot," n.d., unpublished manuscript in author's possession.

28. Interview with Barkay.

29. Interview with Ruth Lask Rasnic.

30. Ruth Lask Rasnic, "Amittai," n.d., unpublished manuscript in author's possession.

31. Ruth Lask Rasnic, "To All Mothers," 1966, unpublished manuscript in author's possession.

32. Interview with Rasnic.

WORKS CITED

Archives and Special Collections

American Colony Archives
Central Zionist Archives (CZA)
Chester Archives, UK
Evelina de Rothschild School Collection, Jerusalem Municipal Archives (JMA)
Faitlovich Collection, Sourasky Library, Tel Aviv University
Hadassah Archives, American Jewish Historical Society (HA)
Hartley Collection, University of Southampton (HC)
Israel State Archives (ISA)
London Metropolitan Archives (LMA)
Middle East Collection, Saint Anthony's College, Oxford (MEC)
National Library of Israel (NLI)
Papers of Helen Bentwich, Women's Library, London (HB)
Rothschild Archives London (RAL)
Ruth Woodsmall Collection, Smith College Library
Sir Ronald Storrs Collection, Pembroke College, Cambridge
Yellin Archive for Jewish Education, Tel Aviv University

Private Papers

Ethel Levy Collection
Landau Family Papers
Shalva Weil Collection

Newspapers

Jerusalem Radio: The Only Radio Publication in Palestine
Jewish Chronicle
Jewish Standard (American Jewish Archive, Hebrew Union College, Cincinnati)
Palestine Post

Interviews Conducted in Israel, 2007–2009

Elisheva Shifman Baram, July 2008
Shoshana Heineman Bar Ilan, August 2008
Adaya Hochberg Barkay, July 2007, August 2008
Miriam Ochana Guini, July 2008
Masha Weingarten Kaplan, July 2008
Lea Steinhardt Keller, August 2008
Shulamit Kishik-Cohen, August 2008
Michal Harrison Modai, July 2007
Hannah Aaronson Newman, December 2009
Rachel Harris Babad Pirani, July 2007
Ruth Lask Rasnic, July 2008
Rachel Levin Reinitz, July 2007
Marta Zayonce Shamir, August 2008
Yvonne Astruc Sitton, July 2007
Liza Slutsky, July 2008
Daisy Ticho, January 2008
Adina Shoshani Toklaty, July 2008
Shulamit Lilienfeld Verner, January 2008
Rivka Weingarten, July 2007
Rivka Zweig Winograd, July 2007

Selected Bibliography

Agnon, S. Y. *Only Yesterday*. Princeton, NJ: Princeton University Press, 2000.

Almog, Oz. *The Sabra: The Creation of the New Jew*. Berkeley: University of California Press, 2000.

Amery, L. S. *The Leo Amery Diaries*. Edited by John Barnes and David Nicholson. London: Hutchinson, 1980.

Andrews, Fannie Fern. *Memory Pages of My Life*. Boston: Talisman Press, 1948.

Antonius, George. *The Arab Awakening: The Story of the Arab National Movement*. London: Kegan Paul, 2000.

Ashbee, C. R. *Jerusalem, 1918–1920: Records of the Pro-Jerusalem Council*. London: John Murray, 1921.

Avery, Gillian. *Childhood's Pattern: A Study of the Heroes and Heroines of Children's Fiction, 1770–1950*. London: Hodder and Stoughton, 1975.

Badt-Strauss, Bertha. *White Fire: The Life and Works of Jesse Sampter*. New York: Arno Press, 1977.

Bar-Chen, Eli. "Two Communities with a Sense of Mission: The Alliance Israélite Universelle and the Hilfsverein de Deutschen Juden." In *Jewish Emancipation Reconsidered: The French and German Models*, edited by Michael Brenner, 111–28. Tübingen, Germany: Mohr Siebeck, 2003.

Bentwich, Norman De Mattos. *The Evelina de Rothschild School, Jerusalem, 1864–1964*. London: Anglo-Jewish Association, 1964.

———. *For Zion's Sake: A Biography of Judah L. Magnes, First Chancellor and First President of the Hebrew University of Jerusalem*. Philadelphia, PA: Jewish Publication Society, 1954.

———. *My 77 Years: An Account of My Life and Times, 1883–1960*. Philadelphia, PA: Jewish Publication Society, 1961.

Bentwich, Norman, and Helen Bentwich. *Mandate Memories, 1918–1948: From the Balfour Declaration to the Establishment of Israel*. New York: Schocken Books, 1965.

Ben-Yehuda, Hemda. "Palestine before the War." In *Jerusalem: Its Redemption and Future*. New York: Christian Herald, 1918.

Bernstein, Deborah S., ed. *Pioneers and Homemakers: Jewish Women in Pre-State Israel*. Albany: State University of New York Press, 1992.

Black, Gerry. *Living Up West: Jewish Life in London's West End*. London: London Museum of Jewish Life, 1994.

Blumberg, Arnold. *A View from Jerusalem: The Consular Diary of James and Elizabeth Anne Finn*. Rutherford, NJ: Fairleigh Dickinson University Press, 1980.

Blyth, Estelle. *When We Lived in Jerusalem*. London: J. Murray, 1927.

Bowman, Humphrey Ernest. *Middle East Window*. London: Longmans, Green, 1942.

Brehony, Kevin J. "English Revisionist Froebelians and the Schooling of the Urban Poor." In *Political Visionaries: Women, Education and Social Progress, 1790–1930*, edited by Mary Hilton and Pam Hirsch, 183–99. New York: Longman, 2000.

Cailingold, Asher. *An Unlikely Heroine: Esther Cailingold's Fight for Jerusalem*. London: Vallentine Mitchell, 2000.

Caroline Franklin: Tribute to Her Memory. London: Frome, Butler and Tanner, 1936.

Chisholm, Edwin, ed. *The Jolly Book for Girls*. London: Thomas Nelson & Sons, n.d.

———. *Old Testament Stories*. London: T. C. and E. C. Jack, n.d.

Cidor, Peggy. "The Odd Couple." *Jerusalem Post*, June 21, 2007.

Committee of the Palestine Exhibition and Bazaar. *Awakening Palestine*. London: Committee of the Palestine Exhibition and Bazaar, 1912.

Eban, Abba Solomon. *Abba Eban: An Autobiography*. New York: Random House, 1977.

Elboim-Dror, Rachel. "British Educational Policies in Palestine." *Middle Eastern Studies* 36, no. 2 (April 2000): 28–47.

———. *Hebrew Education in Eretz Israel, 1854–1914* [in Hebrew]. Vol. 6. Jerusalem: n.p., 1986.

———. "Israeli Education: Changing Perspectives." *Israel Studies* 6, no. 1:76–100.

Endelmann, Todd. *The Jews of Britain: 1656–2000*. Berkeley: University of California Press, 2002.

Fawcett, Millicent Garrett. *Easter in Palestine, 1921–22*. London: T. Fisher Unwin, 1926.

———. *What I Remember*. Honolulu, HI: University Press of the Pacific, 2004.

Finn, Elizabeth Anne McCaul. *Reminiscences of Mrs. Finn, Member of the Royal Asiatic Society*. London: Marshall, Morgan and Scott, 1929.

Finn, James. *Stirring Times, or Records from Jerusalem Chronicle of 1853–1856*. London: n. p., 1878.

Firestone, Michael. *Beit Mahaniim*. Historic Preservation Report. Jerusalem: Israeli Ministry of Education, 1995.

Flaskerud, Ingvild, and Inger Marie Okkenhaug, eds. *Gender, Religion and Change in the Middle East: Two Hundred Years of History*. Oxford, NY: Berg, 2005.

Fleischmann, Ellen L. *The Nation and Its "New" Women: The Palestinian Women's Movement, 1920–1948*. Berkeley: University of California Press, 2003.

Frankel, Jonathan. *The Damascus Affair: "Ritual Murder," Politics, and the Jews in 1840*. Cambridge, UK: Cambridge University Press, 1997.

Gibson, Shimon. *Jerusalem in Original Photographs, 1850–1920*. London: Stacey, 2003.

Gidney, W. T. *The History of the London Society for Promoting Christianity amongst the Jews: From 1809 to 1908*. London: London Society for Promoting Christianity amongst the Jews, 1908.

Gilbert, Martin. *Jerusalem in the Twentieth Century*. New York: John Wiley & Sons, 1996.

Glass, Joseph B., and Ruth Kark. *Sephardi Entrepreneurs in Jerusalem: The Valero Family, 1800–1948*. Jerusalem: Gefen, 2007.

Glenday, Nonita, and Mary Price. *Reluctant Revolutionaries: A Century of Headmistresses, 1874–1974*. London: Pitman, 1975.

Glynn, Jennifer. *Tidings from Zion: Helen Bentwich's Letters from Jerusalem, 1919–1931*. London: I. B. Tauris, 2000.

Goodall, Norman. *A History of the London Missionary Society, 1895–1945*. London: Oxford University Press, 1954.

Goodrich-Freer, Adela. *Inner Jerusalem*. New York: Dutton, 1904.

Government of Palestine. *Department of Education Annual Report, 1926–1927*, Jerusalem, n.d.

Greenberg, Ela. "Between Hardship and Respect: A Collective Biography of Arab Women Teachers in British-Ruled Palestine." *Hawwa* 6, no. 3 (2008): 284–314.

———. "Educating Muslim Girls in Mandatory Jerusalem." *International Journal of Middle East Studies* 36 (2004): 1–19.

———. *Preparing the Mothers of Tomorrow: Education and Islam in Mandate Palestine*. Austin: University of Texas Press, 2010.

Halaby, C. Mona Hajjar. "School Days in Mandate Jerusalem at Dames de Sion." *Jerusalem Quarterly* 31 (Summer 2007): 40–71.

Hananel, Moshe. *The Jerusalemites: The British Mandate Telephone Book, 1946* [in Hebrew]. Tel Aviv: Eretz, 2007.

Harrop, Sylvia. *The Merchant Taylors' School for Girls, Crosby.* Liverpool, UK: Liverpool University Press, 1988.

Hattis, Susan Lee. *The Bi-National Idea in Palestine during Mandatory Times.* Haifa, Israel: Shikmona, 1970.

Henriques, Robert. "Centenary Evelina de Rothschild School: Vision and Fulfillment." *Jewish Chronicle* (Supplement), June 18, 1965.

Holliday, Eunice. *Letters from Jerusalem during the Palestinian Mandate.* London: Radcliffe Press, 1997.

Hunt, Felicity, ed. *Lessons for Life: The Schooling of Girls and Women, 1850–1950.* Oxford, UK: Basil Blackwell, 1987.

Hyamson, Albert Montefiore. *Palestine: The Rebirth of an Ancient People.* London: Sidgwick & Jackson, 1917.

———. *Palestine under the Mandate, 1920–1948.* Westport, CT: Greenwood Press, 1976.

Jacobson, Abigail. *From Empire to Empire: Jerusalem between Ottoman and British Rule, 1912–20.* Syracuse, NY: Syracuse University Press, 2011.

———. "From Empire to Empire: Jerusalem in the Transition between Ottoman and British Rule, 1912–20." PhD diss., University of Chicago, 2006.

"Jerusalem Girls' College." *New York Times,* April 30, 1922.

Jerusalem Girls' College magazine. Jerusalem: Jerusalem Girls' College, 1938.

Jerusalem Radio: The Only Radio Publication in Palestine. Vols. 1–3. Jerusalem: n. p., n.d.

Kadish, Sharman. *'A Good Jew and a Good Englishman': The Jewish Lads' and Girls' Brigade, 1895–1995.* London: Vallentine Mitchell, 1995.

Kagan, Helena. *The Voice That Called.* Jerusalem: n.p., 1978.

Kaplan, Isaac. *The Wandering Jew.* Jerusalem: Teper, 2004.

Kark, Ruth, and Michael Oren-Nordheim. *Jerusalem and Its Environs: Quarters, Neighborhoods, Villages, 1800–1948.* Jerusalem: Hebrew University Magnes Press, ca. 2001.

Kark, Ruth, and Yaakov Israel. "Messianism, Holiness, Charisma and Community: The American-Swedish Colony in Jerusalem, 1881–1933." *Church History* 65, no. 4 (1996): 641–57.

Kendall, Henry. *Jerusalem, the City Plan: Preservation and Development during the British Mandate, 1918–1948.* London: H. M. Stationery Office, 1948.

Khalidi, Rashid. *Palestinian Identity: The Construction of Modern National Consciousness.* New York: Columbia University Press, 1997.

Kheimets, Nina, and Alek D. Epstein. "Languages of Science in the Era of Nation-State Formation: The Israeli Universities and Their (Non)Participation in the Revival of Hebrew." *Journal of Multilingual and Multicultural Development* 26, no. 1 (2005): 12–36.

Kisch, Frederick Hermann. *Palestine Diary*. London: Victor Gollancz, 1938.

Kleinberger, Aharon F. *Society, Schools and Progress in Israel*. New York: Pergamon Press, 1969.

Kroyanker, David. *Jerusalem: The Street of Prophets, the Ethiopian and Musrara Quarters, 1850–2000* [in Hebrew]. Jerusalem: Keter, 2000.

Kushner, David, ed. *Palestine in the Late Ottoman Period: Political, Social and Economic Transformation*. Jerusalem: Yad Ben-Zvi Press, 1986.

Lazar, Hadara. *Out of Palestine: The Making of Modern Israel*. New York: Atlas, 2011.

Levy, Ethel. "One Hundred Years of the Evelina School." *Jewish Observer and Middle East Review*, June 25, 1965.

Lipman, V. D. *A Century of Social Service, 1859–1959: The Jewish Board of Guardians*. London: Routledge and Kegan Paul, 1959.

Loewe, Louis, ed. *Diaries of Sir Moses and Lady Montefiore*. London: Jewish Historical Society of England, 1983.

Malino, Frances. "The Women Teachers of the AIU, 1872–1940." In *Jewish Women in Historical Perspective*, 2nd ed., edited by Judith Baskin, 248–69. Detroit: Wayne State University Press, 1998.

Malleyron, Yona. *You Will Get Out of Here* [in Hebrew]. Jerusalem: Yad Vashem, 1980.

Manneberg, Eliezer. *The Evolution of Jewish Educational Practices in the Sancak of Jerusalem under Ottoman Rule*. Ann Arbor, MI: University Microfilms, 1976.

Ma'oz, Moshe. *Ottoman Reform in Syria and Palestine, 1840–1861: The Impact of the Tanzimat on Politics and Society*. Oxford, UK: Clarendon Press, 1968.

McCarthy, Justin. *The Population of Palestine: Population History and Statistics of the Late Ottoman Period and the Mandate*. New York: Columbia University Press, 1990.

Meinertzhagen, Richard. *Middle East Diary, 1917–1956*. London: Cresset Press, 1959.

Melman, Billie. *Women's Orients: English Women and the Middle East, 1718–1918; Sexuality, Religion and Work*. Basingstoke, UK: Macmillan, 1995.

Nardi, Noah. *Education in Palestine*. Washington, DC: Zionist Organization of America, 1945.

Nashashibi, Nasir al-Din. *Jerusalem's Other Voice: Raghib Nashashibi and Moderation in Palestinian Politics, 1920–1948*. Exeter, UK: Ithaca, 1990.

Newton, Frances E. *Fifty Years in Palestine*. Wrotham, UK: Coldharbour Press, 1948.

Okkenhaug, Inger Marie. *The Quality of Heroic Living, of High Endeavour and Adventure: Anglican Mission, Women and Education in Palestine, 1888–1948*. Leiden, Netherlands: Brill, 2002.

Ophir, Daniel, ed. *The House on Montefiore Street* [in Hebrew]. Petah-Tikvah, Israel: Frumkin, 2010.

Robinson, Charles Henry. *History of Christian Missions.* New York: Scribner's, 1915.

Rodrigue, Aron. *French Jews, Turkish Jews: The Alliance Israélite Universelle and the Politics of Jewish Schooling in Turkey, 1860–1925.* Bloomington: Indiana University Press, 1990.

Rogers, Mary Eliza. *Domestic Life in Palestine.* London: Kegan Paul, 1989.

Rosenbloom, Noah. "Religious and Secular Co-Equality in S. R. Hirsch's Educational Theory." *Jewish Social Studies* 24, no. 4 (October 1962): 223–47.

Rothschild, Mrs. Leopold de, ed. *An Appeal to Jewish Women on Behalf of the Anglo-Jewish Association.* London: Jewish Chronicle, 1911.

Sacks, Oliver. *Uncle Tungsten: Memories of a Chemical Boyhood.* New York: Vintage Books, 2001.

Safir, Marilyn P., and Barbara Swirski, eds. *Calling the Equality Bluff: Women in Israel.* New York: Pergamon Press, 1991.

Sakakini, Hala. *Jerusalem and I: A Personal Record.* Amman, Jordan: Economic Press, 1990.

Samuel, Herbert Louis. *Memoirs by the Rt. Hon. Viscount Samuel.* London: Cresset Press, 1945.

Schneer, Jonathan. *The Balfour Declaration: The Origins of the Arab-Israeli Conflicts.* New York: Random House, 2010.

School magazine. Jerusalem: Evelina de Rothschild School, 1935–1940.

Schor, Laura S. *The Life and Legacy of the Baroness Betty de Rothschild.* New York: Peter Lang, 2006.

Segev, Tom. *One Palestine, Complete: Jews and Arabs under the British Mandate.* Translated by Haim Watzman. London: Little, Brown, 2000.

Shahid, Serene Husseini. *Jerusalem Memories.* Beirut, Lebanon: Naufal, 1999.

Shamir, Martha Zayonce. *Daughter of the Generation of 1948* [in Hebrew]. Jerusalem: privately printed, 2003.

Shapira, Anita. *Land and Power: The Zionist Resort to Force, 1881–1948.* Stanford, CA: Stanford University Press. 1992.

Sherman, A. J. *Mandate Days: British Lives in Palestine, 1918–1948.* Baltimore, MD: Johns Hopkins University Press, 1997.

Shilo, Margalit. "A Cross-Cultural Message: The Case of Evelina de Rothschild." In *Jewish Women in Pre-State Israel,* edited by Ruth Kark, Margalit Shilo, and Galit Hasan-Rokem, 167–79. Waltham, MA: Brandeis University Press, 2008.

———. *Princess or Prisoner? Jewish Women in Jerusalem, 1840–1914.* Waltham, MA: Brandeis University Press, 2005.

———. "Women as Victims of War: The British Conquest (1917) and the Blight of Prostitution in the Holy City." *Nashim: A Journal of Jewish Women's Studies and Gender Issues* 6 (Fall 2003): 72–83.

Shvarts, Shifra. "The Development of Mother and Infant Welfare Centers in Israel, 1854–1954." *Journal of the History of Medicine and Allied Sciences* 55, no. 4 (2000): 398–425.

Silver-Brody, Vivienne. *Documentors of the Dream: Pioneer Jewish Photographers in the Land of Israel, 1890–1933*. Jerusalem: Hebrew University Press, 1998.

Slutsky, Liza. "The Evelina de Rothschild School during the Yishuv" [in Hebrew]. Paper presented at the Schecter Center seminar, Jerusalem, 2006.

Smart, Rich. *Bedford Training College, 1882–1982*. Bedford, UK: Bedford Training College, 1982.

Stockdale, Nancy L. "Gender and Colonialism in Palestine, 1800–1948: Encounters among English, Arab and Jewish Women." PhD diss., University of California, Santa Barbara, 2000.

Storrs, Ronald. *The Memoirs of Sir Ronald Storrs*. New York: G. P. Putnam and Sons, 1937.

Szajkowski, Zosa. "Conflicts in the Alliance Israélite Universelle and the Founding of the Anglo-Jewish Association, the Vienna Allianz and the Hilfsverein." *Jewish Social Studies* 19 (1957): 29–50.

Tibawi, Abdul Latif. *Arab Education in Mandatory Palestine: A Study of Three Decades of British Administration*. London: Luzac, 1956.

United Hebrew Congregations of the British Empire. *Authorized Daily Prayer Book*. Jerusalem: Zuckerman, n.d.

Vester, Bertha Spafford. *Our Jerusalem*. Jerusalem: Ariel, 1988.

Wallach, Yair. "Readings in Conflict: Public Texts in Modern Jerusalem, 1858–1948." PhD diss., University of London, 2008.

Wasserstein, Bernard. *The British in Palestine: The Mandatory Government and Arab-Jewish Conflict, 1917–1929*. Oxford, UK: Basil Blackwell, 1991.

———. *Divided Jerusalem: The Struggle for the Holy City*, 3rd ed. New Haven, CT: Yale University Press, 2008.

———. *Herbert Samuel: A Political Life*. Oxford, UK: Clarendon Press, 1992.

Weissman, Deborah. "Beis Ya'akov as an Innovation in Jewish Women's Education: A Contribution to the Study of Education and Social Change." In *Studies in Jewish Education*, edited by Walter Ackerman, 278–99. Jerusalem: Magnes Press, 1995.

Woodsmall, Ruth Frances. *Moslem Women Enter a New World*. New York: Round Table Press, 1936.

Yachin, Ezra Elnakam. *The Song of Shulamit* [in Hebrew]. Jerusalem: Ezri, 2000.

INDEX

attendance and punctuality, 39, 52, 75–76, 110, 130–31

Augusta Victoria (German Hospital, Jerusalem), 46, 85, 103, 105, 111

Awakening Palestine (1912), 72–73

Bagrut exam, 111, 225, 227, 228, 254

Balfour Declaration, 82, 100, 159, 163

Barkay, Adaya Hochberg, 142, 211, 220, 221, 227, 251–57, 258, 261

Behar, Fortunée, 7–8, 29, 31–33, 35–36, 39, 41–46

Ben-Gurion, David, 222, 225

Ben-Yehuda, Eliezer and Hemda, 74, 78, 93

Ben Yehuda Street bombing (1948), 221, 254–55

Bentwich, Helen, 88–89, 92–94, 96–97, 100–101, 103, 108–10, 112, 117–19, 136

Bentwich, Norman, 88, 94, 117, 205

Berger, Sophie, 88–89

Bezalel Academy for Art and Design, Jerusalem, 67, 72, 209

bilingual education at Evelina School, xiii, 1, 46, 74, 88, 90–91, 108, 121, 153, 162, 227–28. *See also* English instruction; Hebrew

Bishopsgate Ward School, London, 23, 24, 31, 48

bombs and bombings, 146–47, 214–15, 218, 221, 222, 254–55

Bondi, Sophie, 57, 65

Bowman, Humphrey Ernest, 98–99, 112, 120

British authorities: anti-Jewish prejudice, 156–57, 248; Arab boycott (1936-1939) and, 146, 147–48, 154; Balfour Declaration, 82, 100, 159, 163; departure of, 216–17, 222; education standards set by, 98–99, 106; employment of Evelina School graduates by, 85–86, 111,

123, 124, 156–57, 248; establishment of Mandate, 82; infrastructure and services under, 89–90, 91; Landau's and Evelina School's relationship with, 83–86, 99; Landau's loyalty to, 147–48, 158, 183–84; opposition to, 202; prostitution problem and, xiv, 81, 83, 86–89; refugees from Arab riots of 1929 and, 118; unrest of 1945-1947, 212–16; White Paper on Palestine, 159

British character of Evelina School, 7, 44, 46, 53, 84, 131, 147–48, 183–88

Bromberger, Batia (née Salasnik), 143, 235

Cailingold, Esther, 142, 222–23

Canaan, Tawfiq, 93–94

Carlsbad conference (1921), 100

Carpenter, Boyd, 55–58, 125

Caspi, Ziona, 144, 172–73, 186–87, 196–97, 273n37

Central Foundation School, London, 184

Chaikin, Bertha, 129, 238

chaluka, 3, 4, 61, 119, 228

Chanukah, 47, 50, 160, 213, 230

cheder, 3, 6, 34, 243

chemistry instruction, 12, 111, 113, 135, 142, 227

cherem, 46–47, 58

Chisholm, Edwin, 135–36

Christian missionary schools in Jerusalem, xii, xiii, 30–32, 33, 47, 75, 101, 112, 113, 116–17, 160

Cohen, Alfred, 29–32

Cohen, Shulamit (later Kishik-Cohen), 237–43, 246, 252, 261

Cohen (teacher at Evelina School), 46, 57

commercial classes at Evelina School, 86, 126–27, 128, 155, 199

community service, Evelina School tradition of, 138, 140, 159, 199, 230, 234

coronation of George VI, 147–48, *185*, 185–87, 276n19

curriculum of Evelina School, 1, 7–8, 19, 28, 44–45, 53, 62, 99, 127–28, 230, 234

Damascus Affair (1840), 4
d'Avigdor-Goldsmid, Osmond, 99, 110–11
d'Avigdor, Olga, 41–46, 62
Diab (gardener at Evelina School), 130, 147, 153
domestic science classes at Evelina School, 46, 47, 49, 54, 126, 199
Drosdovsky, Shoshana, 191–92

early marriage of pupils, efforts to delay, xiiii, 10, 44, 62, 86
earthquake of 1927, 111–12, 126
Eban, Aubrey (later Abba Eban; nephew of Landau), 22, 114, 205, 226
Eden, Elka, 175–76
Eden, Menuha, 130, 144–45
Eder, David and Edith, 98, 102
education of girls and women: Anglo-Jewish Association on, 29, 157–58; common contemporary objections to, xii; in England in late 19th century, 23–26; Landau on, xi, xiv, 1–4, 8–9, 11, 66, 157–58, 262; in Landau's family, xii, 15–16, 18–19; Landau's own education, xii, 20, 23–27. *See also specific schools*
embroidery. *See* needlework, sewing, and embroidery
employment opportunities for Evelina graduates, 61–64, 65, 67, 76–77, 85–86, 91, 123–24, 155–57, 209, 225–26
English Children's Hour, Palestine Broadcasting Service, 144, 213
English High School for Girls. *See* Jerusalem Girls' College
English instruction: at Anglo-Jewish Association school in Mogador, Morocco, 29; at Evelina School, xiv, 8, 12, 31, 32, 35, 43, 44, 54, 56–57, 61, 67, 74, 85, 91, 101–2, 108, 111, 124, 135, 235;

free elementary education, bilingual programs excluded from, 227–28; in Mandate Palestine, 91; Palestinian Language Strike, 74, 120–21; ultra-Orthodox suspicion of, 88; Zionist opposition to, xiv, 67, 74, 91, 92, 101, 120–21, 124
Ephrata Secondary Girls' School, Evelina School merger with, 234
Eretz Israel, 165, 170, 171, 184
Evelina de Rothschild School: Abrahams report on, 36; accounting and administrative issues, 32, 39, 41–42; under Behar (1854-1899), 28–36; British character of, 7, 44, 46, 53, 84, 131, 147–48, 183–88; Carpenter report on, 55–58; Cohen report and, 29–32; continued survival of, 235; crowding at, 56, 58, 70; d'Avigdor report, 41–46; goals of, 1–2, 6, 158, 227; historical exhibit on tenth anniversary of state of Israel, 233; Israel, importance of school to modern state of, xi, 2, 13, 119; joint teaching of Ashkenazi and Sephardi girls at, 6, 28; Landau as teacher at (1899-1900), xiii, 36, 38–40, 41, 43; Landau's appointment as headmistress (1900-1901), xiii, 7–8, 46–48; Landau's early years as headmistress (before World War I), 52–77; Landau's reports on, 48–52, 58–59, 61, 64, 65, 66, 75, 76–77, 201; legacy of, 11–13, 236–37, 262; Levy as successor to Landau as headmistress, 1, 13, 208–18 (*See also* Levy, Ethel); magazine of (*See School* magazine); merger with Ephrata Secondary Girls' School, 234; modern educational practices and standards, adoption of, 97–99, 106; origins, history, and fortunes of, xii, 5–7, 28–36; post-World War I reopening and restoration of, 81, 82–91; Princess Mary, visit of (1928),

114–15; school crest and motto, 132, 162; school spirit, school rituals, and school day, 128–34, 189–99; stability provided by, in times of crisis, 117–24; student body, 62, 112–13, 116; wider world, engagement with problems of, xiv–xv; in World War I, 77–81

exams: Bagrut, 111, 225, 227, 228, 254; London University matriculation examination, 106, 110–11, 127–28, 139, 152, 155, 183, 193–94, 197–99, 202, 224–27, 228

expulsion from Evelina School, 121, 134, 154

extracurricular activities at Evelina School, 96–98, 136, 232. See also Girl Guides

fees and tuition at Evelina School, 30, 32, 46, 47, 48, 50, 65, 75, 79, 102, 103, 110, 111, 113, 118, 135, 149, 213, 215, 227, 228, 231

Frankel, Rachel, 185–86

Frankfurt, Germany: destruction of Frankfurt synagogue, 168–69; Hirsch School, Landau's studies at, xii, 20, 24–26; refugee pupils from, 148–57; Leah Schoenberger's memories of, 167–69

Franklin, Caroline, 24, 77, 88

Fredkin, Mordecai, 14. See also Landau, Marcus Israel

free elementary education in Israel, establishment of, 227–28

free meals. See social benefits provided by schools

Frutiger House: bombing damage to (1946), 215; decorated for coronation of George VI (1937), 185; Department of Education in, 13, 230; expansions, renovations, and new buildings, 69, 103, 109, 155; final departure of Evelina School from (1948), 218–20; as High Commissioner's residence, 111, 126; Landau's apartment in, 68, 126, 128, 203;

leased for income purposes, 71, 84, 102; purchase for Evelina School, 7, 33–34; return of Evelina School to, 126, 127; in World War I, 80, 83–84

fundraising and acceptance of donations by Landau for Evelina School, xiii, 2–3, 47, 49–52, 64–65, 67, 72, 77, 102–3, 202–3

further education for Evelina School graduates, 126, 209, 224–25, 231–32, 235, 257

geography instruction, xiii, 23, 25, 28, 29, 47, 54, 65, 67, 101–2, 111, 135, 141, 167, 190, 249

George V (king of England), 106, 147, 183, 184–85, 187

George VI (king of England), 130, 147, 160, 185–87

German and Eastern European refugees, xv, 12, 142, 143, 148–57, 163–71, 191–93, 209–12, 253

German Colony, Jerusalem, 68, 161

Girl Guides, Rangers, and Brownies: 1917-1929, 96–97, 99, 101, 109, 114, 116, 119; in 1930s, 135, 136–38, 137, 148, 161, 184, 195; 1941-1960, 205, 214, 234, 247, 248, 255; School magazine and, 184, 195

Girls' Jewish Orphanage, Frankfurt, 149, 150

Goldstein, Pnina (later Moed), 122, 235

Goltmann, Miss, 43, 57

Goodman, Lea, 120–21, 129, 140

governesses, Evelina School graduates as, 65, 66

Graystoke Teachers' Training College, 26, 27, 94

Hadassah Hospital, 147, 221, 223, 244, 245

Hadassah Medical Unit, 87, 90, 118

Hadassah nurses, 75, 77, 80, 92

Hadassah School of Nursing, 209, 244

anniversary in Jerusalem, celebration of, 183; health problems of, 22, 54, 60, 109, 203, 206; as hostess and socialite, xiv, 68, 70, 91–96, 106–10; Jewish immigration to Palestine, support for, 148; Jewish nationalism, evolving views on, 148, 157–60, 183–84; legacy of, 261–62; name, choice of, 20–21; OBE received by, 106; Ottoman authorities, relationship with, 9; photos, 182, 204; religious observance of, 20, 27–28, 95–96, 207; return to Jerusalem following World War I, 81, 83; romantic life, apparent lack of, 124; school reports of, 48–52, 58–59, 61, 64, 65, 66, 75, 76–77, 201; siblings and half-siblings, 15, 21; student's feelings about, 114–16, 122, 123, 183; teacher training, certification, and first teaching job, 26–28; twenty-fifth anniversary in Jerusalem, celebration of, 106–8; wider world, engagement with, xiv–xv; Zionism, lack of identification with, xiv, 60, 66–67, 93, 108, 148, 158, 182

Landau, Chaya (née Kohn; mother), xi–xii, 14–20, 24, 105

Landau, Marcus Israel (Mordecai Fredkin; father), xi–xii, 14–20, 24

Lange, Marta and Hermina, 150, 151, 210, 212

Lask, Ruth (later Rasnic), 131, 258–61

Lebanon, Shulamit Kishik-Cohen in, 241–43

Leon, Eva, 75, 77

Levin, Rachel, 105, 113–16, 128–31, 134–36, 142, 147, 155–56

Levy, Ethel (née Ofstein): change at Evelina School under, 227–35; at daily school entrance ceremony, 129; on death of Landau, 206, 208; Kabbalat Shabbat program continued by, 130; marriage of, 94–95; Old Girls' Club and, 140; on

Palestinian Language Strike, 121; photo, 204; posture of, 134; on refugee pupils from Hitler's Europe, xv, 152; refugees of Arab riots of 1929 and, 119; reports to Anglo-Jewish Association, 212–13, 215, 232; retirement of (1960), 234–35; Scharf, Yona, recollections of, 210–12; as successor to Landau, 1, 13, 208–18; as teacher at Evelina School, 99, 125; as temporary replacement for Landau in 1925, 109; during War of Independence (See War of Independence)

Lilienfeld, Miriam, 148–49

Lilienfeld, Shulamit, 142, 148–49, 224–25

Lionel de Rothschild Technical School, Jerusalem, 29, 35

London Committee for Training Jewish Teachers, 36

London Jews' Society School for Girls, Jerusalem, 30, 47, 75

London University matriculation examination, 106, 110–11, 127–28, 139, 152, 155, 183, 193–94, 197–99, 202, 224–27, 228

ma'abarot, 230, 231, 232

Maccabi Hatzair, 220, 225, 254, 256

MacInnes, Rennie, Mary Anne, and Campbell, 82, 87, 218–19

maestras, 3, 34, 183

Magnes, Judah and Beatrice, 94, 108, 109, 159, 205

Mandatory government. See British authorities

manners and formal behavior at Evelina School, 128–34

marriage: early marriage of pupils, efforts to delay, xiiii, 10, 44, 62, 86; interfaith marriage, 141

Marx, Jonas, 80, 83

Mary (princess, daughter of George V of England), 114–15

mathematics and arithmetic, xiii, 6, 16, 18, 23, 25, 28, 29, 47, 54, 57, 101, 135, 142, 143, 190, 211, 227, 235

medical issues. *See* health and hygiene

Meiroff, Hannah, 104–5

Meyuhas, Yosef, 35, 43, 53, 54, 74, 80, 87, 92

Midsummer Night's Dream (Shakespeare), Evelina School performance of (1925), 103–5

milk distribution program, 139, 172–73, 217, 231

Miss Landau's School. *See* Evelina de Rothschild School

missionary schools in Jerusalem, xii, xiii, 30–32, 33, 47, 75, 101, 112, 113, 116–17, 160

Mitshanik, Rivka, 67–69, 78, 80

Moed, Pnina (née Goldstein), 122, 235

Money, Arthur, 86, 89, 93

monitors, 52, 116, 122

Montefiore, Claude, 9, 36

Montefiore, Sir Moses and Lady Judith, 3, 5, 9

moral responsibility, inculcation of, 35, 48, 64, 71–72, 88

Morgenthau, Henry, Sr, and Josephine., 77, 78

mothers of pupils, Landau's relationship with, 9–10

Muharram, 178–79

music program at Evelina House, 12, 19, 23, 29, 35, 56, 97, 105, 136, 141, 143, 144, 151, 155, 213, 247, 262

Musrara neighborhood, Jerusalem, 93, 118, 153–54, 216, 217

Nashashibi, Ragheb Bey and Laila, 34, 92, 109, 112

Nathan Strauss Health Center, 90, 118, 126, 127, 152

nationalism, Arab, 89, 91, 100, 117, 147

nationalism, Jewish. *See* Zionism and Zionists

Nazis, refugees from, xv, 12, 142, 143, 148–57, 163–71, 191–93, 209–12, 253

needlework, sewing, and embroidery: before World War I, 6, 23, 28, 29, 35, 39, 43, 44, 45, 57, 59, 61–64, 70, 72, 77; after World War I, 89, 102, 126, 209, 231, 233; lace and lacework, 34, 43, 59, 62, 63–64, 69, 70, 72, 73, 77; millinery classes and workrooms, 59, 62, 64, 70

Nissim, Nellie, 71, 80

Nurock, Bertha and Max, 95, 103, 108, 119

nurses, Evelina graduates as, 13, 46, 61, 67, 75, 152, 209, 231, 235, 243–45

Occupied Enemy Territory Administration (OETA). *See* British authorities

Ochana, Miriam, 142, 220, 225, 226

Ofstein, Ethel. *See* Levy, Ethel

Old Girls and Old Girls' Club, 10–11, 63, 64, 139–41, 143, 149, 183, 199, 203, 207, 212, 215, 228–29, 230–31, 235

Order of the British Empire (OBE), Landau receiving, 106

Ottoman (Turkish) authorities, 5, 9, 33, 36–38, 71, 77–81

Palestine Broadcasting Service (PBS), 91, 144, 155, 188, 189, 207, 212–13, 217, 253, 273n37

Palestine Bulletin, 119, 127

Palestine Exhibition and Bazaar (1912), 72–73

Palestine Post, 159, 160, 205, 220, 230

Palestinian Language Strike, 74, 120–21

Passover, 4, 15, 36, 51, 99, 114, 119, 151, 197, 222, 247

Philanthropin, 15, 24–25

Pitman tests, 85, 126, 155, 199, 202

Plumer, Lord and Lady Herbert, 109–10, 111, 112, 114, 136

population of Palestine, 61, 73, 86, 267n29

poverty in Jerusalem, 55, 58, 61, 76, 80–81, 82, 86

prefects, 116, 122, 129, 138–39, 216, 237–38, 239

prizes and awards, 28, 52, 53–54, 115, 116, 127, 131, 133, 135, 136, 142, 184, 214, 250

Pro-Jerusalem Society, 90, 94

prostitution, xiv, 81, 83, 86–89

punctuality and attendance, 39, 52, 75–76, 110, 130–31

Purim, 17, 47, 140, 160, 166, 232, 233

Rackover, Dvorah, 231–32

radio broadcasting: Evelina School and, 144–45, 155, 188–90; PBS (Palestine Broadcasting Service), 91, 144, 155, 188, 189, 207, 212–13, 217, 253, 273n37

Rasnic, Ruth Lask, 131, 258–61

Red Crescent, 71, 268n64

Red Cross, 71, 83, 87, 89, 201, 205

refugees: from Arab riots of 1929, 117–19; from Hitler's Europe, xv, 12, 142, 143, 148–57, 163–71, 191–93, 209–12, 253; Jewish immigrants to Israel, 233, 234–35, 244; Jewish immigration to Palestine, 99–100, 148, 177–78, 202, 274n51; ma'abarot, 230, 231, 232; Zionist removal of Jewish girls from London Jews' Society School, 74–75

Rehavia, Evelina School's move to, 218–20, 230

Reider, David, 123, 129, 141, 142, 198, 205, 227, 235, 246

Reinman (teacher at Evelina School), 46, 57

Reis, Walter, 143, 205, 227

religion and spirituality at Evelina School, 19–20, 48, 54, 108, 115, 116, 129–30, 160, 232, 252

Rosenbaum, Tova (later Menirav), 53–54, 85

Rosenwald, Augusta and Julius, 77, 90

Rothschild, Baroness Evelina de, 5. *See also* Evelina de Rothschild School

Rothschild family, 3, 5–7, 23, 25, 28, 29, 31, 33, 35, 36, 65, 69, 77, 99, 150, 202–3

Rothschild Hospital, Jerusalem, 6, 8, 28, 32, 59, 64, 124

Rubovitz, Margalit, 177–78

Sabbath observance, 19–20, 26–27, 95–96, 130

Sacks, Oliver (nephew of Landau), 22

Salasnik, Batia (later Bromberger), 143, 235

Saloman, Esther and Karl, 144, 213

Samuel, Lady Beatrice, 89, 96, 99, 103, 105

Samuel, Sir Herbert, 89, 91, 95, 100, 103, 105, 106, 109, 110, 207

Scharf, Yona, 209–12

Schick, Conrad, 34, 98

Schiff, Jacob, 67, 102

Schneller Orphanage (Syrian Orphanage), Jerusalem, 146, 264n20, 269n10

Schoenberger, Leah, 167–69

Schonberg, Helena, 141, 142

School magazine, 12, 116, 162–200; Arabs in, 171, 173, 174, 175–80, 243; Britain, attachment to, 183–88; on Evelina School culture and spirit, 189–99; in Evelina School exhibit, 233; Jerusalem in, 178–81, 188–89, 243–44; photo of Landau from, 182; praise of Landau in, 183; on radio broadcasting, 188–90; refugee girls, poems and essays by, 163–71; years in publication (1935-1940), 162; Zionism and Jewish nationalism in, 162–63, 170, 171–83

school uniforms, 88, 114, 115, 122, 128, 131–34, 132, 136, 149, 189, 192, 193, 230, 232

Schwartzstein, Ella, 26, 57, 59, 65, 78, 80, 149, 161

Schwartzstein House, 150–52, 205, 209, 210, 221, 224